fourth edition

POLITICAL ISSUES DEBATED

an introduction to politics

HERBERT M. LEVINE

Prentice Hall, Englewood Cliffs, New Jersey 07632

Library of Congress Cataloging-in-Publication Data

Levine, Herbert M.
    Political issues debated : an introduction to politics / Herbert
M. Levine.—4th ed.
        p.   cm.
    Includes bibliographical references and index.
    ISBN 0-13-681644-4
    1. Political science.   I. Title.
JA66.L46   1993
320—dc20

92-33201
CIP

FOR MARVIN MAURER

Acquisitions editor: Julie Berrisford
Editorial/production supervision and
    interior design: Alison D. Gnerre
Copyeditor: Ann Hofstra Grogg
Cover design: Jayne Conte
Prepress buyer: Kelly Behr
Manufacturing buyer: Mary Ann Gloriande

Printed in the United States of America
10   9   8   7   6   5   4   3   2   1

ISBN 0-13-681644-4

Prentice-Hall International (UK) Limited, *London*
Prentice-Hall of Australia Pty. Limited, *Sydney*
Prentice-Hall Canada Inc., *Toronto*
Prentice-Hall Hispanoamericana, S.A., *Mexico*
Prentice-Hall of India Private Limited, *New Delhi*
Prentice-Hall of Japan, Inc., *Tokyo*
Simon & Schuster Asia Pte. Ltd., *Singapore*
Editora Prentice-Hall do Brasil, Ltda., *Rio de Janeiro*

Contents

II   FORMS OF GOVERNMENT   33

3   Democracy and Dictatorship   35

III   IDEOLOGY   65

4   Liberalism, Conservatism, and Fascism   67

11 Parliamentary and Presidential Systems   224

12 Bureaucracy   245

VI   INTERNATIONAL POLITICS   263

13   International Politics: Motivations   265

14   International Politics: Instruments and Constraints   278

Instruments of Power 281

Alliances, 281 *Balance of Power, 282*
Economic Measures, 282 *Military Force, 283*
Collective Security, 284 *Disarmament and Arms Control, 284*
Diplomacy, 284 *International Law, 285*
International Organization, 285 *Intelligence, 286*

Constraints on Power 286

Moral, 286 *Legal, 287* *Pragmatic, 287* *Political, 287*

Preface

When college students become involved in politics, it is often because issues are of vital concern to them. At times these issues may directly affect their lives, such as a decision by government to register young people for the draft or to send them to war, or, less seriously, to increase their tuition at state-supported universities. At other times, moral considerations compel college students to become involved in issues of vital concern to others, such as the isolation of human rights abroad or eliminating capital punishment.

This book focuses on issues in the hope that the excitement of politics, which comes from its subject matter and the controversy it generates, will interest students to learn more about politics. To that end, the book deals with subjects of great complexity and importance, such as the purpose of government, the reality of democracy, the nature of socialism, the poverty of distant nations, and the prospects of disarmament. The book examines twenty-six issues, some of

long-standing concern, such as the relationship between interest groups and the public interest, the possibility of participatory democracy, and the superiority of the British parliamentary system over the American presidential system of government. Other issues are of more recent relevance, such as whether television news has a unique impact on public opinion, and whether the West should redistribute its wealth to Third World countries.

The issues have been selected because of their controversial character. The intent of the author is to introduce subjects that will stimulate student interest in the study of politics. Background information is provided for each chapter. This material is designed to present the subject matter to students so that they will have the facts necessary to understand the debates. The length of the background information varies considerably, since the amount of information included depends upon the breadth of the subject matter considered in the debates. A list of Recommended Readings at the end of each chapter provides additional sources that students may consult to improve their understanding of an issue. Questions are offered to encourage a discussion of the issues, and Key Terms are cited to focus attention on important concepts and definitions.

The purpose of the book and the nature of the format dictate an approach to the subject matter that is not methodologically rigorous. It is the belief of the author that students must first become interested in politics before they concern themselves with methodological matters.

The debate approach offers several educational benefits. First, students who are accustomed to believe in the truthfulness of the printed word will be encouraged to use their own critical talents, since opposing viewpoints are presented. Second, the debate format is a useful way for students with a limited background in politics to become interested in the subject matter of politics. Third, the instructor will have many possibilities in lecturing and giving assignments. Lectures can be presented that highlight the background information or take one or both sides of a debate. Classroom participation can be encouraged by dividing the class into groups that argue different sides of an issue.

A debate format is not without problems, however. First, students may be encouraged to think that there are only two sides to every argument, when often there are several worthy of consideration. Second, a certain amount of information about politics, which ordinarily is included in an introductory course, may have to be left out or treated briefly. The instructor must determine how to minimize the risks through lectures and class discussions.

The fourth edition of *Political Issues Debated* has retained the structure and most of the debate topics of the third edition. The astonishing developments since the publication of the third edition in 1990—most notably the collapse of communism,

the end of the cold war, the expansion of liberalism and democracy, and the greater acceptance of capitalism—are reflected in three new debates:

- Are liberal democracies the final form of political system that will usher in an era of peace?
- Does the demise of communism mean that socialism is dead, too?
- Should the United States adopt an isolationist foreign policy?

A civil liberties issue that has emerged since the last edition is considered in a fourth new debate:

- Should hate-speech codes be adopted at public universities in the United States?

The material in all chapters has been updated and revised to present additional information and to refine arguments. In some cases, separate Questions and Recommended Readings are supplied for issues in addition to those covering general subject matter.

ACKNOWLEDGMENTS

In preparing the fourth edition of this book, I had the professional help of several people in both the academic and publishing communities. I am grateful to them for their assistance.

The editorial consultants for the book were Professors J. J. Hendricks, California State University, Stanislaus; Dennis A. Schmidt, Iona College; and David Nicholas, Montclair State College.

Karen Horton and Julie Berrisford were the political science editors, and Dolores Mars and Nicole Signoretti assisted them. Alison Gnerre was the production editor. Ann Hofstra Grogg was the copyeditor.

Although I had the assistance of many people, I accept full responsibility for any mistakes that may appear in the book.

ABOUT THE AUTHOR

Herbert M. Levine is a political scientist who taught at the University of Southwestern Louisiana for twenty years. He is the author or editor of several debate books in political science. His recent books include *What If the American Political System Were Different?* (M. E. Sharpe) and *Point-Counterpoint: Readings in American Government* (St. Martin's Press). He is currently a writer based in Chevy Chase, Maryland.

part I

POLITICS, GOVERNMENT, AND NATIONS

What government is and what government does are of interest to everyone who cares about goals such as physical security, economic well-being, health, and education. In the twentieth century, governments throughout the world have increased the services they perform to achieve these goals and the numbers of people they employ to provide those services. People differ about the priority of these goals and about the allocation of resources. Government plays a prominent role in setting public priorities and in allocating scarce resources.

Chapter 1 discusses the way in which people attempt to achieve their goals through public policy. Politics and government are defined before consideration is given to the necessity of government.

Chapter 2 focuses on nations, which have become a battleground for political activity. Distinctions are made between nations and states. Debates center on nationalism: its divisiveness, its tendency toward war, and its obsolescence.

chapter 1

Politics and government

The term *politics* has many definitions and many uses. To some it is a disparaging word. "He got his job through politics" might mean that "connections" rather than "competence" was the reason for his selection. Along similar lines, a *politician* is distinguished from a *statesman* to the extent that the politician is concerned with catering to the interests of a narrow constituency while the statesman serves the interests of the country.

Not everyone, however, has used *politics* and *politician* in a derogatory manner. It is essential when defining a term with such emotional connotations to find suitable objective ways to describe it. Recognizing that the term **politics** has many varied definitions, we shall use it to mean subjects dealing with (1) the state, (2) power, and (3) public policy.

THE STATE

Politics has been traditionally concerned with the state. The term *politics* is in fact derived from the Greek word **polis**, which means "city-state" or "organized community." As used in this chapter, the *state* is a legal entity equivalent to a country. The United States is a state; so, too, are France, Spain, and more than 185 countries throughout the world. Americans are accustomed to thinking of regional units of their country as states—California, Louisiana, and New Jersey. These are, however, equivalent to provinces or districts in other countries. We shall define a **state** as a political entity that possesses people, territory, a government, and sovereignty.[1]

People

The people who live in a country may vary in religion, race, language, and ethnic composition. When people identify with others who live within the state, they constitute a nation. Nations are discussed in

[1] See Chapter 2 for a more elaborate description of states and nations.

3

Chapter 2. Here it is only necessary to point out that the number of people who reside within states varies considerably. Liechtenstein, one of the world's smallest states, has a population of twenty-eight thousand people, and the People's Republic of China, the world's most populous state, contains more than 1 billion people.

Territory

Every state contains a specific piece of territory that distinguishes it from other states. That bounded geographical area may be in one continuous land unit, or it may be separated by other states or large bodies of water. The United States contains among its regional units Alaska and Hawaii—both of which are separated by vast distances from their continental base. States vary in size as they do in population. Until its breakup in 1991, the Soviet Union, occupying one-seventh of the world's surface, was the largest state in the world. States such as Malta and Singapore are among the smallest. Some states are so small—either in area or in population—that they are known as **microstates**.

Government

Government is the social organization that has authority to rule the state. Government is, however, different from other social organizations, such as a family or group. It makes laws that affect all the people within its territory. Its rules are binding upon the people whether they wish to be bound by such rules or not. Institutions other than government, such as churches, village elders, and companies, have made rules binding upon their members in the past and do so now. Today, however, such institutions tend to be limited in authority to a segment of a society rather than applicable to the entire society.

One of the most important features of government is that it is the only social organization that has the legal authority to use force. To be sure, groups ranging from "organized crime" to vigilantes use physical coercion in an unauthorized manner—which is to say that they resort to violence—but such an application of violence by these groups or individuals is regarded as illegal.

Among the major sources of instability in the world today is conflict over which group of people should constitute a government of a state. The problem of maintaining **authority** (the establishment of formal power) and **legitimacy** (the acceptance of authority) is a major difficulty of our times. Northern Ireland, Israel, Lebanon, and Yugoslavia provide recent examples of guerrilla warfare resulting from rival claims to government authority and legitimacy.

Sovereignty

The term **sovereignty** means total legitimate power. It was first used in the sixteenth century by the French political philosopher Jean Bodin. As originally conceived, the term meant that the monarch had total authority to make rules for all the people within the kingdom. In more recent centuries, however, the term has been applied to government's authority rather than the monarch's authority.

The state, then, is the legal entity containing all these elements of people, territory, a government, and sovereignty. Although the state had its origins in antiquity, its modern form arose in Europe between the fourteenth and seventeenth centuries. Powerful monarchs, such as Louis XIV of France and Elizabeth I of England, centralized power in the state. The power of the monarchs declined from the eighteenth century on—in some cases violently through revolution and in other cases peacefully through the establishment of popularly elected institutions—so that the state in the twentieth century is quite different from what it was in the seventeenth century.

Today, students of politics concern themselves with the state. Many are interested in the principal institutions of the state, such as the legislature, the executive and bureaucracy, and the judiciary (see Chapters 11 and 12). In practice, however, the role of these institutions is often not sharply circumscribed, and how each operates in a state varies on the basis of tradition and the realities of power. In focusing on the state, students of politics are also concerned with the relationships between the central government and its regional units (see Chapter 10).

POWER

Although students of politics have been concerned with the institutions of the state, such interest is only a partial preoccupation of their research. One could not hope to understand how American government works, for example, by looking solely at the political institutions of the president, Congress, the courts, and the regional governments.

Students of politics consequently are concerned with power. **Power** is the ability to influence people to do things they may not want to do. In this context, power may (but need not) have anything to do with government. When a criminal threatens a person with physical injury unless he or she complies with the criminal's demands, that is power. A teacher's pledge to give high grades to students for superior academic work is another kind of power that students disregard at their peril. Power carries with it a sanction: in the case of the criminal, physical safety; in the case of the teacher, a grade.

In every society power is distributed unevenly among its members. Power is derived from different sources, such as information, wealth, force or threat of violence, position, and organization. In international relations, for example, precise information about the strength of an ad-

versary's armed forces is of enormous significance to a state. Wealth may not buy happiness, but it may be used to gain political power. The knowledge that the police may legitimately use force to stop a motorist is a deterrent to speeding. The use of violence by terrorists, moreover, has influenced the behavior of diplomats as much as airline passengers. A formal position, such as governor, judge, or teacher, carries with it power for those affected by its decisions. A small, well-organized conspiratorial organization, as the Russian revolutionary V. I. Lenin contended, may have much more power than a weak association of the disorganized masses.

In the context of politics as power, politics, is, to use the political scientist Harold Lasswell's expression, the study of who gets what, when, and how.[2] Politics arises from the fact that the goals of human endeavor, such as health, economic security, prestige, and jobs, are limited. More people want such goals than are available.

Politics, then, can determine who at a hospital can be treated with a rare but vital medicine, who in a university becomes a tenured professor, who in a philanthropic organization becomes humanitarian of the year, and who in a corporation becomes chief executive officer. In none of these cases does the process of selection involve a government decision.

PUBLIC POLICY

In addition to the application of the term *politics* to the state and to power, *politics* is used to refer to **public policy**—the laws, rules, regulations, and decisions that governments make about particular subjects. In modern societies government has come to play an increasing role in allocating resources. Government may improve the quality of health of some citizens through

[2]Harold Lasswell, *Politics: Who Gets What, When, and How* (New York: Peter Smith, 1950).

supporting programs to increase the number of doctors, mandating immunization, and financing public hospitals. It may promote the economic security of some individuals by setting minimum wages, imposing tariffs and quotas, or granting monopolies. It may enhance prestige by giving recognition to the contributions that people have made to society. It may provide jobs by appropriating funds to employ people who seek work. To be sure, the beneficiaries of government may vary. Some people may be taxed so that others may benefit. Government, moreover, may engage in programs that do not achieve the purposes for which they have been established. Whether for good or evil, government has the authority to allocate scarce resources—the prizes of politics.

Students of politics, then, are concerned with how government decides to allocate scarce resources. They seek to understand the behavior of individuals and groups who demand from government such prizes as recognition, economic resources, health, and welfare.

In contrast, government may make demands upon individuals and groups. When President John F. Kennedy said in his inaugural address, "Ask not what your country can do for you; ask what you can do for your country,"[3] he was suggesting that self-sacrifice be a part of citizens' obligations to their country. Most political leaders demand that some expression of civic consciousness be demonstrated by the people who benefit from living in the community. This expression may take the form of jury duty, military service, or loyalty to the state.

Political systems differ as to what is the proper relationship between the state and the people. Some dictators argue that the individual is subservient to the state. Those people who are committed to democracy, however, contend that the state should be subservient to the individual (see Chapter 3). For our purposes, it is essential to note that politics involves the study of how resources are authoritatively allocated in society.

[3] John F. Kennedy, Inaugural Address, January 20, 1961, in "Text of John Kennedy's Inaugural Outlining Policies on World Peace and Freedom," *New York Times*, January 21, 1961, p. 8.

ISSUE

Government plays such a prominent role in our lives that we find it difficult to imagine a society existing without it. In our contemporary period, government promotes military security, encourages economic well-being, and extends welfare benefits.

The record of government's success in these areas is mixed, however. Support for government is also mixed. Ancient Greeks saw the state and government as a natural and necessary part of human experience, and modern liberals generally approve of government (see Chapter 4). There is, however, a tradition in Western thought that has viewed government in hostile terms. **Anarchists** look upon any authority, and particularly the state, as essentially harmful to people. More recently, **libertarians**, who believe that individual liberty is paramount and that the state is an oppressive institution, have made the strongest objections to government. Some socialists, moreover, perceive that government under certain conditions is evil because it is an instrument of oppression against the masses of people (see Chapter 5). Is government, then, an institution that is avoidable?

1/YES IS GOVERNMENT AVOIDABLE?

Government has such a pervasive presence in society that most people regard it as a natural phenomenon, like the air they breathe. After all, they ask, what else but government can furnish the essential prerequisites of a community, such as order, security, and welfare?

From the city-state of ancient Greece to the superstate of the modern world, however, government has been marked by two horrendous features: (1) its enslavement of people, and (2) its suppression of societal needs. Wherever government has been established—whether it called itself democratic, monarchial, aristocratic, or communist—there human beings have suffered.

Enslavement of People. People ought to be free to do what they want to do provided they do not harm others. Governments, however, have been established for the purpose of both preventing people from doing what they want to do and encouraging them to cause injury to others. Such an accusation can be substantiated when we consider murder and theft.

Most of us condemn the acts of murderers and thieves. If a person takes another person's life, that act is quite properly condemned as a heinous crime. So, too, is the taking of another person's property. If a thief enters somebody's home and steals a television set, personal computer, and other valuable items, most of us would agree that the individual should be apprehended, compelled to return the stolen property, and punished.

Those actions that are condemned as contemptible when committed by individuals, however, are often condoned when committed by government. By definition, government is the only institution in a society that has the legitimate right to exercise force and to make binding rules upon all individuals who reside within its jurisdiction. Government, consequently, can legitimately kill and steal.

Governments have had much experience and success in killing. Since government alone possesses the legitimate right to use force, it has often exercised this right through foreign wars. Government takes young men away from their homes and puts them into military service, often

against their will. It tells them that it is an honor to engage in violence against the government's foes. The greatest mass murders in history, such as those resulting from the saturation bombing of Dresden and the dropping of atomic bombs on Hiroshima and Nagasaki in World War II, were government-ordered acts, as have been many other acts of war throughout the ages.

Even wars employing conventional weapons take a heavy toll on life. For example, a recent eight-year war between Iran and Iraq had left 1 million dead, 1.7 million wounded, and 1.5 million in flight as refugees, and cost $400 billion, according to some estimates.[4]

Government, too, kills within its own jurisdiction. It establishes a criminal justice system that enforces its will against those who do not abide by the rules it determines. It puts down rebellions that challenge the governing authorities.

Government also engages in constant theft. It does not label as theft its acts of taking people's property forcefully; instead, it calls these acts taxation. Taxation is taking money that has been duly earned by an individual and spending it for purposes that benefit either government or others. Often the justification for such theft is that society benefits when government redistributes income or concocts programs ostensibly aiding the poor and the disadvantaged. Such an argument, however, is ludicrous, as it is based on the notion that the government, rather than the people, is the better judge of society's needs. Is it not, then, proper to call anyone who kills a murderer and anyone who steals a thief—whether that "anyone" is an individual or government? We think so, unless one adopts a double standard of justice.

Societal Needs. Government acts in ways that are detrimental to social well-being. Among the most important elements of such well-being are physical protection, economic security, and welfare. In all these areas, government has shown that it is not only incapable of achieving

[4] Fox Butterfield, "8-Year Gulf War: Victims But No Victors," *New York Times*, July 25, 1988, p. A1.

these societal goals but that its existence is a real hindrance to achieving them.

Billions of dollars are spent each year for police protection, yet crime—particularly violent crime—remains high. Government has established so many restrictions on people's liberty that the police must devote their attention to punishing offenders of victimless crimes rather than pursuing real, hardened criminals. Why should government interfere in the private lives of its citizens? If an individual wishes to use drugs, see a pornographic film, or engage the services of a prostitute, why should the government try to enforce its own vision of morality?

In nearly every country in the world, however, government is involved in devoting considerable resources to curbing victimless crimes. It is no wonder, then, that murderers, looters, and thieves are not apprehended, given the misdirection of government expenditures. It is no surprise either that people have come to rely on private rather than public security services for their physical protection. The growth of private detective services, private police personnel, and private television surveillance is a reflection of the failure of the government to protect life and property of the citizenry.

Like physical protection, economic security is a societal goal. Wherever government intervenes, however, it inhibits rather than enhances such security. Such a poor economic record is seen from government's direction of the economy and from government's own industrial management.

In an attempt to "do good," government offers all kinds of economic benefits to favored groups. It institutes a variety of programs designed to favor one group of citizens at the expense of others. It offers subsidies to farmers, import quotas for domestic firms facing competitive foreign products, and bailouts for inefficient businesses. Instead of allowing market forces to operate and, consequently, bring prices down, it interferes to keep prices high. Such intervention harms consumers, who are penalized through high prices.

In many countries, moreover, government itself has taken over control and management of industries. When government becomes the employer, mismanagement can be guaranteed. The United States Postal Service is but one case in point. It is inefficiently run. Any private company wishing to compete with the government's monopoly of mail delivery is prevented from doing so because the government has determined that it does not want any competitors—at least for the delivery of regular mail. Such lack of competition has meant constantly rising prices for first-class mail. Special-interest users of mail, such as producers of books and magazines, are subsidized so that their rates are kept low while ordinary people must pay for these subsidies either with higher mailing rates or higher taxes.

What is true for the United States Postal Service is true for other industries managed by government as well. If government obtains a monopoly in any field, there is no competitive reason why it must operate that industry in an efficient manner. Government's inefficiency, consequently, means rising prices to the ordinary citizen.

Government, too, has failed to promote welfare. The term *welfare* connotes many things. In this context, we mean not *relief* but services such as health care, education, and housing.

An individual ought to be free to go to any doctor he or she chooses. The increased role of government in matters of health care, however, has meant that in many countries not only is the choice of doctors severely restricted but the quality of health care is poor. Public hospitals are generally inferior to private hospitals. Talented young men and women are deterred from entering careers in medicine, moreover, because of government controls on doctors' salaries. The quality of medical care, consequently, is low. In Great Britain, a country that has **socialized medicine** (government control of medical care), people have to wait for years, in some cases, to have operations because of a shortage of medical facilities.

Education is another of government's failures. In the United States, for example, the costs of public education are rising. More money is spent for public school education than ever before, yet the reading ability of students—a major factor in how well students perform—is poor. Parents are often so frustrated with the large classes, crime in the schools, and the poor quality of education their children are receiving that they take their children out of the public schools and send them to private schools. Such an action constitutes double taxation, since the parents pay taxes for schools that will not be used by their children as well as pay tuition to private schools. Attempts to strengthen private schools are resisted by the public school teachers and administrators so as to restrict private choice.

Good housing, too, has been wrecked by government. Government is responsible for poor housing in many ways. When inflation occurs (largely because of government spending), government institutes rent controls. The effect of rent controls is to reduce the profits of landlords. If landlords have profits, they reinvest those profits into new housing construction. Because of government interference, however, landlords use whatever money they make in more profitable nonhousing enterprises in which the return on investment is high.

Government programs involving public housing, moreover, cause many social problems. Government puts up skyscrapers that often become crime ridden. The major beneficiaries of public housing are not the poor but the well-to-do, such as property developers and promoters.

The cases of health care, education, and housing show that when government intercedes, its ostensible generosity and caring are misdirected. Government should avoid messing up people's lives, and the well-being of society will then prevail.

Alternatives to Government. Government, then, is an encumbrance placed upon society.

It is self-serving and inefficient. If we recognize government's inadequacies, we can begin to look for an alternative: the elimination of government and the restoration of power to the people. Instead of government making decisions for people, the people can make their own decisions about how they wish to solve their problems. They can build their own homes, educate their own children, and provide for their own health care.

Those who favor government, however, say that such a society is utopian. Such partisans of government have a paternalistic attitude toward people. They believe that people are incapable of providing for these essential needs of physical protection, economic security, and welfare. We have already shown that government has not been able to achieve those goals and that in many cases people are paying double taxation to provide for some of them, such as police protection and education. It is time now to eliminate government intervention and restore the people's control of their own lives.

1/NO   IS GOVERNMENT AVOIDABLE?

In modern times we are so often conscious of the weaknesses and evils of government that we neglect the positive contributions government makes to society. The existence of government is a natural consequence of the increasingly complex nature of human relationships in society. A society without government is neither desirable nor possible.

It is certainly true that throughout history some governments have enslaved their people and pursued policies which hindered, rather than helped, society in achieving some of its vital objectives, such as physical protection, economic security, and welfare. The more notorious examples in this century alone include Adolf Hitler's persecution and mass extermination of the Jewish people, Joseph Stalin's liquidation of millions of people in the Soviet Union, and Pol Pot's massacre of his own Cambodian citizens. There are, however, many governments that have found such actions to be reprehensible and have acted to extend the range of freedom for their people. They have served their citizens well. Let us look

more closely at the *Affirmative*'s charges that government acts to enslave its people and to thwart societal needs so that we may more properly evaluate the record of government.

Enslavement of People. Although government uses force and collects taxes, it is misleading to view such behavior as murder and theft. Government, to be sure, has the legal monopoly to use force. It is unrealistic to assume that without government there would be no use of force or that private individuals could be expected to cope with dangers to their security.

Much of the criticism directed against government is based on the notion that human beings are essentially good but that government makes them bad. Is such a view valid? We think not. Are human beings more or less likely to break the law in the absence of government? To answer that question, we should imagine what would happen if the police went out on strike permanently. Is it not reasonable to assume that there would be more looting, mugging, and other violations of persons and property than would occur with the presence of government?

The *Affirmative* argues that conscription is evil because it violates individual liberty. Such a view overlooks the character of a political system. In some political systems, such as democracies, the government is responsive to popular wishes (see Chapter 3). If duly elected officials determine that an armed force is needed to protect the people of a country and decide that conscription is the best way to constitute a military organization, then government is acting in ways the people themselves would choose. It is wrong to think that because government creates an army it is acting in a manner contrary to popular wishes.

Taxation could possibly be regarded as theft if the money raised from taxes were used for the benefit of the government. Tax money is more often used, however, for the benefit of society as a whole. People demand services, such as education, housing, welfare, and police security, and they expect government to provide them. To do so, they understand there must be taxes. If they did not believe that government should provide these services, they could—in democracies at least—vote the spenders out of office and replace them with nonspenders.

It is certainly true that taxpayers' revolts have occurred from time to time. For the most part, however, these revolts have been directed at the level of taxation rather than at the principle that government has a right and duty to impose taxes to achieve social objectives. Taxation, consequently, is not theft; it is the taking of funds from individuals to secure legitimate objectives.

It is wrong, too, to regard the very existence of government as an obstacle to human freedom. There are many cases in which government has been responsible for expanding human freedom. The government of the United States, for example, was in the forefront of human freedom when it used its power on behalf of black people and against such private racist organizations as the Ku Klux Klan and the White Citizens Council. That same government, moreover, has extended the freedom of women against acts of discrimination in the free market.

Societal Needs. Government has acted in many cases to provide physical protection, economic security, and welfare for its people. Police forces throughout the world do provide protection to people. Much attention is paid to the fail- ures of police agencies rather than to their successes. If, in spite of large expenditures on police protection, there is still much crime, that situation is not the fault of the police but is rather the result of social and economic factors beyond the control of the police.

Government has been blamed for establishing, as criminal, acts that should not properly be so designated. Specifically, laws relating to prostitution, drugs, and pornography are cited. It is wrong to argue, however, that these are "victimless crimes," because these crimes do produce victims and because society has a right to determine for itself what are its fundamental values. Government should assist society in maintaining those values.

Should adolescent girls be encouraged to engage in prostitution? In a totally free society without any government regulation, such a freedom would be assured. Does not common sense, however, dictate that there should be severe penalties imposed on those who entice young women into the world of prostitution? We think so.

Drugs, moreover, are harmful to human health. What good is it to say that human beings should be free to do as they wish if, as a result of such freedom, people become incapable of exercising their drug-damaged brains? When government imposes regulations against the possession and sale of drugs, it is acting in a way that most people approve. Fighting against drugs is a pressing social need.

One need not agree with the extremes of censorship rules to favor restrictions on pornography. Should a pornographic movie house be permitted next door to a church? Only the most extreme advocate of freedom would say so. Society has a right to impose certain restrictions on pornography as it seeks to maintain its traditional values. Government becomes society's agent when it acts in this manner.

Government involvement in the economy is a necessity when it serves society's needs. Public benefits to health, security, and fair play require a government role in the economy, for example.

Individual entrepreneurs may manufacture products that cause illness to unsuspecting consumers. In many countries of the world, food processing is supervised by government to assure that the products measure up to health standards. If cost becomes the single most important factor in the processing of foods, then, quite conceivably, cost saving could be induced by sacrificing health standards. Government establishes health agencies to prevent that from happening.

In the past private companies cared little about water or air pollution. They disposed of chemical wastes in ways that poisoned the air and the rivers. It became essential for government to intervene to make certain that people would not be injured by dangc.ous chemicals, which could produce long-term genetic defects and even death.

Government is essential to provide security for people. If poor people must pay for their own private security forces, then they will surely suffer the harshness of what will be, for them, a lawless society. The police must serve rich and poor alike in any just society, and economic affluence should not be the criterion for people's safety.

Fair play, too, requires government intervention in the economy. Minority groups and women have long been subjected to discrimination in paid employment. In the United States, for example, blacks, Jews, Catholics, Hispanics, Chinese, Native Americans, and women have been denied corporate positions not because they lacked competence but because companies would not hire them for important jobs. Such discrimination is morally reprehensible. Theoretically, a person who experiences discrimination is free to find another job. In fact, however, the person may be relegated to an inferior position everywhere because of patterns of discrimination in the corporate world. Government should provide an opportunity for a redress of grievances, for the sake of justice.

Government's involvement in the economy, then, can be beneficial to society. So, too, is government's role in promoting the welfare of society, such as in matters of health care, education, and housing.

It is certainly true that some mismanagement and unwise decisions have characterized public health matters, but the principle of government involvement in health is a good one. Thanks to public immunization programs supported by government research and money, for example, some illnesses have been virtually eliminated, smallpox and polio being two prominent examples.

Government involvement in health care is based upon the principle that society should provide health care to anyone who is unable to afford it. If an individual develops a serious handicap because of reasons beyond his or her control, that person should be able to receive medical care. Elderly people particularly experience illness at a time in their lives when they may no longer be capable of working. Are the elderly to be discarded like so much garbage after they have reached their "golden" years? To be sure, people should save for a rainy day, but in many cases they cannot prepare for every contingency. Some forms of medical treatment, moreover, require more money than a person could possibly save. How else should elderly people be helped but with government support?

Many of the government programs for sick people have benefited them (and, incidentally, made them economically productive people in society because of their restored health). We may properly object to the bad management practices under socialized medicine, and attempts should be made to improve medical services rendered to the people. We should, however, recognize that people are in better health because they are permitted to obtain medical service at public expense than would be the case if they could not afford to pay for such care.

Public education in many countries has been an outstanding success. Millions of people have moved up the economic ladder because of the educational opportunities opened up to them, not only at the elementary school level but also at secondary schools and universities.

It is certainly true that public schools are not always the perfect educational institutions they should be and that they often do not succeed in enhancing social mobility. Many of the charges against public education are not, however, valid. When critics of public education point to declining reading scores and the rise of crime within the schools as evidence for their case, they are providing misleading information.

A major reason for the low reading scores and the rise of crime in the public schools is the rise of private schools. Public schools must accept every child: the bright and the dull, the sick and the healthy. More affluent parents have an alternative of sending their children to private schools. If they would only send their children to public schools, the reading score average of the public school would increase. No doubt crime would decrease with the infusion of more serious students, as adequate resources would be provided to control crime.

Government has played a positive role with respect to housing, too. Without rent controls, private, greedy landlords would take advantage of any situation to gouge tenants with exorbitant increases in rent. People would then be "free" to find luxury apartments at high rentals, but that quest would result in the denial to themselves and their families of many other essentials of well-being.

As far as public housing is concerned, it is often better than the rat-infested housing it replaced. It is certainly true that big-time property developers take advantage of public housing programs, but that is not a sufficient argument against public housing. Public housing still offers benefits to those who cannot find adequate private housing. If the public housing units are run poorly, it is because not enough money is appropriated for the maintenance of public housing. *More* government, not less, would be the solution to the problem of poor housing.

Government, then, can be a force for good. The cases of health care, education, and housing show that although government does have weaknesses, it is a vital force in serving societal needs.

Alternatives to Government. People who talk about a society without government are offering utopian solutions to real problems. Given the complex nature of society, human beings through voluntary associations could not cope with the essential needs of society. Government has at times been oppressive. Oppression, however, is not a necessary ingredient of government. How government, in fact, can be made responsive to popular needs is a matter to which we should devote our attention (see Chapter 3).

KEY TERMS

Anarchists
Authority
Government
Legitimacy
Libertarians
Microstates
Polis

Politics
Power
Public policy
Socialized medicine
Sovereignty
State

QUESTIONS

1. Who would be harmed and who would be helped if the state were dissolved? Why?
2. What functions that government performs could be better performed by private individuals? Why?
3. What functions that private individuals perform could be better provided by government? Why?
4. Should government regulate pornography? Why?
5. What effect would the abolition of government have on war? Why?

RECOMMENDED READINGS

BARNES, BARRY. *The Nature of Power*. Urbana: University of Illinois Press, 1988. An account of power in society.

BOULDING, KENNETH E. *Three Faces of Power*. Newbury Park, Calif.: Sage Publications, 1989. An analysis of power.

CAPORASO, JAMES A., ed. *The Elusive State: International and Comparative Perspectives*. New-

bury Park, Calif.: Sage Publications, 1989. Analyses of the state.

CRICK, BERNARD. *Socialist Values and Time*. London: Fabian Society, 1984. A defense of socialism.

———, and TOM CRICK. *What Is Politics?* Baltimore: Edward Arnold, 1987. A concise overview of the subject.

DAHL, ROBERT A. *Modern Political Analysis.* 5th ed. Englewood Cliffs, N.J.: Prentice Hall, 1991. A study of politics.

———. "Power." *International Encyclopaedia of the Social Sciences* (1968), 12:405–15. An introduction to the subject.

FRIED, MORTON H. "The State: The Institution." *International Encyclopaedia of the Social Sciences* (1968), 15:143–50. An overview of the subject.

FRIEDEN, KARL. "Public Needs and Private Wants." *Dissent* 34 (Summer 1987): 317–25. An argument against the stereotype of government as inefficient.

HALL, JOHN A., and G. JOHN IKENBERRY. *The State.* Minneapolis: University of Minnesota Press, 1989. An analysis of the historical origins of the state, theories of state power, and the ways that states interact with other sources of power.

HARRINGTON, MICHAEL. *Socialism: Past and Future.* New York: Arcade Publishing, 1989. A case for socialism.

KAYDEN, XANDRA. *Surviving Power: The Experience of Power—Exercising It and Giving It Up.* New York: Free Press, 1990. A study of what power does for people and what happens when power is lost.

LASSWELL, HAROLD. *Politics: Who Gets What, When, and How.* New York: Peter Smith, 1950. An examination of politics as the study of influence and the influential.

LEFTWICH, ADRIAN, ed. *New Developments in Political Science: An International Review of Achievements and Prospects.* Aldershot, England: Edward Elgar Publishers, 1990. An overview of political science.

LUKES, STEVEN, ed. *Power.* New York: New York University Press, 1986. A collection of articles analyzing power.

MACHAN, TIBOR, ed. *The Libertarian Reader.* Totowa, N.J.: Rowman and Littlefield, 1982. Essays on libertarianism.

MEIER, CHRISTIAN. *The Greek Discovery of Politics,* trans. David McLintock. Cambridge, Mass.: Harvard University Press, 1990. An examination of political life in ancient Greece and an assessment of why Greek civilization gave birth to democracies.

WATKINS, FREDERICK M. "State: The Concept." *International Encyclopaedia of the Social Sciences* (1968), 15:150–57. A survey.

WOODCOCK, GEORGE. *Anarchism: A History of Libertarian Ideas and Movements.* Cleveland: Meridian Books, 1962. A study of anarchism.

Nations

If we have to start over again with another Adam and Eve, then I want them to be Americans and not Russians, and I want them on this continent [North America] and not in Europe.[1]

When United States Senator Richard Russell uttered these words during a debate on military preparedness, he was criticized for his belief in a patriotism bordering on madness. What difference does it make, his critics asked, what the nationality is of the last two survivors of a nuclear holocaust that destroyed the lives of billions of people?

However, farfetched the notion of preserving nationality after a nuclear catastrophe may be, the hazards of nationalism are widespread in the world. Examples from the Middle East and Eastern Europe illustrate the dangers.

In the Middle East, the plight of the Kurdish people highlight the perennial problems of nationalism. The Kurds are an ancient people with a three-thousand-year history. They share common ethnic, cultural, linguistic, and religious characteristics that distinguish them from Iranians, Turks, Arabs, and other Middle Eastern peoples. In all, there are about 20 million Kurds, constituting the fourth largest group in the Middle East.

For all of their unity, the Kurds lack a country of their own, which Kurdish nationalists think of as "Kurdistan." Instead, most Kurds live in a contiguous area of 500,000 square kilometers that is divided among four countries: Iran, Iraq, Syria, and Turkey. In each, the Kurds are a minority people. There are also small Kurdish communities in Azerbaijan, Armenia, Lebanon, and Western Europe.

Kurds were part of the Ottoman Empire. At the close of World War I, the right of an independent Kurdistan was recognized in the Treaty of Sèvres in 1920. But independence never was achieved. Instead

[1] Richard Russell, quoted in *New York Times*, January 22, 1971, p. 43.

a new treaty, the Treaty of Lausanne of 1923, revoked the right of self-determination for the Kurds.

Kurdish nationalists continue to seek an independent Kurdistan, but the countries with Kurdish minorities see their movement as a threat. Iran, Iraq, Syria, and Turkey have battled with Kurdish nationalists, and Iraq's leader Saddam Hussein even used poison gas against them.

With the demise of communism, national conflicts have also threatened the peace of Eastern Europe, where the "hodgepodge" of nationalities has long been a potential time bomb. In 1991, Croatia and Slovenia broke away from Yugoslavia and became independent countries after a fierce civil war. Other parts of Yugoslavia—Macedonia and Bosnia-Herzegovina—moved toward independence in 1992 after bloody fighting with Yugoslav forces. Hungary and Romania clashed over the Magyar minority in Transylvania. Relations between Turkey and Bulgaria deteriorated over the conditions of the Bulgarian Turks. And minorities in the former Soviet republics experienced discrimination as the republics sought independence. Ethnic and national conflicts continue to threaten the economic development and political stability of the area.

Whatever one's view of **self-determination**—the right of a group of people to determine for themselves the state in which they will live and the form of government they will possess—there is no doubt that nationalism has become one of the most important political forces of our times. So dynamic is this force that it has swept through every continent and influenced every major political ideology. An understanding of nationalism, then, is essential to evaluate one of the most important influences on political stability and change in states and governments today.

Historians, philosophers, political scientists, and policy makers differ about the meaning of nationalism. The term *nation* derives from the Latin verb *nasci*, meaning

"to be born." Originally, *nation* referred to a group of people born in the same area of the world, although no limit on the basis of the size of territory was associated with the term. Today, **nation** refers to a group of people who identify with a state. **Nationalism** may be defined as an ideology in which a people, regardless of their race, class, or religion, feel that they have more in common with each other than they have with other people and give their highest loyalty to a state or to part of a state that may eventually become a separate state.

In this century nationalism has been expressed in a variety of forms—from acts of violence to demonstrations of cooperation. At its worst, nationalism is the basis of the expansion of a country into the territory of others. Adolf Hitler's attempt to unite German-speaking people under Nazi rule is but one of many examples. More recently, acts of terrorism have been performed in the name of nationalism. Palestinian nationalists, for example, have hijacked airplanes and held innocent passengers as hostages.

Nationalism does not, however, always express itself in violence. For many it is an association of different groups in a common effort. To be sure, conflict is often a characteristic of nationalism, but in some countries—such as the United States, Switzerland, and India, for example—diverse **ethnic groups** (people possessing characteristics that distinguish them from other groups)[2] have, albeit with major exceptions, worked in relative peace and harmony.

In discussing nationalism we deal with some difficult concepts. As we shall see, the world is not an ethnically "tidy" place. That is to say, ethnic groups have moved and been moved because of war, economic factors, discrimination, and personal reasons. In only about 10 percent of the countries of

[2] Benjamin Akzin, *State and Nation* (London: Hutchinson University Library, 1964), pp. 30, 46.

the world do ethnic boundaries of a single ethnic community coincide with state boundaries. As a result there are sizable communities of Germans in Austria as well as Germany, of Indians in East Africa as well as India, and of Italians in the United States as well as in Italy.

In Chapter 1 the term *state* is defined as a political entity that possesses people, territory, a government, and sovereignty. When we talk about a state, we are, then, referring to a *political* or legal entity. A state may or may not contain people who feel especially attached to other members of the state. The term **nation-state** is sometimes used to mean a political institution combining the concepts of nation (an anthropological notion) with state (a legal idea).

Examples of giving one's highest loyalty to the state are varied. It means that an American citizen of German descent would fight for the United States in a war against Germany, or that a British capitalist would terminate a commercial relationship with an Italian capitalist if their two countries were at war, or that a French factory worker would rather support a French capitalist than a Dutch factory worker.

In the twentieth century nothing seems more natural than that a Greek citizen should feel a stronger attachment to Greece than to Turkey, or that a French citizen should feel especially loyal to France; but this feeling of attachment to the state is of recent vintage, dating only from the late eighteenth century. The contrast between the prenational and national periods is striking. In medieval times, to be identified as a religious heretic was regarded as one of the most heinous crimes, a category that in the twentieth century is reserved for a traitor to one's country. In the first half of the eighteenth century, moreover, a foot soldier felt no attachment to his own state but fought for any monarch who paid him. The soldier found nothing extraordinary about switching allegiance from the army of one country to the army of its rival. Today, such switching

would be regarded as treason, punishable by death or imprisonment.

Historically, nationalism is only one of many group loyalties that people have held. In the past people gave allegiance to forms of social and political organization other than the nation, such as a tribe or clan. In ancient Greece, people respected their *polis*, or city-state, but citizenship was restricted by birth and was rarely acquired. Athenian citizenship excluded women, children, resident aliens, and slaves. Certainly the citizens of Athens, one of the most important of the Greek city-states, felt no special attachment to the Athenian slaves. Although empires of antiquity ruled over people of diverse ethnic backgrounds, there was no universal attachment to the empire comparable to the popular loyalty directed by the nation today.

In medieval Europe, people showed loyalty to a variety of entities: a guild, a village, a province, a region, and a church. There was little sense of camaraderie among people of diverse classes, a sense that they had more in common with each other than they had with peoples of other regions. A French, Prussian, or Croatian lord felt that his horse was more a part of his "nation" than were the peasants who worked his lands. In the period prior to the French Revolution, the "nation" was sometimes identified with the ruling class—the sovereign and the aristocracy.

Although forerunners of the nation go back at least to ancient times, nationalism as a force stems mostly from the period of the French Revolution in the late eighteenth century. It began in Western Europe and North America and has moved gradually to include the peoples of the entire world.

Throughout the centuries, many explanations have been put forward to describe the origin and continuation of nations. One of these is that God created the nation. Although much attention has been given to the idea that the Jewish people trace their nationality to God's will, American, German, and French writers have made similar claims for their nations. Another explanation was offered by the conservative eighteenth-century writer Edmund Burke, who contended that the nation was formed from mystical forces linking past to future generations.[3]

Most scholars today, however, argue that a variety of factors has contributed to creating a feeling of nationalism, although not every factor was involved in shaping national consciousness in each case. The most important features include common political system, territory, enemy, language, history, people, religion, economy, and culture.

POLITICAL SYSTEM

It is often the case that a common political system serves as a basis for building nationalism. In this sense, the state precedes the nation. First a legal entity, the state, is created, and then a feeling of nationalism develops within the context of the state.

In seventeenth- and eighteenth-century Europe, strong states existed for the most part without a popular national consciousness. So lacking was a feeling of nationalism in this period that monarchs transferred territory with diverse ethnic populations without taking into account the ethnic composition of the people included in the transfer. In the late nineteenth and twentieth centuries, however, such transfers were less likely to occur.

Jordan is an example of how national boundaries were shaped by a common po-

[3] For these and other explanations, see Boyd C. Shafer, *Nationalism: Interpreters and Interpretations*, 2d. ed. Service Center for Teachers of History, Publication 20 (Washington, D.C.: American Historical Association, 1963), pp. 5–6. For a discussion of recent interpretations of nationalism, see Ernst B. Haas, "What Is Nationalism and Why Should We Study It?" *International Organization* 40 (Summer 1986): 707–44, and the books mentioned by Haas.

litical system. There was no Jordanian nationalism in the sense of a Jordanian people in existence when Jordan (then known as Transjordan) was created after World War I. Its boundaries were shaped largely by the major colonial powers in the Middle East— Britain and France—rather than through the assertion of a Jordanian national consciousness. Once the political entity of Jordan was created, however, Jordanian national consciousness emerged.

What was true for Jordan was also true for other British colonies in Asia and Africa. The British created the basis of political integration through the maintenance of law and order, administrative unity, social and political values, a common English language, and fiscal and economic integration. Nationalism emerged within the political units that Great Britain had shaped, such as India, Kenya, and Nigeria.

The process by which a common political system can serve as a basis of nationalism is clear. First, a political system creates laws governing the people who reside within a geographical area. Then, as certain forces such as war or industrialization mobilize a society, a feeling of nationalism arises out of the common political system.

TERRITORY

Nationalism is associated with a particular territory, even though the boundary lines of states have often shifted. Common territory is often distinguished by peculiar geographical configurations. The Pyrenees Mountains, for example, provide a natural barrier between France and Spain, and the English Channel separates France from Great Britain.

Nationalism is the fusion of the idea of a group unity with a particular territory. Even when territories were under foreign rule, as were Poland for two centuries and Palestine for two thousand years, the national ideal was tied to specific geographical regions.

ENEMY

Nothing may unite a people more quickly than attack by a hostile power. Divisions along class, regional, and ideological lines may disappear if there is a sense of danger from outside forces. For example, when Napoleon's armies marched across Europe, they aroused not only fear but a sense of unity in resistance. Spanish and Russian nationalism, in particular, grew in response to the foreign danger.

Just as invasion and mobilization sparked feelings of nationalism in Europe in the early nineteenth century, so, too, did similar actions mark the African and Asian experience in the twentieth century. During the world wars European powers such as Great Britain and France took into their armies people from their colonies. Once Africans and Asians were mobilized and trained in military skills, it was only a matter of time before they used those skills against their colonial mentors. After the world wars were over, the colonial peoples perceived their imperial rulers as foreigners and enemies. Colonial peoples tended to unite across ethnic and regional lines against the European power. In this way a common enemy united a people. After the imperial power was defeated, however, fragmentation and civil war often characterized the political life of the former colonial people in their newly independent country.

LANGUAGE

People who speak the same language communicate with each other more easily and often than with people who speak other languages. Language is thus a feature that serves to distinguish or separate one group of people from another. The fact that the people of France speak French and the people of Spain speak Spanish means that unless people from each of these countries are bilingual, they will tend to communicate and associate with people who speak the same language. A common language, consequently, may promote a feeling of nationalism and a solidarity among people who can literally understand each other. Language, however, may become an instrument of introducing competitive national symbols, as French has served in promoting a sense of separatism in the Canadian province of Quebec.

HISTORY

The fact that people share a common history over a long period of time is an important force strengthening nationalism. For example, the English people developed their institutions over centuries and feel that they have more in common with each other than they have with other people. Since the thirteen American colonies had in many cases a similar history brought on by more than one hundred years of British rule, a sense of nationalism among the colonial Americans was created as well.[4]

Every people have their own heroes, sometimes from legendary sources, and their own historical memories. Often, however, the historical events they remember are carefully selected to nurture a sense of nationalism rather than to portray internal differences. Recollections of American history, for example, often reflect the "melting pot" idea, in which people from all over the world emigrated to the United States and developed American values. The racial, ethnic, and religious conflicts that characterized American history are often downplayed or forgotten in the national memory. It has been well said that "a nation is a group of persons united by a common

[4]Although the term *Americans* can refer to people from North or South America, it is used here to mean people from the United States.

error about their ancestry and a common dislike of their neighbors."[5]

PEOPLE

Every nation is composed of a people, although the number of people constituting a nation varies. Sometimes a people is made up of different ethnic groups. It is often difficult to recognize a people, since we tend to ignore some characteristics and pay attention to others.

Race, however, is one element used often to distinguish a people. Although the black people of South Africa spoke many languages and came from different ethnic backgrounds, many of them felt a sense of black nationalism that united them in opposition to the government of white-ruled South Africa. In spite of efforts by the Portuguese to integrate the native Africans living in the colonies of Angola and Mozambique, a black consciousness developed in opposition to the Portuguese.

Racial and ethnic similarities have often been used in distinguishing one people from another. For the most part, however, the concept of a people is a psychological one. In effect, a people is any group that thinks of itself as a unique community. People with similar racial characteristics have sometimes chosen to identify with different states. Conflict between black African nations, such as marked the relationship between Uganda and Tanzania for many years, is a case in point.

RELIGION

Religion is a factor that can contribute to a sense of nationalism. The Jewish people have had an ancient religious history that has been a source of solidarity. Although

the Jewish people were expelled from Palestine for a period of nearly two thousand years, the Jewish religion has been essential to the creation and continuation of the Israeli nation. Religion was the basis for the establishment of the state of Pakistan, with its predominantly Muslim population, out of British India with its predominantly Hindu population.

ECONOMY

Economic factors have also served to unify nations. The tearing down of tariff barriers and the strengthening of commercial ties among the thirteen states of the United States after the defeat of the British in the American Revolutionary War helped to unite people into one nation. Similar patterns of economic cooperation appeared in other countries.

There seems to be a relationship between the rise of industrialism and the emergence of nationalism, although it is not clear that the former is a cause of the latter. Preindustrial society was generally characterized by limited movement of people either geographically or socially and by relative separation of government from the daily lives of the masses of people. In contrast, industrialization may be looked upon as a component of **modernization**, which is the application of technology by extensive social interdependence, organization, literacy, social mobility, and other factors.[6] The industrial revolution produced vast social upheavals in which people moved from the countryside to the cities, causing social, economic, and psychological disruptions in their lives. Industrial society required that people of diverse racial, religious, and social backgrounds work together for a common purpose. The nation provided the

[5] Karl W. Deutsch, *Nationalism and Its Alternatives* (New York: Knopf, 1969), p. 3.

[6] Claude E. Welch, Jr., ed., *Political Modernization: A Reader in Comparative Political Change* (Belmont, Calif.: Wadsworth, 1967), p. 2.

conditions of military security and economic unity under which industrialism could flourish. Previous forms of social organization—tribes and empires, for example—could not provide those conditions.

The exact relationship between economics and nationalism is most controversial. Marxists believe that nationalism will disappear and that it has no real basis for existing once the socialist revolution occurs (see Chapter 5). Other political advocates have had different ideas of the role of economics in nation building. However difficult they may be to measure, economic factors undoubtedly have been important in shaping nations.

CULTURE

The idea of nationalism is often the creation of intellectuals who give expression to a **culture**, which may be defined as a core of traditional ideas, practices, and technology shared by a people. The German philosopher Johann Gottlieb Fichte heralded a German nationalism. Theodore Herzl, a Hungarian Jewish journalist, became the founder of **Zionism,** a philosophy that identifies the Jewish people with a homeland in Palestine. The concept of a Pakistani nation separate from India was mostly a creation of a group of intellectuals in the 1930s.

Nationalism also has roots in the cultural traditions of ordinary people through their customs, songs, and style—all are factors that have strengthened nationalism. To the extent that the state increased its power over society in the past two centuries, national symbols of culture have often been encouraged. Public schools in the nineteenth and twentieth centuries also became promoters of cultural unity.

ISSUES

Because of its continued impact on society, nationalism remains a controversial ideology and political movement. Its defenders see it as a force for unity; its detractors condemn it as a force for divisiveness and war.

Three principal questions arise prominently in dealing with this subject: (1) Is nationalism divisive? (2) Does nationalism lead to war? (3) Is the nation-state outmoded at the end of the twentieth century?

2/YES   IS NATIONALISM DIVISIVE?

Nationalism is divisive because of its ambiguity and its **ethnocentrism**—belief that one's group or nation is of universal importance. With nationalism so pervasive, it is almost inevitable that the world should remain chaotic.

Ambiguity. The ideal model of a nation, according to the political scientist Rupert Emerson, is

a single people, traditionally fixed on a well-defined territory, speaking the same language and preferably a language all its own, possessing a distinctive culture, and shaped to a common mold by many generations of shared historical experience.[7]

The problem, however, is that no such nation ever existed.

The elements that go into making each nation are often vague and varied. For example, a com-

[7] Rupert Emerson, *From Empire to Nation: The Rise to Self-Assertion of Asian and African Peoples* (Cambridge, Mass.: Harvard University Press, 1967), p. 103.

mon political system may include peoples of diverse languages and cultures. Switzerland, with its French, German, and Italian peoples, is a case in point. At the same time, many nations speak the same language but give no thought to uniting. The United States and Great Britain are an example. The Irish-born playwright George Bernard Shaw once quipped that the Irish and English are separated by the same language.

Wars, dynastic marriages, discovery, territorial purchases, migrations of peoples, and historical accident have all contributed to creating a world in which peoples have become scattered in such a way as to prevent the construction of neat categories clearly distinguishing nations. Hardly any land in Europe exists that did not once belong to a neighboring state. The legacy of such territorial change is a residue of ethnic minorities all over the continent. German populations can be found in Austria, Poland, and Switzerland. Italian people are located in Yugoslavia and Austria. Greeks inhabit Cyprus as well as Greece.

There are, moreover, few natural frontiers such as the Alps and Pyrenees Mountains. Many a country could, with the logic of geography, be made into two or more nations. The Mississippi River and the Rockies could be regarded as natural frontiers, yet neither prevented the United States from becoming one nation. The Nile River, moreover, unites rather than divides Egypt.

Clearly, the components of nationalism are diverse. There is no objective way to distinguish one nation from another, and overlaps produce rivalry over territory.

Ethnocentrism. Although there is no clear-cut definition of what constitutes a nation, a more serious divisive quality of nationalism is the ethnocentrism it produces. So powerful is nationalism that many of the values people acquire derive from the nation-state. Americans, for example, are taught at an early age to respect national authority. They attend public schools and study their national heritage. They learn the national anthem and the pledge of allegiance. From cradle to grave, Americans as well as people from all over the world discover that the nation is the strongest symbol of loyalty.

People, consequently, think of themselves in national terms, as Americans, Italians, Kenyans, or Japanese. They emphasize those characteristics that separate them from other people. Such a preoccupation with what separates people is basically harmful to the global community.

What is really important is not what separates people but what unites them. Human beings everywhere have similar needs: personal happiness, physical safety, and economic security. Since the world is composed of *people*, the abstract national designation labels like American, Russian, or Chinese are a disservice to humankind. Without the ideology of nationalism Americans would feel the same sense of compassion for victims of famine in sub-Saharan Africa as they do for victims of Mississippi floods. Nationalism is partially responsible for a people's insensitivity to the needs of other peoples of the world.

2/NO   IS NATIONALISM DIVISIVE?

Ambiguity. Nationalism may indeed be an ambiguous concept, but that ambiguity has not necessarily promoted divisiveness among people. Nationalism has often served to unite people. There are many illustrations of this point. The United States began as thirteen states along the Atlantic seaboard. At the time of its independence from Great Britain, it had a population of about 3 million people. Today the United States is composed of fifty states containing more than

250 million people with many diverse ethnic groups. Even Hawaii, which has a minority Caucasian population, is entirely integrated into the American nation. The American ideal is one of the "melting pot."

Germany offers a different example. In the nineteenth century, Prussia became the champion of German unity. Prussia was able to strengthen that unity through creation of the North German Confederation in 1866. A few years later, in 1871, Germany became a unified country, incorporating many states into one nation. After forty-five years of division following World War II, Germany reunited into a single state. Italy, too, was once composed of many principalities that united into a single Italy. For the peoples of Africa and Asia the nation represents not a force of disintegration but a force uniting the many diverse and smaller ethnic or tribal groups into a larger political unit.

The unifying element of nationalism may best be seen by examining its economic aspects. Although the components that help shape a nation are diverse, it is clear that there is a relationship between the emergence of nationalism and the rise of the modern industrial state. As indicated above, to a considerable extent the underlying ideal behind industrialism and nationalism is similar: namely, that people should work together for some common goal.

Peaceful relations among diverse groups within a nation must exist if the political system is to become strong and integrated. There must also be a basic respect for law and a feeling that the rules are equitable for all citizens.

Industrial development requires many of the same things. There can be no economic development without peace. No one will invest money in building a factory if social tensions are so great that the factory is in danger of being blown up. If industrial society is to progress, moreover, the best talent—regardless of race, gender, or religion—must be obtained. To be sure, discrimination has marked hiring practices in industrial societies, but often at the expense of economic development.

The emergence of the nation-state in Europe served to strengthen economic development in a variety of ways. It produced internal order through its control of the armed forces. It established tariffs, which strengthened the domestic market. It gave incentives to industries in the form of subsidies and grants for economic development.

Many Third World countries in Africa and Asia today are experiencing similar benefits from the nation. Some of these states have unusual difficulties because of their enormous poverty and scarce resources. The nation-state often is helpful in devising planning instruments to manage these scarce resources and the economy generally. To the extent that many of these new nations can get people from varying ethnic groups to work together for common goals, to that degree will there be an improvement of the economy. The destruction of the nation-state would, then, undermine economic development.

Although much has been said about the divisiveness of nationalism with references made to secessionist groups agitating for self-determination, it is important to keep in mind that most states have been able to control or contain these militant groups. In spite of the behavior of militant nationalist groups, including Basques, French Canadians, Corsicans, Puerto Ricans, and others, states have rarely been destroyed as a result of nationalist agitation. Recent developments of national independence in the former Soviet Union and Yugoslavia are the exceptions rather than the rule. Nationalism is not as divisive as its critics contend.

Ethnocentrism. There is a big difference between attachment to one's political community and intolerance toward others. Patriotic symbols unite diverse people. Loyalty to one's country does not necessarily mean indifference to other loyalties of religion, class, or profession.

Americans who collect money for the relief of famine-stricken Ethiopians display compassion for fellow human beings regardless of nationality. Patriotism does not preclude sensitivity to the needs of foreigners.

Chew Sock Foon, a specialist in ethnic studies, argues that in multiethnic states ethnic identity is compatible under certain conditions with national loyalty. She contends that if a government pursues congruent public policies designed to implement the core supraethnic values, such as official recognition and encouragement of minority languages *and* tolerance for the cultures of all resident ethnic groups, "then national identification might well be heightened, even as ethnic identification persists at significant levels."[8]

[8]Chew Sock Foon, "On the Incompatibility of Ethnic and National Loyalties: Reframing the Issue," *Canadian Review of Studies in Nationalism* (Prince Edward Island) 13 (Spring 1986): 7.

3/YES   DOES NATIONALISM LEAD TO WAR?

Because of the realities of power, nationalism has often led to bitterness and war. When economic and military interests take precedence over considerations of nationalism, the consequence is conflict.

The problem of the conflict between national and other considerations became particularly acute during the Versailles Peace Conference that was organized to settle the future of the defeated powers after World War I. The victors had their own military security and economic interests, and when these goals conflicted with the principle of national self-determination, then the latter principle was denied, compromised, or minimized. The effects of the peace settlement that resulted had much to do with the evils of the next two decades. The nationality question of the German minorities in Europe was an important factor contributing to the coming of World War II.

The Versailles Treaty illustrates the difficulty of applying the principle of nationalism when other considerations are important. One major example deals with Czechoslovakia. The peace treaty created Czechoslovakia but based its territorial configuration on factors other than ethnic homogeneity. Had Czechoslovakia been created to unite the northern Slav peoples previously under Austro-Hungarian rule, it might have been a more politically viable state. Western political leaders, and Czechs and Slovaks themselves, however, believed that a large section of Bohemia containing 3.1 million Germans would allow the country to be militarily secure and economically viable. A further complication was that the new country had 750,000 Hungarians in Slovakia and Ruthenia plus 460,000 Ukrainian peasants with loyalties outside of Czechoslovakia.[9] When Adolf Hitler determined to unite all German people by force, the dismemberment of Czechoslovakia was inevitable.

In addition to producing political mayhem at Versailles, the principle of nationalism portended political chaos ahead. The revolutionary impact of the principle of national self-determination, in which every people has its own state, was clearly recognized during the immediate post–World War I years. Robert Lansing, Woodrow Wilson's secretary of state, criticized the principle as "loaded with dynamite." He added:

It will raise hopes which can never be realized. It will, I fear, cost thousands of lives. In the end it is bound to be discredited, to be called the dream of an idealist who failed to realize the danger until too late to check those who attempt to put the principle in force. What a calamity that the phrase was ever uttered! What misery it will cause.[10]

Even in the post–World War II period, the principle of national self-determination led to enormous problems. The struggle against Western imperialism was made in the name of national self-determination. "Algeria for the Algerians," "Nigeria for the Nigerians," "Angola for the Angolans," and similar nationalist slogans became the battle cries of the opponents of French, British, and Portuguese imperialism. It became increasingly difficult for Western countries, particularly democracies, to continue colonial rule for many reasons. One of the factors that contributed to the decline of Western imperialism, however, was the moral appeal to national self-determination. How could Western policy makers challenge with conviction the principle of national self-determination that they themselves had asserted on behalf of their own nation-states and their European allies?

Once they had achieved freedom from colonial rule, however, the newly independent countries of Africa and Asia faced challenges from among their own people. These countries themselves were not homogeneous but were, rather, **multinational states**—composed of diverse ethnic groups that cluster within identifiable geographic regions. When the "nations" within these states called for separation on the principle of national self-determination, they were opposed by the very governments that had previously used the principle against their former colonial

[9]Glen St. J. Barclay, *Twentieth Century Nationalism* (New York: Praeger, 1971), p. 26.

[10]Robert Lansing, *The Peace Negotiations: A Personal Narrative* (Boston: Houghton Mifflin, 1921), pp. 97–98.

masters.[11] In that manner they were following in the footsteps of the European experience. When Poland achieved independence from Russian, German, and Austrian rule in 1919, it had to defend that independence against the German, Ukrainian, and White Russian minorities within its borders. These minorities constituted one-third of the entire population.[12]

Nigeria experienced a severe civil war, which may have cost the loss of more than 1 million lives, after the Ibos, one of the three largest ethnic groups in the country, sought independence as the Republic of Biafra in 1967. The Bengalis of East Pakistan successfully seceded from Pakistan to establish Bangladesh. More often than not, however, the smaller ethnic groups within the newly independent states have not succeeded in achieving independence and forming separate states.

Such restiveness was played upon after World War II by the United States and the Soviet Union as superpowers in their own struggles and for their own purposes. Nationalism, as both American President Woodrow Wilson and Soviet leader V. I. Lenin early recognized, is a powerful political force. It is not only powerful but so disruptive of international order that it should be eliminated from the face of the earth.

Political leaders who inculcate values of loyalty to the nation often cannot draw the line between patriotism and chauvinism. **Patriotism** is love of country. **Chauvinism** is excessive, almost obsessive, patriotism and may best be illustrated in this toast by American Admiral Stephen Decatur in 1816: "Our country! In her intercourse with foreign nations may she always be in the right; but our country right or wrong." One wit may have been on much sounder footing when he cited the Decatur toast as the moral equivalent of "My mother, drunk or sober!"

Once the values of nationalism are put forward, it is difficult to draw limits. It is but a short step from saying, "My country is different from yours," to proclaiming, "My country is better than yours." Nationalism, consequently, has produced wars of **irredentism** (national agitation by an ethnic group opposed to foreign rule and demanding incorporation into a country with a similar ethnic composition), wars of imperialism, and wars of self-determination. Major examples of nationalism turning warlike and expansionist in this century are Adolf Hitler's Germany and Benito Mussolini's Italy. Both dictators espoused ideologies that revered the nation-state. Mussolini stressed the classical Roman heritage of Italy as the basis for expansion into Ethiopia. Hitler heralded the superior German nation or race as the justification for expansion into the countries of Europe. Nazism and Italian fascism (see Chapter 4) were logical outgrowths of the age of nationalism.

Even if the fascist examples of Italy and Germany are not considered, nationalism and **total war**—a war fought for unrestricted goals with all available instruments of power—seem to have emerged at the same time. In the eighteenth century, monarchs conducted wars fought by professional soldiers, and it was possible to distinguish between a soldier and a civilian. Even during periods of warfare, citizens of the belligerent countries could travel to the enemy states. Wars were thought to be the province of governments and armies rather than the people. With the emergence and strengthening of nationalism in the nineteenth and twentieth centuries, the character of war changed to include not only the armed forces but also the civilian population. In essence, the age of nationalism became the age of total war and affected every sector of society, separating the peoples of each country and obliterating the distinction between soldier and civilian. Now the enemy became entire peoples, consequently enlarging the battlefield to include not only factories but apartment complexes.[13] Nationalism has made war more devastating and should, therefore, be brought to an end.

[11] Walker Connor, "Self-Determination: The New Phase," *World Politics* 20 (October 1967): 30–53.

[12] Hans Morgenthau, "Nationalism: Dilemma," in *Nationalism and International Progress*, ed. Urban G. Whitaker, Jr., rev. ed. (San Francisco: Chandler, 1961), p. 180.

[13] Edward Hallett Carr, *Nationalism and After* (London: Macmillan, 1968), pp. 26–27.

3/NO   DOES NATIONALISM LEAD TO WAR?

Critics who berate nationalism as a force for war overstate their case: (1) they ignore the many factors that cause conflict; and (2) they do not see that the nation-state is a stepping-stone to a larger political organization.

Causes of War. In addition to promoting peace within a country, nationalism can create a pattern of cooperation and peace rather than war among nations. In fact, this idea stems from the heyday of European nationalism. In the nineteenth century the Italian liberal Giuseppe Mazzini was only one among many liberals in Italy and elsewhere who believed that a world organized on the principle of national self-determination would be a peaceful world. The reason for war, the Italian nationalist contended, was an absence of national self-determination; when every people has its own nation, then there will be no further basis for conflict.

Woodrow Wilson, another liberal, also believed in national self-determination, although he had hoped to apply it to Europe rather than to the colonial world. A world organized under the principle of one nation, one state, he believed, would provide a sufficient basis for peace. He urged that the League of Nations be organized under such a principle.

Because of the attention given to wars based on the national principle, many people have equated wars with nationalism. It is important to remember that people were slaughtering each other long before the emergence of the nation-state. In the Thirty Years War, fought in the seventeenth century, some 30 percent of the German people were killed. In that instance religious difference was a strong causal factor of violence.

People kill for many reasons, among which are economic advantage, psychological maladjustment, ethnic differences, religious commitment, and ideological fervor. In fact, many observers contend that there are more people killed in internal than in external wars. About 500,000 people were killed in Indonesia in 1965 in an internal nonnational conflict. Millions of Soviet citizens were put into slave-labor camps in the 1930s. Many of these people were liquidated by the Soviet leader Joseph Stalin not because of considerations of nationalism but because of the need to maintain power for a privileged class—or possibly because Stalin was insane.

There is no reason to believe that the nation-state, consequently, is the cause of turmoil. Long before the nation appeared, human beings killed each other. Nationalism as a force has been unfairly criticized for many of the wars and acts of violence in the past few centuries. For whatever its defects, nationalism has been more beneficial than harmful to the global community.

Stepping-Stone. Political institutions are in a constant state of flux. They exist because of some important economic or social need. Throughout most of recorded history, there has been no feeling of nationalism. Is it not plausible to believe that the nation-state is not permanent but is, rather, a necessary step toward some higher form of political association? And does not the higher form constitute a wider community in which people will live in cooperative relationships?

For many people the nation-state represents a higher association than they had been accustomed to, for example, family, tribe, city-state, or feudal unit. Many Americans in the late eighteenth century identified with their smaller state units, with Georgia or New York; today, they think of themselves more as Americans than as Georgians or New Yorkers. Military and economic power, moreover, has been transferred to a considerable extent from local and regional units to a larger national unit.

Cannot we assume that at a certain stage of economic development, countries will abandon their national aspirations for some larger political unit in the manner of the American experience? The European Community is clearly an illustration of this trend and evidence of remarkable change. For about nine centuries the French and Germans prepared for war against each other, but they have now stopped thinking along these lines. In the words of one scholar of nationalism: "For the first time in many centuries Western Europe is now a pluralistic security community in some ways comparable to Scandinavia. This is a change of large potential implications."[14]

With the end of Soviet domination of Eastern Europe, many Eastern Europeans have sought to join the European Community. It may be

[14]Deutsch, *Nationalism and Its Alternatives*, p. 35.

that the European Community will eventually include all of Europe.

The **European Community** was organized in 1958 to reduce tariff barriers and stimulate trade among the member nations. Now with 12 members, it is also a political institution that makes binding rules governing the member states. Although the European Community has had problems of political integration, it continues to have the support of its members. A European parliament in which the people of each member country directly elect their own representative is a sign of an evolutionary, peaceful transformation beyond the nation-state. It may well be the case that as the countries of the world climb upward on the industrial ladder, they, too, will follow the advanced industrial nations of the European Community, abandoning their narrow national attachments for larger regional groupings.

4/YES   IS THE NATION-STATE OUTMODED AT THE END OF THE TWENTIETH CENTURY?

Perhaps a case can be made for the past existence of the nation-state system. The military and economic reasons for the emergence of nations have already been pointed out. What is clear, however, is current military, economic, and environmental factors make the nation-state outmoded.

Up to the end of World War II, military power was dispersed among many countries. In the past few centuries no single state has become so powerful as to conquer all others. To be sure, the great disturbers of the peace—Louis XIV, Napoleon, Kaiser Wilhelm, and Adolf Hitler—have all been crushed by alliances of states. Great Britain, acting as the balancer in a world in which military strength was dispersed among several great powers, was able to throw its naval forces to the other side when it appeared that one side was becoming too strong.

In 1945 the nuclear age was born. The American atomic bombs dropped at Hiroshima and Nagasaki were a thousand times more powerful than the large, conventional bombs used in World War II. Today nuclear weapons are available that are millions of times more powerful than the conventional bombs of World War II.

Nuclear weapons are far more dangerous than conventional weapons not only because of their immediate effects but also because of their long-term consequences. Most of the larger nuclear weapons not only destroy valuable property and millions of lives but also produce radioactive clouds that move across the world, descending as rain on neutral countries. These radioactive clouds, containing poisonous chemicals such as strontium 90 and cesium 137, can cause death, cancer, and genetic damage.

For a period of four years the United States was the only country to possess these weapons, but the nuclear monopoly was broken by the Soviet Union in 1949. By 1992 membership in the nuclear club had grown to include Great Britain, France, the People's Republic of China, and India. It is widely reported that Israel possesses these weapons, although the Israelis have not tested them. Pakistan and South Africa are believed to be close to producing nuclear weapons. Estimates of more states joining the nuclear club by the year 2000 are frequently made by military experts.

The knowledge of how to construct these weapons is readily available, and the raw materials they require are relatively easy to acquire. For example, arms control authorities were shocked to discover after the Persian Gulf war in 1991 that Iraq had been in the process of constructing nuclear weapons with equipment and designs regarded as so antiquated that the United States had already declassified them. The implication of this discovery was that other countries could use similar information to build nuclear weapons secretly, just as Iraq was trying to do. Since developing countries are now producing missiles capable of carrying nuclear weapons over long distances, moreover, it is possible that many countries might in the near future possess both nuclear weapons and the means to deliver them anywhere in the world.

As more countries move into the industrial and postindustrial ages, the proliferation of nuclear weapons is a foregone conclusion. Moreover, political turmoil in the former Soviet Union will likely increase proliferation further. Some of the republics have indicated that they want to have their own military forces rather than surrender their forces and equipment to a central government in Moscow. If these republics retain nuclear weapons, then the number of nuclear-weapons states will rise considerably.

For the first time ever, weapons have become so powerful as to make the nation-state obsolete. The cannons that destroyed feudal castles paved the way for the modern state. Is it not clear that nuclear weapons are so dangerous as to pave the way for world government? Since in the nuclear age there is no such thing as military security in any traditional sense of the term, is it not clear that the nation-state today is a detriment to the global community and must be abolished along with the idea of nationalism, or the separateness of one people from another?

Economic arguments support the military realities of our times that oppose the continuation of the nation-state. In a less complex era, it was easier to talk about a country's self-sufficiency. In an industrial and postindustrial world, there is a much greater interdependence among states.

Complex societies need raw materials to support their national machinery. Oil, particularly, is a vital component of a modern society. Without oil, the economies of countries would die, causing severe unemployment and social unrest. Advanced industrial societies need to import that oil primarily from the Middle East, South America, and Africa to run their economies. In turn, the oil-producing countries need the sophisticated technologies and know-how of the advanced societies in order to modernize their economies.

Countries are more and more dependent on each other for goods and expertise. Trade between Western and Eastern Europe has increased rapidly now that Eastern Europe has moved to adopt a free market economy. The development and strengthening of multinational corporations, such as International Telephone and Telegraph (ITT), Ford Motor Company, and International Business Machines (IBM), moreover, are further demonstrations of interdependency.

Multinational corporations have already demonstrated the decaying quality of the nation-state. A **multinational corporation** (MNC) is a large enterprise with offices and/or branches in numerous countries conducting business operations across state lines. MNCs in many cases have resources exceeding those of most countries. Faced with restrictions imposed by a country, many MNCs can move their operations to another country. The nation-state, consequently, is at a disadvantage in dealing with the MNC. The existence of MNCs makes the creation of transnational political institutions essential if goods and services are to be produced for the benefit of the people of the world rather than for the benefit of the few engaged in private enterprise.

Tariff barriers, import controls, and restrictions on the flow of labor from one country to another all impede the rapid economic development that would be advantageous to all. The development of the European Community is an indication of the necessity for transcending national boundaries. The nation-state is now an impediment to economic development and must be abolished.

Although military and economic factors alone are sufficient arguments against nationalism, environmental reasons, too, contribute to the necessity of condemning the nation-state principle. If more than 185 countries in the world continue to pursue their own selfish interests, harmony will not result. The pollution of oceans, rivers, and seas caused by the reckless dumping of waste material can only be controlled by actions transcending nation-states. Similarly, the destruction of rain forests in one country may contribute to global ecological disaster.

The nation-state, then, is obsolete. Military, economic, and environmental factors have contributed to the weakening of the nation-state and the strengthening of newer, transnational institutions.

4/NO   IS THE NATION-STATE OUTMODED AT THE END OF THE TWENTIETH CENTURY?

For all the talk about how the nuclear age has made the nation-state irrelevant, it is important to remember that no country has used nuclear weapons in war since 1945. Even during more than four decades of intense hostility between the Soviet Union and the United States, **deter-** **rence**—a policy that discourages states from pursuing policies in opposition to the wishes of the deterring state—rather than defense became the cornerstone of nuclear policy.

Deterrence is based on the recognition that there would be no winner in a nuclear war, a thought sufficient to prevent a country from going too far in making demands on an adversary. The possession of nuclear weapons by independent states, consequently, may serve the cause of peace.

It is important to remember, too, that nuclear weapons are not the only component of military force. Conventional wars have been fought even in this nuclear age. Formal or informal alliances of independent states have been successful in protecting South Korea and Zaire. Traditional alliances based on military support can serve to enhance the security of many people.

The notion that changes in military technology are bringing about a transformation in the state's traditional independence is based upon a false assessment of the independence of states in the conduct of war. Commenting on European states, Anthony D. Smith notes that in the past they nearly always acted in concert and few were strong enough to "go it alone." Recognizing the possible exceptions of Prussia-Germany and Napoleon's France in this assessment, he observes that few states had the wealth, skill, and leadership to convert temporary military power into political hegemony. He adds:

The "wars of states" and the "wars of nations" of the eighteenth and nineteenth centuries were carried on within a tight framework of interdependent polities just as today's superpower blocs are locked into a similar geopolitical balance. If today's nation-states can no longer act as "world policemen" (if they ever did so), several of them can still defend their own political interests, by force if necessary, as recent examples in Chad or the Falklands make clear.[15]

From an economic point of view, it is clear that the nation-state is not outmoded. There is nothing about the nation-state system that requires two states not to cooperate. Indeed, Canada and the United States are great trading partners, as are Japan and the United States. The multinational corporation has been able to work within the context of the nation-state system as an instrument of economic development.

Much has been made of the power of the MNCs. It is true that MNCs are powerful economic institutions, but nation-states have been

able to exercise control of them. Some of the MNCs are vulnerable because they have huge fixed investments in mineral development and buildings that they cannot pick up and move from one country to another. They and other less vulnerable MNCs have been forced to make accommodations to the demands of nation-states, such as in the employment of host nationals, the reinvestment of part of their profits in host countries, and joint ventures in which the state has significant financial shares. The nation-state shows no sign of eroding because of the MNC challenge.

Much has also been said about the interdependence of nations along economic lines. The real story, however, has not been interdependence but increasing economic independence. The Arab oil embargo of 1973 stimulated energy-hungry countries to become independent of foreign energy supplies. Indeed, the American program was named Project Independence. Western European countries and Japan rushed into all kinds of research and production efforts to avoid dependence upon foreign oil.

There is sufficient evidence to indicate that the control of the state over its economy is increasing rather than decreasing. Twentieth-century improvements in communications and public administration have facilitated collecting taxes, imposing tariffs, and regulating private companies, for example.

The system of separate states, moreover, has not necessarily meant that states cannot cooperate in solving environmental problems. Because the states of the world have worked together in health matters, smallpox—a dreaded disease that decimated communities for centuries—has been eliminated from the face of the earth. Many countries have entered into agreements about nuclear wastes, health, and pollution—all within the context of the nation-state system. It is foolish to change a system when it works.

Like the achievement of security and economic well-being, the achievement of human freedom is one of the great problems of our times—a problem that concerns citizens of every country in the world. In the twentieth century totalitarian political philosophies (see Chapter 3) have threatened to rule the world. Communism is one of the more important examples of totalitarianism.

Communism is discussed in Chapter 5. For our purposes it is important to note that communism as an ideology was nothing more than a

---

[15] Anthony D. Smith, "History and Liberty: Dilemmas of Loyalty in Western Democracies," *Ethnic and Racial Studies* (London) 9 (January 1986): 44.

modern version of classical Russian expansionism, the work of Russians czars continued by Soviet commissars. When at the conclusion of World War II, the army of the Soviet Union occupied considerable parts of Eastern Europe, the Soviet leader Joseph Stalin established communist governments sympathetic to him. According to basic communist philosophy, there is supposed to be no conflict among people under communist rule; the only basis for conflict is economic differences between classes. So long as capitalism is eliminated and communist regimes are established, it is impossible to have conflict among communist countries.

But nationalism served to weaken and ultimately destroy Soviet Communist party control of Soviet society. From its very beginnings in 1917, Soviet leadership made accommodations to the nationality principle in the form of the federal system (see Chapter 10) and limited cultural autonomy. Soviet leaders hoped that the Communist party would provide a powerful force unifying diverse nations and nationalities into a supranational Soviet state. The hope was never realized. The collapse of communism in the Soviet Union, which began in the late 1980s, was brought about in part by a surge of ethnic conflict in the republics and by calls for independence.

Even before the collapse of communism, Soviet leaders also had to deal with the nationality problem in its relations with other communist states. Under Stalin the idea of communist solidarity was used as a subterfuge to rid the communist states of governments hostile to Stalin, whether real or imagined. The communist countries of Eastern Europe were treated in the same manner that Western imperialist powers had dealt with their colonies, with the exception that the West often permitted dissent and peaceful protest movements. According to Stalin, the nonviolent protests of Soviet or other Eastern European dissidents would not only be crushed but would go unnoticed since they would not be reported by Western journalists, who would be barred from covering the stories.

But nationalism undermined Stalin's all-embracing communist ideology. First, Josip Broz Tito, the Yugoslav leader, challenged Soviet domination and later called for national roads to communism. Other signs of nationalism appeared, destroying the pretense of universal communist solidarity. In 1953, East Berlin riots were put down by Soviet forces. In 1956, the Hungarian people rose in opposition to Soviet domination. In that same year there were demonstrations in Poland. Perhaps the most severe challenges to the ideology of universal communism came from Mao Zedong's People's Republic of China. Mao denounced the claim of the Soviet leaders that the Soviet Union was the leader of the communist world, and fighting, subsequently, erupted along the Sino-Soviet border. The movement by trade unions in Poland in the 1980s for greater freedom was partly a rejection of Soviet domination of that country. In Afghanistan, rebel forces continued to fight a communist regime imposed by Soviet military power. Relying on the help of some countries, most notably the United States and Pakistan, the rebels succeeded in inflicting enough damage to compel the Soviet Union to withdraw its forces from the region by 1989, thus undermining the existing communist regime there.

Nationalism played a central role in the breakup of the Soviet Union itself. With the changes brought on by Mikhail Gorbachev after 1985, the Baltic Republics—Estonia, Latvia, and Lithuania—tried to withdraw from the Soviet Union and become independent states. Their movement began a process that led not only to their own independence but also to the independence of other Soviet republics.

Nationalism has been a more powerful force than communism. Nationalism has, consequently, contributed to the erosion of a totalitarian political ideology.

Nationalism serves not only to weaken global totalitarianism but also to strengthen freedom and dignity. Particularly to the peoples of Africa and Asia who have been under colonial rule, nationalism conveys a dignity that was lacking in the old colonial world. In the nineteenth and early twentieth centuries many people in the West regarded themselves as superior people. Some thought about their responsibilities to "take up the white man's burden" or "civilize" the non-Western peoples.

The victors in World War I had no desire to liberate their own colonies. They established a system of **mandates** (countries held in trust by advanced industrial countries) for the colonies of the vanquished European powers. Even as late as 1945, Charles de Gaulle, leader of the French forces, and British Prime Minister Winston Churchill proclaimed that victory over fascist imperialism did not mean that the French and British colonies would become independent.

For many of the peoples of Africa and Asia, then, nationalism became associated with independence from colonial rule. It meant an end to racial discrimination and the notion of a superior Western people. Representation at the United Nations put the new countries on a par with the more industrially advanced states. The principle of **sovereign equality**, in which all states are equal in law, characterized the voting procedure at the General Assembly of the United Nations and was an important element of self-respect. With the influx of newly independent countries into the United Nations in the 1950s and 1960s, the major powers were compelled to court the favor of the former colonies. Today both African and Asian countries often actually vote in opposition to their former colonial rulers. All of this has worked to provide a sense of dignity for the leaders and people of new states.

The nation-state, then, has demonstrated that it is a viable institution. It retains its military and economic effectiveness. It serves, moreover, as a force for human freedom.

KEY TERMS

Chauvinism
Culture
Deterrence
Ethnic groups
Ethnocentrism
European Community
Irredentism
Mandates
Modernization
Multinational corporation

Multinational states
Nation
Nation-state
Nationalism
Patriotism
Self-determination
Sovereign equality
Total war
Zionism

QUESTIONS

1. What are the factors that help create a feeling of nationalism?
2. What are the problems of trying to structure the world under the principle "one nation, one state"?
3. Create a case study in which a particular territory has been claimed by different parties, such as the Falkland Islands, Northern Ireland, Israel, or Kashmir. Make a case for one side on the basis of what you know about nationalism.
4. Does the nation create the state, or does the state create the nation? What are the reasons for your answer?
5. What effect would the elimination of nationalism have on world politics?

RECOMMENDED READINGS

AKZIN, BENJAMIN. *State and Nation.* London: Hutchinson University Library, 1964. A study of the relationship between the political phenomenon of the state and the ethnic phenomenon of the nation.

ALTER, PETER. *Nationalism,* trans. Stuart McKinnon-Evans. London: Edward Arnold, 1989. An introduction to nationalism.

BIRCH, ANTHONY H. *Nationalism and National Integration.* London: Unwin Hyman, 1989. An analysis of the process and problems of national integration.

COBBAN, ALFRED. *The Nation State and National Self-Determination.* London: Collins, 1969. A revised and updated version of an earlier work presenting a history and political analysis of national self-determination.

COMMITTEE ON INTERNATIONAL RELATIONS OF

THE GROUP FOR THE ADVANCEMENT OF PSY-CHIATRY. *Us and Them: The Psychology of Eth-nonationalism*. Report 123. New York: Brunner/Mazel, 1987. An examination of the psychology of ethnicity.

DEUTSCH, KARL W. *Nationalism and Its Alterna-tives*. New York: Knopf, 1969. An analysis of how the problems of nationalism are devel-oping in the contemporary world.

———. *Nationalism and Social Communication: An Inquiry into the Foundations of Nationality*. 2d ed. Cambridge, Mass.: MIT Press, 1966. A theory relating nationalism to social commu-nication.

EMERSON, RUPERT. *From Empire to Nation: The Rise to Self-Assertion of Asian and African Peo-ples*. Cambridge, Mass.: Harvard University Press, 1967. An analysis of nationalism in Asia and Africa with attention to the philoso-phy and history of nationalism in the West.

ENTESSAR, NADER. "Kurdish Identity in the Middle East." *Current World Leaders* 34 (April 1991): 270–82. A survey of Kurdish history and an assessment of the prospects for inde-pendence.

FOON, CHEW SOCK. "On the Incompatibility of Ethnic and National Loyalties: Reframing the Issue." *Canadian Review of Studies in Na-tionalism* (Prince Edward Island) 13 (Spring 1986): 1–11. An argument that ethnic iden-tity may be compatible under certain condi-tions with national loyalty in multiethnic states.

GOLIK, RICHARD D., and RANDALL W. HEATHER. "Canada: Will the Center Hold?" *Defense and Diplomacy* 9 (May/June 1991): 53–61. An analysis of secessionism in Canada.

GRODZINS, MORTON. *The Loyal and the Disloyal: Social Boundaries of Patriotism and Treason*. Chicago: University of Chicago Press, 1956. An examination of loyalty and disloyalty.

HAAS, ERNST B. "What Is Nationalism and Why Should We Study It?" *International Organiza-tion* 40 (Summer 1986): 707–44. A review of four books on nationalism.

HALLIDAY, FRED. "The Beast Awakes." *New Statesman and Society* 86 (March 30, 1990): 12–15. A critical appraisal of nationalism.

HAYES, CARLTON J. H. *Essays on Nationalism*. New York: Macmillan, 1926. A classic book by one of the leading scholars on national-ism.

———. *Nationalism: A Religion*. New York: Mac-millan, 1960. A summing up of the author's research on nationalism with special atten-tion to Europe.

JAMES, ALAN. *Sovereign Statehood: The Basis of International Society*. London: Allen and Un-win, 1986. A rigorous analysis of sovereign statehood in the modern international sys-tem.

KEDOURIE, ELIE. *Nationalism*. 3d ed. London: Hutchinson University Library, 1966. An analysis of nationalism.

KOHN, HANS. *The Idea of Nationalism: A Study in Its Origins and Background*. New York: Collier Books, 1967. A historical treatment of na-tionalism.

KRÓL, MARCIN. "A Europe of Nations or a Uni-versalistic Europe?" *International Affairs* (London) 66 (April 1990): 285–90. An argu-ment that the prospects of stability and de-mocracy in Eastern Europe are dim because of revitalized nationalism.

LINDEN, RONALD. "The Appeal of Nationalism." *Report on Eastern Europe* 2 (June 14, 1991): 29–34. A study of the forces of nationalism at work in Eastern Europe.

MAYALL, JAMES. *Nationalism and International So-ciety*. New York: Cambridge University Press, 1989. A study of the implications of the na-tional idea to international society.

NAIRN, TOM. "Beyond Big Brother." *New States-man and Society* 119 (June 15, 1990): 29–32. An argument that the future belongs to na-tions.

PREMDAS, RALPH R; S.W.R. de A. SAMARASIN-GHE, and ALAN B. ANDERSON, eds. *Secessionist Movements in Comparative Perspective*. New York: St. Martin's Press, 1990. A study of secessionist movements.

SHAFER, BOYD C. "Debated Problems in the Study of Nationalism." *Canadian Review of Studies in Nationalism* (Prince Edward Island) 11 (Spring 1984): 1–19. An overview of the major problems of nationalism.

WALKER, R.B.J., and SAUL H. MENDLOVITZ, eds. *Contending Sovereignties: Redefining Political Community*. Boulder, Colo.: Lynne Rienner Publishers, 1990. A consideration of the changing character of sovereignty.

WHITE, PHILIP L. "What Is a Nationality?" *Cana-dian Review of Studies in Nationalism* (Prince Edward Island) 12 (Spring 1985): 1–23. A historical investigation of the concept of na-tionalism.

part II

FORMS OF GOVERNMENT

Political systems may be compared in many ways in order to understand their relationship to the level of citizen participation in political affairs, the establishment of a just society, and the kinds of policies that a government produces. In ancient Greece, for example, Aristotle classified government in terms of the number of people who ruled and whether that rule was for the benefit of the polity or for the benefit of the political rulers themselves.

Other distinctions have been made throughout the ages between arbitrary government and constitutional government, rule by intellectuals and rule by the masses, and monarchy and republic. In the twentieth century a prominent distinction in classifying governments is made between democracy and dictatorship. Chapter 3 deals with defining and debating issues concerned with such a distinction.

chapter 3

Democracy and dictatorship

It started as a trickle, like the drops of water emptying into a river. The river became a torrent. The torrent was democracy. One by one, from the mid-1970s to the early 1990s, governments that had ruled with an iron fist and symbols of terror were replaced by political systems based on law and freedom. Seemingly rigidly controlled structures crumbled—sometimes violently but more often peacefully. So dramatic was the change that by 1991, Freedom House, an organization concerned with the expansion of freedom throughout the world, reported that for the first time since it began keeping records on the subject in 1955, liberal democracies far outnumbered any other political system.[1]

Such was the reality of 1991. If words were taken at face value, however, the tran-

sition to freedom would merit scant notice. Since World War II, popular support for democracy has been so widespread that almost all governments described themselves as democratic, even when they did not behave like democracies. In the 1970s and 1980s acclaim for democracy was so broad as to appear in nearly all bands of the political spectrum. Communists heralded their system as an expression of democracy. Conservatives condemned as violations of democracy the suppression of dissent in the communist Soviet Union, Cuba, and East Germany. Liberals complained about the restrictions on democracy in Chile and Taiwan. Capitalists pointed to the free enterprise system as an example of democracy, and socialists argued that only with socialism can there be real democracy. Terrorists hijacked planes, bombed buildings, and assassinated elected officials in the name of democracy. Many of those who praised democracy denounced dictator-

[1] R. Bruce McColm, "The Comparative Survey of Freedom: 1991," *Freedom Review* 22, no. 1 (1991): 5.

ship but differed markedly about whom they regarded as dictators.

Although today there is more of a global consensus about the meaning of *democracy*, it is essential to examine this term and its antonym, *dictatorship*. After these concepts are presented and analyzed, issues that highlight the character and differences between democracy and dictatorship will be explored.

DEMOCRACY

Democracy is literally derived from two Greek words: *demos*, meaning "the people," and *kratein*, meaning "to rule." **Democracy** is popular sovereignty, or rule by the people, and it is a form of government distinguished from rule by a king or queen (**monarchy**), rule by a hereditary nobility (**aristocracy**), rule by the most educated, rule by the elders, and rule by religious leaders (**theocracy**). To say that democracy means rule by the people, however, does not reveal enough about the meaning of democracy. For a better explanation, it is necessary to look at three of the principal uses of the term *democracy*: participatory (direct) democracy, representative (indirect) democracy, and economic democracy. These are by no means the only forms of democracy, but they are among the most prominent.

Participatory Democracy

Participatory democracy, or **direct democracy**, is a form of government that emphasizes three features: (1) popular participation, (2) majority rule, and (3) political equality. It has its origins in Athenian experience, which was different from the form of government that many Americans today regard as their own democracy. The major differences reflect geography, participation, and the relationship between citizen and state.

Democratic rule today generally involves a community containing millions of people scattered throughout large geographic regions. The democracy of the United States, for example, governs a transcontinental territory of more than 250 million people. In the fifth and fourth centuries B.C., Athens was a city-state (*polis*) with a population of from 300,000 to 400,000 people—about the same number of people as in Omaha, Nebraska, in 1992—and a territory of about one thousand square miles—roughly the size of Rhode Island. Since many Athenian citizens knew each other, spoke the same language, shared political, religious, moral, and cultural values, and constituted a small political unit, there was a good deal of mutual trust and a real sense of community among them.

Political participation in ancient Athens involved only citizens—that is, male property owners. Women, slaves, youth, and foreigners were excluded from citizenship. The citizens in Athens constituted a minority of the population of the city-state—only about 20,000 to 40,000 men, according to most estimates.

Citizens were expected to participate actively in the actual making of laws, administration of laws, and dispensing of justice. The political institutions of the day—the Assembly, Council, and juries—were set up in such a way as to give the greatest scope for citizen participation. There was no permanent governing unit in the sense in which today the United States has a Congress and a president charged with the responsibility of making and enforcing laws. All Athenian citizens were expected to play a political role. Rotation in office at one- or two-year intervals and selection by lot for those offices were designed to enhance participation by all citizens rather than only by a permanent governing group of representatives. There were no elections, since elections were regarded as aristocratic devices of choosing "the best people" instead of placing government in the hands of the people.[2]

In ancient Athens, moreover, there was no distinction between state and society. Citizens, consequently, possessed no rights against certain acts of the state. The Greek city-state encompassed political, social, and cultural life. In theory, there were no limits on what actions the state could take against its citizens. In fact, however, there was more freedom in Athens for citizens than in undemocratic Greek city-states of ancient times and in many political systems of later centuries. Varying controversial opinions were offered at the Assembly, and even those people who disagreed with the fundamental principles of Athenian democracy were free to voice their own beliefs. For example, the philosopher Plato established his own school in Athens, the Academy, where he taught for a generation. His views were critical of traditional Athenian beliefs and values, yet he was free to advocate his ideas.

The system of decision making was based on majority rule. A majority of the citizens present at an assembly or jury decided on matters within their jurisdiction and punished individuals as they so chose, sometimes brutally. Majority rule itself was based on the principle of **political equality**, or one person, one vote, as it is referred to today, in which each person's vote is counted equally.

In the contemporary world, participatory democracy in the Athenian sense is virtually nonexistent on the national level. Certain practices of participatory democracy, however, can be found in contemporary political systems. The **New England town meeting**, in which the citizens of a small town get together to decide policy, is one example of the contemporary participatory approach. Swiss cantons have similar practices. The Israeli *kibbutz* (agricultural commune) is yet another example of participatory democracy. Jury duty in courts, in which ordinary citizens judge the legal cases, continues in modern democracies, although professional judges preside.

Direct participation in law making exists on a national level, but its scope is confined. The **referendum**, in which the people of a political unit—sometimes national and at other times regional—are asked to decide directly on an issue, is one example. In American states and cities, bond issues involving the authorization of bonds to raise money for the construction of schools and hospitals are often considered in this manner. The United States, however, is one of the few democratic countries that does not permit a national referendum. Ireland and Italy had national referendums on divorce. President Corazon Aquino submitted the 1986 Philippine constitution to the people for ratification. The Spanish people voted in a national referendum on remaining in the North Atlantic Treaty Organization. The British people voted to remain in the European Community. Switzerland holds popular votes on many issues.[3]

Another example of direct democracy is the **initiative**, in which citizens can propose legislative or constitutional changes by filing formal petitions to be acted upon by either the legislature or the entire electorate.

In the 1960s and 1970s, advocates of participatory democracy focused their efforts on **decentralization** (transferring decision making from a central source to smaller or local units) and the direct involvement of amateurs in decision mak-

---

[2]M. I. Finley, *Democracy Ancient and Modern*, rev. ed. (New Brunswick, N.J.: Rutgers University Press, 1985), pp. 19–20; David Stockton, *The Classical Athenian Democracy* (Oxford, England: Oxford University Press, 1990), chap. 3.

[3]Thomas E. Cronin, *Direct Democracy: The Politics of Initiative, Referendum, and Recall* (Cambridge, Mass.: Harvard University Press, 1989), p. 4.

ing.[4] A key slogan became "power to the people," which to the advocates meant taking power away from national structures of government and placing it at the "grassroots" level. It was this emphasis on participatory democracy that characterized the radical groups known as the New Left.

Today advocates of participatory democracy talk about **empowerment**, by which they mean that the people who are affected by public policy should be given the power to make decisions about that policy. Thus parents should help make school policy for their children. Poor people living in public housing should not only make their own rules for their buildings but even own their dwellings. In each case the role of government would be minimized.

Participation is also a feature of decentralization in the workplace. In the 1980s some advocates of participatory democracy argued for worker involvement in decision making. Yugoslavia established a system of workers' councils in which workers contributed to decision-making processes affecting their own work. These councils gave workers some control of policy in factories in such matters as plant expansion and the distribution of profits. Western capitalists and socialists have at times allowed for greater participation by workers in the solving of production problems.

Representative (Indirect) Democracy

Participatory democracy is at least possible in small communities, but is it possible in large political entities? That is a question that will be considered. What is important at this point, however, is that with the emergence over the past few centuries of political communities containing diverse ethnic, religious, and racial groups, larger numbers of people, and more sophisticated

[4]Terrence E. Cook and Patrick M. Morgan, eds., *Participatory Democracy* (San Francisco: Canfield Press, 1971), p. 4.

economies, a different kind of democracy has developed: representative democracy.

A representative democracy, or indirect democracy, possesses some of the features of direct democracy but is different in some important ways. Characteristics that are somewhat similar are popular participation, political equality, and majority rule. Representative democracy is different from direct democracy in that it is a system of representative government based on free elections and a system of limitations on state activity (constitutionalism).

Representative democracy is based on the principle of popular sovereignty. Although modern representative democracy requires popular participation, the scope and form of that participation are different from Athenian democratic practices in two ways. First, the number of people included in the political community is larger. Today, representative democracies claim maximum popular participation and have extended the right to vote to include everyone except criminals, youth, the insane, and noncitizens. Modern representative democracies, moreover, are characterized by **pluralism**—the existence of a variety of associations that are autonomous, or independent from government domination.

Second, although most citizens play no direct role in making laws (except for referendums and initiatives), other forms of political participation are permitted. Some citizens join interest groups for the purpose of influencing elected officials and appointed bureaucrats to act in particular ways. Citizens also work in the political campaigns of candidates who favor their views. They conduct meetings, write pamphlets and articles, take out newspaper advertisements, and hold peaceful demonstrations—all with the goal of influencing policy.

In modern representative democracies, the principle of political equality remains, but various devices have been used to prevent a complete realization of this goal. In many countries, Great Britain and the

United States being examples, representation has at various times been based on a geographic region rather than population. In England, a system of "rotten boroughs" developed in which it was possible for one member of Parliament to represent a few hundred people while another member represented hundreds of thousands of people. A somewhat similar (but less extreme) system of **malapportionment** (in which legislative districts contained unequal numbers of people) worked also in the United States to benefit rural areas at the expense of heavily populated urban areas. Some legislative bodies do not recognize the principle of political equality in their systems of representation. The United States Senate, for example, consists of two senators per state regardless of the size of population, because the men who wrote the Constitution intended that senators represent the states rather than the people. Gradually, however, the worst evils impeding political equality have been eliminated, and today most democratic systems operate under the principle of political equality.

Majority rule is applied in deciding both who the law makers will be and whether bills will become laws. The majority principle has sometimes been by-passed even in these areas. In some instances (usually important matters), a two-thirds or three-fourths vote is necessary to enact laws or constitutional amendments. Legislative devices, such as the **filibuster** (in which United States senators can talk a bill to death by preventing a vote from being taken) or the tying up of a bill in committee, can prevent a majority from deciding law. **Judicial review** (in which a court can declare any act of the legislature or the executive as unconstitutional) can also thwart the will of the majority. The principle of majority rule, however, is generally the accepted norm in representative democracies.

Although popular participation, political equality, and majority rule are adapted with variations from the Athenian experience, representative democracy in contem-porary practice has two new components: a system of representation based on free elections conducted at specified periods and constitutionalism.

Indirect democracy is based on the principle of representation, but there are differences of opinion about what representation means: a mirror image of the population, a reflection of the groups who elected the representative, or a trustee relationship in which the elected official decides issues on the basis of his or her conscience. What is generally agreed, however, is that the representative is elected in competition with one or more people for the same office, that the election is for an agreed maximum period of time, and that if the official is defeated for office, he or she turns over that office in a peaceful manner to the winner of the election.

Constitutionalism may mean many things, but in the context of representative democracy it means that the acts of government are limited by written laws and by custom—even if these acts clearly represent majority wishes. Constitutionalism is fundamental to liberal ideas (see Chapters 4 and 7). *Liberalism* is a political philosophy that makes a distinction between society and the state. According to liberal theorists, individuals possessed natural rights before the state was established. Governments are created by people to protect people's rights.

Some writers argue, consequently, that there is a conflict between democracy and liberalism. According to them, democracy means majority rule *without limitations*. The majority may decide anything, even to deny rights of political participation to the minority. A "tyranny of the majority" is, thus, consistent with democracy. Liberalism, however, assumes that there are limits to what the majority may decide. The majority is not free to suppress freedom of speech and assembly, for example. It is this concern with individual liberty that ties representative democracy to liberalism, so **liberal democracy** is often equated with representative democracy.

Still other writers argue that rights need not be justified according to a belief in liberalism. They contend that a system based on popular participation and political equality assumes that people should be free to participate in the political process and that, regardless of their views, they should be allowed to try to organize majorities. A political system that suppresses freedom to participate, consequently, cannot be classified as democratic. Rights, according to this view, are inherent in democracy.

Both the argument based on liberalism and the argument based on democracy, then, accept the view that there are limits to what the majority can do.

In summary, recognizing that the definition is not without its critics, we will use the terms **representative democracy** (or **indirect democracy**) to mean a system of government characterized by popular participation in the political process, political equality, majority rule, representative government based on free elections, and constitutionalism.

While these are the features of representative democracy, they do not constitute its only model. In some countries, cultural, religious, or ethnic differences may be so strong that special powers must be given to different groups lest civil disorder, or possibly civil war, occur. The political scientist Arend Lijphart notes that majority rule is only one model of democracy and may not be applicable to all conditions. He devised another model, **consociational democracy**, in which "majority rule is replaced by consensual rule." In such a system, the working principles are "grand coalitions, mutual veto, proportionality, and segmental autonomy."[5] Consociational systems exist, for example, in Austria, Belgium, the Netherlands, and Switzerland. It has also been suggested that some Eastern European countries

with strong ethnic divisions devise constitutional systems applying the consociational model.

Economic Democracy

Participatory democracy and representative democracy are generally referred to as *political democracy*. The basic premise about political democracy is that government can do whatever it wishes *and remain democratic* so long as its duly elected officials act in accordance with approved methods. In principle, at least in the minds of some supporters of democracy in its political form, all that democracy signifies is a *method* by which majorities (either the people directly or their representatives) make decisions affecting public policy.

In the past century growing attention has been given to broadening the understanding of democracy beyond method. What does it matter, some partisans have asked, if people can vote but the effect of voting makes no real difference in the quality of their lives? According to this line of reasoning, voting may make no difference because government may exclude certain economic decisions from its consideration. To the extent to which a free enterprise economy allows private individuals to make economic decisions that create conditions of inequality of wealth, then many people—most notably the poor, the unemployed, and the targets of racial, religious, and gender discrimination—will be losers in the political process. These people would vote, but their vote would not change their dismal situation.

Those who contend that democracy should be more than a method use the term **economic democracy** to describe a system of government that distributes the material resources of society so as to maximize equality and improve the quality of life for the masses of people. People who support economic democracy call for government programs to minimize inequalities: taxes and other programs that work to redistrib-

---

[5] Arend Lijphart, "Majority Rule Versus Democracy in Deeply Divided Societies," *Politikon* 4 (December 1977): 118.

ute income from the wealthy to the poor, public education to give poorer people who do not attend private schools equal opportunities to learn, and government-sponsored health care programs to provide all people with the benefits of health care regardless of their income.

Attention to economic equality has raised the issue among democrats of the relationship between liberty and equality. Most supporters of democracy argue that democracy means liberty *and* equality. Some writers argue, however, that liberty and equality are inherently in conflict. If liberty means freedom to do what one wishes without interference from the state, then efforts to redistribute income are a denial of liberty. Other writers contend, however, that the two principles are not inconsistent. They argue that the standard of living in representative democracies is generally higher than it is under other forms of government. Low-income people live well in representative democracies, and the affluence of the few does not depend upon the poverty of the many. In fact, there is a large middle class in representative democracies.

Two prominent groups support economic democracy: social democrats (or democratic socialists) and communists. Although these groups are described more fully in Chapter 5, here we indicate that social democrats argue that democracy requires *both* the features of political democracy *and* economic democracy. They favor free elections, a free press, freedom of speech, and pluralism, but they also support the welfare state.

Communists contend that economic democracy is *the only* element of democracy. By economic democracy they mean the abolition of the free enterprise system and the installation of a socialist economy. Political democracy, in their view, is a sham, since it is capitalists who really control the system. Communists do not, consequently, support free elections, a free press, freedom of speech, and pluralism.

Although the use of the term *economic democracy* is associated with socialism and communism, the linking of the character of an economy to a political system is not exclusive to those ideologies. Some advocates of the free enterprise system regard the character of an economy as a feature of democracy, but they focus on economic freedom. They hail **democratic capitalism** as a system that combines economic freedom with political freedom. Without economic freedom, they contend, political freedom is unlikely.[6]

DICTATORSHIP

Today, in spite of the rise in the number of countries that are liberal democracies, most people live in political systems that do not possess attributes of liberal democracy—namely, representative government, majority rule, political equality, and constitutionalism. It is important to understand the political system in a variety of these undemocratic governments in order to see the contrast between democracy and dictatorship.

Like the term *democracy*, the term *dictatorship* encompasses different meanings.[7] Many concepts have been associated with dictatorship, and it is useful to clarify related concepts, such as autocracy, absolutism, despotism, tyranny, authoritarianism, and totalitarianism.

Dictatorship may be broadly defined as a political system of arbitrary rule by an individual or small group that is not constitutionally responsible to the people or their

[6]See, for example, Michael Novak, *The Spirit of Democratic Capitalism* (New York: Simon and Schuster, 1982). For a critique of democratic capitalism, see Samuel Bowles and Herbert Gintis, *Democracy and Capitalism: Property, Community, and the Contradictions of Modern Social Thought* (New York: Basic Books, 1986).

[7]Franz Neumann, *The Democratic and the Authoritarian State: Essays in Political and Legal Theory* (Glencoe, Ill.: Free Press, 1957), p. 235.

elected representatives. Dictatorship is derived from a practice of ancient Rome in which extraordinary power was entrusted to a single leader for a term of no more than six months to promote public order or guarantee military security in a situation of great emergency. At the conclusion of the stipulated period, the dictator would relinquish his power, and constitutional government would be restored. In many respects, this practice is similar to modern **crisis government**, in which extraordinary powers are temporarily given to an elected official to meet an obvious danger. The power given to Winston Churchill in Great Britain during World War II is an example of crisis government. Elections were suspended in Britain during that war. Once the war against Germany was won, however, elections were held (and Churchill's government was defeated).

Autocracy is rule by an individual who governs without constitutional limits. **Absolutism** is a system in which one or more persons govern with unlimited powers. **Despotism** refers to rule by an absolute leader governing for himself or herself rather than for the common good. **Tyranny** means a system of government in which laws are made for the benefit of those who govern rather than for the common good.

Authoritarian Government

Terms such as *autocracy, absolutism, despotism,* and *tyranny* remain imprecise, although it may be said that they all connote dictatorship. Two modern descriptives of dictatorship, authoritarian and totalitarian, deserve attention as contemporary dictatorships.

The term *authoritarian* is derived from the word *authority,* which has been defined as the establishment of formal power (see Chapter 1). A police officer in a free society, consequently, has the authority to make an arrest when someone is committing a crime. *Authoritarianism* refers to a belief in a political system that emphasizes authority and tradition instead of individual liberty.[8] An **authoritarian government** is based on principles hostile to democracy, such as rule by a select few, suppression of opposition, and reliance on physical coercion rather than law.

Rule by a Select Few. Any government—authoritarian or not—is rule by a select few, but authoritarian government limits its ruling elite very narrowly and does not permit free elections that would allow new leaders to come to power. In an authoritarian system the government is responsible to itself rather than to the general public. This is not to say that authoritarian regimes are not responsive to change and do not take into account the principal groups that make up the political system. Most governments, in some ways at least, reflect the interests of the dominant groups of society lest they be toppled from power. The scope of the opposition in authoritarian regimes, however, is limited, and the opposition's political behavior is confined to a narrow range, as determined by the ruling few.

Suppression of Opposition. Authoritarian regimes fear opposition that may culminate in a new government. They often act to restrict the opposition in many ways. They may declare any opposition political party illegal and may in fact imprison those party leaders; shut down newspapers and magazines that print stories unflattering to the regime; censor books that they believe to be dangerous to the government; persecute students and faculty members who meet to challenge the existing political and social order; and break up peaceful protests and imprison the leaders of protest groups.

Physical Coercion. Authoritarian regimes often display the symbols of their

[8] Michael R. Curtis, "Dictatorship," *Encyclopedia Americana* (1979), 9:82.

strength: the army and the secret police. In many authoritarian countries the leader himself is a military officer, such as António Salazar in Portugal, Anastasio Somoza in Nicaragua, and Francisco Franco in Spain. The army and the secret police support the regime at home and abroad. The secret police use techniques varying from assassination and torture to economic pressure and psychological threats to stop potential dissidents from engaging in activities hostile to the regime.

Authoritarian regimes emphasize the need for order rather than the quest for liberty. They usually justify their actions in terms of the benefit to the people and rely on the symbols of democracy, such as elections, but these elections are rigged to benefit the government. The paradox of dictatorship in authoritarian and other forms is that the government seeks popular support but suppresses dissent.

Authoritarian leaders may want to change society by bringing on rapid industrial development, but they do not indoctrinate the people with a particular ideology pervading all aspects of their lives. The late shah of Iran is cited as an example of an authoritarian leader. He relied upon the army and Savak (a brutal secret police) for his rule. He actively sought to eliminate any opposition to his rule through ruthless means.

Totalitarian Government

In the twentieth century a form of dictatorship that is often regarded as new has appeared: totalitarian government. The prototypes of the totalitarian state are Joseph Stalin's Soviet Union and Adolf Hitler's Germany (see Chapters 4 and 5). Benito Mussolini's Italy is often cited as an example of a totalitarian dictatorship in part because Mussolini coined the term *totalitarian state* to describe his rule. Mussolini's state, however, was never really in the same league as Stalin's or Hitler's. Carl J. Friedrich and Zbigniew K. Brzezinski, two leading scholars of **totalitarian government**, summarize its central features as follows:

- **Ideology.** An elaborate ideology covers all aspects of life, and everyone in the society must adhere to it. The ideology is directed at producing a "perfect society," a utopia.
- **Single Mass Party.** A single party is usually led by one person, the dictator, and constitutes a small part of the population (up to 10 percent). The party promotes the prevailing ideology and is typically superior to or completely intertwined with the government.
- **Terror.** A secret police uses terror to prevent any challenge to ruling authorities. Terror is applied to restrict and prevent dissident activity within the party and by groups outside the party.
- **Control of Mass Communication.** The government controls the entire media. No independent media sources are permitted.
- **Control of the Armed Forces.** The weapons of war and the armed forces are under near-complete government domination.
- **Central Direction of the Economy.** The government dominates the entire economic system.[9]

Some writers contend that there is a qualitative difference between authoritarian and totalitarian systems. Their argument is as follows: Authoritarian leaders impose a dictatorship and are content to rule. So long as individuals and groups do not challenge the government, they are generally left alone. In contrast, totalitarian leaders, while accepting the fundamental practices of authoritarianism, go beyond authoritarianism and seek to change the character of human beings. For example, Stalin promoted "the new Soviet man" who would behave in accordance with communist ideology. In totalitarian systems everything must be subordinated to the prevailing ideal,

[9]Carl J. Friedrich and Zbigniew K. Brzezinski, *Totalitarian Dictatorship and Autocracy*, 2d ed., rev. by Carl J. Friedrich (New York: Praeger, 1965), p. 22.

and the regime is concerned not only with the way citizens behave politically but with what they *think* as well. Hence, government emphasizes ideological orthodoxy and indoctrination in education, economics, culture, athletics, and science.

According to Friedrich and Brzezinski, there have been precursors to totalitarianism, such as the dictatorships of ancient Greece, of which Sparta was a leading example, and the Oriental despotisms, but these were *totalist* rather than totalitarian. That is, they lacked the technological underpinnings that made modern totalitarianism possible. Without a modern technology, the scholars contend, it is not possible to maintain control over the armed forces, impose total terror, and centralize the direction of the economy; nor is it easy to induce active participation of the masses in the goals of the dictator.

Some authors criticize the concept of totalitarianism as a useful category to describe certain kinds of dictatorship. They argue that most modern dictatorships—whether they be communist, fascist, or military—have similar goals. These could include the strengthening of the autonomy of the state, the destruction and integration of existing political institutions and structures, and the quest for popular legitimacy and support. They contend that even Stalin's Soviet Union and Hitler's Germany were really authoritarian.[10]

These authors assert that the single party in both cases was never monolithic, for example. Even Friedrich and Brzezinski refer to autonomous units, or "islands of separateness," such as the family, the church, the army, the professions, and ethnic groups that maintain their separate identity in spite of the dictatorial pressures to impose uniformity.

Some observers note that whatever uniformity of opinion the totalitarian governments of the past sought to impose on a society, ordinary people never accepted it in full. According to this view, political terrorism may have influenced their behavior but *not* their thinking. And so, when, in the late 1980s, the Soviet government turned to reforming its system at home and backed away from control over communist regimes in Eastern Europe, the people of Eastern Europe rose up to denounce communism with such vehemence that they must never have believed in it. According to the political scientist Ellen Frankel Paul, once the people of Eastern Europe recognized that military force would not be used against them, they showed their true feelings: "The 'New Man' of Marxism-Leninism, forged in the crucible of an education of indoctrination, censorship, and loyalty to the party, now marched in the streets demanding liberty, free elections, and even a return to private property and capitalism."[11]

Critics of the concept of totalitarianism argue further that use of the term tends to blur the many differences between the two most prominent totalitarian systems. Although Stalin's communist and Hitler's Nazi systems were dictatorships, they differed in political philosophy and support[12] (see Chapters 4 and 5). Communism purported to be rational and scientific. It sought the abolition of the state and the creation of a classless society. To the extent that it believed in rapid industrialization, it was revolutionary. Totalitarian nazism, in contrast, was irrational, antiscientific, and

[10]See, e.g., William S. Allen, "Totalitarianism: The Concept and the Reality," in *Totalitarianism Reconsidered*, ed. Ernest A. Menze (Port Washington, N.Y.: Kennikat Press, 1981), pp. 97–106.

[11]Ellen Frankel Paul, "Introduction," in *Totalitarianism at the Crossroads*, ed. Ellen Frankel Paul (New Brunswick, N.J.: Transaction Books, 1990), p. 3.

[12]Michael Curtis, "Retreat from Totalitarianism," in *Totalitarianism in Perspective*, ed. Carl J. Friedrich, Michael Curtis, and Benjamin R. Barber (New York: Praeger, 1969), pp. 109–110.

if it had a utopia at all, it was certainly different from the communist utopia. It revered the state, the nation, and a superior race. To the degree that it was anti-industrial and antiurban, it was in conflict with the professed goals of communism. The Nazis drew their main strength from the lower middle class and the military, whereas the communists drew from the intelligentsia and the working classes.

Although the critics of totalitarianism have made telling points, particularly in arguing against scholars who attempt to describe all communist governments as totalitarian, there remains much that is useful in the concept. It serves as a model that some dictators seek to achieve. Totalitarianism, consequently, connotes something qualitatively different from authoritarianism despite imprecisions in describing actual political behavior in any political system.

THE FUTURE OF DEMOCRACY

Political democracy in the early 1990s is in ascendancy. Dictatorships lack an ideological justification for denying democratic practices. With the virtual collapse of communism as a believable ideology, there is a broad consensus today about the definition of democracy that accepts at the minimum a political application of the term and at the maximum the social democratic application of economic democracy. But whether liberal democracy is the wave of the future is uncertain, and it is a subject to which we will return in Issue 11 in Chapter 4.

ISSUES

The discussion of democracy and dictatorship has suggested that there are complex problems involved in dealing with these classifications of political systems. Some of the essential issues include the character of governments that profess to be democratic in the political sense of the term. Other questions deal with the relative merits of democracy when compared to dictatorship.

This chapter considers five issues central to the topic: (1) Do representative democracies represent the interests of the powerful few rather than the people? (2) Should representative democracies represent the judgment of elected leaders rather than the people? (3) Is participatory democracy desirable? (4) Does democracy produce worse government than dictatorship produces? (5) Are dictatorships better able to deal with foreign policy than are democracies?

5/YES — DO REPRESENTATIVE DEMOCRACIES REPRESENT THE INTERESTS OF THE POWERFUL FEW RATHER THAN THE PEOPLE?

That representative democracy does not reflect popular opinion is clear to all who are willing to look at facts rather than engage in idle philosophical speculation or recite empty slogans. The principal arguments in support of this view are: (1) voting turnout in democracies is low; (2) the masses of people are poorly informed on issues and allow experts to rule; and (3) people are easily manipulated to believe what the ruling classes want them to believe.

Voting Turnout. One of the facts of voting behavior is that there is a significant proportion of the voting population that does not vote. This is true for the United States, France, Great Britain, and other democracies. In the United States, for example, only 52.6 percent of the voting-age population actually voted in the 1980 presidential election. This was the lowest percentage of a turnout for a presidential election in thirty-two years. After much talk by both liberal and conservative activists about increasing the number of people registering and voting for the 1984 presidential election, the percentage increased ever so slightly—to 53.3. Then in 1988 the turnout percentage was 48.7. In state and local elections the turnout is even lower. In the 1990 congressional elections, only a little more than one-third of the 186 million Americans eligible to vote actually exercised their right to do so. On some referendums, only 10 percent of the electorate cast ballots.

To be sure, some people do not vote because they are ill or otherwise occupied, but many people choose not to vote. Why? Voting behavior studies show that the people who do not vote are disproportionately the economically poor and relatively uneducated.[13] Many of these people do not vote because they feel that voting does not mean anything and they consider themselves powerless to deal with an insensitive political system. To the extent that large numbers of people choose not to vote because of a feeling of powerlessness, then clearly the representatives do not reflect popular wishes. If anything, they reflect the judgment of the more affluent members of society.[14] If all citizens voted, then the representatives would enact laws that would cater more to the needs of the poor and the disadvantaged.

Some observers contend that nonvoting is an expression of happiness with the existing state of affairs. But as Frances Fox Piven and Richard A. Cloward observe, "No one has satisfactorily explained why 'the politics of happiness' is so consistently concentrated among the least well off."[15]

Information. For as long as polling groups have concerned themselves with public opinion, there has been realization that the masses of people lack information on important political issues.[16] Even when people give a Yes or No answer to a pollster, the response to follow-up questions usually reveals a great ignorance of details.

Lacking information, the masses depend on the experts who control information and who manipulate the choices available to the people. What can a janitor tell a military officer about weapons' technology? How does a factory worker (in contrast to a professional economist) understand the intricacies of the money supply, the balance of payments, or the national debt? Clearly, the masses of people are dependent upon the experts who rule.

Manipulation. Ordinary people can be easily swayed through scientific marketing techniques. Selling political candidates and programs is as scientific today as selling automobiles and soaps. Professional market research experts use clever techniques to sell their political "products." Given the publicity resources available to President John F. Kennedy, for example, the American people became enthralled with a program to send a man to the moon within a decade. On reflection, however, many ordinary citizens preferred that government spend tax money on police so that they could walk to the supermarket without being mugged. But the space program received so much publicity that many other ordinary citizens did not even recognize their own true interests. And many polls showed that Ronald Reagan's approval rating was much higher than that of the policies he advocated. Yet, he was able to win astonishing electoral victories in 1980 and 1984.

The radical philosopher Herbert Marcuse was on target when he described how propaganda is seductive in getting people to work against their own true interests. One need not necessarily agree with his solution of **repressive tolerance** (in which "progressive" ideas can be put forward but "reactionary" ideas can be suppressed) to accept his description of how public opinion is formulated and enticed. Since the propaganda machine is largely in the hands of the well-to-do and the politically important, ordinary people do not have a chance to make an effective independent judgment.

Money is a great unequalizer in the political

[13] Frances Fox Piven and Richard A. Cloward, *Why Americans Don't Vote* (New York: Pantheon, 1988); Carol Jean Uhlaner, "Electoral Participation: Summing Up a Decade," *Society* 28 (July/August 1991): 35.

[14] E. E. Schattschneider, *The Semisovereign People: A Realist's View of Democracy in America* (Hinsdale, Ill.: Dryden Press, 1975), p. 103. The book was originally published in 1960.

[15] Piven and Cloward, *Why Americans Don't Vote*, p. 13.

[16] Angus Campbell, Philip E. Converse, Warren E. Miller, and Donald E. Stokes, *The American Voter* (New York: John Wiley, 1960).

process. In many representative democracies rich corporations use their wealth to diminish popular rule. They give campaign contributions to candidates favorable to their own views. The rich hire public relations experts to push their own interests. They even move beyond the confines of their own country to influence the governments of other countries through bribery of public officials, and they sometimes conspire to destroy the democratic process itself. The poor and the weak, in contrast, have little to offer. Unskilled, unorganized, and uninformed, they are shunted aside by the affluent and their agents. If elected representatives are beholden to the rich, then the system cannot be called democratic in the sense of reflecting the popular will.

An **elite** (a small group of powerful people) actually rules in so-called representative democracies, as it does in practically all systems of government. Many theorists have made this assertion, although they have differed about the details and whether real democracy is possible at all. Marxists contend that representative democracy is a sham, since government is nothing more than a dictatorship of the capitalists. Anarchists argue that a form of government other than a society of equals without the existence of a state is an **oligarchy**—that is, a system of rule by the few for their own benefit. The sociologist C. Wright Mills, a radical critic, identifies politicians seeking election, military leaders desiring promotion, and corporations pursuing profits as a U.S. power elite that builds a war machine to pursue its own interests rather than responding to the wish of the masses of people for peace. Other elite theorists, such as Robert Michels,

Gaetano Mosca, and Vilfredo Pareto, argue that democracy is impossible because the few always rule. In their view, the elites in any large organization have assets of organizational skill, cohesion, and leadership that enable them to rule by ignoring the wishes of their members in most instances.

Students may differ as to which of these specific elite interpretations has the most truth, but it is evident that democracy in practice means rule by the few for their own benefit. Tax laws in the Western democracies work to the advantage of the affluent, who hide behind various "tax shelters." In wartime those who serve in the armed forces—particularly in the more dangerous combat zones—are likely to be from poor and minority groups, while members of the middle and upper classes are often deferred because they are engaged in "sensitive work" needed for the defense effort. Even programs purporting to serve the poor work, in fact, for the benefit of the affluent: contractors, realtors, bureaucrats with high salaries, and stockholders. Democracies, moreover, get involved in neocolonial wars halfway around the world not because the people want war but because war serves the interests of the ruling few.

Representative democracies offer the appearance and not the reality of true, democratic government. Low voting turnout, widespread ignorance of political information, and manipulation of the masses by the elite demonstrate that representative democracies represent the interests of the powerful few rather than the people.

5/NO   DO REPRESENTATIVE DEMOCRACIES REPRESENT THE INTERESTS OF THE POWERFUL FEW RATHER THAN THE PEOPLE?

The historical record shows that democracies have been responsive to popular will. An evaluation of the same points—voting turnout, information, and manipulation—will substantiate the case.

Voting Turnout. What is often missed in the discussions about voting turnout is that in the broad sweep of history, the voting population has increased in the Western democracies. As

the size of the electorate has expanded to include more and more people, so, too, have the kinds of laws enacted changed to reflect the aspirations of the new voting population. This change may best be seen in economic and social matters.

In Great Britain, as a case in point, voting was at first limited to landowning males. The laws that were enacted, such as those dealing with taxation and representation, served the interests of these property owners. By the Reform Act of 1832, prosperous middle-class males were granted the suffrage. Subsequent legislation reflected middle-class views, such as free trade, illegality of trade unions, and weak government to give strength to a free enterprise economy. In 1867, most urban workingmen were given the franchise, a right extended to rural workingmen in 1884. With the inclusion of the working classes into the electorate, the **welfare state** (in which government promoted programs dealing with education, health, social security, and welfare) became a reality.

Every advanced industrial democracy has become a welfare state in spite of the holding of public office by leaders calling themselves conservatives or liberals. The support that masses of people give to low-cost housing, public education, and inexpensive health care shows up in the welfare laws of countries such as Sweden, the United States, Belgium, Holland, and Switzerland. What forces the political leaders to move in the direction of the welfare state is the fear that large segments of the voting public will vote for an opposing candidate who promotes and delivers more of what people want.

The direct effect of voting on social and political matters can also be seen. So long as black people were excluded from participation in the American political process, there was no need for elected public officials to be responsive to their needs. When blacks were assured that they could exercise their freedom to vote without intimidation, the elected public officials responded to the realities of political power.

This transformation may be seen in the person of George Wallace, an arch-segregationist of the 1960s. As governor of Alabama, he was a national leader opposing the federal government's intervention to end racial discrimination in the United States and the symbol of resistance to civil rights laws. When he ran for governor again in 1982, many years after blacks in the South had been enfranchised, he successfully courted the black vote by promising to support laws and appoint officials favorable to black people. After his victory, he carried out his promises.

Laws are a reflection of popular will on the local as well as the national level. In predominantly fundamentalist Baptist areas, for example, local laws ban the sale of alcohol and theaters are forbidden to show X-rated movies. In areas where alternative life-styles are accepted, laws opposing gay rights, nude bathing, and pot smoking have either been struck down or liberalized. Clearly, when government acts in such a manner, it is reflecting the prevailing views of the political community. The record shows that democracy works to reflect the will of the people.

If some people do not vote, it should not be assumed that democracy is not working or that the people feel they are powerless. Many people choose not to vote because they are *satisfied* with the way things are going or because they find some views of each candidate to be worthy. **Cross-pressures**, felt by a voter who finds that some of his or her views are reflected by one candidate and some by the other, may keep a voter from voting, but they do not indicate that the voter is alienated. On the contrary, cross-pressures are evidence that candidates in a democracy seek votes from diverse interests.

Even those who choose not to vote are often regarded as potential voters by the contending campaigners in an election. It is true that voters exercise more influence than nonvoters. Even nonvoters, however, can become voters when an issue becomes important enough.

The fact that so much legislation benefiting disadvantaged, poor, or uneducated people (many of whom do not vote) has been enacted in the Western democracies reveals that the weak are not ignored. Indeed, the record of Western democracies shows that the causes of the weak are often taken up by the people who are educated members of the middle class, especially those with university education. In the words of the political scientist Raymond E. Wolfinger: "I don't think it [low voting turnout] is a measure of the health of the Republic. . . . Switzerland is one of the best governed countries in the world and [it has] a lower turnout rate than we do."[17]

Finally, it is not necessarily the case that nonvoters differ significantly in political preferences from voters in a manner that works against the poor and disadvantaged. According to the political scientists Stephen Earl Bennett and David Resnick, "Studies of the policy preferences of voters and nonvoters [in the United States] indicate that, with the possible exceptions of 1980 and 1984 . . . , had nonvoters gone to the polls, neither Democrats nor liberal policies would

[17]Raymond E. Wolfinger, quoted in Ronald Brownstein "Do Voter Numbers Matter?" *Los Angeles Times*, November 21, 1990, p. A1.

necessarily have benefited."[18] And a New York Times/CBS News Poll revealed that had nonvoters in the 1988 presidential election cast their ballots, not only would the actual winner, George Bush, have still won, but his margin of victory would have risen from 8 percentage points to 11 over his Democratic rival Michael S. Dukakis. The same poll showed that nonvoters were not more cynical about government than voters and that both voters and nonvoters were equally inclined to see government as being run by "a few big interests."[19]

Information. It is certainly true that many people are uninformed about government. But many people are informed. Citizens of democracies may not have the time to understand the ramifications of each and every issue, but they certainly do concern themselves with the issues most important to them. Veterans, for example, know a good deal about government programs benefiting veterans. The same applies to workers who know about occupational safety laws, to business people who know about taxes, and so on.

People affected by decisions, moreover, often join groups whose leaders inform them about what government is doing. Many people, consequently, receive their information in this manner and keep informed on issues through their group leaders.

Those who emphasize the lack of information of the masses and the dominance of the experts misunderstand the relationship between the expert and the masses. A janitor does not have to know the intricacies of weapons' technology to know that a war is being won or lost; battlefield casualties speak clearly on this point. A factory worker does not have to understand about the money supply, the balance of payments, or the national debt to know that the economy is experiencing inflation; a visit to the supermarket will reveal this immediately. What democracy means, then, is not that the masses of people have expertise, but rather that they evaluate the work of the experts.

[18] Stephen Earl Bennett and David Resnick, "The Implications of Nonvoting for Democracy in the United States," *American Journal of Political Science* 34 (August 1990): 775.

[19] E. J Dionne, Jr., "If Nonvoters Had Voted: Same Winner, But Bigger," *New York Times*, November 21, 1988, p. B16.

Manipulation. The view that ordinary people are easily manipulated cannot be substantiated. Are people so stupid that they cannot recognize their true interests? Millions of dollars might be spent on proclaiming the virtues of a commercial product, but the consumers soon know if the product is good or bad. Corporations with enormous funds and marketing research techniques have gone bankrupt because they could not convince consumers as to the desirability of their products. The wizards of soda pop in Atlanta were certain in 1985 that Americans would happily switch to the new Coca-Cola™ after a media blitz would entice them with images of a new magic liquid formula. The expensive campaign fizzled, as Americans demanded and received a return to the old Coke (renamed Classic Coke™).

Ordinary people may make mistakes (as experts do), but it is incorrect to confuse expertise with wisdom. Wisdom is a quality available to the well-informed and the poorly informed alike.

The view that an elite actually governs for its own interest in a representative democracy is not correct in the sense that elite theorists have asserted. The Marxist case in particular is historically inaccurate. Democratic government is not a capitalist dictatorship. Capitalists did not want trade unions to form and to have power, but these organizations of workers did form and do have power in every Western democracy. Capitalists resisted the welfare state with its demands for high taxes. They also opposed government regulations protecting workers from industrial accidents and from substandard wages. They fought the environmental protection laws requiring them to introduce costly machinery to eliminate or reduce pollution. They battled the laws passed on behalf of consumer protection. If a capitalist elite rules the Western democracies, it is acting in a noncapitalist manner. Perhaps it is the capitalists, rather than the ordinary people, who do not know what their true interests are!

Nor is there validity to the arguments of the non-Marxist elite theorists, such as Michels, Mosca, and Pareto. Although there is variation in what each says, the gist of their argument is that democracy is impossible, rulers rule as they see fit, and there is an ultimate separation of interests between the rulers and the ruled.

Although clearly the leadership of some organizations in the democracies has acted in the manner the elite theorists describe, such is not the case in most organizations. If individuals are not happy with their leaders, they can vote to change them or they can leave those private associations and join others.

At the government level, voters are free to vote for opposition parties. In those instances in which the parties come too close together, new parties form to reflect the views of those who feel excluded from representation. When the Republican and Democratic parties in the 1880s ignored the pleas of the farmers and workers for

reform, for example, the Populist party was established. The Democratic party adopted the platform of the Populist party in 1896 and thus effected a realignment of the parties.

When the elitists argue that democracy is impossible, what they really mean is that participatory democracy is impossible. This, however, is another matter. What we contend here is that representatives do reflect popular judgment, and the evidence is clear for this assertion.

6/YES SHOULD REPRESENTATIVE DEMOCRACIES REPRESENT THE JUDGMENT OF ELECTED LEADERS RATHER THAN THE PEOPLE?

Democracy has been described by some writers as a system of government that expresses the common will of a political community. Such a description is labeled the classical formulation of democracy by the economist Joseph A. Schumpeter. Specifically, he characterizes the classical view as "that institutional arrangement for arriving at political decisions which realizes the common good by making the people itself decide issues through the election of individuals who are to assemble in order to carry out its will." Schumpeter challenges the view that democracy means government *by* the people in the same sense that the people as an entity decide issues through their elected representatives. According to Schumpeter, the people do not hold definite and rational opinions about every individual question of public policy, and they do not, consequently, give effect to this opinion "by choosing 'representatives' who will see to it that that opinion is carried out."[20]

Schumpeter suggests that a different definition of democracy, one that conforms to the democratic world as it in fact exists, is appropriate. He proposes a reversal of the classical relationship between leaders and the people. The role of the people in a democracy is not to make policy but to produce (elect) a national executive or government. Democracy as it exists, then, can be defined as a *method*: "that institutional arrangement for arriving at political decisions in which individuals acquire the power to decide by means of competitive struggle for the people's

vote." So long as interest groups and political parties are free to compete in the political process and so long as contending members of the political elite abide by the "rules of the game" (rigorous adherence to constitutionalism), a system is democratic. In this view, popular participation is limited to accepting or rejecting the people who are to rule them.[21]

The political scientist Robert A. Dahl has built upon this perception of democracy put forward by Schumpeter. In so doing, he is one of the exponents of pluralism. Dahl prefers to use the term **polyarchy,** meaning the rule of multiple minorities, to describe representative democracy as we know it in practice.[22] Dahl argues that Western democracies are characterized not by majority rule but by minorities rule. Not all groups are interested in every aspect of public policy, he asserts. In Western democracies, individual groups have an ability to influence laws and administrative actions through their involvement in the specific policy areas for which they have special concern. Religious groups, consequently, exercise influence over religious matters, educational groups over education, and so on. Democracy, according to Dahl, does not mean majority rule but rather a system in which "all the active and legitimate groups in the population can make themselves heard at some cru-

[20] Joseph A. Schumpeter, *Capitalism, Socialism, and Democracy,* 3d ed. (New York: Harper and Brothers, 1950), p. 250.

[21] Ibid., pp. 269, 285.

[22] Robert A. Dahl, *After the Revolution? Authority in a Good Society,* rev. ed. (New Haven: Yale University Press, 1990), p. 60. See also Robert A. Dahl, *Democracy and Its Critics* (New Haven: Yale University Press, 1989), chaps. 15–18.

cial stage in the process of decision."[23] What distinguishes democracy from dictatorship, then, is that democracy is government by *minorities* and dictatorship is government by a *minority*.[24] According to Dahl, a polyarchy, in contrast to a dictatorship, greatly extends "the number, size, and diversity of the minorities whose preferences will influence the outcome of governmental decisions."[25]

Many other social scientists have supported this interpretation focusing on elites rather than the masses of people. It is neither necessary nor desirable that popular participation be massive for democracy to exist. In fact, too much popular participation will cause instability that may threaten the viability of the democratic system itself.

In this regard, the sociologist Seymour Martin Lipset notes antidemocratic tendencies in lower-class groups. He finds from data from a number of countries that such groups have been supporters of demagogues such as Adolf Hitler and Senator Joseph McCarthy. The lower strata may be more liberal in support of welfare state measures, higher wages, graduated income taxes, and trade unions, he asserts, but they are more intolerant than the rest of society on civil liberty matters.[26]

Lipset and other social scientists, consequently, find that there are advantages of stability that assist the system in contemporary representative democracies. The upper-activist strata tend to be more tolerant than the rest of society and are more committed to preserving the "rules of the game" by which a democracy is governed. This is not to say that popular participation is detrimental to stability; but too much participation may undermine the possibility of governing effectively and coherently. So we can see that representative democracy should represent the judgment of elected leaders rather than the people.

[23] Robert A. Dahl, *A Preface to Democratic Theory* (Chicago: University of Chicago Press, 1956), p. 137; see also pp. 145, 150.

[24] Jack Lively, *Democracy* (New York: St. Martin's Press, 1975), p. 20.

[25] Dahl, *A Preface to Democratic Theory*, p. 133.

[26] Seymour Martin Lipset, *Political Man: The Social Bases of Politics*, expanded ed. (Baltimore: Johns Hopkins University Press, 1981), p. 92

6/NO SHOULD REPRESENTATIVE DEMOCRACIES REPRESENT THE JUDGMENT OF ELECTED LEADERS RATHER THAN THE PEOPLE?

Democracy should require maximum participation of the people rather than reliance on elected leaders. We base our case on three points: (1) voting power is not a sufficient democratic resource of the people; (2) participation in politics has a positive impact on the personality of the participants and, consequently, on the stability of the democratic system; and (3) greater participation will produce better laws.

Voting. Voting power is influential only at the time that citizens cast their ballots. Citizens exercise their voting power only once every few years and, thus, relinquish to representatives power and authority to do what they wish once they are in office.

Many people do not participate in the political process because they come to feel that their vote is not important. Constitutional arrangements in representative democracy create impediments to popular rule, as the examples of an overpowering bureaucracy and an imperial judiciary in the United States attest. Laws are sometimes written in a vague manner, allowing bureaucrats discretion to interpret them. Judges who do not even have to compete in elections are able through statutory or constitutional interpretation to prevent the popular will from being implemented, moreover. It is no wonder that many citizens do not vote.

Voting does not mean much in reflecting the wishes of the masses, and that is why there has been a decline in the percentage of voters casting ballots. What the political scientist Benjamin R. Barber notes about the United States may also be applied to other countries: "In a country where voting is the prime expression of citizenship, the refusal to vote signals the bankruptcy of democracy."[27]

Participation should mean more than voting. It should include active popular involvement in the discussion of political issues as well as a direct voice in making decisions about laws and policies. Citizens cannot be expected to vote if they do not think of themselves as involved in all aspects of the political process.

Personality and Stability. More popular participation in government is desirable because of the effect it has on the character of people and, consequently, on the stability of the democratic system itself. To the extent that the individual participates in the political process, he or she develops those qualities of character that are healthy for the individuals themselves and for the community.

Mass participation signifies a sense of community. Civic action helps to generate a feeling of involvement, commitment, and obligation. When people participate actively in all facets of the democratic process, their self-esteem and self-confidence grow. Elitists who argue for limited mass participation ignore the beneficial consequences of participation on the character of citizens.

Much has been made of the antidemocratic tendencies of people who do not participate actively in the political process. Elitists fear these tendencies, but they fail to recognize the democratizing spirit that participation generates. If people are encouraged to participate, they will become more familiar and supportive of the democratic rules of the game. As Ronald M. Mason observes, "These rules of the game would include tolerance of differing opinions, protection of minority rights, and other libertarian principles."[28] We should not believe, then, that the enlargement of participation brings a greater susceptibility to dictatorship.

The effect of participation on character in a democracy is political stability. People who do not participate in the political process feel alienated from the community. They then become easy prey for demagogues, who enflame their frustrations and feelings of powerlessness and encourage undemocratic practices. Nonparticipants will be treated shabbily by political leaders. They will, consequently, lose self-esteem and become hostile to the system that rejects them.

John Stuart Mill wrote, "The most important point of excellence which any form of government can possess is to promote the virtue and intelligence of the people themselves."[29] A political system is important, consequently, not only because of the laws it produces but also because it produces better people.[30] That is why maximum popular participation is necessary in a democracy.

Laws. The elitist view is essentially a *status quo* position concerned with the maintenance of the system rather than with expansion of democratic ideals. The result of the elitist view is that masses of people are unrepresented. As indicated previously, the more advantaged groups tend to participate in the political process. The poor and the disadvantaged, consequently, remain either unrepresented or underrepresented.

Greater participation produces better laws. Widespread popular involvement in politics assures that more voices are heard, more viewpoints expressed, and more government responsiveness to the people that government is committed to serve.

Perspectives on democracy that minimize popular participation give support to a continuation of policies favorable to the more affluent members of a society. The fact of a large nonvoting population in Western democracies, particularly the United States, signifies nothing more than a sickness of democracy.[31]

[27] Benjamin R. Barber, *Strong Democracy: Participatory Democracy for a New Age* (Berkeley: University of California Press, 1984), p. xiii.

[28] Ronald M. Mason, *Participatory and Workplace Democracy: A Theoretical Development in Critique of Liberalism* (Carbondale, Ill.: Southern Illinois University Press, 1982), p. 40.

[29] John Stuart Mill, *Representative Government*, in his *Utilitarianism, Liberty, and Representative Government* (New York: Dutton, 1951), p. 193. The book was originally published in 1861.

[30] Lively, *Democracy*, p. 132

[31] Schattschneider, *Semisovereign People*, p. 96.

7/YES   IS PARTICIPATORY DEMOCRACY DESIRABLE?

Supporters of elements of participatory democracy come from a variety of viewpoints. Liberals favor more participation from the poor and the disadvantaged when they call for reform of the system. Conservatives urge greater "local control" on occasions. Anarchists and the New Left make participatory democracy a cornerstone of their political philosophies. Although it is difficult to come up with a single political philosophy tying these groups together, we can support some of their main arguments in favor of participatory democracy.

Participatory democracy is both necessary and possible. Participatory democracy is necessary because big government organizations are not able to understand the problems and needs of the people they ostensibly serve. There is something wrong, for example, when transportation policy is made by people who do not ride public transit; when education policy is made by people who send their children to private schools; and when war policy is made by people who are themselves too old to fight.

So poorly does government function in representative democracies that present-day systems are said to be ungovernable. If nations and regional units in representative democracies are ungovernable, it is because the masses of people have not been able to participate actively in decision making. How else to explain that billions of dollars are spent for education, and yet many students are poor readers; that billions are spent for welfare, and yet the welfare problems become worse; and that billions are spent to fight crime, yet urban neighborhoods are unsafe?

There is much opportunity for greater popular participation in all sectors of government and society. At the national level, referendums should be put forward so that the people themselves can decide some issues of concern to them.

Ballot issues have often mobilized people to participate in the political process. The political scientist Thomas E. Cronin notes that Idaho voters paid more attention to a right-to-work referendum which would prohibit making union membership a qualification for employment than to U.S. Senate and gubernatorial races in 1986. And in Oregon, some popular ballot issues have produced more voters than any other statewide races.[32] Ballot issues, moreover, are sometimes successful in defeating established interests. Bottle bill initiatives, which would require deposits for glass bottles, were approved in Maine and Michigan in spite of industry opposition.[33]

Popular participation can be encouraged particularly in regional and local matters. In addition to increased use of the referendum, the New England town meeting approach to local problems can be expanded. Other forms of popular participation can be broadened through community boards, neighborhood councils, local school boards, and other units of civic action at the neighborhood level.

There should be greater citizen participation in nongovernmental organizations. Workers can participate in management decisions. Universities, too, can have more participation from their principal constituents—students and faculty. Students can play a role in hiring faculty and designing curriculums. Teachers can participate in deciding administrative issues.

Why shouldn't the poor be consulted about poverty programs, since they are the people who are affected by government decisions about poverty? Why shouldn't the people who live in a neighborhood decide whether their community should be broken up so that a new civic center can be built where their homes now stand? Why shouldn't young people be asked if they really want to fight in Panama or Kuwait? These are legitimate questions raised by critics of democracy in its representative form, thus suggesting that there is merit in the participatory model of democracy.

[32] Cronin, *Direct Democracy*, p. 67.

[33] Kenneth Jost, "Initiatives: True Democracy or Bad Lawmaking?" *Editorial Research Reports*, August 17, 1990, 1:464.

7/NO   IS PARTICIPATORY DEMOCRACY DESIRABLE?

Modern society is too complex for widespread popular participation in government. Even dedicated and conscientious law makers do not have the time to read and comprehend the words in every bill introduced in the legislature. There must be a division of labor in a democracy in which the experts read and interpret the issues and inform the masses about the best options. All democracy requires is that the people choose officials who understand the issues and debate them openly.

Group leaders understand the issues. It is their responsibility to understand them. Clearly, a labor leader in a democracy monitors all legislation dealing with labor matters and reports back to union members. A leader of a feminist group considers every administrative action pertaining to women's rights and informs the members of the feminist association. In the real world at the end of the twentieth century, specialization demands that the masses of people work through their leaders.

Ordinary people do not have time to participate in the political process in the way that group leaders do. As the political scientist Gerald Pomper notes, "Voters have too many pressing tasks, from making money to making love, to follow the arcane procedures of government."[34]

Besides, if the masses of people become so heavily involved in politics, then the system would become so politicized as to produce great social tensions. Because most people are concerned with their private rather than their public lives, governments are able to work effectively.

The problems of modern society, moreover, cannot be solved by participatory democracy schemes of the modern type. Decentralization cannot cope with the problems of environmental protection (in which poisonous chemicals from one area of a country are used in other areas of the country), the well-being of the economy (in which matters affecting a national market must be decided from a central source), or war (with its global connotations). Decentralization is irrelevant to these and other matters.

Initiatives and referendums are not the answer to active citizen involvement. Turnout for referendums is generally less than for elections, and when referendums are on the ballots for state elections, 5–15 percent of those who vote for candidates do not vote on the referendum questions.[35] This disparity is called **drop-off**— the percentage of voters who vote in an election but fail to vote on proposals (or candidates) found lower down on the ballot. Nor do initiatives and referendums necessarily represent the people's will. Often they reflect the desires of those groups that have the money such campaigns require. Tobacco companies, nuclear power interests, and bottling corporations have spent millions fighting initiatives that would be detrimental to their well-being.

Often the wording of initiatives and referendums is difficult for voters to understand in the short time that they have in the voting booth. Moreover, voters often have to consider several questions at once. In 1990, for example, California voters were faced with thirteen initiatives on a single ballot. Although special interests are sometimes defeated, the exceptions prove the rule.[36]

Finally, when we really take a close look as to what some supporters of decentralization mean by participatory democracy, we can see that they do not mean "power to the people" but rather transferring power from one group of leaders to another. When segregationists in the United States called for local control in deciding racial issues, what they meant was that local segregationists rather than central government integrationists should decide policy. When community action leaders ask for participation by the poor, what they really mean is participation by the more politically active leaders who live in the community and speak in the name of the poor. In the name of participatory democracy, then, many sins are committed in which power is given to an unrepresentative few.

[34] Gerald Pomper, "The Contribution of Political Parties to Democracy," in *Party Renewal in America*, ed. Gerald Pomper (New York: Praeger, 1980), p. 7.

[35] Cronin, *Direct Democracy*, p. 67
[36] Jost, "Initiatives," p. 464.

8/YES DOES DEMOCRACY PRODUCE WORSE GOVERNMENT THAN DICTATORSHIP PRODUCES?

We need to go no further than to read the morning newspapers to see that democracy produces bad government. We can see every day that democracy creates poor leadership, corruption, and inefficiency.

Leadership. The masses of people are envious of superior people and seek lackluster leaders to govern. It is no accident, then, that democracies choose leaders of no outstanding qualities or accomplishments.

Because leaders must respond to popular whims, democracies subject themselves to leadership by **demagogues**—leaders who rely on highly emotional and usually irrational appeals to attract the immediate approval of the masses rather than to serve the needs of the country. It is no wonder, then, that democracies have their share of demagogues like Huey Long and Joseph McCarthy.

Particularly in a modern, complex society, we need knowledgeable people to run the government. Specifically, we need experts who understand the technical intricacies of the problems of our society rather than leaders adept at pandering to mobs. We may ask ourselves, for example, if before expert doctors perform an operation, they must consult with patients, orderlies, nurses, and janitors in the hospital about the proper surgical techniques. Shouldn't the doctors, because of their many years of experience in the study of medicine, be entitled to perform the surgery as they deem fit? Similarly, we would not regard it as rational for the passengers of a ship to tell the captain how to run the ship. In a comparable way, it is foolish to expect the masses of people to select expert leaders when they do not know the first thing about governing.

In a democracy even leaders of great ability must pander to popular tastes and are not free to act in the public interest because of the democratic reverence of equality. The people of a country are not equal in intelligence, strength, or character. By enshrining the principle of equality, men and women of great ability are leveled to the standards of the mediocre. In political campaigns, for example, they must travel to the "grass roots" and engage in such ridiculous tokens of leadership as wearing Indian headdresses, eating kosher hotdogs, and dancing Polish dances, none of which has anything to do with good government.

The principle of equality is dangerous to the well-being of society because of the leveling tendencies of society. In a dictatorship, people trained for leadership and excellence receive the prizes a polity has to distribute: political leadership, social prominence, and economic prosperity. In a democracy, in contrast, the masses demand *equality of results* rather than *equality of opportunity*. Those concerned with results oppose talent and ability and are not satisfied if they are left out of top positions. They demand redistribution of income to their own class, and they destroy the incentive of more qualified, intelligent, and innovative people. They ask for **affirmative action** programs in which government can demand that citizens create special recruitment opportunities for minorities and other groups which have previously suffered from discrimination. These programs are no more than an egalitarian attack against merit. The masses of the mediocre, consequently, vote only for those officials who pass laws giving the mediocre advantages that they do not deserve. The result is a society of the mediocre, of unprofessional professionals: teachers who cannot teach, doctors who know little about medicine, and lawyers who do not understand law. Paradoxically, such a society is detrimental to the masses of people who are dependent upon poorly qualified teachers, doctors, and lawyers. How would any sane human being feel about the prospect of undergoing brain surgery by a surgeon who flunked Brain Surgery 101 in medical school but was given a medical license anyway because of egalitarian pressures?

Corrupt Government. Corruption in democracies is widespread. "To the victor belong the spoils," said William L. Marcy, a U.S. Senator from New York in the administration of President Andrew Jackson. That slogan has been made acceptable at the highest and lowest levels in democracies. The corruption revealed in investigations following the Watergate break-in implicated not only cabinet figures but the president of the United States. Illegal campaign contributions to the Committee to Reelect the President (CREEP) were given by big corporations in return for political favors. Watergate signified not only financial corruption but the abuse of power by both the president and many of his appointed advisers.

At the regional and local levels, moreover, corruption is widespread. Payoffs to police to allow criminals to engage in drug sales, prostitution, and gambling are a matter of common knowledge. As government has become big at all levels, it has accumulated more rewards to distribute—contracts, tax loopholes, and jobs—and the scope of corruption has expanded accordingly. The democracies of Germany, Italy, the United States, and Japan, for example, have in recent years received prominent attention because of major acts of corruption by leading political figures.

Inefficiency. Although a case can be made that government itself is inefficient, it is clear that democratic governments in particular are highly inefficient. Too many bureaucratic agencies and interest groups must be consulted and enticed in a democracy. So slow is the laborious process of criticism and debate, moreover, that inefficiencies are bound to result. There is no central authority with the strength to break through the maze of obstacles to action.

Road construction, for example, must be approved by the political leaders from areas not actually involved. The result in this and other policies is duplication and administrative overlapping—two features of an inefficient system. In a dictatorship, in contrast, someone at the top can cut through the red tape and get things moving.

8/NO   DOES DEMOCRACY PRODUCE WORSE GOVERNMENT THAN DICTATORSHIP PRODUCES?

To be sure, democracy has some weaknesses, and these are often pointed out by supporters of dictatorship. Criticisms of democracy producing bad government are revealed as flawed, however, when a close examination is made of the data. We may best think of democracy in the same way that the late French entertainer Maurice Chevalier thought about old age at a time in his life when he was old, "Old age is all right," he said, "especially when you consider the alternative." We can say, then, that in spite of the imperfections, democracy produces good government. We can deal with the issues raised by the *Affirmative.*

Leadership. The argument that bad leaders are chosen by an ignorant electorate is wrong because it confuses the relationship between leaders and people and also because it is factually incorrect. It is certainly true that the masses of people are poorly informed about issues, but this does not mean that they are stupid or unwise. To begin with, ordinary people have common sense and wisdom and are aware of the consequences of government laws and policies. A political leader may say, for example, that a government will soon win a war, but ordinary people know the daily battle casualties and the economic costs of pursuing victory. They can

make a sound judgment based on the costs and sacrifices.

Ordinary people in democracies, moreover, have often chosen great leaders possessing intellect and judgment. American presidents such as Abraham Lincoln, Theodore Roosevelt, and Woodrow Wilson have made outstanding contributions to good government. Thomas Jefferson was one of the most brilliant of American presidents and an accomplished political leader, architect, musician, and philosopher. Other democracies, too, have produced outstanding leaders: Benjamin Disraeli and Winston Churchill in Great Britain, and Georges Clemenceau and Charles de Gaulle in France, for example. The masses of people have not shown hostility to excellence in political leadership. The fact that so many experts are recruited for high-level administrative posts is a reflection of this popular support of expertise.

Dictatorships have produced their share of demagogues and leaders who lacked expertise. Adolf Hitler purged the universities of their eminent scientists. Joseph Stalin liquidated many competent leaders, some of whom were even loyal communists. Both these leaders and other dictators brought their countries to ruin or near-disaster. The record of democracies is better.

Much has been made of the egalitarian evils

of democracy. It is essential to note, however, that there is much confusion about democracy. The main egalitarian component of democracy is *political equality*: Each person's vote is counted equally. That concept is based on a respect for the individual. Proponents of democracy contend quite properly that regardless of talent, intelligence, and ability, every individual has a right to be an active participant in the political process and make whatever contributions he or she deems desirable.

It is certainly true that the people—whether they be disadvantaged, poor, or sometimes unqualified—have made demands on democratically elected officials, but this is often because of the past history of discrimination and deprivation and not because of a desire to reward the unworthy.

Dictatorships do not, in fact, bring the "best" people to positions of eminence. Let us take a look at authoritarian aristocracies as a case in point. In European countries of the seventeenth and eighteenth centuries, aristocratic rule dominated the political system. It was the landed gentry who actually ruled. Were these people "the best"? Certainly the aristocratic system produced people of great merit in politics, science, and the arts. It also, however, produced incompetents who only maintained their positions because of their privilege, not their abilities. We can look at the officer corps of the aristocratic armies as a case in point. To be an officer in the army it was essential to be of the nobility. Any relationship between military competence and royal blood was often a mere happenstance. In the nineteenth century, in contrast, the aristocratic barriers to the officer corps were removed in many countries, and military careers were thrown open to talent. Where an openness of competition was permitted, the quality of armies improved.

Corrupt Government. Like the charge of poor leadership, the accusations by antidemocracy advocates about corruption are oversimplified. It is certainly true that corruption exists in democracies, but the nature of the democratic system is such as to minimize it. A political system reflects a social system; and if the character of a people is corrupt, no government can improve it.

The features of a democracy, however, make it likely that corruption will be minimized. Constitutional democracies require open and responsible government. Part of the oldest traditions of these constitutional democracies is the right of a legislator to inquire of the government (through its responsible cabinet minister, for example) about impropriety in office. A free press, moreover, also serves to expose corruption. A reporter in a free society seeks the acclaim—perhaps even a Pulitzer Prize or its foreign equivalent—for uncovering a scandal involving political leaders. In reporting the information leading to the revelations about Watergate, Bob Woodward and Carl Bernstein were continuing a long tradition of independent journalism. It is no wonder, then, that elected officials of all political persuasions—from liberal Democrats to conservative Republicans—have criticized the overzealousness of the press.

Dictatorships do not permit Woodwards and Bernsteins to roam around government corridors in search of information about government wrongdoing. Graft, corruption, and abuse of power exist even when unreported, however. Without the constraints imposed by a free society—an independent legislature and a free press, for example—corruption is likely to get out of hand. Reports of corruption in dictatorships, such as Iran under the shah, Germany under Hitler, and Romania under Nicolae Ceauşescu, have been documented after the fact. It is wrong to believe that democracies have more corruption because they publicize their problems.

Inefficiency. The notion that dictatorships are efficient is a myth. Supporters used to comment that at least Benito Mussolini made the trains run on time and Hitler got the economy moving again to point out the achievements of dictatorship. Dictatorships, however, are often inefficient. Hitler's political and economic system seemed to many to run like a well-oiled machine. In fact, however, the Nazi regime displayed tremendous inefficiency as government agencies overlapped in authority and competed with each other.[37] Hitler's minister of armaments and munitions, Albert Speer, claimed that Hitler was too frightened to call upon the German people to make the same kinds of sacrifices as those demanded by Franklin D. Roosevelt and Winston Churchill of the American and British people, respectively. As a result, Speer observed, the

[37] H. R. Trevor-Roper, *The Last Days of Hitler*, 3d ed. (New York: Collier Books, 1962), p. 64.

German war effort could not be mobilized to the greatest efficiency.[38]

The inefficiency of dictatorships is also inevitable because of the relationship between the dictator and subordinates. Dictators want their immediate subordinates to be good—but not too good—lest the dictators no longer be needed to

[38] Albert Speer, *Inside the Third Reich*, trans. Richard Winston and Clara Winston (New York: Macmillan, 1970), p. 214.

save the nation. The dictator of a country must seem to be indispensable and so must purge associates who are achieving too much eminence. Subordinates, consequently, are reluctant to make decisions that the dictator may envy or may not like. There is a press toward decision making at the top. The mere volume of decisions that must be made forces incessant delays pending consideration by the dictator. Instead of delegating power, dictators concentrate it into their own hands and make government inefficient. Dictatorships, then, do not produce better government than democracies.

9/YES ARE DICTATORSHIPS BETTER ABLE TO DEAL WITH FOREIGN POLICY THAN ARE DEMOCRACIES?

Whatever may be said on behalf of democracy in a domestic political context, certainly there is no good case to be made for democracy in matters pertaining to the conduct of foreign policy and national security. The sanctity of the national interest in foreign policy, the requirements of war, and the need to maintain secrecy in a dangerous global setting all point to the weaknesses of democracy.

National Interest. The conduct of foreign policy requires the highest attention to the protection of the national interest. Now, as in earlier centuries, national security is the paramount feature of national interest and affects citizens of a state regardless of class, religion, or race. As such, political leaders must take whatever actions are essential to protect that security.

There are many possible goals for a nation to pursue in the conduct of foreign policy: economic, ideological, or military, for example. Only a political leader who does not have to suffer the political constraints imposed by democracy can act properly to serve the security interests of the state.

In the realm of foreign policy, political leaders have been hamstrung by popular legislatures and the popular press. Each of these institutions has injected popular sentiment into foreign policy deliberations and has forced policy makers to act in ways detrimental to the national interest. The passion to engage in modern "holy wars" is difficult to resist, for example. The "yellow press" encouraged wars of imperialism. The role of the press in promoting the Spanish-American War of 1898 is a case of popular interference in the conduct of foreign policy.

The 1990s provide many examples of national security being risked by the pursuit of other goals. From a security point of view, the United States needs strong ties with China. China is a nuclear power, capable of exporting weapons, such as ballistic missiles, to areas of the world that are politically volatile and of great significance to the United States.

But when the Chinese government cracked down on the democracy movement in 1989, liberal interest groups concerned with human rights pressured the United States government to take punitive measures against the government of China. These included retracting China's status as a **most-favored nation**, in which it received preferential tariff terms. Only with great difficulty was President George Bush able to resist the domestic pressures that would have put the United States on a collision course with China.

Ethnic groups have also exerted influence on U.S. foreign policy. Groups in the United States with strong ties to other countries, such as the American Irish with Ireland, the American Jewish community with Israel, and African Americans with African states, have pursued their own agendas at the expense of U.S. security interests. Similarly, economic groups, such as corporations and trade unions, have injected their goals into foreign policy in a manner not in accord with U.S. security interests.

War. Dictators who are trained for leadership are less susceptible than others to the passions of either war or peace. They are able to put events into proper perspective. Democracies, in contrast, require the firing up of people's minds and hearts if citizens are to go voluntarily to war. There is a need, consequently, to engage in propaganda and to make entire nations appear to possess inhumane characteristics. And so the Germans were referred to as Huns during World War I, for example, recalling the bellicose Germanic ancestors of modern Germany. George Bush's firing up of Americans against Saddam Hussein in 1990–91 is a recent case. Once such popular forces of agitation are released, it is difficult for statesmen to engage in moderation or to bring a war to its end. Commenting on how democracies foment emotionalism in war compared to dynastic wars of earlier centuries, the writer Hoffmann Nickerson notes, "It has been well said that the grenadiers of Maria Theresa did not have to be told that Frederick the Great was a Sodomite, or those of Frederick that Maria ate babies."[39]

Similarly in democracies, when the mood is for peace, it is difficult to get the country to prepare for war or to engage in military acts deemed vital to national security. Great Britain in the 1930s may be used as an example. Public opinion was hostile to rearmament in spite of the rearmament of Germany under Adolf Hitler. The British government was weak in responding to Hitler's expansionist policies because of popular opposition to military measures. If British leaders could have acted without the democratic pressures, the country would have been better able to cope with the dangers to its national security.

War, too, reveals yet another limitation of democracy. Because so many people have to be consulted—legislators, administrators, and opinion leaders—it is difficult to engage in war in defense of the national interest. Legislatures have constantly acted in a fashion detrimental to the purely military conduct of a war. As commanding general during the American Revolution, George Washington suffered from constant investigations by the Continental Congress. The congressional Committee on the Conduct of the War restricted Abraham Lincoln in a similar way in the Civil War.

Secrecy. One of the great weaknesses of democracy in foreign policy and national security policy has to do with the openness of democracy. Members of Congress reveal classified information harmful to the national security when that information serves their own interests, whether personal, political, or ideological. A free press embarrasses the government by disclosing in advance secret military operations or activities deemed vital to the national interest. All that an enemy of a democracy has to do is to read the daily newspaper, study published government debates, and question the participants, and he or she then can determine much about a democracy's foreign policy. The publication of the classified *Pentagon Papers* by the *New York Times* in 1971 is but one example of a democracy revealing its own secrets.

A dictatorship can keep secrets from a democratic adversary. Its agents can operate at home and abroad without fear that some journalist interested in winning a reporter's trophy will publish a list of names and addresses of intelligence agents. A dictator's secret police, moreover, have great discretionary powers in serving the national interest. Why should a democratic country put itself at such a disadvantage? As Soviet exile Alexsandr Solzhenitsyn indicated, democracies can be suicidal when it comes to protecting their legitimate foreign policy needs.

Alexis de Tocqueville, the great French observer of the American political scene, noted in his monumental *Democracy in America* the weaknesses of democracy in the conduct of foreign policy. His words are as true today as they were when the book was published in 1835:

A democracy finds it difficult to coordinate the details of a great undertaking and to fix on some plan and carry it through with determination in spite of obstacles. It has little capacity for combining measures in secret and waiting patiently for the result. Such qualities are more likely to belong to a single man or to an aristocracy. But these are just the qualities which, in the long run, make a nation, and a man, too, prevail.[40]

[39] Hoffmann Nickerson, *The Armed Horde, 1793–1939: A Study of the Rise, Survival and Decline of the Mass Army* (New York: G. P. Putnam's Sons, 1940), p. 12.

[40] Alexis de Tocqueville, *Democracy in America*, ed. J. P. Mayer and Max Lerner, trans. George Lawrence (New York: Harper and Row, 1966), p. 211.

9/NO ARE DICTATORSHIPS BETTER ABLE TO DEAL WITH FOREIGN POLICY THAN ARE DEMOCRACIES?

Although we do not attribute to democracy any divine wisdom, we can appreciate democracy best by putting it in perspective. Democracy is not only good for domestic policy, but it serves foreign policy interests equally well.

National Interest. It is certainly true that democracies have suffered reverses in foreign policy. It is not true, however, that national security either must be or is more likely to be undermined in a democracy than in a dictatorship. First, it is not always true that dictators act in the security interests of their countries. They, too, are subject to ideological pressures and occasionally even to insanity. Communist China under the control of Mao Zedong pursued policies designed to isolate the People's Republic of China internationally. It seems clear in retrospect that Mao's policies were detrimental to the security interests of his country. When Pol Pot, the leader of the communist Khmer Rouge, came to power in Cambodia, he proceeded to butcher his own people, a horror that can be compared to the Nazi elimination of the Jews. As a result of this genocide, Cambodia left itself vulnerable to attack by another country, Vietnam.

Second, national security is a difficult concept to identify. It is often associated with the school of foreign policy known as **Realpolitik**, which focuses on power considerations as a guide to policy making. *Realpolitik*, or **realism** as it is also called, is often contrasted to **idealism**, which is concerned with other considerations, such as human rights, economic development, and welfare. Often, however, idealism is far more "realistic" about foreign policy than is realism. As World War II came to an end, for example, "realists" like Winston Churchill and Charles de Gaulle believed that Western imperialism could resume operations in Africa and Asia. It was the idealist Franklin D. Roosevelt who accurately foresaw the clamor for national self-determination in Africa and Asia and the consequent decline of Western colonialism. What is good for the security interests of a country, therefore, is best determined by the give-and-take of debate that characterizes a democratic society.

Third, there are other objectives besides security that nations may properly pursue. The goals of foreign policy are not necessarily contradictory to each other. It may be true, for example, that the security interests of a country may require it to ally itself with a dictatorship. The domestic pressures of the democracy toward liberalization of the dictatorship may work to the betterment of both the security interests of the democracy and the increasing popular support of the dictatorship. Let us examine the case of Iran as an example. Iran, under the leadership of the shah, was a dictatorship complete with secret police and persecution of a free press. The shah did little to broaden the base of support but relied instead on the police, the army, and a thin segment of Iranian society. Once faced with a rising opposition, he lacked strong and wide support. The shah's government, which had been so friendly to the United States, was toppled and replaced by a government more neutralist in its foreign policy. American power, consequently, suffered a loss of influence in the Persian Gulf.

In commenting on the affair a year after the fall of the shah, former Secretary of State Henry Kissinger told a group of reporters that if the United States had to do it over again, it should have put pressure on the shah to broaden his base of support. Had the political pressures in the United States been strong enough to compel the administration to apply its influence on the Iranian government, the shah might possibly have retained power, and the position of the United States in world affairs would have been stronger. Iran would have remained a friend of the United States throughout the 1980s and early 1990s instead of being an enemy.

We should keep in mind the success of the United States in rallying around Corizon Aquino and toppling Ferdinand Marcos as leader of the Philippines in 1986. By backing Aquino the United States was able to win the support of a popular and democratic government rather than suffer the opprobrium of propping up a corrupt and unpopular leader. A stable and democratic Philippines, consequently, serves the security interests of the United States.

War and Secrecy. If foreign policy, in general, can benefit from democracy, the same can be said about the conduct of war. People who live in democracies have been willing to temporarily give up certain freedoms during periods of war. Many Western democracies in World War I and World War II, for example, suspended elections and censored the press. Once the wars were over, however, it was business as usual for the democracies.

Democracy, moreover, has much to contribute in the conduct of a war. War requires the cooperation of the people who fight them, so that if there is no means by which popular sentiment can be expressed, then the prospects for victory may be dimmed. The tactics of British and French generals in World War I called for massive frontal assaults against superior enemy firepower, for example, and resulted in the loss of millions of lives. It was duly elected political figures, such as David Lloyd George and Winston Churchill in Great Britain and Georges Clemenceau in France, who forced the professional military leaders—the experts—to rethink the tactics they had adopted. Similarly, it was duly elected political leaders who complained that the United States could not win the Vietnam War it fought in the 1960s and 1970s. Had there not been an outlet to voice disapproval with the war, even more casualties would have been experienced by both Vietnam and the United States.

One other example of democratic rule in matters pertaining to war concerns weapons systems. We often think, incorrectly as it turns out, that dictatorships make good decisions about armaments since they can more readily cut through red tape. Closer examination of dictatorial conduct of war, however, reveals top-heavy development and bungled decision making. Adolf Hitler, for example, shunned development of jet aircraft and delayed production of ballistic missiles, both of which appeared too late in the war to serve the Nazi cause.

The democratic United States established a good record in developing new weapons, as the case of the atomic bomb illustrates. When scientists told Franklin D. Roosevelt about the possibility of building the atomic bomb, Roosevelt was receptive to the idea. It has been argued that had Roosevelt not supported the development of this new super-weapon, no doubt the scientists would have tried to convince Congress and the press. In a dictatorship, there would have been little recourse to such independent sources of decision making. A comparison of the two systems shows that democracy possesses strengths in weapons procurement, an area vital for national security.

The record of dictators in the conduct of war, moreover, is not as good as the record of democratic leaders. Hitler's decision to move heavily into the Soviet Union and his orders for German troops not to withdraw led to a destruction of Germany's Sixth Army at Stalingrad. The case of Joseph Stalin as a war leader is equally instructive. Soviet leader Nikita Khrushchev revealed (although long after Stalin had died) that Stalin was responsible for great military disasters in World War II, which he attributed to "Stalin's annihilation of many military commanders in the years 1937–41."[41] Clearly, the war record of dictatorships is marked by bad decisions. To be sure, democracies, too, make errors, but there is no case to be made for the overwhelming superiority of dictatorships in the conduct of war.

The record of U.S. foreign policy in the decades since the end of World War II suggest that de Tocqueville was wrong about the qualities of democracy in the conduct of foreign policy. As the political analyst Josef Joffe observes: "In the decades of the postwar era the United States not only executed a 'vast design' by singlehandedly erecting a new order on the ashes of the old; it also 'persevered' in spite of serious obstacles, to use Tocqueville's terminology." Joffe cites the accomplishments by the United States during this period: the building of a global trading system, a global monetary system, an interlocking security system, and initially, at least, a global institution (the United Nations) dominated by the United States. Joffe adds that the United States did not lack the "patience" of a long-term policy. A tough containment policy of the United States toward the Soviet Union lasted for at least a quarter century.[42]

It is possible, then, to conclude that it was not de Tocqueville, but another foreign observer of the American scene—James Bryce—who accurately described the role of democracy in the conduct of foreign policy. He wrote in his *Modern Democracies* (1921):

[41] Robert Conquest, "De-Stalinization and the Heritage of Terror," in *Politics of the Soviet Union: 7 Cases*, ed. Alexander Dallin and Allan F. Westin (New York: Harcourt, Brace and World, 1966), p. 48.

[42] Josef Joffe, "Tocqueville Revisited: Are Good Democracies Bad Players in the Game of Nations?" *Washington Quarterly* 11 (Winter 1988): 164.

In a democracy the People are entitled to determine the Ends or general aims of foreign policy.

History shows that they do this at least as wisely as monarchs or oligarchies, or the small groups to whom, in democratic countries, the conduct of foreign relations has been left, and that they have evinced more respect for moral principles. . . .

Whatever faults modern democracies may have committed in this field of administration [foreign policy], the faults chargeable on monarchs and oligarchies have been less pardonable and more harmful to the peace and progress of mankind.[43]

[43] James Bryce, *Modern Democracies* (New York: Macmillan, 1921), 2:283.

KEY TERMS

Absolutism
Affirmative action
Aristocracy
Authoritarian government
Autocracy
Consociational democracy
Constitutionalism
Crisis government
Cross-pressures
Decentralization
Demagogues
Democracy
Democratic capitalism
Despotism
Dictatorship
Direct democracy
Drop-off
Economic democracy
Elite
Empowerment
Filibuster
Idealism
Indirect democracy

Initiative
Judicial review
Kibbutz
Liberal democracy
Malapportionment
Monarchy
Most-favored nation
New England town meeting
Oligarchy
Participatory democracy
Pluralism
Political equality
Polyarchy
Realism
Realpolitik
Referendum
Representative democracy
Repressive tolerance
Theocracy
Totalitarian government
Tyranny
Welfare state

QUESTIONS

1. Is student participatory democracy possible in a college? What might be the strengths and weaknesses of such an approach?
2. What effect would the denial of constitutional freedoms in representative democracy have on economic democracy?
3. If an elite rules in representative democracies, what influence do the masses have on it?
4. What role should experts play in public policy matters in democracies?
5. What are the strengths and weaknesses of dictatorship?
6. Why do dictatorships perish?
7. Why do democracies perish?
8. Do civil liberties strengthen or weaken a democracy? Why?
9. Is the distinction between authoritarianism and totalitarianism meaningful? Why?
10. What are the strengths and weaknesses of democracies in their conduct of foreign policy?
11. What are the consequences to democracy of greater popular participation in political affairs?

RECOMMENDED READINGS

ARBLASTER, ANTHONY. *Democracy*. Minneapolis: University of Minnesota Press, 1987. A brief introduction to the subject.

ARENDT, HANNAH. *The Origins of Totalitarianism*. New ed. New York: Harcourt Brace Jovanovich, 1973. A philosophical treatment of totalitarianism.

AVEY, MICHAEL J. *The Demobilization of Voters: A Comprehensive Theory of Voter Turnout*. New York: Greenwood Press, 1989. An argument that nonvoting is caused by the behavior of politicians in the political system and not by the characteristics of voters.

BACHRACH, PETER. *The Theory of Democratic Elitism: A Critique*. Washington, D.C.: University Press of America, 1980. An argument asserting that many twentieth-century social scientists who study democracy ignore the necessity of greater political participation by the masses of people. First published in 1967.

BARBER, BENJAMIN R. *Strong Democracy: Participatory Democracy for a New Age*. Berkeley: University of California Press, 1984. A democrat's criticism of liberal democracy.

BENNETT, STEPHEN EARL, and DAVID RESNICK. "The Implications of Nonvoting for Democracy in the United States." *American Journal of Political Science* 34 (August 1990): 771–802. An analysis of nonvoting.

BROWNSTEIN, RONALD. "Do Voter Numbers Matter?" *Los Angeles Times*, November 21, 1990, pp. A1, A18. A presentation of differing views on the subject.

CLINTON, DAVID. "Tocqueville's Challenge." *Washington Quarterly* 11 (Winter 1988): 173–89. An assessment of democracy in the conduct of U.S. foreign policy.

CRONIN, THOMAS E. *Direct Democracy: The Politics of Initiative, Referendum, and Recall*. Cambridge, Mass.: Harvard University Press, 1989. An argument that the initiative, referendum, and recall have worked reasonably well in the United States.

CURTIS, MICHAEL. *Totalitarianism*. New Brunswick, N.J.: Transaction Books, 1979. A brief analysis of totalitarianism.

DAHL, ROBERT A. *Democracy and Its Critics*. New Haven: Yale University Press, 1989. A wide-ranging study of the theory and practice of democracy.

———. *A Preface to Democratic Theory*. Chicago: University of Chicago Press, 1956. An analysis of polyarchy as a modern form of representative democracy.

FINLEY, M. I. *Democracy Ancient and Modern*. Rev. ed. New Brunswick, N.J.: Rutgers University Press, 1985. An examination of democratic Athens and the relevance of Athenian democracy to the contemporary world.

FRIEDRICH, CARL J., and ZBIGNIEW K. BRZEZINSKI. *Totalitarian Dictatorship and Autocracy*. 2d ed. rev. by Carl J. Friedrich. New York: Praeger, 1965. A landmark book on totalitarianism.

GREGOR, A. JAMES. *The Ideology of Fascism: The Rationale of Totalitarianism*. New York: Free Press, 1969. A philosophical assessment of fascism.

GROTH A. J. "Totalitarians and Democrats: Aspects of Political-Military Relations 1939–1945." *Comparative Strategy* 8, no. 1 (1989): 73–97. A comparison of military-political relationships between democracies and dictatorships.

JOFFE, JOSEF. "Tocqueville Revisited: Are Good Democracies Bad Players in the Game of Nations?" *Washington Quarterly* 11 (Winter 1988): 161–72. An assessment of the strengths and weaknesses of the United States as a democratic country in the conduct of foreign policy.

JOST, KENNETH. "Initiatives: True Democracy or Bad Lawmaking?" *Editorial Research Reports*, August 17, 1990, 1: 462–75. An overview of initiatives in the United States.

KORNHAUSER, WILLIAM. *The Politics of Mass Society*. New York: Free Press, 1959. A case favoring the existence of independent elites and groups as a prerequisite for democracy.

KRAUTHAMMER, CHARLES. "The Price of Power." *New Republic* 196 (February 9, 1987): 23–25. An assertion that there is a conflict between democracy and foreign policy.

LAPHAM, LEWIS H. "Democracy in America?" *Harper's* 281 (November 1990): 47–49. An argument that democracy is in decline in the United States.

LAQUEUR, WALTER. "Is There Now, or Has There Ever Been, Such a Thing as Totalitarianism?" *Commentary* 80 (October 1985): 31–39. A survey of the research on totalitarianism. See also "Letters from Readers: Totalitarianism." *Commentary* 81 (February 1986): 2, 4–6.

LIVELY, JACK. *Democracy*. New York: St. Martin's Press, 1975. An evaluation of analytical and empirical theories of democracy.

MAGLEBY, DAVID B. *Direct Legislation: Voting on Ballot Propositions in the United States*. Baltimore: Johns Hopkins University Press, 1984. An argument that features of direct democracy in the United States have not worked well.

MENZE, ERNEST A., ed. *Totalitarianism Reconsidered*. Port Washington, N.Y.: Kennikat Press, 1981. Differing perspectives on totalitarianism.

PATEMAN, CAROLE. *Participation and Democratic Theory*. Cambridge, England: Cambridge University Press, 1970. A critique of contemporary theories of democracy

PAUL, ELLEN FRANKEL, ed. *Totalitarianism at the Crossroads*. New Brunswick, N.J.: Transaction Books, 1990. Essays on communism as a form of totalitarianism.

RUBIN, BARRY. *Modern Dictators: Third World Coup Makers, Strongmen, and Populist Tyrants*. New York: McGraw-Hill, 1987. An explanation of why dictatorships emerge in the Third World.

SARTORI, GIOVANNNI. *The Theory of Democracy Revisited*. Vol. 1, *The Contemporary Debate*; Vol. 2, *The Classical Issues*. Chatham, N.J.: Chatham House, 1987. A major work in democratic theory.

SCHATTSCHNEIDER, E. E. *The Semisovereign People: A Realist's View of Democracy in America*. New York: Holt, Rinehart and Winston, 1960. Reprint. Hinsdale, Ill.: Dryden Press, 1975. A critique of modern empirical theories of democracy and a call for greater participation in the American political system.

SCHUMPETER, JOSEPH A. *Capitalism, Socialism, and Democracy*. 3d ed. New York: Harper and Brothers, 1950. Part IV contains a critique of the theory of democracy.

STOCKTON, DAVID. *The Classical Athenian Democracy*. Oxford, England: Oxford University Press, 1990. A description and analysis.

TREADGOLD, DONALD W. *Freedom: A History*. New York: New York University Press, 1990. A history of freedom on a world scale.

TULLOCK, GORDON. *Autocracy*. Dordrecht, The Netherlands: Kluwer Academic Publishers, 1987. An inquiry into the nature of dictatorships.

WALKER, JACK L. "A Critique of the Elitist Theory of Democracy." *American Political Science Review* 60 (June 1966): 285–95. A description of how democracy works.

WIESELTIER, LEON. "Democracy and Colonel North." *New Republic* 196 (January 26, 1987): 22–25. A case for the relevance of democracy in the conduct of foreign policy.

See also Recommended Readings in Chapters 4 and 5.

part III

IDEOLOGY

In political life ideas play important roles. When during World War II, for example, Germany experienced reverses on the battlefield, Adolf Hitler continued to divert enormous resources from military purposes toward the implementation of Nazi policy to liquidate the Jews. The appeal of liberal values to some Western intellectuals, moreover, led them to urge the United States into the war against Germany although Germany had not committed an act of war against the United States.

The political ideas that influence people and events are diverse and are used to justify acts of liberty and slavery, free enterprise and socialism, war and peace, and strong government and weak government. When these ideas are put into a coherent structure to describe, explain, predict, and justify political behavior, they are known as **political ideology**.

Ideology is more than a collection of political beliefs, which are unsystematic preferences individuals hold about politics. Ideology, rather, is an entire system of ideas that is designed to guide behavior. Often, consequently, ideology is a pattern of ideas that some individuals hold as a matter of fundamental conviction.

Political ideologies serve different purposes in a political system. They are sometimes used to legitimize the system of political rule. In every modern political system a few people rule the many. When the masses of people accept the way the rulers come to power and exercise their power, then the government is said to be a **legitimate government.** Governments find great difficulty in sustaining their rule only by force, so they must rely on popular support to be effective. An ideology that has wide popular support for the basis of rule, consequently, allows government to act effectively.

Another purpose of ideology in a political system is to legitimize the interests of various groups in the society. Individuals who benefit from weak government, for example, sometimes promote an ideology like classical liberalism, which justifies weak government (see Chapter 4). Individuals who benefit from strong government, in contrast, sometimes favor socialism or communism (see Chapter 5). Not all who espouse an ideology, however, do so for their own immediate economic benefit.

Another function of ideology is to undermine the legitimacy of a political system. In the age of imperialism, for example, the ideology of nationalism undermined colonial rule (see Chapter 2). When V. I. Lenin became leader of the Soviet Union, moreover, he established an international communist organization, the Comintern, and asserted that henceforth communists throughout the world had a legitimate right to overthrow noncommunist regimes (see Chapter 5).

Ideology is important in a political system because of its influence on public policy through laws and executive actions. Ideological concerns have much to do with the stability of political systems and the relationship between individuals and the state.

Part III examines a few of the most influential ideologies of the past two centuries. Chapter 4 discusses liberalism, conservatism, and fascism. Chapter 5 considers capitalism, socialism, and communism. They are by no means the only important ideologies, but they do relate to some of the most vital political ideas of our times and suggest some important contemporary issues.

chapter 4

Liberalism, conservatism, and fascism

The ideologies of liberalism, conservatism, and fascism have been among the most powerful political ideologies guiding the conduct and beliefs of statesmen, political philosophers, and ordinary citizens. Although liberalism and conservatism owe more to the eighteenth and nineteenth centuries and fascism more to the twentieth century, they are discussed together here because of the contrasts they show and the issues they raise.

LIBERALISM

The terms *liberal* and *liberalism* are labels used in describing not only political but other matters as well. In politics, **liberalism** today connotes certain values, such as a commitment to individual freedom, an opposition to militarism, and a support of the welfare state. *Liberal*, however, is also used as a synonym for "generous," as in the portions of food offered at a restaurant; for

"reformist," as in reforming church hierarchy by including women in the clergy; or for "experimental," as in trying new forms of educational techniques.

Any understanding of liberalism requires a knowledge of its origins. Liberalism as a political philosophy originated in the latter part of the seventeenth century and remains strong today, although its tenets have been somewhat modified. In the seventeenth century, however, it presented a challenge to the rule of government based on the theory of the **divine right of kings**—the belief that the monarch exercises authority by gift from God. Liberals sought to limit the power of the state and to maximize the rights of the individual against arbitrary rule.

The seventeenth-century English writer John Locke was the foremost early exponent of the liberal ideal. Positing a **social contract**, in which government is created with the consent of the governed as a means of combining individual freedom with the benefits of social cooperation, Locke established the foundation of liberalism. In Locke's view, individuals in a state of nature lived harmoniously but voluntarily chose to establish a government. Other social contract theorists such as Thomas Hobbes and Jean-Jacques Rousseau differed with Locke's view about the character of the society and the nature of the social contract. But Locke's social contract is most clearly associated with liberalism and influenced government not only in England but also in the United States, France, and other countries.

The views that Locke and later exponents of liberalism put forth between the seventeenth and nineteenth centuries are often referred to as **classical liberalism**, as distinguished from its later, twentieth-century version. As a doctrine and political program, classical liberalism developed most fully in England in the period between the Glorious Revolution of 1688 and the Reform Act of 1867. Although there were many differences among classical liberals, the central tenets of classical liberalism are: the preservation of individual liberty is the primary concern of any polity; human beings by nature are good; reason will solve problems; progress can be expected; equality of opportunity is desirable; people are the same everywhere; government is a dangerous but necessary evil; and the free market economy will produce the best social order.

Individual Liberty

Liberalism has always regarded individual liberty—whether in politics, economics, or religion—to be the primary concern of any polity. Institutions that might endanger that liberty—government, churches, and the army—must be restrained. John Stuart Mill, one of the leading nineteenth-century liberals, emphasized individual liberty in his writing. Modern liberals often look to the writings of Mill for insights in the defense of liberty.

Human Nature

To liberals, human beings are by nature good. Locke depicted men in the state of nature as essentially free and decent. They choose government, according to Locke, to take care of basic minimal needs that each could not deal with alone—in other words, as a convenience and not to control evil impulses and actions.

Reason

Liberals understand that there remains much conflict in the world. War, terrorism, and crime exist, but liberals attribute the causes to ignorance, bad social conditions, and superstition. Professor J. Salwyn Schapiro puts it succinctly, "Man, according to liberalism, is born ignorant, not wicked."[1] Liberals believe that if people use reason they will be able to solve most problems. They contend that institutions that demand obedience to authority because of reverence for tradition, revelation, or faith—rather than reliance on reason— are, consequently, threats to social progress.

Specifically in this connection, wars come about because of the misunderstanding that results from the inadequate use of reason, and liberals try to maximize the channels of communication to avoid that misunderstanding. Crime happens not because people are bad but because of miserable social conditions. Crime will be eliminated when people prosper and achieve a stake in society, according to liberal premises.

Progress

Liberals have an optimistic belief in progress. They argue that by expanding knowledge and perfecting reason, and

---

[1] J. Salwyn Schapiro, *Liberalism: Its Meaning and History* (Princeton, N.J.: D. Van Nostrand, 1958), p. 12.

by improving economic conditions, humankind will advance. People ought to turn away from superstition based on religious doctrine or rote patriotism. Eliminate the old attitudes and replace them with the new, and progress will ensue, the liberals say.

Equality

Classical liberals believe in equality of opportunity. In the nineteenth century the belief in equality did not extend to universal suffrage. Liberals contended that democracy was dangerous and, consequently, favored property restrictions on voting. Classical liberals argue, however, that conditions promoting equality of opportunity should be encouraged.

Universalism

Classical liberals believe that liberal values are relevant throughout the world. They talk about "the rights of man," echoing the French Declaration of the Rights of Man and of the Citizen (1789), or "**human rights**" rather than the rights of Englishmen or Frenchmen. These are universal rights. Liberals should support them everywhere.

Government

Liberalism was founded on the premise that the protection of the individual against arbitrary government restriction is paramount. Thomas Paine, a pamphleteer of the American Revolution, expressed in his *Common Sense* (1776) the liberal hostility toward government: "Society in every state is a blessing, but government, even in its best state, is but a necessary evil."[2]

[2] Thomas Paine, *The Political Works of Thomas Paine* (New York: Worthington, n.d.), p. 7. *Common Sense* was first published in 1776.

Economic Freedom

Classical liberals support a free enterprise system, or *laissez-faire* (see Chapter 5). In the seventeenth century, they were reacting against the privileges of mercantilism with its monopolies granted to strengthen the state. Classical liberals believe that economic freedom and political freedom are both essential in any free society.

Contemporary liberals continue to accept the principal tenets of classical liberalism on most matters other than economics. The basic political philosophy supporting individual liberty remains the same, but the means to achieve that liberty in the economic sector has changed.

Contemporary liberals accept the necessity of the powerful state to regulate business and to establish the welfare state. In this context, they have adapted to changed economic and social conditions. As the character of capitalism has been transformed, with large corporations undermining the small competitive companies of the early nineteenth century, so, too, has liberal philosophy changed. Now liberals support the state to maintain competition in the face of monopoly and to ensure that consumers are not harmed by unfettered capitalism.

Contemporary liberals, moreover, favor the growth of social programs to eliminate the evils produced by a complex industrial society. Now liberals believe that there are *government* solutions to social problems. If people are ill housed, liberals contend that government should provide housing. If people cannot find jobs, then government should employ them. If people are ignorant, then public schools should educate them. Government can solve these and other problems, such as crime, the urban crisis, inadequate health care, and malnutrition. As Professor Charles Frankel notes, "To put it starkly, but I think exactly, liberalism invented the idea that there are such things as 'social problems' "[3] Whether or not contemporary liberals invented social problems, they continue to believe that with the proper application of reason and money, social problems can be solved. This emphasis on government solutions to problems, however, distinguishes contemporary liberals from their classical forebears.

CONSERVATISM

If *liberalism* lends itself to a variety of meanings, so, too, does *conservatism*. A liberal might define a conservative as "someone who believes nothing should ever be done for the first time."[4] Conservatives could correctly note, however, that they have often initiated policies. It was the British conservative Benjamin Disraeli who extended the vote to large segments of the British working class in 1867 and the American conservative Richard Nixon who led the United States in improving relations with the People's Republic of China.

Conservative has been used to mean "reactionary," "cautious," "gradualist," "moderate," and "slow." As a political philosophy, conservatism originated in the latter part of the eighteenth century, although its roots go back to Plato in ancient Greece. The British philosopher and politician Edmund Burke is unquestionably the founder of conservatism, although he never used the term. Much of his and early conservatism was a response to the French Revolution. Writing in *Reflections on the Revolution in France* (1790), Burke expressed horror about the premises underlying that revolution. He predicted accurately the political instability and dictatorship that were

to arise out of the more moderate phase of the revolution.

The classical conservatism of Burke and others included a variety of beliefs. It was impossible in Burke's time, as it is today, to define precisely the conservative philosophy or program. It is best to look at **conservatism** as a set of general principles. In essence, these conservative principles include: order and stability must be maintained; human beings are by nature wicked; it is essential to rely on experience rather than reason; gradual change is desirable; liberty is more important than equality; diversity rather than universalism should be promoted; and government is a necessary institution.

Order and Stability

Conservatives believe that without order and stability there can be no liberty or civilization. Order and stability are maintained to the extent that authority is respected. Traditional authority based on religion, birth, and patriotism, consequently, must be protected. Those who undermine authority endanger the well-being of civilization.

Wickedness of Humankind

Unlike the liberals who believe that human beings are by nature good, conservatives derive their philosophy from a different analysis of the human condition. Some conservatives attribute human wickedness to original sin, although other conservatives do not rely on a religious formulation. Many find admirable the writings of Thomas Hobbes, the seventeenth-century English thinker who portrayed a society without government as chaotic and bestial. Unless restraints are imposed on human beings through laws and religious practices, conservatives argue, the evil nature of human beings will express itself

[3] Charles Frankel, *The Case for Modern Man* (New York: Harper and Brothers, 1956), p. 33.

[4] As disparagingly cited by Robert Schuettinger in his anthology, *The Conservative Tradition in European Thought* (New York: G. P. Putnam's Sons, 1970), p. 11.

through war, conquest, violence, and rapacity.

Experience

Conservatives prefer to rely on experience over reason. This does not mean that conservatives are irrational. Rather, they prefer to use reason to counter a belief that reason can solve all problems. Conservatives are intellectually and temperamentally opposed to any grandiose scheme, such as a blueprint for revolutionary change, since they are pessimistic about the perfectability of humankind. They are skeptical about the usefulness of social programs to change the character of society quickly.

Gradual Change

Those conservatives who are against all changes involving new ideas and programs are correctly labeled **reactionaries**. Most conservatives, however, do not want to return to some golden age. They favor moderate changes and the formation of policy based on the observation of how well these moderate changes work out. Edmund Burke, for example, supported the American colonists against Great Britain in their quest for securing the "rights of Englishmen" in the New World. He saw in the American Revolution an acceptance of free institutions that he could cherish—unlike the French Revolution, which challenged all established institutions.

Liberty

Conservatives are opposed to equality, viewing it as a danger to liberty. Traditionally, they have supported government based on nobility of birth. Initially, they opposed the capitalists who sought power on the basis of wealth. They also resisted the egalitarianism implicit in democracy,

perceiving democracy to be a danger to the established order.

Diversity

Conservatives revere diversity rather than universalism. The same laws that worked well in England could not be transported to every other country, according to them. Separate development of different nations and different races is desirable because the experience of different peoples is never the same.

Government

Traditionally, conservatives were not hostile to government. Conservatives received privileges from government and sought to retain those privileges. They opposed the liberal critics who wanted to deny them these privileges. Besides, government was essential to maintain order and stability, according to the conservative view.

In the twentieth century, conservatism has changed. The traditional principles of conservatism—its beliefs in order and stability, wickedness of humankind, experience, gradualism, liberty, and diversity—remain. Contemporary conservatives, however, are more like classical liberals in their economic ideas than like traditional conservatives. Modern conservatives tend to reject or be skeptical about the welfare state and government management of the economy.

The fact that modern conservatives support at least a respect for free enterprise is one essential modification of conservatism. Another change is the growth since the late 1960s of a philosophy called **neoconservatism** or **New Conservatism**. Neoconservatism is an American political philosophy that maintains the temperament of conservatism, supports the existence of capitalism and a mixed economy, and is critical of some elements of the welfare state.

The major figures of neoconservatism are former liberals who have modified but not rejected all the tenets of liberalism. They are, consequently, critical of programs that they perceive as harmful to the groups the programs intend to benefit. Some neoconservatives argue, for example, that many welfare programs encourage people not to work; that attempts to promote racial and sexual equality in the professions through affirmative action programs are wrong; and that busing to promote racial integration actually encourages segregation. Among the leaders of this school of thought are Irving Kristol, Nathan Glazer, and Jeane J. Kirkpatrick.

Perhaps in response to the emergence of neoconservatism, a new movement—neoliberalism—has appeared in the United States in the 1980s. **Neoliberalism** is a political philosophy that accepts modern liberal values, such as a belief in civil liberties, civil rights, and equality of opportunity. It attempts to provide what it considers to be a more pragmatic or realistic approach to current issues than that offered by most liberals since the New Deal programs of President Franklin D. Roosevelt. Neoliberals assert that they are concerned with economic growth more than with redistribution of income; that they favor over national planning and regulation an industrial policy in which government, business, and labor cooperate closely; and that they support a stronger national defense rather than a weaker one. Charles Peters, the editor of *Washington Monthly*, is perhaps the foremost neoliberal. It was he who coined the term *neoliberalism*.[5]

Liberalism and conservatism, then, are best described today in terms of disposition rather than in terms of a fixed ideology or program. It is often the case that a particular person accepts part, but not all, of the

agenda of an ideology—whether it be liberal or conservative. A person may hold liberal views on economic issues, for example. In the past few decades American liberalism and conservatism have included both economic and social dimensions. Such a development has created major strategic problems for both the Democratic and Republican parties.

Although differing in temperament, both liberals and conservatives in the twentieth century share a commitment to constitutional government. Both liberals and conservatives, moreover, accept political democracy in stark contrast to the advocates of the political philosophy of fascism.

FASCISM

Like *communism*, the words *fascism* and *fascist* have been used in imprecise ways to describe many kinds of behavior. In the past two decades, for example, the term *fascist* has been used to refer to a geneticist engaged in scientific research relating race to I.Q. scores, American intervention in the Vietnam War, and even to anyone who voted for Ronald Reagan in the presidential elections of 1980 and 1984. In this century, moreover, *fascism* has been applied to capitalists, socialists, soldiers, the police, churches, and even the Boy Scouts.

A term with such varied uses can have no analytical utility. To get at a better understanding of the meaning of *fascism*, it is essential to look at the historical roots of this ideology. Fascism as an ideology is a twentieth-century phenomenon. It originated in Italy with the *fasci d'azione rivoluzionaria* of 1914–15 and the *fasci di combattimento* of 1919. The early *fasci* (or political groups organized for limited purposes) were formed in World War 1 to end Italian neutrality and make Italy join the war. Although he had practically nothing to do with setting the goals of these organizations, Benito Mussolini, whose intellectual heritage was socialist, became the

---

[5] For a description of neoliberalism, see Randall Rothenberg, *The Neoliberals: Creating the New American Politics* (New York: Simon and Schuster, 1984).

dominant figure in Italian fascism. *Fascism* appeared in popular usage in 1919 with the emergence of Mussolini as a major political figure.

The term *fascism* is derived from the Latin word *fasces*, which means "bundle." In ancient Rome a bundle of rods bound around an ax was the symbol of authority.

Although Italy was a pioneer of fascism, other regimes became associated with this ideology. Spain under Francisco Franco and Portugal under António Salazar are two notable examples. In more recent times the military regime of General Augusto Pinochet in Chile was regarded by some as fascist. Many people have described the political system of **National Socialism** (or **nazism**) under Adolf Hitler in Germany as a prime example of fascism, but some scholars see significant differences between Mussolini's fascism and Hitler's nazism. To be sure, all of these regimes are correctly identified as dictatorships, but there are so many differences among them that scholars cannot agree on a universal definition.[6]

In spite of the different kinds of regimes that are regarded as fascist, we may distinguish some of the most salient features of **fascism** found in most systems so classified. These are: supremacy of the state over the individual, intense nationalism, antiliberal democracy, militarism and terrorism, rule by a dictator, and anticommunism.

State

A central feature of fascism is a belief in the state as more important than the individual. Fascism, consequently, is a political ideology that is antiliberal in its most fundamental tenet. Liberals believe that

the function of the state is to serve the interests of individuals. For fascists, individuals must serve the state.

The state, consequently, is totalitarian (see Chapter 3). It plays a role in every aspect of society. Its economy is centrally directed. In Italy—in theory if not in practice—the central direction of the economy was expressed by Mussolini's concept of the **corporate state**, in which business and labor would work in cooperation with the supreme state acting as arbiter. Such a notion was in sharp contrast to the view of Marxists, with their emphasis on class struggle. Under fascism, class cooperation under state dominance is the primary theme. The state, too, purports to control other institutions of society, such as schools, libraries, and social organizations. Leaders of these organizations accept the views of the dictator.

Nationalism

In contrast to socialism in which class solidarity is supposed to transcend national barriers, fascism reveres nationalism. The nation is sometimes equated with a people or a race. All nation-states encourage and promote patriotic respect for national symbols, such as the flag, independence day, and the national anthem. Fascism, however, requires more than the mere patriotism that every nation promotes, for fascists make intense demands on people to support national symbols above everything else.

Antiliberalism

Fascism is antiliberal not only in its conception of the state but also in its criticism of institutions such as parliamentary government and civil liberties. Fascists reject the notion of constitutionalism with its constraints on power. They regard opposition parties as unnecessary and indeed dangerous to the strength of the all-embracing state. Fascist states are one-party states with

[6]See Renzo de Felice, *Fascism: An Informal Introduction to Its Theory and Practice* [an interview with Michael A. Ledeen] (New Brunswick, N.J.: Transaction Books, 1976), pp. 72, 89; Noël O'Sullivan, *Fascism* (London: J. M. Dent and Sons, 1983), pp. 4–5.

no opposition tolerated. Individuals are denied the basic liberal freedoms of religion, speech, assembly, and the press.

Militarism and Terror

Fascism reveres strength both in foreign policy and on the domestic front. Mussolini's invasion of Ethiopia in 1935 was the beginning of Italian fascist militarism. As Mussolini put it, "The program of Fascist foreign policy can be given in one word: expansionism."[7] Hitler's rearmament efforts in violation of the Versailles Treaty restrictions were another reflection of militarism and expansionism.

In fascist Italy and Germany, symbols of terrorism created fear at home. Opposition political leaders were arrested, and some were assassinated. Meetings of dissidents were broken up, and the independent news media were suppressed. Secret police were charged with maintaining fascist supremacy.

Dictator

Fascism requires a supreme leader (in Italy, *Il Duce*), who imposes his imprint on the political system. Sometimes the leader is seen as head of the fascist political party, and sometimes he is superior to it. In Nazi Germany, for example, soldiers had to take a personal oath to Adolf Hitler (*Der Führer*, or "leader") rather than to a constitutional government, as is the case in a liberal democracy. The fascist dictator's role is celebrated in paintings, photographs, and sculptures prominently displayed throughout the country. The dictator in a fascist regime is depicted as endowed with creative genius and is said to be always correct and capable of miraculous feats of leadership and heroism.

[7]Benito Mussolini, quoted in A. James Gregor, *The Ideology of Fascism: The Rationale of Totalitarianism* (New York: Free Press, 1969), p. 162.

Anticommunism

Fascism historically has been anticommunist. Although Mussolini began his life as a socialist, he had rejected socialism by 1914. He and Hitler were strongly anticommunist, although such a belief does not, in fact, mean that communism and fascism have no similarities. For many supporters of Hitler and Mussolini, however, fascism was seen as a worthy opponent of communism (and of democratic socialism, too). Fascism is often portrayed in Marxist sources, consequently, as nothing more than a counterrevolutionary ideology designed to keep entrenched bourgeois forces in power. Many scholars, however, question this evaluation of fascism. They contend, in contrast, that fascism and communism spring from similar historical sources and are kindred totalitarian systems.

While these six characteristics of fascism are generally found in most fascist systems, German fascism, or National Socialism, had an additional feature of *racism* that distinguished it from other fascist systems. Early in his career Hitler became an ardent anti-Semite. In his book, *Mein Kampf* (My Struggle), written in 1924, he argued that the Nordic Aryan race was the superior race because of its culture-giving qualities. He advocated a policy of racial supremacy of the Aryans over all other races, or civilization would end. The German nation was the highest expression of Aryanism, he contended. He attacked the Jews as being responsible for the evils that had befallen the world. He called for persecution of the Slavs and their domination by Germans. He maintained that German blood must remain pure, "uncontaminated" by "inferior" races.

Unlike Hitler, Mussolini was not at first a racist. When he used the term *race* he generally meant it as a synonym for "people" or "nation" rather than in a biological sense. It was not until the late 1930s, when

Italy moved closer to allying with Nazi Germany, that Mussolini began supporting anti-Semitic causes. Under the Nazis, Jews were denied citizenship rights. Books written by Jewish authors were burned. Eventually, Jews in Germany and in German-occupied countries had their property confiscated. The extermination camp and the gas chamber ultimately liquidated 6 million Jewish people for the offense of being Jewish.

Racism, then, may be viewed as a characteristic of fascism, especially if nazism is regarded as its prototype. The demise of Hitler did not bring an end to racism. Until the early 1990s, South Africa practiced a system of **apartheid** (or separateness) in which strict racial separation laws were en-

forced by the white minority over the black majority. In Europe political parties appealing to racism have appeared in Austria, France, Germany, Norway, and Switzerland. In the Federal Republic of Germany, the Republikaner Partie, established in 1982, has demanded the expulsion of foreigners and appealed to racist fears. The National Front in France and similar parties in Europe have viewed immigrants to their countries as weakening indigeneous culture. These right-wing parties talk about the dangers of the "Islamicization of Europe." In the United States, such groups as the American Nazi party, the Aryan Nation, and the Ku Klux Klan continue to attack minorities, especially Jews and blacks.

ISSUES

As ideologies, liberalism and conservatism are guides to action. Liberals, however, are rarely united as a group in applying their views to particular policy prescriptions. Nor are conservatives in agreement among themselves about issues. Yet liberals and conservatives have distinct outlooks.

This chapter considers two questions with liberal and conservative themes: (1) Should the United States avoid making human rights an objective of foreign policy? (2) Are liberal democracies the final form of political system that will usher in an era of peace?

The first debate deals with moral concerns in foreign policy. Many, if not most, conservatives would argue that the United States should avoid making human rights an objective of foreign policy. Many, if not most, liberals would challenge that view.

The second debate is inspired by a highly

controversial article in the journal *National Interest* by Francis Fukuyama, a former official in the U.S. State Department's Policy Planning Staff. Fukuyama argued that the developments of recent years show that the world has reached what he called "the end of history." According to the author, liberal democracy had now shown that it is superior to any other form of government and that it will envelop the world.[8]

Couched in ideas of the German philosopher Georg Hegel, the article provoked serious attention not only in the United States but throughout the world, as it was translated into many languages. The debate considers the central thesis about the future of liberal democracy and the consequences of liberal democracy to peace.

[8] Francis Fukuyama, "The End of History?" *National Interest*, no. 16 (Summer 1989): 3–18.

10/YES   SHOULD THE UNITED STATES AVOID MAKING HUMAN RIGHTS AN OBJECTIVE OF FOREIGN POLICY?

Political atrocities in the world—such as the planned extermination of the European Jews by Adolf Hitler, the destruction of millions of peas-

ants by Joseph Stalin, the massacre of the Cambodian people by the communist leader Pol Pot, the persecutions inflicted on the Ugandan people by Idi Amin, the use of poison gas by Iraqi leader Saddam Hussein against Iraq's Kurdish population, and the massacre of peaceful protesters in Tiananmen Square in Beijing in 1989—have called the world's attention to horrors that civilized people hoped could not exist. Compassionate human beings can only condemn such depraved acts. Given the fact of such horrors, states have had to respond to them—whether by deeds, words, or even silence. For the United States, as a democracy, the question arises as to whether the promotion of human rights is a legitimate objective of foreign policy.

We argue that although dreadful evils do occur in countries around the world, the United States should not regard the pursuit of human rights as a legitimate objective of its foreign policy. Five points substantiate our case: (1) there is no agreement about a definition of human rights; (2) the United States has no right to interfere in the internal affairs of other nations; (3) a human rights policy can only hurt our security goals; (4) a human rights policy is counterproductive; and (5) a human rights policy is hypocritical for the United States to pursue.

Definition. The term *human rights* means different things to different people (see Chapter 7). In classical times, civilizations did not consider that the individual had rights apart from his or her community. The Western world is mostly responsible for the idea that human rights are individual civil liberties that states are created to protect.

As we will see in Chapter 7, however, not everyone in the West accepts the primacy of political rights. Marxists and communists contend that economic rights are essential to any rendering of a definition of human rights. A Marxist interpretation of political rights is that they are part of the superstructure (see Chapter 5). Liberal societies, according to this perception, provide merely the illusion of rights and not the reality, since in modern capitalist economies, the capitalists are really in control anyway. Until capitalism is abolished, consequently, there can be no civil rights, according to this Marxist view.

Although liberalism and Marxism derive from a Western tradition, they are not in agreement about individual rights. The lack of agreement is even more noticeable when the liberal view of rights is contrasted with the political beliefs of African and Asian governments, many of which are steeped in traditions in conflict with the no-

tion of human rights. Given such ambiguity about the definition and desirability of human rights, the United States cannot realistically pursue a human rights policy.

Interference. To be sure, governments have done horrible things to their people. The world, however, is organized into sovereign states. The term *sovereignty* means supreme power and authority. If states can determine what standards must be applied in other countries, the principle of sovereignty will be undermined.

The principle of sovereignty is widely accepted. Article 2, Section 7, of the Charter of the United Nations, for example, asserts that nothing in the Charter will authorize the United Nations "to intervene in matters which are essentially within the domestic jurisdiction of any state." The right to take action to protect a state's sovereignty has a long history that an activist human rights policy would destroy.

If the United States could interfere in the internal affairs of other countries, then it, too, could legitimately be the object of intervention from its enemies. The effect of the right to intervene when applied universally would be to undermine the basis of world order.

Security. In a multistate world system, national security is paramount. In a world without a world government, states must make alliances and enter into agreements with other states that may have abhorrent political systems. If the United States is to survive as a state with its institutions intact, it must act as other states—with security as the primary objective. States that violate human rights may possess a strategic position or scarce resources that the United States needs for its security. The United States cannot assure its security if it requires its allies to pass morality tests.

We may take as examples to prove our point the cases of Spain under the fascist General Francisco Franco, and the People's Republic of China under Mao Zedong. At the conclusion of World War II, the United States and its Western democratic allies feared the military strength of the Soviet army. Although Spain was governed by a dictator, it was anticommunist. Protected in part by a natural frontier, the Pyrenees Mountains, Spain offered a relatively safe location in which to build American bases. Those bases could be used for defense against the Soviet forces invading across Western Europe. Given the Soviet danger, the United States supported the Franco government in spite of its dictatorial character. Security requirements were primary.

Security, too, was a factor involved in American support of the People's Republic of China under Mao Zedong in the 1970s. Between 1949, when the Chinese communists seized control of Mainland China from the Nationalist Chinese government, and the early 1970s, when the Nixon administration sought better relations with the communist Chinese government, the United States and China had been bitter foes. Although a communist country, the People's Republic of China had become engaged in a fierce ideological and political struggle with the Soviet Union by the early 1970s. Border clashes between the two communist countries flared from time to time, and many Soviet divisions were sent to the Chinese frontier. To the extent that Soviet troops were diverted from Europe to meet the Chinese threat, the United States and its North Atlantic Treaty Organization (NATO) allies were made more secure. Had the United States refused to promote good relations with the People's Republic because of China's extensive violations of human rights, American security interests would have been harmed.

States have no friends; they have only interests. The cases of United States relations with Franco and Mao Zedong support the view that the United States must pursue its security interests regardless of how foreign governments treat their own people. By encouraging the promotion of human rights everywhere, the United States has weakened governments that were friendly to it. Iran is a classic case study. To be sure, the leader of that country—the shah—was a dictator who used his secret police to oppress his own people. The shah, however, was pro-West. When an oil embargo was instituted by Arab countries during the Arab-Israeli October War of 1973, the shah ordered Iran to continue to supply the West with oil. For more than three decades, the shah was a friend of the United States.

Iranian opponents to the shah's dictatorship were emboldened by President Jimmy Carter's criticism of the shah for his human rights record. Eventually the shah's regime was toppled by a religious extremist, the Ayatollah Khomeini. The new government was hostile to the West and particularly to the United States. It sought to humiliate the United States when it took American hostages at the American Embassy in 1979 and called for a holy war against American imperialism. The effect of President Carter's human rights policy was to replace the pro–United States government with an anti–United States government. The security consequences of that political transformation were harmful to the United States.

If an activist human rights foreign policy can harm American security interests with respect to its allies, it may also adversely affect those interests in superpower relationships. During the **cold war**—the period between 1945 and the late 1980s when relations between the United States and the Soviet Union were marked by hostility—many Americans found Soviet domestic policy abhorrent. Although the political liberties of Soviet people were constantly violated, the United States found it essential to improve relations with the Soviet Union and concluded arms control agreements with that country. The United States realized that there would be no victor in a nuclear war with the Soviet Union. The result was the strengthening of the security of both states. Had the United States required the ending of human rights violations in the Soviet Union as a basis for any negotiations with that country, it would have created distrust; and agreements dealing with arms control would not have been forthcoming. The security of the two superpowers, consequently, would have been imperiled.

Careless rhetoric about human rights, moreover, may have led to revolution in the communist countries. In the 1950s, for example, some people within the administration of Dwight D. Eisenhower talked about "liberating" Eastern European states from communist rule. When, in 1956, the Hungarians rose up against the Soviet Union, the United States did not intervene to assist the Hungarians after all. Thousands of Hungarians were slaughtered by Soviet tanks and troops, and American prestige among the peoples of communist countries declined. The United States had spoken about liberation, Hungarians felt, but when the crucial moment came, the United States did not act.

Counterproductive Results. The United States confronts the limits of its power when it tries to promote human rights abroad. Quiet diplomacy, as former United States Secretary of State Henry Kissinger pointed out, has achieved more benefits than loud pronouncements about human rights. Kissinger's behind-the-scenes diplomacy was able to increase Jewish emigration from the

Soviet Union to a record annual level of thirty-five thousand. The figure declined sharply once the Carter human rights policy was initiated. Soviet violations of human rights ended with the collapse of communism in the early 1990s, and U.S. human rights policy had very little to do with that collapse.

Hypocrisy. A human rights foreign policy would be hypocritical because the United States could not maintain it consistently or even live up to the civil liberties standard it professes to the world. Such hypocrisy would undermine the country's moral standing in the world.

In the real world of foreign policy, states must finally pursue security rather than moral objectives. When, at the beginning of his term in office, President Jimmy Carter made a strong point about the absolutist character of human rights, he created expectations that could never be realized. In his record as president he showed a constant retreat from that policy. Since the United States needed the oil and support of Iran, for example, the president continued to supply arms to the shah. American arms were sent to dictatorial South Korea as well. Anxious not to upset the arms control and trade ties between the United States and the Soviet Union, President Carter eased off on the human rights rheto-

ric dealing with internal Soviet matters. The effect of such a manipulation of the human rights issue, consequently, was to subject the United States to charges of hypocrisy—the selective use of a moral principle to serve American foreign policy goals.

Perhaps a more significant charge of American hypocrisy can be raised when the American blemishes of human rights are put on stage for the world to view. The violations of human rights in the treatment of American blacks, Hispanics, women, and Indians are well known. Police brutality occurs from time to time. Freedom of speech and the press has been violated, particularly during periods of tension in international relations. The activities of federal government officials during the administrations of Presidents Lyndon Johnson and Richard Nixon in infiltrating antiwar protest organizations were major breaches of civil liberties. How can the United States tell other countries how to behave when *it* violates human rights? The answer is that it cannot, lest it be subject to charges of hypocrisy. Americans should clean up their own house before passing judgment elsewhere. They should follow the advice of John Quincy Adams, who commented, "We are the friends of liberty everywhere, but the custodians only of our own."

10/NO   SHOULD THE UNITED STATES AVOID MAKING HUMAN RIGHTS AN OBJECTIVE OF FOREIGN POLICY?

Human rights must be a goal of foreign policy. Self-professed realists in international politics display a cynicism in analyzing foreign policy that makes them overlook the realism of moral purpose as an objective of diplomacy. We can show by considering the same points as the *Affirmative* that human rights ought to be a goal of American foreign policy.

Definition. To be sure, the term *human rights* has lent itself to different definitions. Those who have wanted to cloud the issue have pointed to the divergencies in the West about civil liberties and the differences in tradition between the West and the non-Western world. Those who revere liberty, however, know that it is political rights, or civil liberties, which are human rights (see Chapter 7). We may have difficulty in accurately drawing the line between individual liberty and the need for public order, but that is a mat-

ter for courts to determine. The political freedoms of speech, religion, the press, assembly, fair trial, and the franchise are the rights at issue.

It is certainly true that these rights originated in the West, but they have often been accepted in the non-Western world as well. When Western countries controlled the world, the anticolonial critique was based on these Western principles. Many of the twentieth-century Third World leaders were educated in the West. They not only accepted Western aspirations about economic development, but they forced Western leaders to apply their own standards to the way they were treating the colonial peoples. When colonial powers imprisoned nationalist revolutionaries in the Third World, the anti-imperialists denounced these violations of civil liberties. The ideological support of human rights helped to undermine Western imperialism both in the

Western imperialist countries and in the colonies and contributed to the rise of self-government for the peoples of Africa and Asia. The *Affirmative*, consequently, is on shaky ground when it says that a Western concept is being imposed on non-Western governments.

One need not necessarily accept this interpretation about the widespread support of the Western idea of human rights to prove its universality. Although the concept of human rights may be a Western value, many of the major violations of these rights are also violations of the religious and philosophical heritage of all peoples. When we consider modern political crimes, such as torture and the persecution of religious and racial minorities, we can see that non-Western traditions have also been hostile to such behavior.

The sociologist Peter L. Berger points out that Cambodia is a Buddhist country, and Buddhism "has as its highest moral tenet the 'respect for all sentient things.'" The atrocities committed by Pol Pot can be condemned, consequently, in Buddhist terms. Berger also notes that when China under the government of Mao Zedong separated children from their parents in the course of communist experiments, it was violating the entire body of Chinese tradition that holds, among other things, that government should be "human-hearted" and that "filial piety" is one of the highest human goods. Berger cites the ethical basis of Islam, moreover, which commands men to be compassionate.[9] Many of the violations of human rights, then, are condemned by universal standards of justice.

Interference. The record of international relations reveals that human rights have been considered as international in scope. As early as 480 B.C. Gelon, prince of Syracuse, upon defeating Carthage, included in the peace terms a provision requiring the Carthaginians to end their custom of sacrificing their children to Saturn.[10] In the twentieth century states have continued to show that certain problems are truly international in scope. Racism, for example, has been held in this light.

Throughout the post–World War II period, Third World countries particularly have viewed the retention of political power by the white minorities in Rhodesia (now Zimbabwe) and South

[9] Peter L. Berger, "Are Human Rights Universal?" *Commentary* 64 (September 1977): 62.

[10] Walter Laqueur, "The Issue of Human Rights," *Commentary* 63 (May 1977): 29.

Africa as a matter of international concern. When white-dominated governments of both those countries denounced the invasion of their sovereignty by outside states, Third World countries pointed to international norms. They correctly did not say that racism was an internal matter.

Human rights now constitute an international norm. Violations of these rights are matters of international concern. Such an international concern has been affirmed in the Charter of the United Nations, the Universal Declaration of Human Rights, and the Helsinki Accords. The U.N. Charter includes in its Preamble a purpose of the organization: "to reaffirm faith in fundamental human rights." Articles 55 and 56 also mention the subject. The Universal Declaration of Human Rights was adopted by the U.N. General Assembly in 1948 without a dissenting vote. The Helsinki Accords of 1975, which had thirty-five signatories, contained "Basket 3" provisions designed to protect and expand human rights. When a norm is given international approval, as in these cases, a country cannot legitimately charge a violation of sovereignty.

Security. In the long run, security will be benefited rather than hurt by a concern with human rights. Concern does not mean preoccupation or fixation. Of course, the United States must reconcile moral with security considerations. It may well be, as the case of Iran in the post–World War II period indicates, that it cannot jeopardize its security and that of its allies by promoting a vocal and inflexible human rights policy. It should, however, do what is within its power to promote human rights abroad. Tactics may vary from public denunciations to quiet, suggestive diplomacy, but its security interests will best be served if it keeps human rights always as a goal. We may take the case of a Third World dictatorship to prove our point.

Governments cannot endure forever without some popular support. The more countries rely on force at home, the more they suppress rather than eliminate dissent. When governments friendly to the United States suppress dissent and imprison people who openly and peacefully disagree with their governments, then the chances are that dissent will grow. Repressive governments holding **political prisoners** (those people who are put in prison for their political beliefs rather than for illegal actions) tend to imprison people from ever more diverse groups in the political community. Eventually, the political leader becomes isolated from his people, and revolution occurs. American security interests would be served if friendly leaders have broad support for their actions. A number of people argued during the 1980s that Ferdinand Marcos, as president of the Philippines, was responsible for the growing communist insurgency in that country although he was an anticommunist. Marcos had engaged in repressive policies against his own people. Many who worked to topple him from power hoped that the democratic government of Corazon Aquino, with its respect for civil liberties, would undermine the communist movement.

Counterproductive Results. The record shows that when the United States and its Western allies have promoted human rights, they have been effective in many cases. Of course, *how* effective depends on the political leverage available to the United States. A country such as South Korea is heavily dependent upon the United States for its security. The United States has interceded for dissidents, and some were released from prison under the South Korean dictatorship of General Park Chung Hee.

The Soviet Union was also pressured successfully. Dissidents such as Anatoly Scharansky may have been released in part because of pressure from outside the Soviet Union. Under Stalin, dissidents were shipped to Siberian prison camps, where many of them died.

Spotlighting human rights violations can bring results. The record shows that it can be effective—perhaps not in every case, but at least in many.

Hypocrisy. It is certainly true that the United States could be judged hypocritical if it were to pursue an activist and absolutist human rights foreign policy. That accusation, however, would not be valid if its policy were consistent with its security goals. Quiet, behind-the-scenes warnings to a friendly country would be one way to deal with the problem. In those cases in which the United States could be effective, however, it can profess a bolder policy. There is nothing hypocritical about such political behavior.

The case of El Salvador is instructive. A communist insurgency threatened to undermine the political system of that country. Widespread abuses of human rights increasingly alienated the people from their government. The United States asserted its influence to prevent such atrocities as the killing of innocent people by right-wing death squads. It also encouraged free elections in which José Napoleón Duarte was elected. Duarte committed himself to social reform and political democracy. Although his government had some failures and Duarte himself was subjected to criticism that he moved too slowly in bringing about social reform, most observers agree that the situation for United States security in El Salvador was better because of Duarte's reforms than would have been the case if someone else who was not committed to human rights had been in power.

Finally, with respect to its own civil liberties, the United States should indicate that it has faults and it has tried to correct them. It should denounce efforts to equate unrelated political phenomena and challenge assertions that the persecution of blacks in the United States, long opposed openly by American political leaders and protest groups, is equivalent to Stalin's slave labor camps, which Soviet political leaders tried to keep secret from the world; that the internment of Japanese-Americans in relocation camps during World War II, which was a temporary wartime measure condemned by American civil libertarians at the time, is on a par with the deportation of the ethnic Chinese into unseaworthy boats by the communist Vietnamese governments, which was a permanent racist effort to remove an entire ethnic minority at a great cost in human life; and that press censorship during wartime, a temporary move monitored by an independent judiciary, is the same as the former Soviet government's control of the press, which is a permanent feature of a totalitarian political system.

It is certainly true that the United States should work to make itself ever more vigilant in promoting civil liberties at home. That does not mean, however, that it should be indifferent to such acts as the extermination of Jewish groups by Adolf Hitler, the liquidation of Cambodian people by Pol Pot, the suppression of dissent in China, the terror imposed by Idi Amin, and the racial discrimination of South Africa. To eliminate or limit evils such as these, the United States should pursue an activist human rights policy.

11/YES

ARE LIBERAL DEMOCRACIES THE FINAL FORM OF POLITICAL SYSTEM THAT WILL USHER IN AN ERA OF PEACE?

Liberal democracy is the dominant system of the present and will continue into the future. It will, moreover, usher in an era of peace. Our view is based on the following arguments: (1) the twentieth century has seen a clear and continuing trend toward the expansion of liberal democracies; (2) liberalism has become the dominant political ideology as other ideologies have been discredited; (3) economic development and political stability in most countries can only be achieved through democratic means; and (4) democracies do not go to war against other democracies.

Liberal Democracies in the Twentieth Century. As indicated in Chapter 3, liberalism and democracy are differing and at times competing concepts. Liberalism at its core is a belief in universal human rights and basic freedoms. Democracy at its core is a system of majority rule and political equality. **Liberal democracy** promotes the notions of political freedom and popular participation but accepts the principle that the majority must not become tyrannical and deny rights to minority viewpoints and interests. Today, however, those systems that combine the features of liberalism and representative democracy are often called, simply, democracies.

It is clear that the twentieth-century trend is toward democracy. Modern democracy has its roots in the West, with democratic regimes established mostly in North America and Western Europe. After World War II, democratic regimes replaced fascist governments in Italy, Japan, and the Federal Republic of Germany. In the 1970s democratic governments supplanted dictatorships in Greece, Portugal, and Spain.

Latin America has also moved toward democracy. Authoritarian military governments have been replaced by elected representative democracies in Argentina, Brazil, Ecuador, El Salvador, Guatemala, Honduras, Peru, and Uruguay. A dictator has also been removed from Grenada. Democratic successes have been notable in Venezuela and Brazil. Chile held elections in 1989 and readopted democratic practices that had been interrupted by years of dictatorial rule. Free elections were held in Nicaragua after long-term Sandinista rule. Costa Rica has had a tradition of democratic government.

In Africa there are signs of change, too. In the decades following World War II, as former European colonies moved to independence, military coups and one-party rule became the order of day. Most countries experienced only a short period of democratic government after which they denied basic civil liberties to their people. South Africa, which was ruled by a minority white government, is now empowering its black population. In 1990–91, nine countries in Africa, including Benin, Cape Verde, and Gabon, held multiparty elections. For most of them, it was the first time they had free elections since they became independent countries. In other African countries, such as Mozambique, Zaire, and the Congo, reforms were instituted that held out hope for such elections. And in 1991, Col. Mengistu Haile-Mariam, whose ruthless acts of dictatorship in Ethiopia took the lives of many of his people, was forced to flee his country by a rebellious army. In assessing the situation in March 1991, Salim Lone, editor of *African Recovery*, observed; "More governments introduced multiparty politics in the last year than in the previous 25 years combined."[11]

In Asia, the democratic revival is seen in countries that have moved from dictatorial to democratic practices, most notably South Korea and the Philippines. Taiwan has made great strides in adopting democratic processes, too.

But it has been in the communist world that the shift to democracy has been the most striking. Following the emergence of Mikhail Gorbachev to power in 1985, fundamental reforms in the Soviet political system were instituted that led to the eventual breakup of the country (see Chapter 5). Most of the republics of the Soviet Union are now adopting democratic processes, including competitive elections.

Eastern Europe had led the way in instituting democratic reforms. In 1989 and 1990 Czechoslovakia, Hungary, and Poland became democracies, and the German Democratic Republic dissolved itself as a separate political entity and

[11] Salim Lone, quoted in Robert M. Press, "Africa's Struggle for Democracy," *Christian Science Monitor*, March 21, 1991, p. 4.

reunited with the Federal Republic of Germany. Romania ousted a dictator, but its new government disappointed those forces favoring democracy.

By 1992, only China, Cuba, North Korea and Vietnam continued to function as communist systems. But the winds of change were clearly evident in China and Cuba, and it would not be surprising to see democracy there in the 1990s.

And so, liberal democracies are in the ascendancy. By the beginning of the last decade of the twentieth century, the direction of history was clearly toward liberal democracy.

Democracy as the Dominant Political Ideology. Ideologies other than liberal democracy have been discredited. The two major challengers to liberal democracy in the twentieth century—fascism and communism—no longer have significant appeal. Fascism failed with the defeat of Germany, Italy, and Japan in World War II.

In the aftermath of that war, communism emerged as the major challenge to liberal democracy. Communism as an ideology was hailed by its adherents as a just system that could bring about economic development and greater equality. But it did not succeed. The Soviet Union was near economic collapse when Communist party supremacy was ended in 1991, following a failed coup by party officials. Shortly afterward, the Soviet Union ceased to exist as an independent country.

With the collapse of both fascism and communism, then, liberal democracy remains the only ideology capable of appealing to the masses of people.

Economic and Political Development. The collapse of communism was only a recent reminder of the weakness of dictatorship in satisfying even basic economic necessities. In one communist country after another, masses of people lined up for hours for the chance of purchasing basic commodities that most people in the West take for granted. An inadequate infrastructure, currency that had little value, and a low standard of living were obvious features of the communist system. It was these features that helped spark the downfall of communism. In contrast, the countries with liberal democratic institutions have achieved the greatest prosperity for their people.

Liberal democracies have their problems, too. Economic decay and political disorder brought on by intergroup conflict within a state can pose serious dangers to political stability. But democracies are more resilient than dictatorships. Although it is true that German and Austrian democracy succumbed to dictatorship after the economic catastrophe of the 1930s, such was not the case in many other countries faced with the same conditions. As the political scientist Juan J. Linz notes:

The world depression that presumably destroyed the democracy in Weimar and Austria created more unemployment in Norway and in the Netherlands and in fact consolidated the Norwegian democracy. The Dutch government was one of the most long-lasting after the depression. The degree of institutional legitimacy was more decisive than the economic crisis.[12]

One can add the United States to the list of countries. Although the depression of the 1930s caused severe unemployment and social disruption, democratic institutions remained intact.

Democracy and War. The establishment of liberal democracies reduces the chances of war. The historical record is encouraging in the twentieth century. For the most part, there have been no wars between democracies in this period. The political scientist Samuel P. Huntington notes that long-lasting problems between countries were moderated when the parties were democratic. He points to the controversies between Britain and Argentina over the Falkland Islands (Malvinas), Guatemala and Spain over the remnants of empire, and Greece and Turkey over Cyprus.[13]

Liberal democracies permit organizations that minimize the prospects of war. Peace movements, for example, are a constant feature of liberal democracies. Governments based on the consent of the people, moreover, are unlikely to support military action that may take lives.

As more countries become liberal democracies, it is likely that their disputes can be resolved peacefully. The fact that in the past democracies have generally not gone to war and that there are institutional constraints on war suggests that war may become an archaic method of resolving differences among democratic countries.

[12] Juan J. Linz, "Transitions to Democracy," *Washington Quarterly* 13 (Summer 1990): 160.

[13] Samuel P. Huntington, "No Exit: The Errors of Endism," *National Interest*, no. 17 (Fall 1989): 6.

11/NO

ARE LIBERAL DEMOCRACIES THE FINAL FORM OF POLITICAL SYSTEM THAT WILL USHER IN AN ERA OF PEACE?

The establishment of liberal democracies since the late 1980s has led to too much euphoria about the future. A close look at the facts shows that: (1) liberal democracies may not last over the long haul; (2) ideologies other than liberal democracy may capture the imagination of people; (3) economic development and political stability can be achieved by dictatorship; and (4) the record of democracies as peace lovers is dismal.

Liberal Democracies in the Twentieth Century. Political developments since the 1970s— and most particularly the extraordinary changes in the communist world since Mikhail Gorbachev came to power—have been astonishing. Democrats everywhere can rejoice at the outpouring of freedom by people whose rights were suppressed for so many years.

It is important, however, that we not be carried away by the euphoria of the moment. Instead, we should apply historical perspective in analyzing these developments. For if the record shows anything, it reveals that the history of democracy does not unfold in a unilinear manner. Rather, it shows that as times and conditions vary, so, too, does the stability of democratic regimes.

The American Revolution and the French Revolution led to movements establishing free republics in Europe and Latin America. But in Europe, Napoleon emerged as a dictator and with his downfall monarchies were restored to power. Dictatorships were established in Latin American countries, too.

World War I was fought, said President Woodrow Wilson, to make the world "safe for democracy." During the war, the Russian czarist autocracy was replaced by a democracy, but within months that democracy was supplanted by a more efficiently run dictatorship that lasted for more than six decades.

After the war democracy was established in Germany, only to be crushed by Adolf Hitler's Nazi minions in the 1930s. Germany experienced economic distress throughout the 1920s as a result of its grappling with *reparations*, the huge sums it was obligated to pay to its former enemies in World War I. And the Great Depression, which started in 1929 and continued into the 1930s, contributed to the decline of democ-

racy not only in Germany but in other countries as well. In the late 1920s, moreover, both China and Japan seemed on course toward becoming democracies, but both soon were governed by dictatorships.

After World War II, many countries of Africa and Asia previously under colonial rule achieved independence. Constitutions establishing democratic governments were put in place. But within a few years, most of the new democratic governments were replaced by dictatorships— either by one-man personal dictatorships (such as Idi Amin in Uganda and Jean-Bédel Bokassa in the Central African Republic) or by one-party or military rule (as in Ethiopia under Col. Mengistu Haile-Mariam).

The backsliding away from democracy, then, suggests that we should be cautious about seeing inevitable trends toward liberal democracy.

Liberal Democracy as a Dominant Ideology. It is true that the major ideologies of the twentieth century have been discredited. Today fascism and communism as mass movements find few adherents. It is wrong to deduce, however, that the failure of these ideologies means the inevitable triumph of liberal democracy.

Alternatives to the liberal democratic tradition are available as replacements for the failed ideologies. Forms of religious fundamentalism are a case in point, with a notable example being Iran under religious clerics who sanction torture at home and terrorism abroad as instruments of power against their enemies.

Nationalism remains a powerful ideological force, and, as indicated in Chapter 2, it is often associated with the conquest and suppression of minorities. The syndicated columnist Charles Krauthammer notes that about a month after Bulgaria abandoned its old dictatorial rule, the majority population demanded the repression of the Muslim minority. He writes, "The country is racked with civil disorder protesting the repeal by the new Communist regime of aggressive anti-Turkish decrees."[14]

[14]Charles Krauthammer, "In Liberated Europe, Liberation May Be the Bane," *Los Angeles Times*, January 14, 1990, p. M7.

Social unrest has caused deaths and violence among ethnic groups in the republics of the former Soviet Union. Rather than promoting freedom for all, many groups took to violence against their ethnic neighbors, as conflicts between Armenians and Azerbijanis, Georgians and Ossetians, Uzbeks and Meskhetians demonstrate. In Yugoslavia, enmity among ethnic groups was so fierce that in 1991 and 1992 parts of the country seceded and became independent states.

Ideologies based on religious fundamentalism and nationalism are not the only ideologies that can capture the support of people. However invidious racism is, it still is a factor that must be reckoned with. And so we should recognize that human beings are capable of producing new ideologies or recreating old ones.

Economic Development and Political Stability. Economic development and political stability are not associated solely with democracy. For all of his reprehensible policies, the dictator Adolf Hitler did succeed in improving the German economy in the 1930s. Ugly ethnic tensions in the former Soviet Union, long suppressed by the dictators of the Soviet communist system, are now recurring and are violent; the conflicts between the Azerbaijanis and Armenians are an example. And Yugoslavia under communist dictator Josip Broz Tito remained unified in spite of its sharp ethnic divisions. But with democratic movements have come ethnic conflicts that have the potential to undermine the existing order, particularly in Yugoslavia.

What is important to keep in mind is that in the overall sweep of history, liberal democracy has been rare. As indicated in Chapter 3, democracy is, with the exception of the ancient Athenian system, a recent development. Dictatorships in one form or another have been the most prevalent form of government throughout history.

The continuation of democracy depends on a variety of cultural, economic, and political factors that do not always come together. From a cultural point of view, democracy requires a tolerant community. The people who lose in elections must not fear that the winners will persecute or liquidate them. In a presidential election in the United States, for example, the people who vote for the losing candidate do not worry that the incoming president will imprison them or close down the offices of the losing parties.

Such tolerance is not taken for granted elsewhere. It is often difficult for hostile ethnic or religious groups in a single political entity to cooperate. Violence between Christians and Muslims in Lebanon and between the Tamils and Sinhalese in Sri Lanka is intense because of basic distrust. The stable democracy of India has been undermined by communal rioting and ethnic conflicts that have caused hundreds of deaths.

Democracy also depends upon favorable economic conditions. Observers as far back as Aristotle noted the importance of a large middle class in maintaining a stable constitutional system. Where a society is polarized into a rigid class structure, with a few people owning or controlling all the wealth and the overwhelming masses languishing in poverty, then democracy is difficult to establish and maintain.

Setbacks to democracy occur during periods of adverse economic conditions, such as depressions and hyperinflation. While a booming economy can satisfy the economic needs of all groups and promote political stability, economic decay can lead to instability. The rise of nazism in Germany in the 1930s owes much to the tensions and chaos generated by hyperinflation.

Even in the early stages of democratization in Eastern Europe, there is severe economic dislocation. Ordinary consumer goods are often in short supply. Often these goods are available only in the black market. A government—even a democratic government—unable to see to it that basic needs are supplied to its people may find its support undermined.

Democracies are also vulnerable because of political factors such as foreign policy. As discussed more fully in Chapter 3, democracies may lose their freedom through defeat. Hitler's Germany destroyed democracy in France and other Western European countries. But democracy can also be destroyed through the militarization required to meet an external threat, since in wartime normal democratic freedoms are more readily dispensed with. Napoleon was the first modern leader to use his military position to create a dictatorship. During wartime governments, even democracies, are pressed to infringe on liberties that they would regard as fundamental during peacetime. The experience of France and Great Britain in the world wars and that of the United States in the Civil War; in World War I and World War II; and in the cold war when it anticipated a war with the Soviet Union, show crisis conditions produce recurring threats to fundamental liberties.

And so, it is well to heed Abraham Lincoln's warning that democracy is always "one generation away from extinction."[15] Democracy remains a fragile system dependent upon conditions that are often difficult to control.

Democracy and War. The relationship between democracy and war has long been a subject of dispute. It is clear, though, that democracies are not inherently peaceful. Even in democratic political theory, democracy means majority rule. And if a majority of elected representatives decide on going to war, a democracy can retain its democratic features and still go to war.

The world has seen many examples of the warlike spirit of democracies. The involvement of the United States in wars against Mexico and Spain is an example. Great Britain and France—two leading democracies of the nineteenth century—embarked upon many imperialist military campaigns. As the writer Leon Wieseltier notes: "Colonialism . . . was largely a liberal policy."[16]

Throughout the twentieth century, democracies have flexed their muscles in acts of liberal **messianism**—belief in the absolute rightness of a cause. And so, as indicated above, Wilson went to war to make the world safe for democracy. Ronald Reagan sent troops into Grenada in 1983 and George Bush ordered military operations against Panama in 1989. Bush, moreover, called up the reserves and turned the United States into the linchpin of a worldwide coalition to reverse the Iraqi conquest of Kuwait in 1990. Bush's actions came not as a response to an attack on the United States or its forces abroad but rather to a perceived change in power relationships in the Middle East. Bush decided that aggression should not be permitted to stand. And the U.S. Congress, duly elected democratic representatives of the American people, authorized the use of military forces for the objectives that Bush had set.

Leaving aside the subject of the inherent peaceful character of democracies, we must consider what history tells us about war between democracies. For as Samuel Huntington notes, the acceptance of democracy by large numbers of countries in the world is a very recent development. In the nineteenth century, wars occurred often among ncighboring countries over issues not related to democracy. And in the twentieth century, Huntington adds, neighboring democratic countries were members of the North Atlantic Treaty Organization (NATO), an alliance of Western democracies. With an erosion of that alliance brought on by the collapse of the Soviet Union, it is possible that war will erupt among some of these members.[17]

And so, even with the establishment of liberal democracies in more countries, we should not take it for granted that peace is a sure thing.

[15] Abraham Lincoln, quoted in "Democracy's Hour," *Christian Science Monitor*, May 23, 1991, p. 20.

[16] Leon Wieseltier, quoted in a panel discussion in *A Look at "The End of History?"* ed. Kenneth M. Jensen (Washington, D.C.: United States Institute of Peace, 1990), p. 58.

[17] Huntington, "No Exit," pp. 6–7.

KEY TERMS

Apartheid
Classical liberalism
Cold war
Conservatism
Corporate state
Divine right of kings
Fascism
Human rights
Legitimate government
Liberal democracy
Liberalism

Messianism
National Socialism
Nazism
Neoconservatism
Neoliberalism
New Conservatism
Political ideology
Political prisoners
Reactionaries
Social contract

QUESTIONS

Liberalism, Conservatism, and Fascism

1. What effect does government intervention in the economy and the expansion of the welfare state have on individual freedom?
2. What are the similarities and/or differences between conservatism and fascism?
3. What positions on domestic and foreign policy matters does one have to maintain in order to be labeled a liberal?
4. How is it possible for people who are committed to the same ideology to differ among themselves in supporting particular government policies or laws?
5. What criteria should be used in evaluating whether the United States is a racist society?

Human Rights

1. What would be the consequences to U.S. security interests if the United States treated violations of human rights by its friends in the same manner as it treats violations of human rights by its enemies?

2. What is the relationship between moral purpose and national security in the conduct of foreign policy?
3. What are the conservative values expressed in the *Affirmative*'s case on human rights?
4. What are the liberal values expressed in the *Negative*'s case on human rights?
5. At what point would liberal values be jeopardized by the United States if it vigorously pursued a human rights foreign policy?

Liberalism, the End of History, and War

1. What are the factors strengthening democracy throughout the world?
2. What are the factors weakening democracy throughout the world?
3. What ideologies now challenge liberal democracy?
4. What lessons from history are useful in determining whether liberal democracy is "the end of history"?
5. How would you compare democracies and dictatorships in the likelihood of going to war?

RECOMMENDED READINGS

Liberalism, Conservatism, and Fascism

ARBLASTER, ANTHONY. *The Rise and Decline of Western Liberalism*. New York: Basil Blackwell, 1987. An analysis, criticism, and history of liberalism.

BERLIN, ISAIAH. *Four Essays on Liberty*. New York: Oxford University Press, 1969. A classic work on liberalism.

BURNHAM, JAMES. *Suicide of the West: An Essay on the Meaning and Destiny of Liberalism*. New York: John Day, 1964. An indictment of liberalism.

DE FELICE, RENZO. *Fascism: An Informal Introduction to Its Theory and Practice* [an interview with Michael A. Ledeen]. New Brunswick, N.J.: Transaction Books, 1976. A discussion of fascism by a leading scholar of the subject.

DUNBAR, LESLIE. *Reclaiming Liberalism*. New York: W. W. Norton, 1991. An assessment of what liberalism should be.

EATWELL, ROGER, and NEIL O'SULLIVAN. *The Nature of the Right: American and European Politics and Political Thought Since 1789*. Boston: Twayne Publishers, 1990. Essays on right-wing thought and policies.

GERBER, WILLIAM. *American Liberalism: Laudable End. Controversial Means*. Rev. ed. Lanham, Md.: University Press of America, 1987. An analysis of liberalism in the United States.

GREGOR, A. JAMES. *The Ideology of Fascism: The Rationale of Totalitarianism*. New York: Free Press, 1969. A classic introduction to fascism.

———. *Interpretations of Fascism*. Morristown, N.J.: General Learning Press, 1974. A survey of social science efforts to explain the fascist phenomenon.

HARRIS, GEOFFREY. *The Dark Side of Europe: The Extreme Right Today*. Savage, Md.: Barnes and

Noble Books, 1990. A description of fascism in Europe today.

HILL, DILYS M., RAYMOND A. MOORE, and PHIL WILLIAMS, eds. *The Reagan Presidency: An Incomplete Revolution.* New York: St. Martin's Press, 1990. Evaluations of the administrations of President Ronald Reagan.

HIMMELSTEIN, JEROME L. *To the Right: The Transformation of American Conservatism.* Berkeley: University of California Press, 1990. A sociological analysis of conservatism in the United States.

HOLMES, STEPHEN. "The Permanent Structure of Antiliberal Thought." In *Liberalism and the Moral Life,* ed. Nancy L. Rosenblum, Cambridge, Mass.: Harvard University Press, 1989. Pp. 227–53. A critique of antiliberal thought.

HONDERICH, TOM. *Conservatism* Boulder, Colo.: Westview Press, 1991. An analysis of conservatism.

KIRK, RUSSELL. *The Conservative Mind: From Burke to Elliot.* 7th ed. Chicago, Ill.: Regnery Books, 1986. A study of the political philosophy, religious thought, and literature of conservatives.

KRISTOL, IRVING. *Reflections of a Neoconservative: Looking Back, Looking Ahead.* New York: Basic Books, 1983. Essays by a leading neoconservative.

MULFILL, JOHN, ed. *The Attractions of Fascism: Social Psychology and Aesthetics of the "Triumph of the Right."* New York: Berg, 1990. Essays on the social psychology of fascism.

NISBET, ROBERT. *Conservatism: Dream and Reality.* Minneapolis: University of Minnesota Press, 1986. A survey of conservative thought.

REICH, ROBERT B. *The Resurgent Liberal (And Other Unfashionable Prophecies).* New York: Times Books, 1989. Chapter 32 contains an essay on a new public philosophy of liberalism.

ROTHENBERG, RANDALL. *The Neoliberals: Creating the New American Politics.* New York: Simon and Schuster, 1984. A history of neoliberalism.

SCHUETTINGER ROBERT, ed. *The Conservative Tradition in European Thought.* New York: G. P. Putnam's Sons, 1970. An anthology with an excellent introductory article.

SKIDELSKY, ROBERT, ed. *Thatcherism.* Cambridge, Mass.: Basil Blackwell, 1990. An assessment of the politics of British Prime Minister Margaret Thatcher.

"The Vision Thing: Conservatism for the Nineties." *Policy Review,* no. 52 (Spring 1990): 4–37. A symposium of thirty-nine conservative leaders on domestic and foreign policy priorities for the 1990s.

"Where To from Here?" *Progressive* 54 (November 1990): 17–32, 34–38. Liberal and left views of domestic and foreign policy priorities for the 1990s.

WILL, GEORGE F. "Last Gasps of Liberalism." *Washington Post,* July 11, 1991, p. A15. A critique of liberalism.

Human Rights

BERGER, PETER L. "Are Human Rights Universal?" *Commentary* 64 (September 1977): 60–63. Yes, says the author.

DONNELLY, JACK. *Universal Human Rights in Theory and Practice.* Ithaca, N.Y.: Cornell University Press, 1989. An explication and defense of human rights as universal rights.

GREENFIELD, MEG. "Beware of Geobaloney." *Newsweek* 94 (December 25, 1989): 84. An argument that human rights are a legitimate concern of foreign policy.

HENKIN, LOUIS. *The Age of Rights.* New York: Columbia University Press, 1990. Contains a discussion of human rights and U.S. foreign policy.

HOFFMANN, STANLEY. "Reaching for the Most Difficult: Human Rights as a Foreign Policy Goal." *Daedalus* 112 (Fall 1983): 19–49. A defense of human rights as a goal in foreign policy.

KAGAN, DONALD. "Human Rights, Moralism, and Foreign Policy." *Washington Quarterly* 6 (Winter 1983): 86–95. An argument that human rights and national interest do not often dovetail.

KIRKPATRICK, JEANE. "Dictatorship and Double Standards." *Commentary* 68 (November 1979): 34–45. A controversial article about human rights.

RENTELN, ALISON DUNDES. *International Human Rights: Universalism versus Liberalism.* Newbury Park, Calif.: Sage Publications, 1990.

An examination of the universality of human rights.

ULLMAN, RICHARD. "Both National Security and Human Rights Can Be Served Simultaneously." *Center Magazine* 176 (March/April 1984): 21–29. An eloquent defense of human rights as a foreign policy goal.

VINCENT, R. J., ed. *Foreign Policy and Human Rights: Issues and Responses*. Cambridge, England: Cambridge University Press, 1986. Essays on the relationship between the two concepts.

YI DING. "Opposing Interference in Other Countries' Internal Affairs through Human Rights." *Beijing Review* 32 (November 6, 1989): 14–16. An argument that human rights matters are not the proper concern of foreign policy.

Liberalism, the End of History, and War

ATLAS, JAMES. "What Is Fukuyama Saying? And to Whom Is He Saying It?" *New York Times Magazine*, October 22, 1989, pp. 38–40, 42, 54, 55. An overview of Francis Fukuyama's article on the end of history.

BAKASH, SHAUL. "Democracy in the Arab World?" *Dissent* 38 (Summer 1991): pp. 332–36. An analysis of the prospects for democracy in the Arab world.

DIAMOND, LARRY. "Beyond Authoritarianism and Totalitarianism: Strategies for Democratization." *Washington Quarterly* 12 (Winter 1989): 141–63. Recommendations to extend democracy throughout the world.

FUKUYAMA, FRANCIS. "The End of History?" *National Interest*, no. 16 (Summer 1989): 3–18. An argument that liberal democracies are the end of history.

———. *The End of History and the Last Man*. New York: Free Press, 1992. An elaboration of the argument set forth in his article in *National Interest*.

———. "A Reply to My Critics." *National Interest*, no. 18 (Winter 1989–90): 21–28. Fukuyama defends his thesis.

GERSHMAN, CARL. "The United States and the World Democratic Revolution." *Washington Quarterly* 12 (Winter 1989): 127–39. A discussion of what role the United States should play in exporting democracy.

GRAY, JOHN. "The End of History—or of Liberalism?" *National Review* 41 (October 27, 1989): 33–35. A discussion of the end of history debate.

HUNTINGTON, SAMUEL P. "No Exit: The Errors of Endism." *National Interest*, no. 17 (Fall 1989): 3–11. A critique of Fukuyama's thesis.

JENSEN, KENNETH M., ed. *A Look at "The End of History?"* Washington, D.C.: Institute of Peace, 1990. Panel discussion of the end of history thesis.

LEWIS, FLORA. "The Return of History." *SAIS Review* 10 (Summer/Fall 1990): 1–11. A discussion of the end of history debate.

LINZ, JUAN J. "Transitions to Democracy." *Washington Quarterly* 13 (Summer 1990): 143–64. An analysis of the subject.

MUELLER, JOHN. *Retreat from Doomsday: The Obsolescence of Major War*. New York: Basic Books, 1989. An argument that war is becoming obsolete among liberal democracies.

"Responses to Fukuyama." *National Interest*, no. 18 (Winter 1989–90): 19–35. Commentaries on the end of history debate.

RUSTOW, DANKWART A. "Democracy: A Global Revolution?" *Foreign Affairs* 69 (Fall 1990): 75–91. An assessment of democracy's prospects.

chapter 5

Capitalism, socialism, and communism

"Capitalism is a system of exploitation of man by man; and communism is the exact opposite," is one of the quips about the two systems. Capitalism and communism have had such vehement supporters and critics over the years that they lend themselves to many humorous remarks. The same is true of another system—socialism. Often, however, the humor about these systems is based on misunderstandings of their central features. The misunderstandings arise because of confusion and disagreement about the definitions of these systems, the need to protect the beneficiaries of these systems, and differing assessments about the consequences of each system to society.

We will begin our discussion of this subject by noting that capitalism, socialism, and communism owe much to the development of industrialism throughout the world. Although receiving their impetus from economic factors, these ideologies go beyond economics and deal with such matters of political philosophy as the role of government in society, the relationship between citizen and state, and the extent of individual liberty.[1]

WHAT IS CAPITALISM?

Throughout much of the world today, capitalism is popular. Capitalism developed in Western Europe and North America and continues to dominate its economic systems, while Eastern Europe rushes to embrace its important practices. And many of the poor countries of Africa, Asia, and Latin America—known as the **Third World** because its industrial development follows the First World (the United States and its industrialized allies) and the Second World (East Europe)—are now vocal partisans of capitalism, too.

[1] Part of the material in this chapter is drawn from the author's *Communism and Democracy: Principles and Practices* (Dubuque, Iowa: Kendall/Hunt, 1971).

Such widespread acclaim of capitalism is unique to most of the twentieth century. Leaders of communist countries traditionally denounced capitalism as synonymous with exploitation of the masses. Noncommunist Third World leaders equated capitalism with Western colonialism. Even in the West capitalism was criticized daily not only for exploitation and colonialism but for greed, pollution, war, and injustice.

To be sure, capitalism is not without its critics, but the critics are much less vociferous and influential than they used to be. And in the past, even in areas of the world where capitalism was under attack, capitalism had its supporters, though they were often on the defensive.

To sort out rhetoric from fact, it is essential first to describe objectively the features of a capitalist system. We can then examine its historical development and note its many changes. We can study some of the principal critics of capitalism and their prescriptions for remedying its evils—evils both real and imaginary.

The term *capitalism* is an invention of nineteenth-century socialists who were critical of business practices. Some commentators prefer to use the terms *free enterprise, private enterprise*, or *market economy* rather than *capitalism*. In doing so, they wish to distinguish between an ideal system of economic organization and the actual behavior of people who call themselves capitalists but who act in ways that conflict with the ideal system. Recognizing that the distinction between the theory of capitalism and the practice of capitalism is a valid one, we shall use the terms *capitalism*, **free enterprise**, and **private enterprise** as if they are the same when discussing the theory of capitalism. We shall define **capitalism** as an economic system characterized by private property, competition, a market economy, and freedom of managerial decision.

Economic System

Capitalism is first and foremost an *economic* system. It should not be confused with a *political* system, such as political democracy. Some observers contend that capitalism is an essential prerequisite of democracy since individuals should be free to spend their own money just as they should be free to vote. In spending and in voting, people are expressing their individual preferences, as required of a free society. If, however, we accept the definition of democracy as characterized by, among other things, a feature such as majority rule, then we can conclude that a majority acting through its representatives can support *either* a capitalist economy *or* some other economic system.

Private Property

A second feature of capitalism is private property. In this context property includes not only land but also such components as tools, factories, ships, and stock. In a capitalist system individuals are permitted to acquire as much property as they are legally capable of acquiring. There are few restrictions imposed by the state. Heavy taxation, particularly, is viewed as theft—the taking away of private property from someone who possesses it and distributing it to others who do not.

Competition

In a capitalist system competition among many units is an important characteristic. A basic feature of capitalism is that buyers rather than monopolists or government bureaucrats are the best judges of what they want. A system that permits individuals to choose how they spend their money and where they work creates a free society in which the consumer is sovereign in the marketplace. Business people (or *entrepreneurs*, as they are sometimes called) are free to enter the marketplace to satisfy consumer demands. Competition assures that prices remain low. If a product is very much in demand, many entrepreneurs will rush to furnish that item or something similar to it, thus reducing prices. The public will be able to get the best goods at the cheapest prices through this arrangement. As Adam Smith, an eighteenth-century Scottish political economist, put it: If each individual seeks to maximize his own self-interest, an "invisible hand" will maximize the economic satisfaction of the entire community.

Market Economy

A market economy, as distinguished from a command economy, is an essential feature of capitalism. A **market economy** is a system in which individuals are free to buy and sell goods and services as they wish with no or few restrictions. A **command economy**, in contrast, is a system in which decisions about production and distribution are centralized in the hands of government or of a few monopolists.

Freedom of Managerial Decision

According to capitalist theory, for society to prosper there must be complete freedom for the entrepreneurs to invest as they deem appropriate. If capitalists invest their savings in things that the public does not want, they lose money and go out of business. A capitalist system, consequently, encourages the most ambitious and innovative individuals to demonstrate their moneymaking talent, and the system rewards those who have proven their ability to satisfy consumers.

Entrepreneurs, then, are free from any government interference in their decision making. They hire and fire workers as they deem fit. They pay whatever wages they choose. If workers are not satisfied with the wages they are earning, then they are free to move elsewhere. Market forces determine if workers are worth more money than they are receiving. Capitalists who choose to discriminate on the basis of race, religion, or gender soon find that they are neglecting the services of a pool of qualified talent, and, consequently, they suffer economically from their prejudices. When tal-

ented people from groups experiencing discrimination are selected by a more intelligent entrepreneur, that entrepreneur's business is more likely to prosper.

Anything that inhibits the entrepreneurs from making decisions based on economic efficiency is detrimental not only to them but to the rest of society as well. Taxes are bad because they curb incentive. Minimum wage laws are harmful because they place restrictions on the freedom of the capitalist. Worker safety laws, legally mandated antidiscrimination policies, and environmental protection rules are all detrimental to society because they impede the freedom of the managers to decide how to direct their companies.

The expression *laissez-faire*, literally "to leave alone," vividly describes managerial freedom. This expression is derived from a French merchant named Le Gendre who, in 1680, suggested to the French government that the best way to promote commerce and industry is for the government to "leave them alone." Today, *laissez-faire* is a synonym for a market economy or free enterprise system.

CAPITALISM AND THE INDUSTRIAL REVOLUTION

The features of capitalism—private property, competition, market economy, and freedom of managerial decision—were described most thoroughly by Adam Smith in his *Inquiry into the Nature and Causes of the Wealth of Nations* (known more commonly by its shortened title, *The Wealth of Nations*), published in 1776. Smith, however, never mentioned the term *capitalism*. In writing his book, which has become the bible of capitalism, Smith denounced the prevailing system of **mercantilism**—an economic system based on the theory that the wealth of a state may be calculated on the basis of the gold, silver, and other precious metals it possesses. Under mercantilism, monopolies, tariffs, and state regulation had become central features. Smith urged that a free economy be established instead of a mercantile system.

Although Adam Smith's concepts became the adopted philosophy of capitalists, the philosophy of capitalism and the practices of capitalism varied over time. It is essential, therefore, to examine the historical development of capitalism.

Capitalism has roots going back to ancient times when individuals owned property and traded for a profit. Trade across continents existed in Greece and Rome, but modern capitalism emerged first in Europe and North America in the late eighteenth century after a long process of development.

Although profit was a feature uniting the old and the new capitalism, what distinguishes the two is that modern capitalism is based on the idea of economic development and growth. That is to say that, in ancient capitalism, profit was perceived as being derived at someone's expense: A gain for someone in a static economy is a loss for someone else. In modern capitalism, it is possible to create wealth that will be beneficial to many people rather than to a select few. According to the British economist Arthur Shenfield, "Capitalism was the first system in human history in which it became possible to become rich by uplifting the poor."[2]

Modern capitalism coincided with the industrial revolution. In fact, capitalism became the first economic system to bring about the industrial revolution. In the twentieth century, the state—rather than capitalists—has played a more important role in bringing on the industrial revolution in developing countries. Because of the role of capitalism as originator of the industrial revolution, we must understand the central features of that revolution.

The **industrial revolution** is the name given to the rapid transformation in economic life brought about by the application of science and technology to the production of goods. The industrial revolution involved methods of production based on the use of new scientific inventions driven by the steam engine.

The industrial revolution started in England and spread elsewhere. Through that revolution, production of goods expanded rapidly. Other major changes took place: Roads were built, canals were opened, steamship services were begun, and railroad operations increased. New markets and sources of raw materials became available as a result of the demands of an industrial society. Banking and finance played important roles in the new economic order.

The industrial revolution did not appear all of a sudden without centuries of slow development in science, technology, philosophy, laws, and business practices. By the nineteenth century, however, it was clear that the processes of industrial development were moving so rapidly that the world would never again be the same. It has been said that the changes in the world brought on by the industrial revolution transformed the world more than anything the world had experienced in all of its preindustrial history.

From the point of view of the development of capitalism, three major changes are notable: the growth of cities and urban life, the formation of new classes, and the creation of a new political world.

Cities and Urban Life

The industrial revolution was marked by the rapid growth of cities. Urban growth was caused by a rise in population brought on by industrial society and economic inducements. The industrial revolution produced a higher standard of living and better health conditions, which extended life expectancy. People flocked from the countryside to the cities because of economic opportunities and because in many cases economic difficulties drove them

---

[2] Arthur Shenfield, *Myth and Reality in Economic Systems*. no. 4 (Washington, D.C.: Heritage Foundation, 1981), p. 7.

from the farms. The new factories in the cities manufactured goods far more efficiently than could individuals at home or in small shops, so there was a rapidly diminishing market for the goods produced outside the factory system.

As millions of people fled to the cities to find work, the quality of life for many people deteriorated. Housing was inadequate, and the cities became marked by slums, poor sanitation, and crime.

Urban life was a misery for many of the factory workers. Conditions in many of the factories were appalling, as often the machinery was dangerous and the working environment was unhealthy. Men, women, and children worked in "sweatshops." There was little that the workers could do to alter these miserable conditions since the laws generally supported the business leaders at the expense of the working class. If workers were injured on the job, for example, their wages were stopped immediately. Children were whipped if they fell asleep at the machines.

Many of the workers were paid low wages, and work was not always available for them. To be sure, there had been poverty in earlier periods of history. What made the poverty of the industrial revolution different was its concentration and visibility to the rest of society. Because the suffering was concentrated in urban areas, it could be seen and deplored.

Formation of New Classes

The two classes that emerged in power and influence as a result of the industrial revolution were the middle class and the working class. The middle class, or **bourgeoisie** as it is sometimes called, consisted of factory owners, bankers, merchants, and lawyers. Gradually, these men took power from the aristocracy, whose influence was based on land and family ties. The bourgeoisie encouraged laws to be passed that expanded the influence of capitalists in economic development. In many cases

these laws hurt the interests of both the aristocrats, whose privileges were based on inheritance, and the factory workers, who were often the victims of rapid economic development.

The political power of the factory workers (or **proletariat**, as they are sometimes called) grew more slowly. In most countries factory workers were initially excluded from certain kinds of political participation, such as voting in elections and organizing trade unions. Labor unions and strikes were illegal in the early stages of the industrial revolution. Typical antilabor statutes of the eighteenth century included the Le Chapelier Law in France and the British Combination Acts, which made unions illegal.

As industrialism developed, the number of factory workers increased and the political power of these workers grew stronger. Gradually, in Western democracies, the factory workers received the franchise and were permitted to form trade unions. Collective bargaining and the strike became legal weapons.

A New Political World

As indicated in Chapter 2, the nineteenth century was marked by the unleashing of the forces of nationalism. Although nationalism cannot be explained exclusively in terms of the rise of an industrial system, there is a close affinity. Industrialization meant a mobilization of society into an immense economic effort. It required a cooperative venture on the part of people of diverse religious, ethnic, and social backgrounds for the purpose of economic development. With the building of better transportation and communication systems, there was much more interaction among people residing within a state than had occurred earlier.

Not all countries adapted readily to the aspirations of the new industrial order. At first, the industrial revolution was limited to Western Europe and North America. It gradually spread to Eastern Europe. By the twentieth century it had encompassed the world. There is scarcely a country that has not accepted the principles of an industrial society, although the pace and style vary from one to another.

THE CHANGING CHARACTER OF CAPITALISM

In Adam Smith's time, capitalism was quite different from what it is today. When we think of capitalism today, we think of giant corporations—Exxon, General Motors, and IBM—businesses so big that they play major roles in their industries. When Smith thought of capitalism, he perceived many entrepreneurs engaged in small-scale operations. In that context, the owner of a factory was usually also its manager.

Even Smith noted storm signals ahead for a competitive economy, observing that free market economy principles could be violated. "People of the same trade seldom meet together," he wrote, "but the conversation ends in a conspiracy against the public, or in some diversion to raise prices."[3]

During Smith's lifetime, joint stock companies were limited in purpose—created to build a railroad or canal, for example—and were often limited in time as well. In the late nineteenth and twentieth centuries, large corporations began to emerge. In these corporations, as Adolf A. Berle, Jr. and Gardiner C. Means observe, there has been a separation between the owners and the managers—a radical change from early capitalism.[4] In the new capitalism the managers play the dominant role in making decisions for the corporation.

Modern capitalists, moreover, differ

[3] Adam Smith, quoted in Robert L. Heilbroner, *The Worldly Philosophers: The Lives, Times, and Ideas of the Great Economic Thinkers*, 6th ed. (New York: Simon and Schuster, 1986), p. 70.

[4] Adolf A. Berle, Jr. and Gardiner C. Means, *The Modern Corporation and Private Property* (New York: Macmillan, 1933), chap. 5.

from their forebears in that they have often tried to avoid price competition. The biggest corporations attempt to provide "market leadership" in price so that competition focuses on the quality of the product, technological innovation, and service. In this manner, cutthroat competition can be avoided. In general, attempts to break up the giant corporations through antitrust legislation have not been successful. Many entrepreneurs with limited resources have lacked the financial base to compete effectively against the giants.

The big corporations have at various times attempted to form **cartels**—organizations of companies controlling supply and demand of products. They have increasingly sought government support through tariffs, government contracts, and subsidies. When facing economic difficulties, they have not let Adam Smith get in the way of requesting government bailouts. In some industries, such as armaments, corporations have become so enmeshed with the state as to really lose their "capitalist" identity. Capitalism in practice, then, differs considerably from capitalism in theory.

THE SOCIALIST CHALLENGE

Socialism is the major ideological challenge to capitalism. Like *democracy*, the term *socialism* is ambiguous and lends itself to many definitions. Communists sometimes refer to socialism as being almost synonymous with communism. Some anticommunists use the term *socialism* to distinguish themselves from communists. No definition of socialism has been universally adopted. Although it is possible to go back to antiquity to find early examples of socialistic communities, socialism is better understood as a modern phenomenon—a reaction to the excesses of capitalism.

Although recognizing that no one definition of socialism will satisfy everyone, we will define **socialism** as a system in which the major economic institutions are in public rather than private hands. Generally, in a socialist system, the state acts as a representative of the public and owns and manages the major economic institutions, such as factories, railroads, and farms. Its planning institutions play a central role in the management of the economy, and the welfare state is prominent. In practice, however, there is much variation in the amount of public ownership and the extent of welfare programs even in countries that profess to be socialistic.

Elements of socialism are found in many democratic systems. And so, western democratic countries have government programs for social security, health, and education, for example,

Like capitalism, socialism is an *economic* system. It is possible for a country to adopt a socialist economy and still be a democracy, if democracy is defined in political terms. The reverse is also true—that is, it is possible for a country to be a dictatorship and have a socialist economy.

As a response to capitalism, socialism has appeared in many varieties. The early socialists of the nineteenth century were utopian socialists The most influential of the nineteenth-century socialists were the scientific socialists (or Marxists). We shall deal with these two groups first and emphasize the Marxist critique because of its significance. We can then look at later socialist philosophies, such as democratic socialism and communism.

Utopian Socialists

Utopian socialists believed that capitalism could be reformed by establishing **utopias** (ideal communities). These communities would be based on cooperation. Frequently, utopian socialists favored the building of communities that were self-sufficient. Their leading proponents were Claude-Henri de Saint-Simon, Charles Fourier, and Robert Owen.

The utopian socialists failed because they all shared the belief that the capitalists would cooperate in the new schemes. The utopian socialists believed in *voluntary* socialism and had no conception of a class struggle between those who owned the means of production and those who did not. As we shall see, this belief in voluntary socialism placed them in stark contrast to Marx.

Marxists

Of the nineteenth-century critics of capitalism, the Marxists made the most enduring and influential attack. Because of his predominant position in the socialist movement, we shall examine the writings of its founder, Karl Marx, in greater detail than we have done with other critics of capitalism.

Marx's writings consist of books, polemical tracts, and newspaper and scholarly articles. No single work by Marx contains a synthesis of all his ideas. In part, this failure to provide a "bible" for his followers resulted from the activist, revolutionary nature of his work. As a leader of *one* faction within the socialist movement, Marx often directed his attention not against established institutions but against other critics of industrial society, such as the utopian socialists. Marx, moreover, stressed different points in arguing against his fellow radicals. Writing over a period of forty years, he was bound to change his mind on various issues and also to sometimes contradict himself. His work, consequently, is filled with many ambiguities and inconsistencies, so that it is possible to find criticisms of Marx in various works written by Marx.

Probably the two best known of all Marx's works are *The Communist Manifesto* (1848) and his unfinished *Das Kapital*, of which the first volume appeared in 1867 and the second and third volumes were published posthumously. During his adult life, Marx wrote constantly, and, in addition to *The Communist Manifesto* and *Das Kapital*, these are considered among his principal writings: *German Ideology* (1845–46), *Theses on Feuerbach* (1845), *Poverty of Philosophy* (1847), *Class Struggles in France* (1850), *Eighteenth Brumaire* (1852), *The Critique of Political Economy* (1859), and *Civil War in France* (1870–71).

Cleared of all ambiguities, certain pillars of thought have come to constitute Marxism, the philosophy of Karl Marx. **Marxism** may thus be defined as a theory of human development that purports to explain all history on the basis of immutable economic laws. Marxists claim their analysis is scientific, hence the term **scientific socialism** to describe their ideas. These main ideas are: historical materialism, the dialectic, the class struggle, a theory of capitalism, revolution, and the inevitable emergence of the classless society.

Historical Materialism.

Historical materialism is an explanation of history in terms of the material or economic foundations of society. According to this interpretation of history, the way in which a society uses its resources and produces its goods determines its political and social structure. If the system of production changes, corresponding changes in politics and society will result. Marx referred to the economic foundation of society as the **substructure** and everything else, such as laws, government, religion, culture, and ideology, as the **superstructure**. If the substructure is changed, so, too, will the superstructure change.

The relationship between substructure and superstructure may be seen from two examples concerned with religion and the state. Christians believe that God created man. A Marxist, in contrast, believes that man created God—or rather the *idea* of God—to serve the interests of a ruling class. A Marxist argues that if a ruling class can convince the masses of people that their kingdom is not of this earth and that their rewards are to come in some heavenly kingdom rather than in the material present, the ruling class will be able to more easily exploit the masses by paying them low wages and providing few benefits. Workers would be happy with the knowledge that they will enter the Kingdom of God. The statement by Marx that "religion is the opium of the people"[5] can be understood in this light.

Marxists view the state with as much disdain as they do religion. In this regard, they are in conflict with a classical view of ancient Greeks, such as that held by Aristotle, who described the state as a natural and essential institution of society. Marxists characterize the state as an artificial creation—part of the superstructure. The state is really an instrument of the ruling class and is consequently an evil institution. Ultimately, the state will wither away if exploited classes are liberated. This hostility to the state is a feature of Marxist philosophy that is shared by anarchists, who are opposed to the very existence of any state.

The Dialectic.

Marx was influenced by the writings of the German philosopher G. W. F. Hegel. Marx derived his notion of the dialectic from Hegel although he used it in a different way. Hegel viewed history as a continuous unraveling of God's design for the world. For Hegel, the real world is a reflection of the world of ideas. History unfolds progressively through a process of the dialectic.

By **dialectic**, Hegel meant the clash of opposites in which every idea is opposed by a contrary idea. The main components of the dialectic are thesis, antithesis, and synthesis. First an idea (**thesis**) is presented, out of which an opposing idea (**antithesis**) is formed. Out of the struggle between the two comes a third idea (**synthesis**), which takes the best aspects of the thesis and the

[5] Karl Marx, "Contribution to the Critique of Hegel's Philosophy of Right," 1844, as excerpted in *Essential Writings of Karl Marx*, ed. David Caute (New York: Collier Books, 1967), p. 87.

antithesis. This process is a continuing one and is dynamic, as the synthesis becomes a thesis, which creates a new antithesis resulting in a new synthesis, and so on.

It has often been said that Marx took Hegel's ideas and turned them upside down. For Marx, the ideal world is a reflection of the real world. Historical development unfolds on the basis of the dialectical process, but is keyed to the driving *economic* forces of the times.

According to Marx, history shows several stages of development, which he described as primitive communal, slave, feudal, capitalist (bourgeois), and socialist. With the exception of the primitive communal, these stages correspond to control over the means of production by particular classes: slave owners, feudal lords, capitalists, and workers, respectively. In the primitive communal state, there is communal rather than private control over the means of production.

According to Marx, history unfolds progressively from one stage to the next as the economic foundations of society change. When too many obstacles impede movement to the next stage, *contradictions* arise. **Contradictions** are problems that cannot be solved without changing the basic structure of society. Revolution is the process that resolves the contradictions.

For Marx, the dialectic works to move historical development forward. For example, **feudalism** (thesis), an economic and social system based on landed privilege and self-sufficient agricultural units, gradually produced a commercial class of entrepreneurs. These entrepreneurs grew stronger with the development of capitalism (antithesis) and eventually challenged the feudal leaders, resulting in a synthesis marking the triumph of capitalism. Capitalism, however, creates a proletarian class. As we shall see, for Marx the dialectical process terminates with the triumph of the working classes over their exploiters—the capitalists—or with the common ruin of the contending classes.

The Class Struggle. According to Marx, the history of all human society, except for primitive communities, is a history of **class struggle**. Marx never defined *class* explicitly. In general, he used the term to mean how groups are related to the means of production. Two major classes are thus distinguished: those who control the means of production and those who do not. It is the conflict between the *haves* and the *have-nots* that moves history forward.

New classes emerge as the forces of production change. The capitalists as a class are created when they are able to manage the new productive forces of society more efficiently than the feudal lords. The capitalists then create a new class—the proletariat, or workers. The proletariat and the capitalists struggle against each other in the same manner as the middle class and the guild workers earlier fought the feudal lords. Eventually, the workers take control of the means of production when the capitalists become unable to administer the productive forces of society efficiently. This is the dialectic applied to economics.

History, then, becomes the end product of the resolution of contradictions through the class struggle. The final class struggle between the proletariat and the capitalists will end either with the victory of the former and the end of exploitation, or in the common ruin of the contending classes.

Theory of Capitalism. Marxism is both a critique of capitalism and a praise of its virtues. The criticisms dealing with the exploitation of man by man have been noted. Marx, however, also extolled the virtues of capitalism. He admired the capitalists because they were able to produce material benefits in such abundance as to control the worst ravages of nature. In *The Communist Manifesto*, he and Friedrich Engels, his collaborator in many of his writings, observed:

It [the bourgeoisie] has been the first to show what man's activity can bring about. It has accomplished wonders far surpassing Egyptian pyramids, Roman aqueducts, and Gothic cathedrals; it has conducted expeditions that put in the shade all former Exoduses of nations and crusades.[6]

Although Marx approved of the achievements of capitalism and thought of the capitalists as providing a necessary historic mission, he condemned them as exploiters of the proletariat. In his view, capitalism was responsible for the destruction of the family, the workers' alienation from their work, and a declining standard of living for ordinary people. He perceived capitalism, however, as containing within itself the seeds of its own destruction. How this was to occur can best be understood by examining Marx's analysis of capitalism. Marx began with the **labor theory of value**, a theory that he drew from other economists. According to this theory, the value of a commodity is equal to the amount of labor-time necessary for its production.

Marx built upon this theory. He contended that capitalism treated the workers as if they were commodities. The workers receive wages that are just enough to provide for themselves and their families. Unlike all other commodities, labor produces a value greater than its own market value. Marx referred to **surplus value** as the value that labor produces over and above the amount that is necessary to produce an item, and viewed it as exploitation. Profit is derived solely from the surplus value created by the proletariat.

In the quest for more profits, the capitalists find themselves in a competitive situation with other capitalists producing similar goods. They are constantly trying to reduce costs of production by lowering the wages they give their workers and by introducing labor-saving machinery. Less

efficient capitalists are driven out of business, and industry becomes concentrated in fewer and fewer companies. Society is polarized into those few who control the means of production and the army of the proletariat thrown out of work by machines. Wages are driven to a point below the subsistence level; many workers are unemployed. When the capitalists are unable to control the forces that they have unleashed, they call upon the state (which, according to Marx, is nothing more than the executive committee of the bourgeoisie) to stop the agitation of the proletariat.

Revolution. At the point in which the crisis is the greatest—when the proletariat is most exploited, when people are out of work, when capitalism and industrialism are most advanced, and when the state is most coercive—a revolution occurs. The revolution is an armed uprising of the proletariat unwilling to tolerate these most wretched conditions. There is nothing the capitalists can do to stop the revolution, since capitalism has created these irresistible forces that will destroy it.

It is important to emphasize that Marx attributed to the proletariat and to no other group the historic revolutionary mission. Because of its organization, cohesion, and numbers, it is that class that has the inevitable historical revolutionary role. The proletariat must be the instrument of the revolution because only the proletariat is capable of becoming masters of the productive forces of society.

The **peasants**, those poor farmers who work the land, play no revolutionary role. Marx viewed the peasantry as a reactionary element in society. He condemned both the "idiocy of rural life" and the peasant quest for private property.[7] Marx also criticized the *Lumpenproletariat*—that class of peo-

---

[6]Karl Marx and Friedrich Engels, *The Communist Manifesto*, trans. Samuel Moore (Baltimore: Penguin Books, 1967), p. 83. *The Communist Manifesto* was first published in German in 1848; Samuel Moore's translation was first published in 1888.

[7]For a discussion of Marx's views on the peasantry, see David Mitrany, *Marx against the Peasant: A Study in Social Dogmatism* (New York: Collier Books, 1961).

ple who cannot find a place in the workers' world (in other words, the unemployable or the "parasite")—as a reactionary force in society.

To provide leadership for the workers, Marx advocated the primacy of the *communists*, a name he gave to his socialist faction to distinguish it as being more radical than others. He indicated, moreover, that there should be some role for intellectuals like himself in helping to educate the proletariat to develop a class consciousness. That class consciousness will arise, however, from economic conditions and not from planned activities of intellectuals.

The Classless Society. It may seem odd that there is scarcely any description in the writings of Marx and Engels as to what is to take the place of the old capitalist system after the revolution occurs. Marxism is as unclear about the end condition as many religions, though its end condition is on earth and not in heaven.

Marx did say that the state will wither away. There is no need for a state apparatus since there will be no classes—no group to exploit others. In other words, there will be a **classless society** based on the principle: "From each according to his ability, to each according to his needs." Marx provided no blueprint for socialism. Those writers and political leaders who came after Marx had to guess as best they could about the future of socialism, since they had scarcely any guidance from Marx's writings.

Marx and Engels did acknowledge that there is a short transition stage between the destruction of capitalism and the establishment of the new order. This stage is labeled the **dictatorship of the proletariat**. This dictatorship exists only for the purpose of eliminating the last vestiges of capitalism. Having completed this "mopping up" operation, the state withers away. Community interest rather than exploiter interest then guides human development in the new classless society.

COMMUNISM

The words *communism* and *communist* create certain familiar images, such as the Soviet Union, Joseph Stalin, Fidel Castro, and collectivism. Communism, however, also means different things to different people. In the early part of this century conservative business people viewed trade unionists as communists if they made demands for higher wages and better working conditions. The *communist* label has also been applied to liberals advocating minimum wage laws, hippies rejecting values of established institutions, civil rights advocates engaged in peaceful protest marches, and even doctors who favor fluoridation.

Etymologically, *communism* is derived from **commune**, a small isolated community. Communes go back to ancient times. Throughout the centuries people have joined communes—religious and seccular—for varying reasons, and *commune* can be used to describe anything from a monastery of orthodox Christian holy men in prayerful dedication to God to a modern urban shelter dedicated to self-realization.

The use of the term *communism* to signify communal living is now somewhat dated. A more modern use appeared in the nineteenth century when *communism* was sometimes applied to the political philosophy of Karl Marx. As we have seen, Marx himself chose *communist* to mean the most radical of socialist groups. Today, however, many Marxists would chastise anyone who would identify them as communists.

Recognizing the ambiguity of the word **communism**, we will use it to mean a political ideology based on the writings of Karl Marx and the Russian revolutionary V. I. Lenin. The term *communism*, then, is synonymous with **Marxism-Leninism**. We have already described the political philosophy of Marx, so we shall now consider Lenin and those communists who came after him. To understand communism, we must first take a look at some of the central economic and political features of the period leading up to Lenin's rise to power. Later we shall examine changes in the communist world from 1917, when the first communist state was established, to the present.

1848–1914: A Period of Prosperity and Reform

The period between 1848 and 1914 in Europe and North America was marked by widespread prosperity, the expansion of the suffrage, the growth of trade unions, the enactment of social reform legislation, the spread of nationalism, and the emergence of imperialism. Such profound changes were bound to have an impact on society.

Marx had predicted severe economic crises with increasing misery for the proletariat—a condition that would lead to revolution. The period between 1848 and 1914 saw, however, widespread prosperity instead of poverty. Rather than experiencing a decline in the standard of living, the workers in advanced industrial countries made gains in real wages.

In many countries, moreover, the franchise was enlarged to include ever greater numbers of people. In Great Britain, for example, the Reform Act of 1832 expanded the franchise to the middle class, and the Reform Act of 1867 gave the vote to part of the working class. By 1884, universal manhood suffrage was almost achieved. By 1928, women, too, were given the vote, and universal suffrage was a reality in Britain.

Not only was the franchise expanded, but restrictions against trade unions were abandoned and the number of workers enrolled in these associations rose. The power of trade unions, consequently, grew. To be sure, throughout this period there were acts of brutality against workers and their unions, but it could not be denied that their power was growing.

Workers and others benefited, too, from more humane state legislation to remedy the evils of uncontrolled capitalism. Child labor laws were passed. Working conditions improved. Germany in particular pioneered in establishing the welfare state based on the notion that the state has a responsibility to guarantee that every citizen is provided educational opportunities, medical care, and social security. The welfare state eventually was adopted by all advanced industrial countries, whatever their political persuasion.

Marx's prediction about the political behavior of the proletariat did not hold true. The workers did develop a class consciousness within their own countries in Europe, but they did not develop a class unity transcending national boundaries. They did not, moreover, achieve a revolutionary consciousness. Workers found that they had a vested interest in maintaining national ties to their state rather than in extending their primary loyalties to a world proletariat.

Another important development in this period was the territorial expansion of Western and other industrial countries into Africa and Asia, a process that was labeled **imperialism** (or colonialism). Great Britain and France led the advanced industrial countries in acquiring enormous overseas territories. The imperialist fever spread to Germany, Italy, the United States, and Japan. Although the motives for expansionism varied, the industrial countries were thus able to secure cheap sources of raw materials for their burgeoning economies.

The Ideological Response to Marx

Prosperity, the franchise, trade unionism, the welfare state, nationalism, and imperialism all became prominent features of the socialist analysis following Karl Marx. A central doctrinal problem of socialists was how to explain the events that were occurring in advanced industrial societies. Two principal views were put forward: the evolutionary and the revolutionary. These views, which had their origins in the latter part of the nineteenth century, continue to split the socialist movement to the present day.

Democratic Socialism. The evolutionary view contended that socialism could be achieved through peaceful and gradual change. Its foremost intellectual spokesman was Eduard Bernstein, a German socialist who had served as Engels's secretary. Bernstein argued that socialists should abandon the idea of violent revolution that could be found in Marx and other socialist writers. According to Bernstein, socialists should form parties of peaceful protest, reform, and democracy.[8] To that end, socialists should continuously wage a protest campaign for improved working conditions, educational opportunity, and political participation. By organizing to vote in free elections, Bernstein contended, the workers could achieve their goals through the ballot box rather than through the turmoil of street barricades. Bernstein's prescription for socialism was to elect public officials responsive to socialist needs. He wrote, "To me that which is generally called the ultimate aim of socialism is nothing, the movement is everything."[9] By this he meant that the final aims of revolution and the creation of a utopian society are meaningless; what really counts is the practical day-to-day improvement of the condition of working people and increased popular participation in political life.

Bernstein also attacked many of the assumptions of Marxist ideology itself. Specifically, he criticized the idea that capitalism was doomed to reduce the standard of living of the proletariat. He questioned the validity of dialectical materialism. Bernstein became the chief proponent of the **revisionists**— those who revised the ideas of Marx. He did more than merely revise Marx's writings,

[8] Eduard Bernstein, *Evolutionary Socialism: A Criticism and Affirmation*, trans. Edith C. Harvey (New York: Schocken Books, 1961). The book was first published in 1899.

[9] Ibid., p. 202.

however; he set forth a clearly new philosophy in conflict with Marx.

Although many writers and political leaders in Bernstein's time and thereafter did not support his entire analysis of the direct assault on Marxism, many agreed with the fundamental principle of achieving socialism through evolutionary and peaceful democratic reform. This approach to socialism is known as **social democracy** or **democratic socialism**. On the continent of Europe the social democratic movement developed in response to Marxist writings. Because of their insular positions and their nonideological approach to politics, many British and American writers and political leaders with similar views argued with little or no reference to Marx, although they reached the same conclusions as Bernstein. Social democrats, then, are champions of social reform and the welfare state through political democracy.

Social democrats today are likely to favor programs that provide greater benefits for medical care, housing, public education, and aid for the poor. When in power in capitalistic economies, social democrats have had to reconcile their desire for economic equality with a need to stimulate economic growth by encouraging market forces. Attempts at such a reconciliation have led to differences among social democrats about whether the goal of social reform is being sacrificed in the quest for political success at election time.

Leninism. The evolutionary approach to socialism was challenged by the more radical sections of the socialist movement. The principal critic was a Russian intellectual, Vladimir Ilyich Ulanov, better known as Lenin.

To understand the man, his ideas, and his policies, it is essential first to look at Russia, the country that Lenin eventually ruled, during the period before World War I. While Western Europe was industrializing its economy and involving more groups in political participation, Russia was slow to change. Economically, it remained dominated by agriculture. Politically, the czar and his close supporters ruled in an authoritarian way over a society consisting mostly of a peasant population.

Economic and political transformation of society was slow in coming. Russian people had difficulty in expressing discontent with the pace of change through legitimate, peaceful expression because of government repression, censorship, and police surveillance. By the end of the nineteenth century, however, certain reforms in the economy were instituted, and Russia embarked on a policy of industrialization. At the time World War I began in 1914, Russia was still a poor country—although an active newcomer to industrialization—with an autocracy ruled by a monarch, Czar Nicholas II.

It was the tragedy of World War I that brought down the czar. Although he played no role in ending czarist rule, Lenin was able to skillfully manipulate popular dissatisfaction with the war, so that his faction—the **Bolsheviks**—eventually came to power in November 1917.

Lenin's contributions to political thought must be considered in relationship to Marxism since Lenin contended that he was actually applying Marxism to conditions of Russia in the twentieth century. Critics of Lenin—including even some Marxists—argue, however, that Leninism is in fact anti-Marxist. Debate on the relationship between Lenin and Marx is made even more complicated because, like the works of Marx, the writings and speeches of Lenin are often contradictory. Lenin, consequently, can be and has been quoted to support nationalism and internationalism, coalition government and noncooperation with noncommunist parties, and peace and war. The essence of Leninism, however, deals with Lenin's ideas on the nature of the Communist party, the dictatorship of the proletariat, the skipping of revolutionary stages, the flexibility of tactics, and imperialism.

COMMUNIST PARTY. Marx had offered no analysis of the nature or role of political parties. The revolution was to occur when economic conditions were ripe, according to Marx. Intellectual leaders, moreover, might help educate the working classes, but economic conditions—not the actions of leaders—would produce revolutions.

Lenin developed a concept of a Communist party in stark contrast to Marx. In his view the party should be small, disciplined, and conspiratorial. Lenin argued that since the Russian police under the czar would not permit a dissenting group to openly criticize the government, the party must of necessity be small and conspiratorial. Even after the czarist government was destroyed, however, Lenin continued to maintain a similar view of the Communist party.

Like Bernstein, Lenin believed that workers left to themselves would find that their economic conditions would gradually improve. Unlike Bernstein, Lenin felt that such a situation was harmful to the cause of the revolution. To the extent that the workers achieved a higher standard of living, education, and health care, they would have a vested interest in the perpetuation of the capitalist system. In other words, Lenin perceived that the workers would not develop a proper revolutionary consciousness.

According to Lenin, it is a Communist party composed of dedicated revolutionaries that possesses the proper revolutionary consciousness. Without the party, it is not possible to achieve communism. The party must be small and disciplined, since its strength comes from its unity and resolve. It is this party that knows what is in the best interests of the masses of people, since the party would not be swayed by false ideologies propounded by the bourgeois publicists. The party would be "the military staff of the proletariat." The basic decision-making principle would be **democratic centralism**. By this Lenin meant that party members could debate issues, but, once a decision was made, every party official had to support it. In this way, top party leaders controlled the government. Although while in power Lenin tolerated debate and lost on some party issues, he instituted actions that restricted opposition not only from non-communists but from Communist party members as well. It was not until actions by his successor, Joseph Stalin, however, that any opposition was crushed.

DICTATORSHIP OF THE PROLETARIAT. Marx had written that the dictatorship of the proletariat, coming soon after the proletarian revolution, would last only for a short transitional period. Its function was to rid society of the last vestiges of the old capitalist order. With its work completed, the dictatorship of the proletariat would disappear, and the state would wither away.

Lenin, however, made the dictatorship of the proletariat and the building of a communist state a central element of his theory. Since the communists came to power not, as Marx had predicted, in an advanced industrial society but, rather, in one of the economically weakest industrial powers in Europe, Lenin argued that the dictatorship of the proletariat would last a long time. It would be the instrument for building the new industrial society. Lenin reinterpreted Marx to mean that when Marx said the state would wither away, he was referring to the bourgeois state, but the proletarian state would be required to build socialism. In power, Lenin constructed a communist state commensurate with his view.

THE SKIPPING OF STAGES. As indicated above, Marx had argued that history would move according to the inevitable historic stages. Although he wrote occasional contradictory comments, the thrust of his argument was that socialism would not be achieved unless capitalism had run its course.

Lenin contended, in contrast, that it was possible to skip stages—to move from feu-

dalism to communism without going through the bourgeois stages of economic and political development. The instrument of that transformation would be the Communist party, which would create an industrial order. Leninism, consequently, provides more flexibility than Marxism for leaders to manipulate events in pursuit of communist goals.

FLEXIBILITY OF TACTICS. At first, Lenin believed that he was to be the leader not of a Russian revolution but of a *world* revolution. It soon became obvious that the world revolution was going to take much longer to come about than Lenin had anticipated. Lenin devised tactics for communist revolutionaries to support, and these tactics were in stark contrast to Marxism.

For Lenin, world communist revolution was the essential goal. Morality consisted of communist victory, and any means used to achieve this objective was acceptable. The task of communists, therefore, was to disrupt legitimate organizations and political parties for their own ends in noncommunist countries.

In 1919, Lenin established the **Third International**[10] (sometimes referred to as **Communist International** or **Comintern**) and set forth the policies that caused social democratic parties to withdraw from the organization of a world socialist movement under the dominance of the Soviet Union—the new name of Russia. According to Lenin, socialists everywhere must subvert reform movements in bourgeois countries for the ultimate goal of communist revolution and identify their cause with the Soviet Union. Such a view was in conflict with the political convictions

[10] The First International was Karl Marx's International Workingmen's Association of 1864–76. The Second International, or Labor and Socialist International, existed before World War I as a loose confederation of socialist and labor parties. The Second International was re-created after World War I with a social democratic orientation.

of anyone committed to political democracy and nationalism.

Social democrats and liberals saw their work as bringing about peaceful reform within a democratic framework. When noncommunist, reform-minded individuals joined associations such as trade unions, peace groups, civil rights organizations, or anti-imperialist societies, for example, they engaged in open, peaceful protest activities. Communists, however, were ordered by Lenin to subvert these groups for communist ends as determined by the communist leaders of the Soviet Union.

We may take peace groups as a case in point and use the American effort before World War II as an example. When Adolf Hitler and Joseph Stalin concluded a nonaggression pact in 1939, communists in the United States were ordered to strengthen the peace cause by helping to keep the United states from rearming. When Hitler violated the treaty and attacked the Soviet Union, American communists were told to use their influence to get America to rearm at once. Genuine pacifists, who continued to urge the United States to stay out of the war, were now condemned by Soviet-oriented communists.

IMPERIALISM. Drawing on the ideas of the British writer J. A. Hobson, Lenin devised a theory of imperialism to help explain why the revolution did not occur in the advanced industrial societies, as Marx had predicted. According to Lenin, capitalism had moved beyond its industrial stage into a new period dominated by monopoly and finance capital. During this new stage, monopolies and cartels were formed. Capitalists carved up spheres of influence all over the world so that capitalism would survive through acquiring cheap sources of raw materials and new markets.

Lenin argued that the reason why prosperity had been rising in the capitalist societies was that the capitalists and the proletariat in the developed societies were profiting from the colonies. Imperialism

was essential to capitalism, moreover, and those countries that could not maintain colonies would be a weak link in the capitalist chain and, consequently, were ripe for revolution.

Leninism, then, is the central core of political views held by a leading communist theoretician. Unlike Marx, however, Lenin was both a theoretician and a political leader of a country. As such, he had to adapt his ideas to the practical needs of his times.

Once in power, Lenin occupied himself with solving concrete problems in domestic and foreign policy. In his first two years, he nationalized industry, confiscated bank and church property, and created a secret police (the Cheka). This period, known as war communism, was also characterized by a civil war, which the Bolsheviks eventually won. Recognizing the need to improve the economy and to regain power, Lenin adopted a moderate pragmatic program, the **New Economic Policy** (NEP), which allowed for some domestic capitalism to operate and for Western capitalists to invest in the Soviet Union.

At the time of Lenin's death in 1924, the beginnings of a dictatorship were apparent. Freedom of the press was suppressed. The Communist party dominated all the political institutions in the country. Lenin refused to permit any non-Bolshevik group to exercise independent power. Even within the Communist party itself, restrictions were placed on the degree of freedom of party members to organize into factions. The secret police were operating in all sectors of society. The seeds of a full-blown dictatorship were planted. It remained for Lenin's successors to fill in the details.

Stalinism. Three years after the death of Lenin, Joseph Stalin rose to undisputed leadership in the Soviet Union. Once regarded as the great leader of an innovative and experimental political system, Stalin lost his place of eminence in communist folklore only after his death. When he ruled the Soviet Union, he could do no wrong—at least so far as all Soviet history books, magazines, and newspapers were concerned. Since his death in 1953, Stalin has become—even for many communists—a symbol of how a noble revolution can be betrayed by one man obsessed with a "personality cult." How much of what the Soviet Union experienced in the period of his rule can be attributed to *Stalin the man* rather than *communism the system* is now, and probably will continue to be, debated by social scientists without ever reaching a definitive answer.

Joseph Stalin, born in 1879 as Joseph Vissarionovich Djugashvili, grew up in Georgia, a region bordering on the Black Sea. Stalin, unlike Lenin, was not an intellectual; nor did he spend most of his time before the Revolution of 1917 outside Russia. Stalin was a shoemaker's son. He entered a theological seminary on a scholarship. Theological studies did not interest him, and he turned his attention to revolutionary activities. Because of these efforts, he was expelled from the seminary. By 1904, Stalin had joined the Bolsheviks, and in 1912 he became a member of their Central Committee. He was exiled to Siberia in 1913 by the czarist government. He went to Petrograd after the March Revolution in 1917 and became editor of the communist newspaper *Pravda*.

Stalin's skills were primarily administrative and organizational, and he maneuvered himself into positions of authority. He was people's commissar for nationalities. He later was the head of the Workers' and Peasants' Inspection, an organization that put the workers and peasants into positions of governmental administration. Stalin served on the Politburo (the small group of party leaders) when it was first set up. In 1922, he became general secretary of the Communist party. Crafty and single-purposed in his desire to come to power, Stalin moved adeptly against his challengers for leadership. By 1927, he had taken command and changed the character of life in the Soviet Union.

The two major ideological innovations of **Stalinism** were: an emphasis on building socialism in one country—the Soviet Union—rather than promoting world revolution, and totalitarianism.

SOCIALISM IN ONE COUNTRY. Under the NEP, the Soviet Union made economic gains but at the cost of making concessions to free enterprise in the industrial sector and to the peasants in terms of individual farms. Thus many communists saw the NEP as a betrayal of socialism. Between 1928 and 1941, however, the Soviet Union embarked on a new program of economic development to radically alter the social and economic life of that country. Stalin had decided to establish "**socialism in one country**." To rapidly industrialize the Soviet Union would be the first goal of the Soviet government, and world revolution would be second to that goal. To achieve socialism in one country, drastic changes were brought about in agriculture and in industry.

Because the peasants were not producing enough agricultural products and the economic efficiency of the peasant small holdings was low, Stalin instituted collectivization of agriculture in 1929. **Collectivization** meant that private ownership of land would be replaced by public ownership or control. Stalin wanted to use the savings from agricultural development to finance major industrialization projects.

In less than a year's time, about 10 million peasants were taken from their land. Some were arrested; others were exiled. Hundreds of thousands perished, and millions were made destitute. The peasants resisted by destroying cattle and crops. Some of the ravages of the resistance produced consequences to Soviet agriculture from which the Soviet Union did not recover. The immediate result of collectivization was to produce a famine, which caused many deaths. As a result of the failure at collectivization, Stalin eased up against the peasants by permitting some private incentives. By the end of the 1930s, however, nearly all the farms were collectivized.

In addition to agricultural programs, Stalin set out in a major effort to industrialize the Soviet Union. The first of the five-year plans (government goals for the economy) began in 1928. Forced labor was introduced into factories. Consumer goods were kept to a minimum as capital was used to develop heavy industry. Penalties for economic "crimes" were made severe. Jail sentences for workers who came twenty minutes late for work were not uncommon. According to Stalin, the Soviet Union would have to modernize rapidly, lest it be vanquished by its enemies.

Under Stalin, the Soviet Union modernized rapidly. Construction in heavy industry, hydroelectric plants, and transportation facilities helped to strengthen the economy in Stalin's time and served as a base for future economic development. Welfare state benefits were established, and educational opportunities were created. The advances in economic development took place at a high cost in human freedom, however.

TOTALITARIANISM. The cost in human freedom was a direct consequence of rapid industrialization and the establishment of a dictatorship. Stalin created the first totalitarian state (see Chapter 3). The Soviet Union became a police state, and communism became the all-encompassing ideology. The Communist party dominated Soviet society. Stalin ruled the Communist party by instituting purges of party members. Dedicated communist revolutionaries who had fought against czarist forces were sent to prison camps. The purges extended into all sectors of government and society. Millions perished as a result of these policies.

Under the control of the government, the news media hailed Stalin as a great leader. Pictures and statues of Stalin ap-peared everywhere, and Stalin experienced no public criticism within the Soviet Union.

Communism since 1953: From Reform to Collapse

Toward the end of World War II, Soviet forces swept over Eastern Europe. When the war ended, communist governments loyal to Stalin were established in most of the areas occupied by Soviet troops. Even before Stalin's death, however, opposition to Soviet domination appeared. In 1948, Yugoslavia successfully asserted its independence from Soviet domination. In 1949, a revolution in China saw the emergence of Mao Zedong and his followers, who were resentful of Soviet practices. Although the rift between the Soviet Union and Communist China did not appear openly in 1949, it grew wider in the 1960s and 1970s.

After a short period of jockeying for leadership of the Soviet Union following Stalin's death, Nikita Khrushchev came to power by 1956. He engaged in de-Stalinization at home and a policy of "peaceful coexistence" abroad.

De-Stalinization. **De-Stalinization** was a policy of blaming Stalin for the evils that the Soviet Union had experienced. Stalin was denounced in a "secret speech" delivered by Khrushchev at the Twentieth Party Congress in February 1956. Khrushchev criticized Stalin for creating a "cult of personality" and committing atrocities against the Soviet people. Khrushchev instituted a certain amount of liberalization in the Soviet Union and a relaxation of Soviet control of other communist countries.

Peaceful Coexistence. The Soviet Union proclaimed a policy of **peaceful coexistence** in which it would seek to engage in peaceful competition with the West and avoid military confrontation. The Soviet

Union, however, did engage in some military confrontations during the period of Khrushchev's rule, which ended in 1964. Nevertheless, the professed goal was nonconfrontation with the West. Although there were periods of confrontation and cooperation after 1964, **détente** (relaxation of tensions) remained the official Soviet goal in foreign policy for more than two decades after Khrushchev lost power. Détente, however, did not mean the elimination of the goal of promoting communism everywhere in the world.

Relations between the Soviet Union and other communist countries, and between the Soviet Union and the communist parties of noncommunist countries, also changed during the regimes of Khrushchev and his successors. At times, the Soviet Union used military force against its communist allies, such as against Hungary in 1956 and Czechoslovakia in 1968. At other times, however, it was unable or unwilling to influence other communist states.

The Gorbachev Era and the Attempt at Reform. In the years before the death of Leonid Brezhnev, the Soviet Union seemed to be in a state of paralysis. An aging leadership resisted changes in the economic, social, and political system, while the economy showed signs of decay. The Soviet Union continued to import wheat from the West since it was unable to produce enough food to feed itself. Its economic growth lagged behind the West and the Pacific Basin countries, such as Hong Kong, Japan, South Korea, and Taiwan. Although it had made impressive gains in production of oil, steel, and electric power, it did not build the kind of sophisticated economy required by what is known as the communications age, with its reliance on computers and electronics.

The Soviet Union ceased to have an ideological appeal to any appreciable extent in noncommunist countries. At the Twenty-second Party Congress in 1961, Khrushchev had boasted that the Soviet

Union would overtake the United States by 1970 and would build a full communist society by 1980. No Soviet leaders were making similar claims in the 1980s. Noncommunist countries turned increasingly to the West as a model for economic development.

Soviet society experienced severe problems—alcoholism, pollution, and corruption. Alone among industrial countries, life expectancy in the Soviet Union actually declined in the 1970s and 1980s.

After the death of Brezhnev in 1983, Yuri Andropov came to power. Although he attempted to make some changes in the Soviet economy through a campaign against corruption, he died soon after he assumed leadership. An aging and ill Konstantin Chernenko succeeded him, but he, too, died soon after he took office. In March 1985, Mikhail Gorbachev became the Soviet leader. Fifty-four years old, he represented the younger political generation that came of age after Stalin died. His meetings with leading political figures in the West and his statements and actions symbolized vigor and change. British Prime Minister Margaret Thatcher, who had a reputation as an ardent anticommunist, was impressed with Gorbachev, as were other Western political leaders, academics, and journalists. *Time* magazine made Gorbachev "Man of the Year" for 1987, and public opinion polls in Western Europe indicated that he was more admired there than the president of the United States.

Gorbachev took a number of steps on the economic, cultural, political, and foreign policy fronts. The key concepts he promoted were *perestroika* (restructuring) and *glasnost* (openness). Although each term lacks a universally accepted definition, in general, ***perestroika*** was an effort to modernize the Soviet economy. ***Glasnost*** was an effort to make Soviet society less secretive and more open to differing and critical viewpoints.

Gorbachev acted to reform the economy. He sought to decentralize economic decision making. Cooperatives were encouraged, and economic viability was to become a key factor in determining whether a factory would continue in operation.

It was clear that capitalism, as such, was not being introduced into the Soviet economy. Soviet citizens still could not hire labor as a business firm does under capitalism. But a cooperative could be formed, and the cooperative's profits could be distributed to its members. Under "moonlighting" laws put into effect in spring 1987, any Soviet citizen could ask local authorities for permission to start a small business. In agriculture, collective farms now sold fruits, vegetables, and potatoes directly to the cities at prices that were between the state prices and higher prices in the free markets in the city, where the products of the private plots were sold. The Soviet government sought to encourage foreign investment in the Soviet Union through joint ventures in which the Soviet Union would have a 51 percent interest and the foreign holder 49 percent. Not permitted were wholly owned foreign plants.

Gorbachev sought to fight the corruption that had become a feature of Soviet society. He also launched a campaign against alcoholism and greatly increased the price of alcohol. Popular opposition to this program made the Soviet leader ease up on the campaign.

Through the policy of *glasnost*, Gorbachev signaled a change in the tolerance of the Soviet government to criticism of the regime. Newspapers carried stories about government wrongdoing. They even reported on the poor quality of medical care in the Soviet Union and on demonstrations and strikes, poverty and vagrancy, and drug abuse. Books that had been banned for decades were now printed, including works by Boris Pasternak, Mikhail Bulgakov, and Vladimir Nabokov. The arts—film, theater, and literature—were opened up to innovators whose works were either politically critical of the regime or were of a kind that Communist party officials had previously believed improper for the Soviet people because of their subject matter or avant garde character. The jamming of some foreign broadcasts was suspended. The government began to report accurate negative social trends. It admitted that maps of the cities of the Soviet Union had been deliberately distorted for reasons of security, thus confusing tourists and others who tried to use them.

In the realm of human rights, the Soviet Union released some prominent dissidents from prisons. Andrei Sakharov, a leading dissident who had been exiled to Gorky, was brought back to Moscow. The number of Jews allowed to emigrate from the Soviet Union increased.

Gorbachev took steps to change the formal governing system. He amalgamated the head of state and the general secretary of the Communist party into a single position. The person holding this office would now be elected for a specific term. Gorbachev sought and successfully enacted in 1988 the establishment of a new parliamentary body, a 2,250-member Congress of People's Deputies. It was scheduled to meet every year to select a smaller full-time legislature, the Supreme Soviet, and also a president, who would serve as the chief executive of the country. The Congress of People's Deputies was elected, with multiple candidacies, from unions and other functional groups, and also from geographical and ethnic constituencies.

Recovering from a quiescent foreign policy of aging Soviet leaders, the Soviet Union under Gorbachev took new initiatives. Gorbachev met with President Ronald Reagan in five summit meetings. Soviet troops, fighting in Afghanistan since 1979, were withdrawn. Gorbachev took steps to conclude arms control agreements with the United States. In 1987, he and Reagan signed the Intermediate-Range Nuclear

Forces (INF) Treaty to eliminate all U.S. and Soviet intermediate-range ballistic missiles. In July 1991, he and George Bush signed the Strategic Arms Reduction Treaty (START) that reduced the strategic nuclear arsenals of both superpowers. In September and October 1991, he and Bush each announced unilateral, parallel measures of massive reduction of short-range nuclear weapons and removed many of their nuclear weapons from alert status, on which they had been for most of the Cold War.

The Fall of Gorbachev and the Collapse of Communism. Despite the reforms Gorbachev instituted in the economy, political institutions, human rights, and foreign policy, he had difficulty juggling the demands of the conservatives (the Communist party, the secret police, the military, and the bureaucracy) with those of the reformers (intellectuals, nationalists, advocates of human rights, and the overwhelming majority of the Soviet people). He tried to maneuver between those who wanted to protect their privileges or maintain the *status quo* and those who yearned to move ever more rapidly into what would have amounted to a revolutionary transformation of the Soviet system and the death of communism. To some extent, Gorbachev was boxed in by political forces from both sides. But he was also constrained by his personal commitment to maintain much of the older system albeit in a modernized form.

Gorbachev had hoped to *reform* the Soviet system and not to destroy it. In 1990, he told a group of intellectuals: "I am not ashamed to say that I am a Communist and am devoted to the socialist idea. . . . My choice was made a long time ago, and it is a final one."[11] And in March 1991, he made a similar comment: "I am not ashamed to

say that I am a Communist and adhere to the Communist idea, and with this I will leave for the other world."[12]

A defining moment came for Gorbachev in 1989, when he rejected the idea of a direct presidential election and permitted himself to be nominated by a bloc of uncontested seats reserved for the Communist party in the Soviet legislature. This move was in sharp contrast to that of Boris Yeltsin, a Russian leader and adversary of Gorbachev, who broke with the party and became in 1991 the first popularly elected leader of Russia in one thousand years. Many analysts believe that in 1989 Gorbachev would have won a popular election had he chosen that electoral path. But as Yeltsin submitted himself to popular appeal and won, he had the moral authority and popular support that Gorbachev lacked.

Up to August 1991, Gorbachev resisted any move to abandon the party. He refused to back the Democratic Platform within the Communist party that tried to fight the entrenched party establishment. Only after a coup against him that month did he resign as general secretary, dissolve the Central Committee of the Communist party, and approve the suspension of Communist party activities throughout the country.

Unable to tear himself away from communism, Gorbachev was nonetheless willing to make great foreign policy and domestic changes. In foreign policy, he led the way not only in ending Soviet domination of Eastern Europe but in encouraging the forces that toppled Eastern Europe's communist governments as well. During his tenure in power, Soviet troops stationed abroad declined from 221,000 to an estimated 28,200. As mentioned above, the Soviet involvement in the war in Afghanistan (often described as the "Soviet Vietnam"

---

[11] Mikhail Gorbachev, quoted in Michael Dobbs, "Reformed Out of a Job," *Washington Post*, December 15, 1991, p. A34.

[12] Mikhail Gorbachev, quoted in Serge Schmemann, "The Soviet State, Born of a Dream, Dies," *New York Times*, December 26, 1991, p. A14.

because it had the same kind of demoralizing effect on the Soviet military that U.S. involvement in the Vietnam War had on the U.S. military) had come to an end. The governments of Eastern Europe were allowed to renounce communism without fear of Soviet military intervention.

The withdrawal from Afghanistan may have been the crucial first step in giving strength to forces for independence and social and economic change. Even before Gorbachev came to power, there had been movements for reform, with Solidarity in Poland being the most prominent example. Anti-Marxist groups emerged in nearly all the communist countries, although often they had to operate partly underground and partly on the fringes of official society. Among these groups were Democratic Forum in Hungary, New Forum in the German Democratic Republic, and Civic Forum in Czechoslovakia. Their goal was to unite people of different social and political positions, intellectuals, and others into a coalition that would bring down their totalitarian governments and create a society based on democratic principles.

The turning point for change came in 1989 and 1990, when the Soviets adopted what came to be known as the Sinatra Doctrine, named after the American singer, Frank Sinatra, who popularized a song called "My Way." Now the Soviet satellite countries were free to choose their future "their way"—that is, to pursue whatever political, social, and economic policies they favored so long as they did nothing to endanger the national interests of the Soviet Union.

Once the fear of Soviet intervention in Eastern Europe disappeared, an anticommunist wave rolled across the region. Gorbachev appeared to support the removal from power of veteran communist leaders, such as Erich Honecker in East Germany, Miloš Jakeš in Czechoslovakia, Todor Zhivkov in Bulgaria, and Nicolae Ceauşescu in Romania. He also endorsed Solidarity's assumption of power in Poland; accepted, if not encouraged, the collapse of the Berlin Wall; and favored free elections in Hungary, which led to the defeat of the communists.

Poland had already begun the process of transformation from communism to democracy. Peaceful protests brought an end to communism in Hungary and Czechoslovakia. And Soviet troops did not intercede to prevent a similar change in East Germany. When the Berlin Wall came tumbling down, thus bringing about the end to the division of Germany, the Soviets still did not intervene, nor did they object when East Germany was amalgamated with the former Federal Republic of Germany. Gorbachev even accepted the new Germany's decision to remain part of the North Atlantic Treaty Organization (NATO). Of the Eastern European countries, only the Romanian transformation was bloody. Street fighting by Ceauşescu partisans was fierce, but the Romanian military supported the revolution. The Romanian leader and his wife were captured and executed by firing squad.

To many who had known only the Cold War, this transformation of world politics was astonishing. Equally astonishing were the foreign policy developments outside of Europe. The Cold War had been a global confrontation. Both superpowers vied for influence in Africa, Asia, and Latin America. When one superpower supported a government in those areas, then the other superpower usually was opposed to that government. Each superpower gave military and economic assistance in part because of its assessment of how the aid would strengthen its global position with respect to the other.

But with Gorbachev's reforms came a settlement of these so-called regional disputes. Conflicts in Angola, Cambodia, Guatemala, and Nicaragua were resolved in part because the Soviet Union no longer had the will or the resources to prop up its allies. Moreover, the Soviet Union supported the efforts of the United States and its allies to fight a war against Iraq in 1991. And it joined the United States in cosponsoring a conference to bring peace to the Middle East between Israel and its neighbors.

Gorbachev's maneuvering in foreign policy was more successful that his dealings at home, where he was moving quickly but not quickly enough. The Soviet people experienced hard times during his leadership. When he left office in December 1991, after nearly seven years in power, the economic condition of the average Soviet citizen was worse off than when he arrived. And so, too, was the economic condition of the country. During Gorbachev's tenure as Soviet leader, the foreign debt quadrupled to $67 billion, gold reserves dropped by nearly 90 percent to 240 tons, oil production fell sharply and oil exports were cut by more than a half, and the official growth rate plummeted from +2.3 percent to −11 percent.[13]

The open criticism of communist leaders that could be made because of reforms Gorbachev instituted now worked against him. *Glasnost* produced greater freedom of speech not only to reform the communist system but to denounce it to the very core. The release of political prisoners and the expansion of human rights meant that ideas that had been suppressed for as much as seven decades were now exploding with the fury of an erupting volcano.

It has been well said that communism in the Soviet Union had prevented the development of a **civil society**—one in which people who have common interests participate in the political life of a polity to form groups and influence the political system. The ideology and practice of communism meant that there could be no accepted independent institutions of power, private or public. And so under communism, industrial groups were dominated by the Communist party, as were social, labor union, national, and ethnic groups.

Thanks to the freedoms instituted by Gorbachev, these groups were now forming in an independent manner and making their claims on society. Newly active religious groups sought religious freedom and the right to practice their faiths; national groups advocated either independence from the Soviet Union or greater autonomy; and economic groups made demands for free market options and less government interference in the economy.

Not least of Gorbachev's problems was trying to keep the fifteen republics of the Soviet Union together. The Baltic Republics of Estonia, Latvia, and Lithuania made the first attempts at independence. These republics had been independent countries between the world wars. In 1939 Stalin made them part of the Soviet Union. Other republics also asked for independence.

To allow for more autonomy, Gorbachev pushed for a federal system on the model of the U.S. federal system (see chapter 10). He was trying to win the support of the republics for a federal union when in August 1991, a coup attempt—made largely by military, party, and secret police leaders—sought to push him from power and restore the old guard to political leadership. Gorbachev was held captive in his summer home.

The coup failed because of the mismanagement of its leaders, the unwillingness of some military factions to support it, and the courageous opposition of Yeltsin and his supporters who rallied the opposition. In spite of the failure of the coup, Gorbachev's position declined rapidly. It was widely recognized that the coup plotters were all people whom Gorbachev himself had appointed, and this fact contributed to the erosion of his support.

One by one, the republics called for independence from the Soviet Union. On December 8, 1991, leaders of Russia, the Ukraine, and Byelorussia—representing 70 percent of the Soviet population and 80

[13] Dobbs, "Reformed Out of a Job," p. A34.

percent of its industrial output—met and announced the dissolution of the Soviet Union as a country. They established a Commonwealth of Independent States. Eight other republics soon joined the commonwealth. The Baltic republics were not among them, choosing instead to return to their independent status. The Republic of Georgia initially refused to join the Commonwealth, too, and soon became enmeshed in civil turmoil. Later, however, it became a commonwealth member.

The allocation of powers for the new confederation were yet to be worked out. The commonwealth lacked the centralizing powers of the federal union. The three founding members of the confederation agreed to devise a system for control of nuclear weapons in which all three would have to agree before a nuclear weapon could be launched. The status of the military remained unresolved, as did many other questions involving currency and trade. The Republic of Russia took over the offices previously held by Soviet leaders.

On December 25, 1991, the Soviet flag was lowered from the Kremlin and replaced by the old Russian flag of czarist days. After sixty-nine years, the Soviet Union had terminated its life as an independent state. Its dominance in Eastern Europe and its standing as a superpower were at an end, and the ideology that guided it and its advocates throughout the world was just about dead in the republics that once made up the Soviet Union.

Out of the ashes of communism, however, emerged countries and leaders committed to change. Traditional conflicts between ethnic groups that had been long suppressed under Soviet dominance had already come to the surface. Although the republics recognized that they had to cooperate to survive, the form that cooperation would take was still unknown.

As far as the rest of the world was concerned, communism was experiencing much the same fate as it had in the Soviet Union. African leaders who had been identified with communism, such as Col. Mengistu Haile-Mariam, had been deposed. The countries of Africa that had found the communist political and economic model attractive began to turn, albeit slowly and incompletely, to pluralism, political democracy, and a market economy. By early 1992, only four countries—China, Cuba, North Korea, and Vietnam—felt an affiliation with the ideology of Marxism-Leninism. China had suppressed, but not destroyed, a democratic movement in a bloodbath in 1989. Castro's Cuba was cut off from the support of its major benefactor, and its economy was languishing. To many observers, Castro's days in power seemed numbered. And North Korea and Vietnam showed some limited signs of moderating their communist policies.

ISSUES

Capitalism remains a strong force in the twentieth century. Socialism retains influence not only in the few remaining communist states but in both former East European communist states and states that were never under communist rule.

Two questions consider capitalism, socialism, and communism: (1) Is socialism better than capitalism? (2) Does the demise of communism mean that socialism is dead, too?

12/YES   IS SOCIALISM BETTER THAN CAPITALISM?

The fact that socialism in one form or another has been adopted in most countries of the world is an indication of its popularity compared to the tarnished image of capitalism. If we consider socialism as it is practiced in noncommunist countries, it is clear that socialism is superior to capitalism because it: (1) promotes equality, (2) serves public needs, (3) plans better, (4) respects individual freedom, and (5) strengthens democracy.

Equality.

No one who can honestly call [himself or herself] a socialist would not agree that equality is the value basic to any imaginable or feasible socialist society; nor that egalitarian behaviour and example is not a necessary part of building any road to socialism.[14]

These words of the political scientist Bernard Crick focus on the essential element in any analysis of society. In a world where material resources are available to improve the condition of humanity, there is no excuse for the wide gaps in income between the rich and the poor. These gaps are a natural consequence of capitalism.

Capitalism works for the wealthy. If, however, an individual has not been born wealthy, capitalism is not so great. Supporters of capitalism argue about equality of opportunity. Anyone with initiative can make it in a capitalist system, they contend. In theory, this may be so; but in practice, social conditions contribute to making the rich richer and the poor poorer.

Minority group members growing up in slums do not have equality of opportunity. They attend inferior public schools, where they learn little. In contrast, wealthy youngsters go to private schools and are taught by Ph.D.'s. Slum neighborhoods are unsafe because of crime, whereas wealthy neighborhoods are better protected against crime. Public hospitals do not provide the same quality of medical services as do private hospitals.

What does equality mean in such socially and economically disadvantaged circumstances?

[14]Bernard Crick, *Socialist Values and Times*, Fabian Tract 495 (London: Fabian Society, March 1984), p. 16.

How can the slum child show initiative? Initiative depends on self-respect, a quality of character difficult to achieve in a slum setting. Socialism, however, would strive to provide equal opportunity to everyone. Schools would be upgraded, and slums would be rebuilt. Socialized medicine would improve medical care for the poor and serve the interests of the masses rather than satisfy the aspirations of the rich and the bank accounts of the private doctors.

Public Needs.

Capitalism assumes that in a society in which everyone pursues his or her selfish interests, the public good will be served. In practice, however, society suffers from such a system. Everyone is encouraged to buy an automobile, for example, so the result is pollution, traffic jams, and billions of dollars spent on highways. Public transportation, consequently, is neglected. Public transportation is far more efficient than private transportation, but the emphasis on the private automobile has resulted in the public's transportation needs being poorly served.

Capitalists pursuing the highest profits engage in other harmful practices. Since cost-effectiveness is their most important consideration, they care little about environmental protection. Strip mining, for example, blights the beautiful countryside because the capitalist is more interested in making a fast buck than in protecting the environment. In pursuing profits, capitalists care not at all about the social consequences of their business decisions, such as unemployment or consumer injury.

Planning.

Although big corporations plan for their futures, capitalist systems do not promote coordinated planning that takes into account the global effects of business decisions. Scarce resources, consequently, are not managed properly, as the experience of the West in the energy crisis of the 1970s attests.

Lack of planning, too, has been responsible for the inconsistent pattern of economic development. Inflation, recession, depression, and unemployment are all features of a capitalist economy because there is no central plan to allocate the resources of a capitalist society in a rational manner. Why should people remain unemployed if they are willing to work? Yet capitalist economies experience high levels of unemployment.

Planning makes it easier to cope with the evils of social disruption caused by profit calculations. To a capitalist, business decisions are made on the basis of efficiency. To the people who work in a factory, however, the human consequences of these decisions are important. If capitalists decide to close down or move their companies, the lives and well-being of their workers, families, and communities will be adversely affected. Socialist planning would avoid such difficulties, as human costs are brought into the plan.

Freedom. Supporters of capitalism like to emphasize the freedom offered by the so-called free enterprise system. The fact is that the free enterprise system is a myth both because of what capitalism actually has become in our times and because the idea that individual consumers can exercise their free will to determine what is produced in the market—**consumer sovereignty**, as it is called—is inoperable.

Big corporations do not believe in free enterprise anyway. Price competition is not the central feature of the capitalist economy as it used to be. In practice, the big corporations use government to prevent competition from overseas suppliers through the imposition of tariffs or quotas on various products; engage in lucrative government contracts to produce munitions and to build roads, schools, and hospitals; and in general manipulate government regulatory agencies for their own benefit. Adam Smith would turn over in his grave if he knew the sins being committed in the name of a market economy.

Lee Iacocca is a case in point. As head of the Chrysler Corporation, he demonstrated keen business skills in turning his company from a big loser to a big winner in manufacturing and selling automobiles. A good deal of his talent is derived, however, from his ability to influence government. At a crucial moment in Chrysler's tough times, he was able to obtain a federally guaranteed loan for his corporation. He and his fellow capitalists along with the auto union exerted influence on the government that resulted in limiting the number of Japanese cars being imported into the United States, thus reducing competition.

The idea of free enterprise, then, is largely a myth in the actual operations of corporations.

The notion of consumer sovereignty is also a myth. In capitalist economies billions of dollars are spent on advertising every year. Consumers are fed large doses of propaganda calculated to make them feel that luxury products are really basic necessities. Instead of keeping a good old car, they are encouraged to buy the latest model from Detroit. Capitalists hawk their products through slick advertisements in television, radio, magazines, and newspapers. The effect of this media blitz is to coerce people into wanting products that they really do not need and that very often are harmful to them. Cigarettes may cause cancer, but the tobacco industry encourages smoking. Chocolate candy may damage teeth, but children are enticed to buy it. Consumers who are bombarded with so much propaganda soon become slaves to the advertisers and do not have the freedom of choice that capitalists say they have.[15]

Democracy. Capitalists often say that democracy requires a market economy. Indeed, some even argue that democracy cannot exist without capitalism. They base their case on consumer sovereignty and the experience of nations.

Voting in the marketplace is different from voting in the voting booth. The only way that consumers can exercise their ballots in the market is for them to *buy* ballots. As the socialist Henry Pachter observes, unless consumers are equipped with purchasing power, producers will be unable to satisfy their desires. "In other words," he notes, "this 'democracy' is based on unequal suffrage."[16]

Democracy, moreover, requires that people or elected representatives be allowed to make choices about important decisions. Business decisions, however, are often made in private—behind closed doors and beyond public scrutiny. If democracy means anything, it means open discussion of issues, not secrecy. Socialism, writes Andrew Levine, "for better or worse,

[15] See John Kenneth Galbraith, *The New Industrial State* (Boston: Houghton Mifflin, 1969), pp. 211–18, 272–73.

[16] Henry Pachter, "Three Economic Models: Capitalism, the Welfare State, and Socialism," in Henry Pachter, *Socialism in History: Essays by Henry Pachter*, ed. Stephen E. Bronner (New York: Columbia University Press, 1984), p. 19. The article was originally published in 1964.

eliminates systemic restrictions upon the scope of public choice."[17]

If capitalism and democracy go hand in hand, we would expect to see democracy flourishing only where capitalism thrives. Such is not the case. Although the Nazi government directed the German economy for military purposes from the early 1930s to the end of World War II, capitalism was able to exist and produce profits.

[17] Andrew Levine, *Arguing for Socialism: Theoretical Considerations*, rev. ed. (London: Verso, 1988), p. 134.

Capitalism in the past existed in other fascist countries, such as Italy, Spain, Portugal, and Greece. Today, capitalists flourish in some of the prominent dictatorships. It is true that socialism does exist in communist dictatorships, but it exists in various forms in vigorously democratic societies, such as Sweden and Holland. Capitalism and democracy do not go hand in hand.

We can see, then, that socialism serves the public good. Its advantages in promoting equality, serving public needs, planning efficiently, respecting freedom, and strengthening democracy are overwhelming.

12/NO   IS SOCIALISM BETTER THAN CAPITALISM?

Capitalism is the least romantic conception of a public order that the human mind has ever conceived. It does not celebrate extraordinary heroism in combat, extraordinary sanctity in one's religious life, extraordinary talent in the arts; in short, there is no "transcendental" dimension that is given official recognition and sanction.[18]

These words of the political philosopher Irving Kristol, a supporter of capitalism, help to explain the unpopularity of that economic system. It is a pity that capitalism has such a bad press especially when its extraordinary accomplishments and the dismal failure of socialism are considered. The issues of equality, public needs, planning, individual freedom, and democracy must be reviewed in order to see the benefits that capitalism gives to a free society.

Equality. Capitalism works for most people who are willing to show initiative and industry. Arguments about poor people in capitalist systems are deceptive. Capitalism has revered equality of opportunity. Under capitalism, millions of people have moved up the economic ladder, rising from poverty to affluence; it is not a case of the rich getting richer and the poor getting poorer.

The slums are a case in point. Immigrants coming to the United States lived in slums. Many rose to positions of eminence in business, the

[18] Irving Kristol, *Two Cheers for Capitalism* (New York: Basic Books, 1978), p. x.

arts, and the professions. Many groups that experienced discrimination, moreover, have achieved prosperity. A rising black middle class is a recent example.

To be sure, there is unemployment in capitalist economies, but some of that unemployment is caused by socialist policies in which government pays people not to work. Even if this point is excluded, however, one cannot judge an entire system by its few failures. There is much that we just do not know about poverty, and any system—capitalist or socialist—would find some of the unemployment problems to be intractable.[19]

Although capitalism does not revere equality, it has been responsible for increasing the standard of living for overwhelming numbers of people it encompasses. The average worker's standard of living in most capitalist economies is high. Under capitalism even people classified as poor often have automobiles, washing machines, and television sets. Henry Ford did not become wealthy building cars for a few wealthy people but by providing good, inexpensive automobiles to the masses. The riches produced by capitalism benefit all classes in the sense that a rising tide lifts all boats.

Furthermore, there is no evidence to indicate that socialist economies are more egalitarian. Wage disparities in socialist economies are

[19] See Edward C. Banfield, *The Unheavenly City Revisited: A Revision of "The Unheavenly City"* (Boston: Little, Brown, 1974).

great. Some observers contend that these disparities are even greater under socialism than under capitalism. The only difference is that the economic benefits go to the elite of government employees rather than to the capitalists.

Public Needs. Capitalism serves public needs better than does socialism. Here, too, it is essential to note that capitalism is not perfect. Capitalists do many harmful things, such as damaging the environment by strip mining and polluting the atmosphere. Laws, however, have been enacted to cope with these evils. It is not necessary to accept socialism as a solution. Pollution exists in socialist countries, too, as often the government does not want to allocate resources away from more short-term productive needs.

Socialists enjoy emphasizing public over private transportation in their war against the automobile. The masses of people, however, prefer the automobile to public transportation. Commuters, for example, will put up with the discomfort of traffic jams and high costs of garages and automobile insurance for the convenience of having a means of transportation that will take them directly between home and work. They enjoy listening to the news on the car radio, chatting with a few friends sharing the ride, and relaxing in an air-conditioned or heated setting. In some urban areas, moreover, people have found there is more physical safety—protection against criminal assault—in the private automobile than in public transport's subways, buses, and stations.[20]

Planning. Socialist planning has been a great failure. In theory and practice, capitalism never professed that its institutions would guarantee that there would be no waste of resources. All it contended was that if capitalist planning was poor, the company responsible for the plan would suffer financially and eventually go out of business.

Under socialism, government does the planning, but government is not very good at it. Government planners do not have the business experience necessary to make good plans. Government, moreover, does not have to abide by a profit-and-loss statement, as does private industry. Socialist economies are notoriously inefficient with their plans.

Socialism, moreover, pretends to solve the problems of unemployment, recession, and depression; but it generally fails. Economic crises do appear in socialist countries. Countries ruled by socialists have at times experienced unemployment, inflation, and high interest rates in part brought on by the enactment of socialist programs.

Freedom. The history of capitalism and the history of freedom are intertwined. The notion of the private company making decisions apart from the state is a central feature of a pluralist democracy. Under socialism, it is easier to put all the institutions of society under government control and, consequently, destroy human freedom.

Consumers, moreover, are free to choose what they wish, whether to buy or sell, or whether to work for a big corporation or change jobs. The ordinary person is not so easily brainwashed. Corporations cannot brainwash consumers if they are not willing to respond to advertising messages. Advertising campaigns have often failed to convince people of the excellence of a product. The ordinary person is not stupid and knows better what is in his or her interest than does some state bureaucrat. Freedom requires that the individual choose, and not the state.

It is strange that socialists believe that ordinary people are so easily manipulated by shrewd advertising campaigns of a capitalist economy. If, in fact, people are so easily duped by product advertising, then is it not reasonable to assume that they are as easily duped by political advertising for this or that candidate and party? What, then, does the advantage of democratic socialism offer to the consumer?

Democracy. A capitalist economy strengthens democratic rule. In the words of Michael Novak, "Political democracy is compatible in practice only with a market economy."[21] When people, rather than government, decide how to use their financial resources, they are, in fact, exercising their ballot and are getting from the market exactly what they voted for. When government, through its use of taxation, spends people's money, people are not getting what they vote for.

[20] See B. Bruce-Briggs, *The War against the Automobile* (New York: Dutton, 1975).

[21] Michael Novak, *The Spirit of Democratic Capitalism* (New York: Simon and Schuster, 1982), p. 14.

In a general sense, it is true that voters cast a ballot for a candidate or a party in a democracy. In complex societies, however, the voter casts a ballot for a "package"—that is to say, for a candidate and party espousing views on many issues. The market, in contrast, allows individuals to zero in on exactly what they want and so strengthens democracy.

We can see, then, that capitalism, for all its faults, is worth retaining. Socialism produces consequences detrimental to society.

13/YES   DOES THE DEMISE OF COMMUNISM MEAN THAT SOCIALISM IS DEAD, TOO?

On Christmas Day, 1991, the flag of the Soviet Union was lowered forever from the Kremlin. The leading communist country had lost its identity as an independent state. The contempt of the people who had endured seven decades of communist misrule produced dramatic scenes of hostility, such as the removal of the icons of Lenin and his cohorts and the repudiation of communism through electoral contests and public demonstrations.

The failure of communism in the Soviet Union and in Eastern Europe was also a failure of socialism. We need not look only at the experience of the communist world to observe the failure of socialism. Noncommunist countries—whether they followed the Soviet or some other model of socialism—demonstrated that both socialism and communism are at a dead end. In contrast, capitalism has once again proven its superiority as a system.

Socialism has failed because: (1) the communist variant of socialism has been discredited; (2) noncommunist countries are abandoning it; and (3) capitalism remains the only system capable of improving the standard of living for the masses of people.

Communism Has Failed. The failure of communism is now obvious. By the beginning of 1992, only a few communist countries remained, and their days seemed numbered. The advocates of communism in Western societies are moving like a plane that has lost its guidance mechanism. The few communist parties throughout the world are weak, and some of them have even abandoned the principles of Marx and Lenin.

Despite these astonishing developments, some apologists for socialism have said that while communism has failed, socialism has not. What is often forgotten in such an assessment, however, is that since 1917, the Soviet Union was seen by many socialists as being the leading socialist state. They pointed to the many achievements of the Soviet Union: its construction of hydroelectric plants and steel mills, its seeming ability to wipe out unemployment and provide each citizen with basic social security for health and old age as well as the other benefits of the welfare state, and its heroic role in fighting Hitler's Germany in World War II.

Some of these same socialists even denied the atrocities committed by Stalin in the name of the lofty communist ideal based on community rather than selfishness. Others simply ignored these atrocities while attacking Stalin's critics as "red baiters." And some socialists did not deny the wrongdoing of Stalin, but they attributed the evils not to communism the system but to Stalin the man, who somehow took an idealistic socialist system and subverted it for his own sinister purposes.

Even after Stalin was dead, many socialists pointed to the Soviet experience as a model Third World countries should follow in their path to economic development. They contended that the transformation of a society from agrarian to industrial was always accompanied by hardship. The early capitalist era in the West also produced dismal conditions for peasants and workers. In sum, economic development was always going to be difficult, but at least the Soviet Union had shown that communism could convert an agrarian society into an industrial power.

What was ignored, however, was that so many of the policies of the Soviet Union under Stalin had nothing to do with economic development. True, the Soviets could point to mighty industrial achievements, such as hydroelectric plants and steel mills. But the establishment of the *gulag*—the Soviet prisons and forced labor camps—that claimed the lives of millions and the loss of life that accompanied the collectivization of agriculture actually inhibited economic development. It was not until years after Stalin's death that there was a general recognition that communism was an inefficient system, one that could not begin to satisfy the needs of the people it was supposed to serve.

Also ignored in the comparisons of capitalism to communism on the road to economic development was the role of political democracy in capitalist societies. People in democracies could protest the evils of capitalism and help to bring about its reform. Such was not the case under communism.

For many socialists, then, communism, for all its faults, was an achievement for socialism. Since these socialists took this position, they should at least now recognize that not only communism has failed but so, too, has socialism.

Noncommunist Countries. One need not look only at the experience of communist countries to see that socialism has failed. Socialism has had a similar outcome in noncommunist countries. After World War II, Great Britain adopted many socialist practices, including the nationalizing of some key industries and the expansion of the welfare state. But the inefficiencies of those industries generated a decline in productivity. When Margaret Thatcher came to power as prime minister, she began to reverse the role of government in society.

Thatcher in Great Britain and Ronald Reagan in the United States became leaders in opposition to socialism with its principal tenet that government is a force for good that can be used to stimulate economic growth and improve the quality of life for its people. Both adopted programs of **privatization**—the transferring of activities from government to the private sector. Among other measures, Great Britain sold shares of British Steel and British Airways to private owners. Thatcher and Reagan sought, moreover, to reduce government involvement in the economy by eliminating some government regulations and cutting funds for regulatory agencies. Some states and localities in the United States sold off their airports and replaced government employees with private firms for running fire and sanitation departments and even prisons.

We can see the wide condemnation of socialism by looking not only at Great Britain and the United States but at other countries as well. In 1990, twenty-five governments in every inhabited continent sold $25 billion worth of state-owned enterprises, bringing the total for the three-year period 1988–90 to $90 billion.[22] Among the items sold were banks, insurance companies, power plants, fertilizer factories, and petrochemical complexes. Also among the items sold or in the process of being sold were twenty-five national telephone systems, more than ten state-owned airlines, and government-owned newspapers. Among the more notable sales were Indian Airlines, Quantas Airlines (Australia), huge shares of the telephone systems of Argentina and Mexico, Pakistan's textile mills and cement plants, and more than a dozen of Turkey's largest industrial concerns.[23]

This worldwide phenomenon of privatization can be seen as a rejection of socialism, with the bloated bureaucracy and undisciplined work force that accompany socialist enterprises. Indeed, the movement toward privatization is recognition that a key element of capitalism—namely, competition—is far more efficient than state-run enterprises and superior in enhancing economic growth.

What is particularly noteworthy is the retreat from socialism in Africa. Upon achieving independence from European colonial powers in the 1950s and 1960s, many governments adopted leftist principles not only in economic management but in politics as well. Julius Nyerere of Tanzania embraced a form of peasant socialism, *ujamaa*, which sought the greatest happiness for the greatest number. But socialist principles left the economies of Tanzania and other countries applying similar models in a shambles. Many are now welcoming investment and allowing for a free market, which will certainly improve the conditions that socialism has created.

Capitalism Triumphant. The failure of socialism throughout the world has directed our attention to the superiority of capitalism. The most prosperous societies are those that have allowed the private sector to flourish with minimum government interference. The impressive gains of economies of countries along the Pacific Basin—most notably Japan, the Republic of Korea,

---

[22] The figures are compiled by Privatization International, a London-based newsletter that tracks the issue, cited by Stuart Auerbach, "Around the Globe, the Sale of a Century," *Washington Post*, November 17, 1991, p. H1.

[23] Ibid., p. H1.

and Singapore—can be attributed in large part to the market economy in those countries.

Capitalism has won. The complex adjustments and incentives of a modern society require a capitalist economy. As the world moves toward the twenty-first century, it rejects socialism of the past for capitalism of the future. Adam Smith was right that the market economy is the best way to secure prosperity for all people. And the world is moving in that direction. There is, indeed, truth to the quip heard about either communism or socialism these days—that it is the longest and most painful road from capitalism to capitalism.

13/NO   DOES THE DEMISE OF COMMUNISM MEAN THAT SOCIALISM IS DEAD, TOO?

The fact that communism has failed is clear. But the collapse of communism in 1991 no more means the end of socialism than the collapse of the free market in the Great Depression that began in 1929 and continued well into the 1930s meant the end of capitalism. Socialism has not failed. It will endure because: (1) socialists are pleased that communism has failed since many, if not most, socialists opposed communism; (2) socialism in noncommunist countries can provide both sound economic development and social justice; and (3) while socialism has its difficulties, capitalism creates problems that cannot be solved by the rhetoric of free enterprise.

Socialism and Communism. It is inaccurate to see socialism and communism as part of the same phenomenon. The biggest enemies of the communists were the socialists. Even in the years before V. I. Lenin's coming to power in 1917, the social democrats were opposed to the theory of communism. And when the communists came to power, social democrats continued their opposition.

Although many governments in Western Europe after World War II were socialist, they supported the establishment of NATO, which was a barrier to Soviet expansion, and they opposed their own home-grown communist parties. While recognizing the need for government intervention in the economy and the welfare state, they did not declare war on capitalism, and they certainly did not engage in the authoritarian practices that were common in communist countries.

Instead, social democracies allowed for democratic processes, such as elections and popular participation in government. They were able to build their economies and at the same time offer their citizens a measure of social justice and economic equality that were lacking in capitalist countries.

As the economist Philip Hanson observes, the social democratic version of socialism is based upon the ideals of equality, social justice, respect for the individual, and wider choice and access to the decision-making processes that govern the life of a community. The communist version of socialism opposes these ideals.[24]

Hanson adds that the communist connection with socialism is twofold: First, communists use the state as a form of social engineering. Socialists do that, too. But communists—unlike socialists—do it without regard to society. Second, Communists use the language of socialism entirely devoid of its content as a means of legitimizing power at home and abroad.[25]

Socialism and communism are at odds, then. And it is wrong to see them as part of the same phenomenon.

Socialism, Economic Development, and Social Justice. While socialists have favored government involvement in the economy and a welfare state, they have not been hostile to market forces. Even in Sweden, which is regarded by many as the premier socialist state, the economy has remained in private hands. In fact, 85 percent of Swedish industry is privately owned, making that economy the least socialized in Western Europe.[26] Since World War II, socialists have controlled the Swedish government most of the time. But they never sought to eliminate

[24] Philip Hanson, "Is There a 'Third Way' between Capitalism and Socialism?" *Report on the USSR* 3 (August 30, 1991): 3.

[25] Ibid., p. 3.

[26] Joanne Barkan, "Sweden: Not Yet Paradise, But . . . ," *Dissent* 36 (Spring 1989): 147.

the private sector in the economy and establish a command economy. And, of course, they never took the horrific steps of communism in destroying democracy, suppressing opposition parties, and filling prisons with political prisoners.

If Sweden is a stellar example of what socialism can achieve in terms of a high standard of living for its people, it is useful to note how its management of the economy differs from that of the command economies of communist countries. Sweden has a wage policy based on centralized bargaining to achieve equal pay for equivalent work nationwide. Businesses that are unproductive are allowed to fail. The prospect of failure means that efficiency is enhanced. Tax incentives direct profits into reinvestment, increasing productivity and creating jobs.[27] Thus Sweden demonstrates that socialism can produce sound, strong economies.

Sweden also demonstrates the achievements of socialism in other areas. There are few crimes of violence and no slums. Impressively, the country offers extraordinary social benefits, such as health insurance, housing subsidies, education, child allowances, sickness pay, workmen's compensation, disability pensions, government-paid parental leave, and day care subsidies.[28]

It is true that these social services require high taxes. Marginal tax rates are 80 percent for people with moderately high incomes, and there is a 25 percent sales tax. But Swedish socialists have been willing to adjust to demands for change without abandoning their commitment to social justice. They have stopped defending every social welfare benefit and government program. They have agreed to allow more freedom of choice within the public sector. And they no longer object to the privatization of local government services.[29]

Sweden is a model socialist state, but it does not stand alone. Even those countries that have rejected socialist economies have accepted the socialist principle that government has a responsibility to provide for the basic security of its people and some role in the managing of the economy.

Even Ronald Reagan and Margaret Thatcher could not dismantle the welfare state. Nor, for that matter, could they reduce government spending. Both reduced the *rate* of government

growth but not its expansion. Reagan could get applause when he spoke about the evils of government, but he would have gone down to defeat if he tried to end social programs that had political support, such as social security and workers' compensation.

Today a majority of the American people are dissatisfied with the system of health care. The costs of health care insurance are high and millions of Americans have no health insurance. Many look to government to provide the solution.

In every advanced industrial society in the world—whether capitalist or socialist—government is regarded as having a role in providing basic security for the well-being of its citizens. This basic security is not military only but extends to health, education, housing and jobs. Even where economic systems are *laissez-faire*, a failure of *laissez-faire* often results in government intervention and the adoption of socialist measures.

Capitalism and Its Problems. While socialism has its problems, capitalism has bigger problems. Primarily, it is chaotic. It has indeed provided material goods to the masses of people who have lived under its system to an unprecedented degree, as Karl Marx noted more than a century ago. But it has not been able to solve the problems of the business cycle and unemployment, nor can it solve social problems.

In theory, capitalism never promised to provide equal benefits to everyone. Its tenets assert that society in general will be better off through a system of private enterprise. But there will always be periods of boom and bust. When people lose their jobs and are forced to remain unemployed for long periods, under capitalism, they have to cope on their own.

In addition to problems of boom and bust, capitalism produces environmental problems. Under capitalism profits come first; there is no incentive for protecting the environment. It is much cheaper for a manufacturer of chemicals to dump waste matter than to build special incinerators to handle pollutants. It is much easier for a manufacturer of plastics to produce foams by old formulas than to shift to biodegradables. And so they do—and leave the mess for someone else to clean up.

Moreover, as even Adam Smith observed, capitalists like to leave little to chance. When they run into trouble—and even when they don't—they try to use government for their own selfish ends. The savings and loan crisis in the

[27] Ibid., p. 147.

[28] Steven Kelman, "Sweden Sour?" *New Republic* 205 (July 29, 1991): 20.

[29] Ibid., p. 22.

United States, in which billions of dollars were siphoned off by dishonest bankers and financiers, is but one example. Taxpayers had to pay the bill for the excesses of business people and their political apologists. The stock market manipulations and illegal insider trading that enriched scoundrels, such as Michael Milken and Ivan Boesky, illustrate that a strong government hand is needed to protect ordinary citizens from being ripped off by capitalists who have special access to money and power.

As capitalist behavior with respect to the environment and finance indicate, the system creates problems for the public at large. Government is the only means not only for solving the problems but, even better, for controlling capitalist behavior in the first place.

Many of socialism's criticisms of capitalism are correct. As the political scientist Robert Dahl notes: "Capitalism is persistently at odds with values of equity, fairness, political equality among all citizens, and democracy." Where socialists went wrong, Dahl adds, was their belief that the cure for the evils of capitalism "could best be solved by abolishing markets, competition among economic enterprises, and the seeming 'anarchy' of the price system" as well as by transferring the ownership and control of the economy to the public or society as represented by the state.[30]

Fortunately, socialism remains a vibrant force in the world. For all its benefits, capitalism left to its own devices causes serious injury to a society that only socialism can cure.

[30] Robert Dahl, "Social Reality and Free Markets," *Dissent* 37 (Spring 1990): 226.

KEY TERMS

Antithesis
Bolsheviks
Bourgeoisie
Capitalism
Cartels
Civil society
Class struggle
Classless society
Collectivization
Comintern
Command economy
Commune
Communism
Communist International
Consumer sovereignty
Contradictions
Democratic centralism
Democratic socialism
De-Stalinization
Détente
Dialectic
Dictatorship of the proletariat
Feudalism
Free enterprise
Glasnost
Historical materialism
Imperialism
Industrial revolution
Labor theory of value

Laissez-faire
Lumpenproletariat
Market economy
Marxism
Marxism-Leninism
Mercantilism
New Economic Policy
Peaceful coexistence
Peasants
Perestroika
Private enterprise
Privatization
Proletariat
Revisionists
Scientific socialism
Social democracy
Socialism
"Socialism in one country"
Stalinism
Substructure
Superstructure
Surplus value
Synthesis
Thesis
Third International
Third World
Utopian socialists
Utopias

QUESTIONS

Capitalism, Socialism, and Communism

1. What would be the consequences to American society if the United States adopted a free market economy in the manner of Adam Smith's prescription?
2. Which system—capitalism or socialism—is better suited to solve the problems of Third World countries? What are the reasons for your answer?
3. Which system—capitalism or socialism—produces greater (a) economic development and (b) equality? Why?
4. Take one policy area, such as civil rights, national health, or defense spending, and determine if the Marxist analysis is valid in explaining the developments in that policy area.
5. In view of the changing character of capitalism from the eighteenth to the twentieth centuries, are Adam Smith's prescriptions meaningful?
6. How would you evaluate whether Marxism is democratic?

7. Is Leninism a variation of Marxism, or is it something different? What are the reasons for your answer?
8. What is the relationship between capitalism and democracy?
9. What is the relationship between socialism and democracy?

The Gorbachev Era and the Demise of Communism

1. What would have happened to the Soviet Union if Mikhail Gorbachev had retained the policies of his predecessors and did not introduce *glasnost* and *perestroika*?
2. What could Gorbachev have done to prevent the breakup of the Soviet Union?
3. Was the fate of communism inherent in the flaws of the ideology? What are the reasons for your answer?
4. Under what conditions could communism reemerge as a powerful force in the the republics that made up the Soviet Union?
5. How could a person like Gorbachev emerge in a communist system?

RECOMMENDED READINGS

Capitalism, Socialism, and Communism

ARBLASTER, ANTHONY. "The Death of Socialism—Again." *Political Quarterly* 62 (January/March 1991): 45–51. An argument that the death of communism does not mean the end of socialism.

AUERBACH, STUART. "Around the Globe, the Sale of a Century." *Washington Post*, November 17, 1991, pp. H1, H9. A description of privatization developments throughout the world.

BARKAN, JOANNE. "Sweden: Not Yet Paradise, But . . . ." *Dissent* 36 (Spring 1989): 147–51. A positive view of the Swedish political and social system.

BERGER, PETER J. *The Capitalist Revolution: Fifty Propositions about Prosperity, Equality, and Liberty.* New York: Basic Books, 1986. An analysis of capitalism.

BERNSTEIN, EDUARD. *Evolutionary Socialism: A Criticism and Affirmation*, trans. Edith C. Harvey. New York: Schocken Books, 1961. A major social democratic work. First published in 1899.

CONQUEST, ROBERT. *The Great Terror: A Reassessment.* New York: Oxford University Press, 1990. Originally published in 1973, this book is an indictment of Stalinist terror during the 1930s.

CRICK, BERNARD. *Socialism.* Minneapolis: University of Minnesota Press, 1987. A short account of the subject.

CUNNINGHAM, FRANK. *Democratic Theory and Socialism.* Cambridge, England: Cambridge University Press, 1987. An inquiry into the reconciliation of socialism and democracy.

DYE, THOMAS R., and HARMON ZIEGLER "Socialism and Equality in Cross-National Perspective." *PS: Political Science and Politics* 31 (Winter 1988): 45–56. An argument based on cross-national research that economic equality depends on a country's level of economic development rather than on the nature of the economic system.

FISCHER, LOUIS. *The Life of Lenin.* New York: Harper and Row, 1964. A standard biography.

FRIEDMAN, MILTON, and ROSE FRIEDMAN. *Free to Choose: A Personal Statement.* New York: Harcourt Brace Jovanovich, 1990. A case for the market economy.

GAY, PETER.*The Dilemma of Democratic Socialism: Eduard Bernstein's Challenge to Marx.* New York: Collier Books, 1962. An evaluation of Bernstein's revisionism.

GILDER, GEORGE. *Wealth and Poverty.* New York: Basic Books, 1981. A defense of capitalism.

GOULD, BRYAN. *A Future for Socialism.* London: Jonathan Cape, 1989. A British view that socialism has a bright future.

HAYEK, FRIEDRICH. *The Road to Serfdom.* Chicago: University of Chicago Press, 1944. A critique of government planning as a form of dictatorship.

HEILBRONER, ROBERT. "The Triumph of Capitalism." *New Yorker* 64 (January 23, 1989): 98–109. An argument that capitalism has proved superior to socialism but that its future is in doubt.

KELMAN, STEVEN. "Sweden Sour?" *New Republic* 205 (July 29, 1991): 19–23. The Swedish economic model with commitments to social services still works.

LEVINE, ANDREW. *Arguing for Socialism: Theoretical Considerations.* Rev. ed. London: Verso, 1988. An investigation of the theoretical standards that should be used in assessing socialism and capitalism.

McCLELLAND, DAVID, ed. *Marxism: Essential Writings.* New York:; Oxford University Press, 1988. A selection of Marxist writings.

McCORD, WILLIAM. *The Springtime of Freedom: The Evolution of Developing Societies.* New York: Oxford University Press, 1965. An argument that dictatorship inhibits economic development.

MARMOR, THEODORE R., JERRY L. MARSHAW, and PHILIP L. HARVEY. *America's Misunderstood Welfare State: Persistent Myths, Enduring Realities.* New York: Basic Books, 1990. A defense of American social welfare programs.

NOVAK, MICHAEL. *The Spirit of Democratic Capitalism.* New York: Simon and Schuster, 1982. A defense of a system characterized by a democratic polity, a market economy, and cultural pluralism.

POLLIN, ROBERT, and ALEXANDER COCKBURN. "The World, the Free Market and the Left." *Nation* 252 (February 25, 1991): 224–32, 234–36. An argument that socialism is more just than capitalism.

PRYBYLA, JAN S. "Why, Where, What, and How." *Problems of Communism* 40 (January/April 1991): 1–17. An argument that the market system is the only viable alternative to the Soviet style of socialism.

SKOUSEN, MARK. "Just Because Socialism Has Lost Does Not Mean That Capitalism Has Won" [an interview with Robert L. Heilbroner]. *Forbes* 147 (May 27, 1991): 130, 132–33, 135. An assessment of capitalism and socialism.

STERN, GEOFFREY. *The Rise and Decline of International Communism.* Brookfield, Vt.: Gower Publishing, 1990. An overview.

TILTON, TIM. *The Political Theory of Swedish Social Democracy: Through the Welfare State to Socialism.* Oxford, England: Clarendon Press, 1990. A study of the Swedish Social Democratic party's vision of society.

The Gorbachev Era and the Demise of Communism

BIALER, SEWERYN. "The Death of Soviet Communism." *Foreign Affairs* 70 (Winter 1991–92): 166–81. An assessment of the reasons for the end of communism in the Soviet Union.

BRZEZINSKI, ZBIGNIEW. *The Grand Failure: The Birth and Death of Communism in the Twentieth Century.* New York: Charles Scribner's Sons, 1989. An assessment that communism has been a failure.

DOBBS, MICHAEL. "Reformed Out of a Job." *Washington Post*, December 15, 1991, pp. A1, A34. An assessment of the Gorbachev era.

GOLDMAN, MARSHALL L. *What Went Wrong with Perestroika.* New York: W. W. Norton, 1992. An economic and political autopsy of *perestroika.*

GWERTZMAN, BERNARD, and MICHAEL T. KAUFMAN, eds. *The Collapse of Communism.* New York: Times Books, 1990. A collection of articles by *New York Times* correspondents covering developments in the communist world in 1988 and 1989.

SCHMEMANN, SERGE. "The Soviet State, Born of a Dream, Dies." *New York Times,* December 26, 1991, pp. A1, A14, A15. A study of the rise and fall of communism in the Soviet Union.

TEDSTROM, JOHN. "Gorbachev the Economist." *Report on the USSR* 3 (August 30, 1991): 10–12. An assessment of Gorbachev's economic policies.

WREN, CHRISTOPHER S. *The End of the Line: The Failure of Communism in the Soviet Union and China.* New York: Simon and Schuster, 1990. A veteran *New York Times* correspondent describes life in the Soviet Union and China in the 1970s and 1980s.

STATE AND CITIZEN

The politics of a society is shaped by the character of the people who reside within the political community. The attitudes and opinions that people hold influence the decisions that government makes. Part IV deals with the relationships between how citizens think and act and the behavior of the state.

Communities vary in terms of their attitude toward government authority, their willingness to accept change, and their respect for their fellow citizens. Chapter 6 examines the ways in which attitudes and opinions are formed.

How citizens behave politically depends in part upon the freedoms that they posses. In some societies individuals and groups are free to articulate their demands to government in an open manner.

In other societies, however, government forbids or severely restricts the amount of political freedom available to individuals and groups. Chapter 7 discusses the rights of citizens against the state.

In most contemporary political systems, political parties and elections are prominent features. The role and nature of these parties vary, as does the amount of freedom that individuals have in electoral activities. Chapter 8 deals with these matters.

An instrument for articulating demands of people is the political interest group. Political interest groups engage in diverse activities. The degree of autonomy they possess, moreover, differs among political systems. Chapter 9 describes these groups and their role in politics.

chapter 6

Political culture, political socialization, and public opinion

As Western countries prepared to grant independence to their African and Asian colonies in the 1950s, many supporters of national independence anticipated that the establishment of Western-type institutions, such as parliaments and federal systems, would result in governments that would be both stable and democratic. Within several years, however, the new institutions proved to be short-lived in many countries and were replaced by governments dominated by military or one-party rule. As military coups and civil wars became frequent phenomena, it became apparent that neither stable government nor democratic systems would be assured by the implantation of Western institutions in the non-Western world. If political stability and democracy were to be achieved, so many chastened commentators now asserted, attention would have to be directed to the sociological and psychological factors that contribute to popular supports for those objectives rather than to formal political institutions.

The attention to the underlying sociological and psychological aspects of a system is not a new development in political science. Since the 1930s, political scientists have been deeply involved in studying not only the mechanics of government institutions but also the patterns of behavior of individuals and groups in different political systems. Such a perspective was essential for analyzing some of the important political phenomena of our times, such as why there are differences among and within political systems in adapting to economic and social change, in participating in civic affairs, in exercising the right to vote, in embarking on militaristic adventures abroad, and in transferring political loyalties from one leader to another.

To understand matters such as these, political scientists have been concerned with the formation of political attitudes by elites and the mass public. Central to this concern are the subjects of political culture, political socialization, and public opinion.

POLITICAL CULTURE

The term *culture* has been defined as a core of traditional ideas, practices, and technology shared by a people (see Chapter 2). **Political culture**, as defined by the political scientists Gabriel A. Almond and G. Bingham Powell, Jr., "is the pattern of individual attitudes and orientations toward politics among the members of a political system."[1] The political culture of a society can be measured through public opinion and attitude surveys.

Political culture varies among political systems. In some political systems, for example, active participation in the political life of the community, such as in voting and in joining private associations established to influence government activity, is regarded as a legitimate and worthy objective. In many traditional societies, however, the masses of people do not play an active role in political life.

Even among countries that are properly called democratic, considerable differences may exist in political culture. In France, for example, the political culture has been marked by sharp ideological differences among its people, whereas Great Britain is characterized by a broad consensus of attitudes about government.

Although variations in political culture often mark different states, they may also appear within a single political system. Ethnic, racial, and generational groups may develop their unique features and are, consequently, labeled **subcultures**. In the 1960s and 1970s, for example, much attention was directed to the attitudes of young people in the United States. Specifically, the term **youth culture** was used to distinguish attitudes, values, and way of life that separate young people from the rest of American society.

[1] Gabriel A. Almond and G. Bingham Powell, Jr., *Comparative Politics: A Developmental Approach* (Boston: Little, Brown, 1966), p. 50.

The orientations that exist in a political culture influence the way a political system works. Social scientists have become particularly concerned with the relationships between orientations and such matters as nation building, political participation, law and order, and trust in government.

Nationalism has been a paramount force in the past two centuries (see Chapter 2). Nation building generally requires the transferring of loyalties from regional and parochial units to national ones. The new states of Africa and Asia have been particularly troubled in building a national consciousness from widely disparate ethnic groups.

A political culture that encourages the development of a passive and submissive population is unlikely to produce a political system in which people participate actively in government affairs. Religious traditions that emphasize fatalism may produce a political culture in which people accept almost any kind of government. In contrast, a cultural norm that reveres participation and control over one's destiny encourages active popular participation in political affairs.

Respect for law and order is another cultural norm that has an impact on political life. In a political system like Great Britain's, respect for law and order has evolved over a period of centuries. In other political systems, such as that in Bolivia, widespread disrespect for law and order has made political stability hard to achieve.

A culture that encourages individual trust among people influences the character of a political system. If, for example, a culture produces elites who develop attitudes of tolerance toward each other, the peaceful transfer of power from one group to another may be easier to accomplish than in a culture distinguished by elite distrust. Both the United States and Great Britain have developed elites that trust each other, while many Latin American countries have not.

POLITICAL SOCIALIZATION

Each society seeks to transmit its culture to its members. The process of doing so is known as **socialization**. In the legal profession, for example, young attorneys are taught how to speak before judges and deal with other attorneys. In education the young student is taught about the proper relationship between students and teachers. In many societies, as feminists point out, women are socialized to a life devoted to family rather than to professional pursuits or to *both* family and professional pursuits.

Political socialization refers to the method in which a culture transmits its political culture to its members. Political socialization is the process of learning about political life, and it is the way in which political cultures are maintained and changed. In this regard people learn to respect or not to respect political authority, to participate or not to participate in political activity, to tolerate or not to tolerate dissenting opinion, and to obey or to defy the law. The study of political socialization is important because it shows how a citizen acquires knowledge, attitudes, beliefs, and opinions about the political system. Such a study, moreover, reveals the way in which individuals not only perceive the political world but also behave politically.

Although the term *political socialization* was first used in 1959,[2] interest in how people acquire political attitudes has ancient roots. One of the earliest philosophers to deal with this subject was Plato, whose *Republic* described how education was to be used to train an elite to rule. In modern political systems, moreover, much attention is given to transmitting the community's knowledge and norms of political behavior. Both democracies and dictatorships share an interest in influencing the political attitudes of their people toward the mechanics and objectives of their respective political systems, although modern totalitarian dictatorships rely more upon indoctrination than do democratic systems.

Students of political socialization are concerned primarily about the types of political learning, the means by which political learning is achieved, and the objectives of political learning.

Types of Political Learning

Three types of political learning are distinguished: cognitive socialization, affective socialization, and evaluative socialization. **Cognitive socialization** refers to how knowledge of the basic structures and rules of politics is acquired. How, for example, does an American become aware of the president, the Congress, and the Supreme Court? **Affective socialization** is the process in which an individual develops feelings of approval or rejection of a political leader, government unit, or political system. The way in which an individual's disposition toward the president, the police, or the bureaucracy is developed, is illustrative of affective socialization. **Evaluative socialization** refers to the process through which one acquires the judgments and opinions about the political system on the basis of some moral criteria. An assessment of how an individual decides government policy should be concerned with national health problems is an example of evaluative socialization.[3] Cognitive socialization supplies the rudimentary underpinnings of popular support, but affective and evaluative socialization tell more about the attitudes of a community toward its political system.

[2] Herbert H. Hyman, *Political Socialization: A Study in the Psychology of Political Behavior* (Glencoe, Ill.: Free Press, 1959).

[3] For a discussion, see Almond and Powell, *Comparative Politics*, pp. 50–51.

Agents of Socialization

The means by which an individual gains knowledge of the political culture are known as the **agents of socialization**. These agents include the family, peer groups, the schools, social groups, and the mass media.

Family. Political socialization begins before adolescence. In most societies the family exerts a major influence on the child. In their study of the political beliefs of children in Chicago, the social scientists Robert D. Hess and David Easton observed that preadolescent children learn to love and identify with the government, and especially with the president, even before they know what the government does.[4] As children reach adolescence, they become more aware of other elements of government. Studies of children's attitudes toward government in other countries, however, indicate that children often do not show affection for the chief executives.[5]

The crucial point in the child's social, psychological, and political development is the period between nine and thirteen years.[6] Cognitive and affective orientations are influenced by the family during this period. Many studies of political behavior reveal, moreover, that the identification an individual has with a political party is heavily influenced by parental attitudes toward parties.

The persistence of political attitudes and beliefs from childhood to adulthood is a subject of controversy among social scientists. Some scholars say that political events and communication by the mass media play an important role in modifying attitudes and beliefs. If this is so, then experiences in adult years may alter people's established political attitudes and beliefs.[7]

Peer Groups. **Peer groups** are face-to-face groups of which an individual is a member. Peer groups include friends, classmates, immediate colleagues at work, and fellow churchgoers. Peer groups may serve to support family attitudes in those cases in which the peer groups are similar in attitudes to the family. Peer groups may, however, socialize individuals away from family values in those instances in which there are considerable differences in socioeconomic orientation. In his study of the attitudes of Bennington College students, the psychologist Theodore M. Newcomb discovered, for example, that students reared in conservative backgrounds tended to become much more liberal because of peer group influences at Bennington College[8]

Schools. In modern societies formal education is an important component of political socialization. Every country uses schools to inculcate the basic values and rules of its political system. Patriotic symbols, such as the flag and national anthem, are glorified in the school years. The political scientists Gabriel A. Almond and Sidney Verba note, moreover, that their five-nation study (United States, Great Britain, Mexico, Germany, and Italy) revealed that

---

[4] Robert D. Hess and David Easton, "The Child's Changing Image of the President," *Public Opinion Quarterly* 24 (Winter 1960): 632–44.

[5] David O. Sears, "Political Socialization," in *Micropolitical Theory*, ed. Fred I. Greenstein and Nelson W. Polsby, vol. 2 of *Handbook of Political Science* (Reading, Mass.: Addison-Wesley, 1975), pp. 99–100.

[6] Fred I. Greenstein, *Children and Politics*, rev. ed. (New Haven: Yale University Press, 1969), p. 1.

[7] For a discussion of persistence in political socialization, see David O. Sears, "Whither Political Socialization Research? The Question of Persistence," in *Political Socialization, Citizenship, Education, and Democracy*, ed. Orit Ichilov (New York: Teachers College Press, 1990), p. 69–97.

[8] See Theodore M. Newcomb, "Persistence and Regression of Changed Attitudes: Long-Range Studies," in *Socialization to Politics*, ed. Jack Dennis (New York: John Wiley, 1973), pp. 413–24.

education was an important factor in political participation and knowledge about government.[9]

Education has always been regarded as important for its influence. In the United States, for example, concern with the subject matter taught in schools has sparked controversy in many communities. In her study of public school textbooks in American history, Frances Fitzgerald notes that each generation has attempted to revise American history in its textbook treatment of the past.[10] And so, during the Progressive period of American history, textbooks reflected the dominant Progressive themes of social reform. Today, groups of varying interests—religious, feminist, racial, libertarian—peruse the textbooks that are under consideration by state educational agencies responsible for selecting textbooks to make certain that the books do not contain what they consider objectionable material.

Social Groups. Political attitudes are much influenced by the associations people make through their trade unions and the professional, religious, and social organizations to which they belong. A union member's voting behavior often shows the influence of union membership on voting, for example.

Mass Media. The **mass media** are printed and electronic forms of communication. Printed sources are primarily newspapers, and electronic media include radio and television. People are influenced by the information they receive. In dictatorships the mass media are controlled by government, which attempts to restrict the factual information reaching the public. In democracies freedom of information is re-

[9] Gabriel A. Almond and Sidney Verba, *The Civic Culture: Political Attitudes and Democracy in Five Nations*, new ed. (Newbury Park, Calif.: Sage Publications, 1989), pp. 317–18. This study was first published in 1963.

[10] Frances Fitzgerald, *America Revised: History Schoolbooks in the Twentieth Century* (Boston: Little, Brown, 1979).

garded as a prerequisite of a free society. Even in democracies, however, some information is restricted because of considerations of national security, morality, and health.

Television, particularly, has become the most prominent media form, as each individual in advanced industrial societies spends on the average several hours a day before the television screen. Even in developing countries television has become an influence in promoting political viewpoints and inculcating patriotic ideals.

PUBLIC OPINION

To some early theoreticians of representative democracy, the voice of public opinion was seen as expressed through democratically elected representatives. The argument was put forward that elected officials actually represent the views of their constituents. In the twentieth century public opinion has been closely examined by political scientists, sociologists, and journalists, and the model of how representative democracy works has had to adjust to the empirical data about public opinion.

When the journalist Walter Lippmann wrote *Public Opinion* in 1922, he became one of the first to portray the ordinary American citizen as ignorant of the major issues of public policy. Other scholars have noted similar findings, not only in the United States but in nearly every other country. One of the most significant findings about public opinion is that the masses of people are ill informed about major political issues. At the height of the Vietnam War, for example, more than 25 percent of the American people could not even identify the North Vietnamese leader Ho Chi Minh in spite of the daily news coverage of the war.

Social scientists are not in agreement about the knowledge ordinary citizens possess about political issues. Although there is a consensus that the masses of people are not well informed, some scholars assert that the amount of political ignorance has been exaggerated. In their view more people in advanced industrial societies are better informed about politics than ever before. They attribute the greater awareness to the expansion of the mass media—particularly television—which increases access to political information; a higher level of education; and political awareness brought on by a larger role that government plays in society.[11]

Revelations of mass ignorance of issues has led to readaptations of democratic theory to take the new data into account (see Chapter 3). Public opinion is still considered to be an important factor in influencing what government does, but now distinctions are made about the different kinds of publics included in public opinion. Studies dealing with systems that are undemocratic, moreover, indicate that public opinion is an important feature in those systems, too.[12]

To better understand public opinion, it is essential to provide a definition, indicate its significant features, show how it is measured, and describe its influence on the behavior of government. Social scientists hold varying opinions about these features, however, although much is now known about them.

Definition

Distinctions are sometimes made among attitudes, beliefs, and opinions. **Attitudes** are dispositions about ideas, policies, and people. **Beliefs** are fundamental commitments, such as religious or philosophical convictions. **Opinions** are attitudes about specific matters. We shall use the term *public opinion* to include attitudes and beliefs, however, since it is often difficult to make hard and fast distinctions.

People have opinions about all kinds of subjects, including political candidates, public policy, movie stars, and baseball teams. **Public opinion**, however, is the attitudes and beliefs that people hold about matters of public concern. Such a definition ordinarily excludes attitudes about movie stars or baseball teams, unless those subjects have become politicized. When an actress such as Jane Fonda organizes antinuclear rallies, for example, then public opinion may involve attitudes about movie stars.

Elected officials and group leaders are concerned with what the people are thinking. In democracies, elected officials normally wish to be reelected, and gauging public opinion accurately is essential for reelection. If the officials endorse policies that do not have popular support, they may find themselves defeated on election day. Group leaders must organize coalitions, and a knowledge of public opinion allows them to more effectively prepare a campaign to broaden their support.

Even dictatorships are concerned with public opinion, although totalitarian dictatorships often ruthlessly squelch dissent through repressive acts, such as liquidation, imprisonment, or torture. Even totalitarian dictatorships must respond to public opinion in some ways, however, less they topple from lack of popular support.

Features

In describing the features of public opinion it is essential to make two distinctions. Quite simply, one distinction refers to public, and the other to opinion.

In early writings about public opinion, a number of commentators described public

---

[11]Russell J. Dalton, *Citizen Politics in Western Democracies: Public Opinion and Political Parties in the United States, Great Britain, West Germany, and France* (Chatham, N.J.: Chatham House Publishers, 1988), chap. 2.

[12]See e.g., Alex Inkeles, *Public Opinion in Soviet Russia: A Study of Mass Persuasion* (Cambridge, Mass.: Harvard University Press, 1958).

opinion as if it were of a single mind. For example, statements were made that the American people were against involvement in a foreign war. More recently, however, distinctions have been made between the mass public and the attentive public. According to the political scientist Gabriel A. Almond, the **mass public** consists of most ordinary citizens who have little information about issues but who react in a rather generalized manner to political stimuli. The mass public constitutes the bulk of the population. Public opinion polls have demonstrated that large numbers of people cannot even identify the names of their legislators, let alone understand the intricacies of issues.

The **attentive public** consists of those individuals who are concerned with public issues and makes up only about 15 percent of the population. The number of people who constitute the attentive public can vary, and individuals previously not concerned about issues can become vitally involved in political matters. In other words, members of the mass public may become members of the attentive public if some issue galvanizes their attention. Many U.S. citizens, for example, were not concerned about Saddam Hussein and Iraq. In fact, many could not even identify Saddam as the leader of Iraq, nor could they locate the country on a map. But when Saddam's armed forces conquered Kuwait in 1990 and U.S. regular and reserve forces were deployed in Saudi Arabia in preparation for war, the heretofore uninformed citizens could never get enough information about the Iraqi leader and the thorny issues of Middle East peace and security.

Some students of public opinion have noted that the mass public often gets its cues from the attentive public in order to form opinions. Such a process is known as the **two-step flow of communication**. The masses of people get their opinion from the group leaders with whom they identify. The media reach these group leaders, who make their interpersonal influence felt on their followers by filtering the information to them.[13] When individuals find support among different group leaders, their opinions become reinforced. When their group leaders differ, the individuals are often subject to *cross-pressures* (political ideas that conflict) that often lead them to avoid expressing an opinion or becoming involved over some issues of public concern (see Chapter 3).

Criticism has been made of the two-step flow theory. Studies have shown that those people who engage in political discussion tend to discuss political issues with people who have equivalent levels of information and knowledge. Evidence does not support the view that there is a flow of information from the top down to the less politically informed. The politically informed follow the media and talk with other politically informed people. Those who are not politically sophisticated neither watch the news nor talk about politics.[14]

The distinction among publics, then, has provided useful insights into public opinion. Other features of public opinion, however, focus on opinions rather than publics. Opinions are studied to determine direction, intensity, and stability.

In determining **direction**, public opinion analysts are concerned with whether an individual is for or against a policy or candidate. A simple Yes or No answer can determine direction. A percentage of approval can be compiled about such matters as: "Is the president doing a good job?" "Should the government adopt a national health insurance program?" "If an election were held today involving Candidate A and Candidate B, would you vote for Candidate A?"

[13.] See Elihu Katz and Paul F. Lazarsfeld, *Personal Influence: The Part Played by People in the Flow of Mass Communications* (Glencoe, Ill: Free Press, 1955).

[14.] W. Russell Neuman, *The Paradox of Mass Politics: Knowledge and Public Opinion in the American Electorate* (Cambridge, Mass.: Harvard University Press, 1986), p. 147.

A simple Yes or No answer does not, however, provide enough information about public opinion. Analysts have, consequently, designed scales of measurement to determine political opinions more precisely. Through such a scale, for example, opinion may be distinguished among those who support different kinds of programs, such as a comprehensive national health plan, a limited national health plan, and a national health plan designed to insure only for catastrophic illnesses.

Direction, however, is not a sufficient measure of public opinion, since the percentage of respondents favoring one or the other position leaves many aspects of opinion still unknown. How strongly people hold their views—that is, the **intensity** of their opinion—is important. Asked by a pollster whether he or she is for or against nuclear energy, a respondent may have little or no interest in the subject. If the respondents have strong feelings, then they are more likely to participate in political affairs for the purpose of influencing political action.

Opinions may be intensely held at various times, but public opinion analysts are also concerned with the **stability** of opinions. Are the opinions held over a long period of time? Sometimes during presidential primary contests, for example, public opinion can fluctuate rapidly, and candidates fade from public prominence as rapidly as falling pop stars lose their staying power on the disc charts.

Measurement

The method used to measure public opinion is the public opinion poll. The idea of a poll is to take a sample of the total population to be investigated (or **universe**, as it is called) for the purpose of determining what that universe is thinking. Often, the actual number of people constituting the sample is quite small. In public opinion polls about presidential preferences, for example, about 1,200 people are polled from a universe consisting of more than 100 million people. A margin of error of 2 or 3 percentage points is estimated, based on the size of the sample.

Sampling technique is essential for accuracy. The **probability sample** is used in which each person in the targeted population has an equal chance of being selected. There are different forms of probability sampling. A **simple random sample** takes the entire universe and selects samples such as drawing names out of a hat or numbers out of a computer. A **systematic sample** uses a random procedure to choose the *first* respondent but a skip interval to select the remaining respondents. In this latter form the random sample determines, say, that the fiftieth person is selected from a list, and then every fiftieth person from the remaining list would be chosen. A **stratified sample** breaks down the universe into classifications, such as region, race, or religion, in the same proportion as they exist in the universe, and then respondents from those classifications are selected.[15]

In addition to making certain that the sample is scientifically drawn, pollsters must solve other problems. They must phrase the question in an unbiased manner and must interpret the responses correctly. The pollster Burns W. Roper observes, "The major source of survey error stems from question wording. The smallest error comes from the most often cited source of error, sampling error."[16]

Critics of public opinion polls have questioned both the technical aspects of poll taking and the uses to which polls are put. The technical criticisms include the size of the sample, the way in which questions are phrased, the subjectivity or professionalism of the interviewer, and the validity of the response of the interviewee.

[15] For a discussion, see Jerry L. Yeric and John R. Todd, *Public Opinion: The Visible Politics*, 2d ed. (Itasca, Ill.: F. E. Peacock, 1989), chap. 3.

[16] Burns W. Roper, "Are Polls Accurate?" *Annals of the American Academy of Political and Social Sciences* 472 (March 1984): 34.

Critics argue that it is impossible to measure the opinions of millions by sampling only 1,200 people. Pollsters argue, however, that the size of the sample is sufficiently large so that, within a margin of error of a few percentage points, an accurate measure of the opinion may be recorded.

Critics argue that the way in which a question is phrased can alter the results of a poll. When a *New York Times*/CBS News poll asked people if they favored an amendment "prohibiting abortions," a majority opposed it. But when asked whether they favored an amendment "protecting the life of the unborn child," some 20 percent of them switched sides.[17]

Critics of polls question the subjectivity and professionalism of the interviewer. Although interviewers are trained to be unbiased, they do not always follow the appropriate guidelines. In some cases, pollsters may rush respondents because of pressures to meet an unspecified quota.

Pollsters defend the scientific quality of their profession. Interviewers trained in polling, or in **survey research** as it is sometimes called, can make certain that the questions are not biased and that their own personal opinions do not affect the outcome of the poll. But pollster critics are not convinced that polling is a science.

Some people who are interviewed respond to questions on subjects about which they know little or nothing simply because they do not wish to reveal their ignorance to a pollster. One group of researchers conducted a poll in Cincinnati and found that 33 percent of the respondents expressed an opinion on the 1975 Public Affairs Act. This law, however, was fictitious, having been "invented" solely for the survey.[18]

Technical questions aside, some of the

most pointed criticisms against polling have been directed toward the political uses to which polls are put. Polling results can become part of the political campaign issues, as candidates search for any issue that will strengthen their support.

Polls are also publicized by candidates to show that they can win, or that they are gaining, or that their opponent is slipping. Moreover, "private" polls, conducted by a candidate's paid pollster can be leaked to the press if they reveal good news. Such uses of polls bring the accuracy of polls generally into question.

Polls can have an influence on the way people vote. During primaries, some people vote for their second choice because the polls indicate that a vote for the first choice would be wasted. There is evidence, moreover, that the early release of **exit polls** (polls conducted of people as they leave the voting booth) may discourage people who have not yet voted from voting because they think the outcome of the election has already been decided. In recent presidential elections, lower turnouts on the West Coast have been blamed on East Coast exit polls. That lower turnout is believed to have influenced the outcome of a number of electoral contests for Congress and for state and local offices.

Influence on Government

As indicated above, public opinion is important in both democracies and dictatorships. In democracies public opinion can be freely expressed. Political leaders who act against public opinion face defeat at the ballot box. Dictatorships that ignore public opinion or attempt to suppress it through terror may discover that their base of support has eroded. They may, however, be cunning enough to make accommodations to some segments of opinion in the community. Joseph Stalin and Adolf Hitler manipulated public opinion by creating scapegoats and fostering a climate of fear.

Although it is difficult to show empirically how public opinion influences govern-

[17] Brock Brower, "The Power of Polls," *Reader's Digest* 133 (July 1988): 53.

[18] George F. Bishop, Robert W. Oldendick, Alfred J. Tuchfarber, and Stephen E. Bennett, "Pseudo-Opinions on Public Affairs," *Public Opinion Quarterly* 44 (Summer 1980): 198–209.

ment behavior in democracies, accounts of tenure by political leaders after they have left public office reveal how greatly they were guided by public opinion. Some political leaders submit readily to every changing whim. Because public opinion is volatile and unstable, some political leaders in democracies attempt to lead public opinion in the hope that they can bring about a change in popular attitudes. Still other political leaders move fearlessly against public opinion when they feel that it is wrong. John F. Kennedy's *Profiles in Courage* (1956), describes political leaders who defied public opinion on matters of conscience.

The attention that political leaders give to polling in democratic societies indicates that the link between opinion and political action is strong. The toppling of dictators throughout the world suggests, too, that those who ignore or neglect popular support risk the loss of power. Political leaders decide for themselves whether to move with or against public opinion. In democratic governments statesmanship requires both a willingness to lead on the basis of objective needs and a responsiveness to opinion. Polls cannot, however, tell a leader what to do.

ISSUE

Since the invention of the printing press, the mass media have had an important influence by informing people about political ideas and events. At first, newspapers and magazines were the principal means of disseminating information to the masses of people. In the twentieth century, however, the electronic instruments of communication have become the dominant media forms. Television particularly, more than radio, newspapers, or magazines, presents news and shapes public opinion in a unique way, and controversy surrounds its effect on attitudes.

14/YES DOES TV NEWS HAVE A UNIQUE IMPACT ON PUBLIC OPINION?

The uniqueness of television derives from three factors: (1) the major political events of the past few decades have been television events; (2) television has intrinsic features that no other channel of communication can duplicate; and (3) the American people have come to depend on television for their news more than on any other of the media.

Politics as Television Events. If events are to have political significance, people must know about them. Since television appeared as a major media form in the 1950s, it has become deeply involved in covering political stories as part of the daily national news broadcasts. To a large extent, television determines what millions of people think of as news. Political campaigns, government wrongdoing, protest movements, civil unrest, acts of war and violence, and diplo-

matic events have become prominent features of the evening TV news in the past few decades.

The reporters decide which candidates to cover and have even made obscure political figures into major national personalities. Moreover, they make political life difficult for a candidate by asking embarrassing questions or revealing information depicting the candidate in a derogatory manner.

TV reporters decide when and how to report the work of government officials. The animosity between TV journalists and Richard Nixon, for example, helped project the Nixon administration's wrongdoing into national prominence. Watergate became a matter of heightened national concern in part because of the daily TV attention given to the illegal acts of Nixon and some of his associates.

Protest movements, too, are made nationally

known through TV coverage. Many activities of the civil rights movement in the 1960s, for example, were television events. TV reporters vividly displayed the intimidation and violence endured by supporters of racial integration. The confrontations in Birmingham and Selma are cases in point. Martin Luther King, Jr., came to be recognized as a national civil rights figure in large part because of TV news coverage.

Civil unrest in the form of urban riots in northern cities in the 1960s was also vividly depicted on the television screen. The riots in Newark and Detroit, for example, became fixed in the minds of millions of viewers as they were taking place. In fact, TV coverage of riots seemed to trigger riots in other cities.

Television is, moreover, particularly graphic in showing acts of war and violence. The Vietnam War was reported on television in a way no earlier wars could be covered by other media forms. The video films of the fighting in that seemingly interminable war helped to shape public opinion about the war.

Acts of terrorism, moreover—whether they are conducted in the United States or abroad—influence the attitudes of people about terrorists and the ability of government to deal with them. In fact, some terrorists use television as a way of getting their messages across to large audiences. A notable example occurred in 1985 with the hijacking of a TWA jetliner to Beirut. In that case, interviews with the hijackers were broadcast, unedited, on TV network news stations in an effort to influence U.S. public opinion.

Foreign political leaders are aware of how they can manipulate the American media in general and television in particular. They have granted interviews only to friendly reporters and forced unfriendly journalists to leave the country. Ze'ev Chafets, an Israeli journalist, even contends that the lives of Western journalists are threatened if the reporters give unfavorable accounts of the Palestine Liberation Organization. In his view Israel gets a bad press in the United States precisely because Israel is a democratic society that allows journalists to report freely.[19] The political scientist Guenter Lewy comments along somewhat similar lines about unbalanced coverage of the Vietnam War:

The Viet Cong were notoriously uncooperative in allowing cameramen to shoot pictures of the disemboweling of village chiefs and other acts of terror, while scenes of South Vietnamese brutality, such as the mistreatment of prisoners, were often seen on American television screens.

Lewy concludes that such reporting biased the coverage of the war against the American side.[20]

Aware of the lessons of Vietnam, the Bush administration was determined to avoid negative reporting of its military operations in the Persian Gulf war of 1991. It denied the reporters access to soldiers unless a press officer was in attendance. Unlike the practice during the Vietnam War, when reporters could move about Vietnam freely, coverage of the Persian Gulf war was constrained by the establishment of *press pools*— groups of selected journalists who were supposed to cover stories for all the journalists in the area and abide by the restrictions of the U.S. government or its allies. With the exception of Cable News Network (CNN) correspondents— most notably Peter Arnett, who was allowed access in Iraq by Iraqi officials—the Pentagon controlled most of the information coming out of the war, at least for most of the time that military operations were being conducted.

The U.S. military gave twice-daily briefings with a pro-U.S. slant on the war. It provided compelling pictures of "smart bombs" hitting targets with extraordinary precision. With the exception of some TV pictures from Iraq revealing civilian casualties, most of the pictures were favorable to the United States and its allies. It is no wonder, then, that President Bush's approval rating in public opinion polls zoomed to unprecedented heights. It was only *after* the war that stories appeared about the American soldiers who died from "friendly fire," the failures of U.S. military intelligence, the bombing of Iraqi targets that had no or little direct military value, and the large number of bombs that had fallen wide of their targets.[21]

---

[19] Ze'ev Chafets, *Double Vision: How the Press Distorts America's View of the Middle East* (New York: Morrow, 1985).

[20] Guenter Lewy, *False Consciousness: An Essay on Mystification* (New Brunswick, N.J.: Transaction Books, 1982), p. 104.

[21] For a description of the criticisms of media coverage of the war, see Howard Kurtz, "News Media Ask Freer Hand in Future Conflicts," *Washington Post*, July 1, 1991, p. A4; Edwin A. Diamond, "Who Won the Media War?" *New York* 24 (March 18, 1991): 26–29.

Diplomacy, too, has become a television event. Summit conferences of leading international figures are now more devoted to public appearances than to private negotiations. The summit meetings between Soviet leader Mikhail Gorbachev and U.S. President Ronald Reagan were "photo opportunities" in which television played a prominent role.

The events of the past decades, then, cannot easily be distinguished from television's reporting of them. The opinions that people formed of politics were shaped by the medium of television.

Intrinsic Features of TV. Some commentators note that American TV journalists are more liberal than the public they serve and that they use television to project their biases onto the public. It is not essential to establish the political attitudes of TV journalists, however, to show that television news is a distortion of reality and influences public opinion. TV journalists, like judges, may, however, restrain their own personal biases because of a commitment to a professional ethic.

What makes television news biased are the characteristics of that medium. Television news has some unique features that distinguish it from other channels of communication, most notably newspapers. These features include a heavy emphasis on pictures, greater attention to interpretation of the news, and an unusually large and captive audience.

Although newspapers pioneered in using pictures to illustrate news stories, television news is much more dependent upon film. A television reporter who sat in front of a camera and just read the news would soon lose the interest of an audience. Television's attraction is that it shows vivid pictures of events as they are unfolding, such as an urban rioter looting a store, an American hostage held captive by terrorists, or civilians wounded by military bombardment. In this respect two students of TV contend that it is television's "insatiable appetite for action, indeed for gross action" that may set it apart from the other media.[22] Television thrives on instant and visual attractions in ways that other media forms cannot duplicate, however much they try.

Almost as important as the reliance of television on action is its ability to recreate that action by multiple showings of the same footage. Some striking examples of this repetition were the destruction of the Challenger spacecraft in 1986 and the beating by Los Angeles police of Rodney King, a criminal suspect, in 1991. The dramatic pictures of the beating led to calls for investigations of police brutality not only in Los Angeles but in other cities, as well.

In addition to its reliance on film, television news depends heavily on the journalist to interpret events. Newspaper reporters are trained to leave themselves out of a story and, consequently, to let the facts speak for themselves. Because television relies so heavily on the visual picture and because each TV news story must be compressed into a time span measured in seconds, TV journalists become part of the story. It is they who interpret the pictures that are displayed on the television screen. Television journalists, consequently, often become popular celebrities. It is not surprising that CBS News TV anchorman Walter Cronkite was long regarded as one of the most trustworthy Americans in the polls—a status he continued to hold years after he retired.

In describing the news, TV news personalities often create a vision of the United States that is designed to attract the attention of viewers. According to the political scientist Michael J. Robinson, television journalism in the United States in the late 1960s and early 1970s promoted images of distrust in the effectiveness of government and a feeling of malaise about the American political system. This vision influenced public opinion and voting behavior, Robinson contends. Were there no television news, he argues, there would have been less political malaise in American public opinion.[23]

Finally, the character of the audience for TV news is different. Not only is it larger (as we shall see below), but it is often inadvertent as well. Studies of newspaper readers show that most people who buy newspapers do not do so primarily to read the political news of the day. Instead, they may be interested in sports, theater schedules, or department store sales. They select the information they wish to read. In television news programs, however, the viewers

[22] Gary L. Wamsley and Richard A. Pride, "Television Network News: Re-Thinking the Iceberg Problem," *Western Political Quarterly* 25 (September 1972): 439.

[23] Michael J. Robinson, "Public Affairs Television and the Growth of Political Malaise: The Case of 'The Selling of the Pentagon,' " *American Political Science Review* 70 (June 1976): 409–32.

interested in one aspect of the news must sit and watch an entire news program. They cannot be selective about what they see. They may want to see a triumph of their favorite football team, but they have to sit through stories about foreign affairs and domestic politics. In that way, they learn more news on television than they do with other media forms.

Before the age of television, many people obtained their information about political matters from intermediary agencies, such as family, friends, group associates, or political parties. Television has displaced these agencies to a significant degree. What is significant here is that people who ordinarily are unconcerned about political matters are exposed to politics through television, and this development has an impact on the political behavior of the masses of people, as we shall see below.[24]

Dependency on TV for News. Studies of the media reveal that in the United States most people depend more upon television for their political information than on any other media form. This dependency marks an important change in the kinds of information about politics that people receive. In the United States most newspapers have been regional, and people have been likely to read the newspapers of their region. Television news, however, is predominantly national, although there are local and regional news broadcasts, too. These local and regional news programs, however, have smaller audiences. Thus, the same evening news on the networks is seen by people across the country. People who used to rely on newspapers and the radio for their information—with the heavy emphasis on local and regional news—now become concerned with issues of national scope that they would have ignored in the pretelevision past.

Children, in particular, are affected by television. The political scientist Austin Ranney notes that from the time children begin watching television (at the age of three months) until the time they finish high school, they "have spent less than 12,000 hours in front of a teacher and more than 22,000 hours in front of a television set."[25]

The political significance of a national audience that includes millions of inadvertent viewers is that attitudes of millions of people will be heavily influenced by this media form. Their political attitudes toward such matters as the effectiveness of political institutions to deal with social problems, the integrity and honesty of government leaders, and the wisdom of political choices will be interpreted in ways determined by TV journalists. Since so much emphasis is placed on interpretation of the news, then, TV news has come to play an extraordinary role in shaping public opinion.

Critics of television news often direct their attacks on the way newscasters express their opinions even through the kind of political issues they choose to highlight. Selection of issues is often subjective. By featuring topics such as the risks of nuclear energy, the plight of the homeless, and the danger of drug addiction, newscasters play a prominent—and often *the* most prominent—role in **agenda setting**—that is, the selection of topics that the general public thinks important. As the political scientist Bernard Cohen notes, "The mass media may not be successful much of the time in telling people what to think, but the media are stunningly successful in telling their audience what to think about."[26]

The political scientists Shanto Iyengar and Donald R. Kinder studied the effect of television on public opinion and concluded that television news powerfully influences which problems viewers regard as the nation's most serious. They write, "Rising prices, unemployment, energy shortages, arms control—all these (and more) become high priority political issues for the public only if they become high priority news items for the networks." These scholars believe, moreover, that the agenda-setting function of television is particularly strong in shaping the judgments of citizens with limited political resources and skills, while those who are partisans, activists, and close observers of the political scene are less likely to be influenced in this manner.[27]

Iyengar and Kinder also note that television

[24]Ibid., p. 426.

[25]Austin Ranney, *Channels of Power: The Impact of Television in American Politics* (New York: Basic Books, 1983), p. 4.

[26]Bernard Cohen, *The Press and Foreign Policy* (Princeton, N.J.: Princeton University Press, 1963), p. 16.

[27]Shanto Iyengar and Donald R. Kinder, *News That Matters: Television and American Opinion* (Chicago: University of Chicago Press, 1987), pp. 4, 60.

news has an effect they call **priming**—the changing of standards that people use to make political evaluations. If television news becomes preoccupied with nuclear annihilation, then many people will judge the president in terms of what he has done to make nuclear war less likely. According to their studies, priming affects the

politically involved as effectively as it does the politically withdrawn.[28]

All of these factors have contributed to making television a unique media form in the United States.

[28] Ibid., pp. 63, 95.

14/NO DOES TV NEWS HAVE A UNIQUE IMPACT ON PUBLIC OPINION?

Television has been blamed for many of the great evils that have fallen on society. Arguments have been put forward that television is responsible for encouraging violent crime, contributing to the decline of reading skills by the nation's youth, and weakening family ties. It is perhaps only a faint remembrance that some early enthusiasts saw television as a means of educating the masses. The ordinary person who might not have time to read the newspaper, so it was asserted, would certainly be able to become informed about political matters through watching fifteen or thirty minutes of TV news each day.

The hope that television news could create an enlightened citizenry has given way to the feeling that the masses of people are misinformed, misguided, and heavily influenced by television reporters. We argue that such an assessment of TV news is not accurate and shall deal with the points raised by the *Affirmative*.

Politics as Television Events. It is certainly true that the major political events of the past few decades, such as political campaigns, protest movements, civil unrest, acts of war and violence, and diplomatic events, have been television events. The fact that television has recorded these events, however, does not mean that they would not have occurred if television had not been invented.

Partisan conflict for political power has long been a prominent feature of democratic politics in the United States. Candidates for public office in the nineteenth century sought campaign success by influencing newspaper journalists, for example, and did not need television to get their message across to the public.

As with electoral contests, the major issues of our time naturally influence public opinion. Long before the Watergate affair, there was much popular interest in honest government and

the uncovering of wrongdoing in office. The Teapot Dome affair in the administration of Warren Harding received as much public scrutiny in 1923 as did Watergate in 1973–74. Investigations of malfeasance in office sparked many a reform crusade in urban politics before television was invented.

It was not so much television, but rather popular interest in remedying the evils of the post–World War II period, that produced the intense political activism of so many people. The civil rights protests developed out of the patterns of segregation and disenfranchisement affecting black Americans. Television did not create an issue that traced its injustices back to the colonial period.

Urban riots were not born in the television era either. Riots occurred in ethnically diverse urban areas with the rise in European immigration to the big cities of the United States around the turn of the century. The existence of slums, relative social and economic deprivation, and lack of hope by unemployed youth played a more important role in generating urban riots than did the television portrayals of those riots.

War weariness is not new to the United States, either. In the Civil War, for example, draft riots swept through some northern states. Antiwar protesters were a feature of the nineteenth and twentieth centuries, and conscientious objectors asserted their beliefs without benefit of network television inducements.

It is wrong to blame television for the political behavior that we condemn. Television news reporting is merely a reflection of our society. If what the mirror reflects is ugly, that is not the fault of the mirror.

Intrinsic Features of TV. Television may possess certain unique features, but these do not result in any special effects on society. As early as Greek antiquity, political theorists like Plato and Aristotle warned about the powers of spellbinding speakers who could move crowds to a frenzy.

More recently, however, other media forms have shown powers of persuasion. The "yellow press" of newspaper magnate William Randolph Hearst one hundred years ago is often blamed for creating the same kinds of sensationalism today often attributed to TV. Newspapers have also been blamed for their prejudiced accounts of German atrocities in World War I and their undue influence in promoting American intervention.

Radio, too, has become a convincing means of influencing attitudes and behavior. In 1938, for example, Orson Welles broadcast a radio dramatization of H. G. Wells's *War of the Worlds*, which depicted an invasion of earth by Martians. So convincing was the dramatization that many people fled from their homes to avoid the "invasion."

Too much attention is given to television's unique emphasis on pictures and news interpretation and its attraction to the inadvertent viewer. These are all qualities that accurately describe television's unusual features, but their significance is overstated.

From the early days of photography, pictures have been used in the dissemination of news. Still pictures of the American Civil War were powerful portrayals of that war. Newsreels shown in movie theaters of fighting scenes in pretelevision-era wars, moreover, were equally powerful in affecting people's attitudes about war. What strengthened the protest movement against the war in Vietnam was not the television screen's bringing war scenes directly into the living room but the growing popular feeling that the United States could not or would not win that war.[29] It is well to remember that Americans had become similarly disenchanted with the Korean War about two years after the United States sent its forces to Korea, and that war was not a television war.

The military analyst Harry G. Summers notes that television news has been unfairly blamed for turning American public opinion against the war in Vietnam. He writes that those who make such

a claim repeat the same kinds of misconceptions of the early proponents of air power, who believed that terror bombing of civilian targets would evoke so much horror that immediate surrender would be assured. "We now know," he writes, "that such terror bombing during World War II only strengthened national resolve." In Summers's view the decline in public support of the Vietnam War came about because the American people believed that the sacrifices required by the war were too high in terms of the goals set by U.S. political leaders. He explains, "By its failure to establish the political object, the government failed to establish the 'value' of the war."[30]

Much has been made of the alleged U.S. government control of the media in the Persian Gulf war. But it is important to keep in mind that the media—and television in particular—provided extraordinary coverage of the events leading up to the war. Among them were the buildup of forces in Saudi Arabia in late 1990, the discussions in Geneva between U.S. Secretary of State James Baker and Iraqi Foreign Minister Tariq Mikhayl Aziz in early January 1991, and the debates and votes in Congress on the war resolutions immediately following the failure of the Baker-Aziz meeting.

While it is certainly true that the U.S. government sought to manage the news, it did not succeed. Peter Arnett's stories and TV picture from Iraq countered the Pentagon's version of events. And late in the war, TV correspondents broke loose from their press pools and went about their task of reporting in an independent manner. It is clear that had the war continued, the range of freedom for journalists would have been widened.

The emphasis on interpretation of the news is characteristic of television. It is clear from the past, however, that radio commentators, such as Walter Winchell, Drew Pearson, and H. V. Kaltenborn in their day, were popular because of their interpretation of the news on national radio programs. Print journalists, moreover, also interpret the news, both in their selection of subject matter and in the prominence they give to a subject. While Fidel Castro was a guerrilla fighter in the Cuban countryside in the 1950s, sympa-

[29] Daniel C. Hallin, "The Media, the War in Vietnam, and Political Support: A Critique of the Thesis of an Oppositional Media," *Journal of Politics* 46 (February 1984): 2–24.

[30] Harry G. Summers, "Western Media and Recent Wars," *Military Review* 66 (May 1986): 12.

thetic accounts of his activities reported by the journalist Herbert Matthews of the *New York Times* gave Castro a popular following in the United States. After Castro came to power, however, and established a communist regime, his image became tarnished. A witty commentary of his early period in power suggested that the *Times* might promote its want-ad sales by using a photograph of Fidel Castro with the caption, "I got my job through the *New York Times*."

Finally, it cannot be denied that people watch television news programs and hear information that might otherwise come from other sources, such as friends, interest groups, and political parties. As we shall see, however, these factors are not as important as they might superficially appear to be.

Dependency on TV for News. It is true that most people do depend more on TV for the news than on any other media form. This is not a crucial fact as far as influencing public opinion is concerned, however, because the mass media do not have much influence on public opinion.

Students of communications have observed that the dominant effect of mass media is reinforcement rather than change of existing beliefs.[31] People are more likely to be influenced by interpersonal relations than by television, no matter how many hours they spend before the television box. Family, friends, and social groups have a greater impact on opinions than do the media. The media ordinarily influence mediators rather than the mass public directly.

Psychologists and sociologists have observed that belief patterns are influenced by the principle of selectivity. **Selectivity** means that people often choose the information they wish to know. In other words, in forming attitudes and opinions, believing is very often seeing, rather than seeing is believing.

Three different kinds of selectivity have been distinguished: selective exposure, selective perception, and selective retention. **Selective exposure** refers to the fact that people choose to see media presentations that are in accord with their predispositions. If a particular news program is biased in a way that viewers do not approve, the chances are that the viewers will turn to another channel. **Selective perception** means that individuals tend to see what they want to see. People who are strong Democrats, for example, may self-censor news that they find in conflict with their predispositions about Democrats. **Selective retention** means that the kind of information individuals remember is also self-censored, so that the information most favorable to their point of view will be remembered and the rest ignored or forgotten.[32]

Much has been said about the role of television news in agenda setting and in priming. What is often ignored, however, is the role of the governing elite in influencing television coverage of the government's agenda.

The Reagan presidency is a case in point. As president, Ronald Reagan appeared frequently on television. It was Reagan and not the television media who set the national agenda in defense issues, as his television speech in 1983 announcing the Strategic Defense Initiative illustrates. The large number of journalists—broadcast and print—who cover regular newsbeats in Washington are dependent upon the government for information. The governing elites are, consequently, able to play a major role in agenda setting and in priming.

Television, then, is limited in its ability to influence opinion. Even journalists who might feel that they want to depict the evils of American institutions cannot be sure that they are achieving their desired effects. Outside the Democratic party national convention in Chicago in 1968, for example, television cameras portrayed scenes of policemen clubbing demonstrators. In spite of TV journalists' criticism of the Chicago police, studies of public opinion revealed that there was overwhelming popular support of the police rather than the demonstrators. The principle of selectivity seemed to apply. Television, then, has not become the ogre that its critics have described.

[31] Joseph T. Klapper, *The Effects of Mass Communication* (New York: Free Press, 1960), p. 15.

[32] Ibid., pp. 19–25.

KEY TERMS

Affective socialization
Agenda setting
Agents of socialization
Attentive public
Attitudes
Beliefs
Cognitive socialization
Direction (public opinion)
Evaluative socialization
Exit polls
Intensity (public opinion)
Mass media
Mass public
Opinions
Peer groups
Political culture
Political socialization

Priming
Probability sample
Public opinion
Selective exposure
Selective perception
Selective retention
Selectivity
Simple random sample
Socialization
Stability (public opinion)
Stratified sample
Subcultures
Survey research
Systematic sample
Two-step flow of communication
Universe
Youth culture

QUESTIONS

Political Culture, Political Socialization, and Public Opinion

1. How do we form our opinions?

2. What are the differences and what are the similarities in political socialization processes in democracies and dictatorships?

3. What kinds of civic education should be part of primary and secondary school programs? What are the reasons for your answer?

4. Should the recitation of the pledge of allegiance be made compulsory in the public elementary and secondary schools? What are the reasons for your answer?

5. Can public opinion be measured scientifically? What are the reasons for your answer?

6. What influence does public opinion have on public policy in democracies and dictatorships? Give examples.

Television News

1. Based on your viewing, is the TV evening news positive or negative in its portrayal of American society and American politics? Describe specific evening news stories to illustrate your argument.

2. What effect does the control over television by a dictatorship have on the opinions of its citizenry?

3. What limits should be imposed on the television news media in covering military and foreign policy matters? What are the reasons for your answer?

4. If a known terrorist were willing to give an interview on a Western television station, should the station be willing to show the interview directly to viewers? What are the consequences of your answer to (a) freedom of the press, and (b) the likelihood that more terrorist acts will be committed?

5. What role do elected public officials play in manipulating the news that appears on television?

RECOMMENDED READINGS

ALMOND, GABRIEL A., and SIDNEY VERBA. *The Civic Culture: Political Attitudes and Democracy in Five Nations*. New ed. Newbury Park, Calif.: Sage Publications, 1989. An examination, using survey research, of the political culture of democracy and the social structures and processes that sustain it. First published in 1963.

————, and ————, eds. *The Civic Culture Revisited*. Newbury Park, Calif.: Sage Publications, 1989. Essays on *The Civic Culture*.

BERGER ARTHUR ASA. *Agitprop: Political Culture and Communication Theory*. New Brunswick, N.J.: Transaction Publishers, 1990. A study of how popular culture relates to political culture.

BRADBURN, NORMAN M., and SEYMOUR SUDMAN. *Polls and Surveys: Understanding What They Tell Us*. San Francisco: Jossey-Bass, 1988. A comprehensive, nontechnical guide to understanding surveys.

BUDANSKY, STEPHEN. "The Numbers Racket: How Polls and Statistics Lie." *U.S. News and World Report* 105 (July 11, 1988): 44–47. A popular account of the subject.

CALVERT, SUSAN, and PETER CALVERT. *Argentina: Political Culture and Instability*. Pittsburgh: University of Pittsburgh Press, 1989. A study of the relationship between political culture and instability in Argentina.

CONVERSE, PHILP E., and MICHAEL W. TRAUGOTT. "Assessing the Accuracy of Polls and Surveys." *Science* 234 (November 28, 1986): 1094–98. An explanation of why polls on similar topics conducted over the same time period or near the same time period vary.

CRESPI, IRVING. *Public Opinion, Polls, and Democracy*. Boulder, Colo.: Westview Press, 1989. A study of the reciprocal influences of polling, politics, and the media.

EXOO, CALVIN E., ed. *Democracy Upside Down: Public Opinion and Cultural Hegemony in the United States*. New York: Praeger, 1987. A critique that public opinion is molded by the dominant economic interests in the United States.

FARAW, TAWFIC E., and YASUMASA KURODA, eds. *Political Socialization in the Arab States*. Boulder, Colo.: Lynne Rienner, 1987. A collection of essays on the subject.

ICHILOV, ORIT, ed. *Political Socialization, Citizenship, Education and Democracy*. New York: Teachers College Press, 1990. Essays on the linkage between political socialization and democracy.

KELLY, RITA MAE, ed. *Gender and Socialization in Power and Politics*. New York: Haworth Press, 1986. An overview of the political socialization of women.

LANGTON, KENNETH P. *Political Socialization*. New York: Oxford University Press, 1969. A cross-cultural study of political socialization.

McCLOSKY, HERBERT, and JOHN ZALLER. *The American Ethos*. Cambridge, Mass.: Harvard University Press, 1984. A study of the values of the American people and the significance of those values in American history.

PYE, LUCIAN W. *The Mandarin and the Cadre: China's Political Cultures*. Ann Arbor, Mich.: Center for Chinese Studies, 1988. A political cultural approach to the study of China.

SIGEL, ROBERTA S., ed. *Political Learning in Adulthood: A Sourcebook of Theory and Research*. Chicago: University of Chicago Press, 1989. Essays focusing on the utility of studying the life-span of an individual, rather than childhood and adolescence, in analyzing political socialization.

Television News

BRAESTRUP, PETER. *Big Story: How the American Press and Television Reported and Interpreted the Crisis of Tet 1968 in Vietnam and Washington*. New Haven: Yale University Press, 1983. A study of reporting in the Vietnam war.

DIAMOND, EDWIN. "Who Won the Media War?" *New York* 24 (March 18, 1991): 26–29. An account of how the Persian Gulf war of 1991 was covered by the media.

GITLIN, TODD. "Blips, Bites and Savvy Talk: Television's Impact on American Politics." *Dissent* 37 (Winter 1990): 18–26. An assessment of television's influence on American politics.

GOLDSTEIN, TOM, ed. *Killing the Messenger: 100 Years of Media Criticism*. New York: Columbia University Press, 1988. Media criticism in historical perspective.

GRABER, DORIS A. *Mass Media and American Politics*. 3d ed. Washington, D.C.: CO Press,

1989. An examination of the pervasive impact of the media on the American political system.

HALLIN, DANIEL C. "The Media, the War in Vietnam, and Political Support: A Critique of the Thesis of an Oppositional Media." *Journal of Politics* 46 (February 1984): 2–24. An argument that the case of Vietnam does not show that American news media shifted to an oppositional stance during the 1960s.

HERMAN, EDWARD S., and NOAM CHOMSKY. *Manufacturing Consent: The Political Economy of the Mass Media.* New York: Pantheon Books, 1988. An argument that mass media in the United States are instruments of U.S. government propaganda.

HERTSGAARD, MARK. *On Bended Knee: The Press and the Reagan Presidency.* New York: Farrar Straus Giroux, 1988. An argument that the Reagan administration manipulated the press.

HOWELL, CASS D. "War, Television and Public Opinion." *Military Review* 67 (February 1987): 71–79. An argument that TV cameras should be banned from the battlefield.

IYENGAR, SHANTO, and DONALD R. KINDER. *News That Matters: Television and American Opinion.* Chicago: University of Chicago Press, 1987. An argument that TV news influences opinion by helping to set the political agenda and affecting the way in which public officials are judged.

KLAPPER, JOSEPH T. *The Effects of Mass Communication.* New York: Free Press, 1960. An analysis of the social and psychological effects of mass communication.

KUPPERMAN, ROBERT, and JEFF KAMEN. "When Terrorists Strike . . .: The Lessons TV Must Learn." *TV Guide* 37 (September 23, 1989): 18–22. An assessment of how television covers terrorist acts.

LANDAU, SAUL. "The Real Nintendo Game." *Progressive* 55 (March 1991): 26–28. A critique of TV coverage of the Persian Gulf war of 1991.

LEVINE, HERBERT M. "What If There Were No Television?" In *What If the American Political System Were Different?*, ed. Herbert M. Levine. Armonk, N.Y.: M. E. Sharpe, 1992. Chap. 4. An assessment of what the American political system would be like today if television had never been invented.

RANNEY, AUSTIN. *Channels of Power: The Impact of Television on American Politics.* New York: Basic Books, 1983. A broad analysis of the subject.

ROBINSON, MICHAEL J. "Public Affairs Television and the Growth of Political Malaise: The Case of 'The Selling of the Pentagon.' " *American Political Science Review* 70 (June 1976): 409–32. An argument that television has a fundamental impact on the political behavior of the mass public.

SMOLLER, FREDERIC T. *The Six O'Clock Presidency: A Theory of Presidential Press Relations in the Age of Television.* New York: Praeger, 1990. A theory of the presentation of television network news coverage of the U.S. presidency.

STARKER, STEVEN. *Evil Influences: Crusades against the Mass Media.* New Brunswick, N.J.: Transaction Publishers, 1989. A defense of the media against the charges of evil influences that have been leveled against them.

SUMMERS, HARRY G. "Western Media and Recent Wars." *Military Review* 66 (May 1986): 4–17. An argument that political forces rather than the media influence popular support of a war.

chapter 7

Civil liberties

- An old widow, living alone, is raped and murdered. The police apprehend a young man and accuse him of the crime. The state is unable to prosecute because a judge says that the evidence obtained by the police was seized in violation of the constitutional rights of the defendant.
- A man sets fire to the American flag in a public demonstration. He is arrested and convicted for the crime of destroying the American flag. Higher courts reverse the decision, and the man is unpunished.
- An American Nazi party official announces that his organization will march through Skokie, Illinois, a city with a number of Jewish people who had been incarcerated in Adolf Hitler's concentration camps.

Events such as these have brought frustration and indignation to many American people. To some, they are the expression of a nation gone mad—one that lets criminals go free while innocent people become their victims, protects a person who desecrates a revered American symbol of patri-

otism, and provides security for one of the most horrendous groups the world has ever known while the survivors of Adolf Hitler's atrocities relive their nightmares.

So widespread has been the dissatisfaction with such seemingly irrational official acts that some Americans have questioned the wisdom of relying on a constitutional system that permits such behavior. Specifically, they direct their criticisms at the elaborate protections to all citizens and residents, protections that are known as *rights*. A **right** is a power to which a person has a just claim. In the United States, many individual rights are enumerated in the Constitution and its first ten amendments (known as the Bill of Rights). These rights constitute the fundamental protections of the American people against encroachments by the federal government. Other amendments, statutes, and judicial interpretations have extended many of these rights to include protections against not only the federal government but against state governments and private groups as well.

The notion that individuals have rights that must be protected by government is a principle found not only in the American Constitution but in other constitutions as well. Even countries that violate individual rights have constitutions that profess in principle the rights they are in fact violating. Some private groups, such as the Ku Klux Klan and the American Nazis, which would destroy individual rights if they came to political power, rely on the rights of a free society for their protection.

Rights, then, are both condemned and honored. Rights are important in determining what the proper relationship is between the citizen and the state. To understand different perspectives about rights, it is essential to specify different kinds of rights, describe their historical development, and then look at the justification and criticisms of a political system that reveres rights. An examination of three issues—civil disobedience, capital punishment, and hate-speech codes—illuminates the complexities involved in any discussion of rights.

WHAT ARE RIGHTS?

Rights have been defined as powers to which a person has a just claim. Rights may be further broken down into political rights and economic and social rights. **Political rights** are defined as those rights that assure an individual freedom of expression, opportunity to participate in the political process, fair treatment in criminal proceedings, and equal treatment under the law. **Economic and social rights** are those freedoms that allow for material security, such as freedom to get a job, good housing, adequate education, social security, and welfare (see Chapter 3).

A great deal of ambiguity marks any discussion of rights, since often the term is used in different ways for different purposes. Political rights are frequently said to be composed of civil liberties and civil rights. The term **civil liberties** describes the rights of an individual against the state, freedom of expression, and rights in criminal proceedings. In general usage **civil rights** consist of those rights that assure minority group equality before the law.

Recognizing the definitional difficulties, we shall include civil liberties and civil rights as synonymous with political rights, as defined above. We shall also introduce an additional term, *human rights*, which we shall define exclusively as synonymous with political rights. Some writers include economic rights in the definition of human rights. They point to the meaninglessness of political rights to those people who cannot achieve at least the basic minimum of health, housing, and employment. So broad a definition of human rights is, however, beyond the traditional use of the term *rights*. More important, perhaps, is that it permits political leaders who imprison their opponents without legal justification, suppress dissent, oppress minorities, and destroy a free press to argue that they are advocates of human rights merely because they provide the benefits of a welfare state. Adolf Hitler and Joseph Stalin could be included as human rights activists in such an interpretation, although each was responsible for the liquidation of millions of people[1] (see Chapters 3, 4, and 5).

It is important to keep in mind that even if political rights are viewed as the only component of civil liberties, the application of those rights varies among free societies. The United States, for example, gives wider latitude to the press to publish confidential government information than does Great Britain. The use of evidence

[1] See Maurice Cranston, *What Are Human Rights?* (New York: Taplinger, 1973), pp. 65–68. For a view that would incorporate economic and social rights into human rights, see Jack Donnelly, *Universal Human Rights in Theory and Practice* (Ithaca, N.Y.: Cornell University Press, 1989), pp. 26–27.

illegally obtained by the police is a basis for dismissing cases against defendants in some free societies and not in others. Many of the political rights described below are drawn from the experience of the United States. We can categorize these rights as freedom of expression, freedom to participate in the political process, fair treatment in criminal proceedings, and equal protection of the law.

Freedom of Expression

Freedom of expression includes freedom of speech, freedom of petition, freedom of assembly, freedom of the press, and freedom of religion.

Freedom of speech refers to the right of an individual to speak in support of any idea, however unpopular it may be. It includes the right to denounce one's government, a political party, a cherished religious institution, and widely held beliefs. It could mean a Republican's right to espouse Republican causes in a predominantly Democratic neighborhood, but extends to the advocacy of controversial ideas, such as nazism and communism in the United States. It protects the scientist whose findings reveal genetic differences in intelligence among different racial groups as much as it does the civil rights activist in a racist district.

Rightly or wrongly, legal limits have been placed on freedom of speech even in democracies. **Slander**, which is the telling of untruths about an individual, is a limit on freedom of speech. Other limitations are **obscenity** (the reciting or portraying in the media of acts regarded as lewd), and **blasphemy** (statements that describe a religion in sacrilegious ways).

Free speech has also been limited in cases in which it presents a "**clear and present danger**" to the public. As asserted by Supreme Court Justice Oliver Wendell Holmes:

The question in every case is whether the words used are used in such circumstances and are of such a nature as to create a clear and present danger that they will bring about the substantive evils that Congress has a right to prevent. It is a question of proximity and degree.[2]

In this connection courts have upheld restrictions of speech deemed contrary to the national interest in times of war.

Freedom of petition is the right to present written statements that criticize or recommend changes to any public official. In many countries such a petition is regarded as **sedition** (an incitement to resist lawful authority) and is punishable by imprisonment or death.

Freedom of assembly includes the right of people to meet in their homes or other meeting places without interference from government. So long as the meeting is conducted peacefully and is not conspiratorial, the freedom to assemble is supposed to be assured. When in China in 1989 opponents of the government peacefully assembled to advocate democracy in their country, they were ruthlessly suppressed. And critics of Iraq's dictator, Saddam Hussein, have been tortured, killed, or imprisoned for any opposition against the government even when expressed peacefully.

Freedom of assembly obligates the police to protect all groups who wish to meet for political purposes, provided their methods are peaceful. Courts have held that government may determine the manner in which such meetings are held, such as time and location. Police, however, cannot legally deny to one group what they allow another merely because they agree with the one and disagree with the other.

The right of groups to meet peacefully, then, is assured in a free society. However, distinctions among dissent, resistance, and civil disobedience often complicate the discussion of those concerned with civil liberties and must be clarified.

Dissent means disagreement. A free society must permit individuals to disagree with prevailing sentiments, no matter how

[2]*Schenck v. United States*, 249 U.S. 47 (1919).

absurd their position. So long as the disagreement is peaceful, government will protect the dissenters.

Resistance is the taking of illegal actions to undermine legal authority. Acts of resistance are not peaceful but violent, such as the assassination of a political leader, the blowing up of an abortion clinic, and the kidnapping of opponents. A political system that permits peaceful dissent has an obligation to prevent resistance. Resisters in a democracy assume that their will is superior to that of the majority as reflected in the laws of the land. The majority has a right to protect the fundamental basis of its rule.

Civil disobedience is an intermediate step between dissent and resistance. It is the taking of a token action in defiance of the law for the purpose of changing the law. People who engage in civil disobedience say, in effect: "We realize that the majority is against us. We feel the law or policy is so bad that we must take this step in violating it in the hope that we shall convince the majority of people to change their minds. We are willing to be punished for our offense."

In the 1960s, the civil rights "sit-ins," in which black people took seats in racially segregated facilities and requested service, were regarded by many as acts of civil disobedience. So were some refusals by young men to register for the draft or to report for duty when called. More recently, anti-abortion activists blocked the entrance to abortion clinics in efforts to prevent abortions from being performed. Whether or not civil disobedience is justified is a matter that is debated below.

Freedom of the press assures journalists the right to report the news as they deem fit. In free societies members of the press are given special privileges to protect their sources because of the belief that the people have "a right to know." Freedom of the press is strengthened when journalists are not restricted by **prior restraint**—the requirement that articles or books must be submitted for government approval before they may be published.

Governments have placed some regulations on the media, particularly on radio and television. Broadcasts must conform to certain standards regarding the way in which religious or sexual matters are treated, for example.

How much freedom reporters have varies from one free society to another. In the United States, the press has published classified government information when it deemed it in the public interest to do so. In Great Britain, in contrast, an Official Secrets Act prevents government documents from being published in an unauthorized manner. Where the line is drawn for freedom of the press differs from place to place. The underlying assumption of freedom of the press is, however, that only when people have all the information can they be expected to make intelligent judgments about what the government is doing.

Freedom of religion includes the right to practice one's religion without interference from others. It is one of the most recent of civil liberties. In seventeenth-century Europe religious tests were a requirement for government service. Gradually, religious toleration has replaced discrimination.

Today, freedom of religion is a fundamental tenet of those who revere liberty. It means that not only do people have a right to choose their own religion but they have a right not to believe in one as well.

Countries differ as to how separate church and state should be. The United States has the greatest separation, with constitutional restrictions limiting government interference. Other countries do not make such sharp distinctions. Even when countries accept the principle that people should be free to practice their own religious faith, they have limited certain religious practices that they have regarded as offensive, for example, human sacrifice, polygamy, and preventing children from being vaccinated.

Freedom to Participate in the Political Process

Civil liberties include those freedoms that permit maximum political participation in the political process. Some of these freedoms coincide with the freedom of expression. The right to assemble peacefully, for example, is essential for a citizenry that has a right to select its political leaders. Of the freedoms to participate in the political process that are not included in freedom of expression, the most notable are the right to vote, the right to fair elections, and the right to form a loyal opposition.

The right to vote must be assured. Restrictions on the basis of race, religion, belief, property, or sex must be eliminated. The history of suffrage is characterized by the enlargement of the electorate, so that today universal suffrage is the goal of a free society.

Elections must be fair. In countries that revere freedom, ballots must be counted honestly. Campaign workers must be permitted to make their appeals for support without harassment from government.

The right to form a loyal opposition must be assured. When out of power, a political party that abides by democratic rules will not be harassed, or its leaders imprisoned, because of their views. It should be regarded as a loyal opposition.

Fair Treatment in Criminal Proceedings

The rights of protection of an individual when charged with a criminal offense are among the oldest of civil liberties. They go back at least to thirteenth-century England, and probably existed for centuries before that time. Today, rights dealing with criminal offenses include the right of habeas corpus, right of trial by impartial jury, right to counsel, right to grand jury indictment, right to be protected from unreasonable searches and seizures, right to confront accusers, due process of law, no self-incrimi-nation, no ex post facto laws, no cruel and unusual punishment, no excessive bail, and no double jeopardy.

The right of **habeas corpus** (literally, "you should have the body"), guarantees that when a public official, such as a policeman or a warden, holds an individual in custody, that official must go before a judge to explain why that individual is being detained. If the judge decides that the imprisonment or detention is authorized by law, the individual in police custody remains in captivity. If not, the judge sets him or her free. According to the legal scholar Zechariah Chafee, Jr., this right is the most important in the Constitution because when imprisonment is possible without explanation or redress, every form of liberty is impaired. "A man in jail," he writes, "cannot go to church or discuss or publish or assemble or enjoy property or go to the polls."[3]

Right to trial by impartial jury assures the defendant of a fair trial. Juries decide the guilt or innocence of individuals on the basis of the facts of the case, and they are supposed to be impartial. In an era of mass communications that sensationalize major crimes, such as the assassination of a popular political figure, it is sometimes difficult to find a jury that has not prejudged the guilt or innocence of a defendant.

Right to counsel assures a defendant that his or her case will be handled by a qualified attorney. While, theoretically, every person accused of a felony is entitled to be represented by an attorney, the quality of legal service available to the poor is obviously much lower than that available to the rich. In the United States, however, indigent defendants are assured the services of attorneys paid out of public funds.

Right to grand jury indictment provides a defendant an opportunity to have the evidence evaluated. A **grand jury** is a body of people who decide whether there is

[3] Zechariah Chafee, Jr., ed., *Documents in Fundamental Human Rights* (New York: Atheneum, 1963), 2:1.

enough evidence for a trial to be justified. Such a body prevents frivolous charges from becoming court cases.

The denial of unreasonable searches and seizures is another bulwark of human freedom. In a free society, an individual is presumed innocent until proven guilty. Police officials are not legally free to go on "fishing expeditions" merely because they do not like an individual. They must secure a **warrant**, which is authorization by a judge to search or seize an individual or his or her property when there is evidence that an individual has committed a criminal offense. If evidence is seized without such authorization, it often may not be used in the criminal proceedings against the defendant. The result may mean that an individual goes free although he or she committed a crime. Those individuals who consider human rights to be paramount contend that although some guilty people may go free because of "legal technicalities," the extreme alternative—a **police state** in which the police are free to act without restriction—is worse.

The **right to confront one's accusers** assures a defendant that he or she knows who the individuals are who are providing damaging testimony. Often, people are more likely to make accusations in secret than in public, and the right to know one's accusers limits hearsay evidence and gossip from being used against a defendant.

Due process of law, though used in different ways, from the point of view of a defendant's rights means that no person may be denied property or freedom without proper legal justification. Such justification includes the statement of the actual provision of the law that the defendant has allegedly violated. The purpose of due process is to prevent arbitrary harassment of an individual by public authorities.

The government does not have the right to force defendants to testify against themselves. In other words, **self-incrimination** is forbidden unless voluntarily accepted by a defendant. The assumption of a just legal system is that an individual is innocent until proven guilty. This means that the burden of proof is on the prosecution, not the defendant. The state must make its case against an individual and respect his or her right to remain silent. Once a defendant's attorney calls his or her client to the stand, however, the state's attorney may cross-examine that person.

Ex post facto laws are regarded as violations of freedom. An **ex post facto law** is one that subjects people to criminal punishment for acts committed at an earlier time when no such law existed. If in 1995, for example, a federal law were enacted that made the consumption of alcohol illegal, an individual could not be tried for having consumed liquor in 1990.

Defendants are protected, too, by the nature of the punishment. The Constitution prohibits "cruel and unusual punishments." Courts have applied this concept in different ways. In the United States this means no maiming, for example. **Capital punishment**, which is the death penalty, has been challenged as cruel and unusual punishment. Countries differ, however, about the legitimacy of the death penalty. However applied, the principle of no cruel and unusual punishment means that there must be some relationship between the crime and the degree of punishment.

No excessive bail assures defendants of freedom while their cases are being considered. **Bail** is the posting of money that will be forfeited if a person accused of a crime does not appear for trial. How high bail is set depends on the nature of the case and the character of the defendant. An alleged murderer may be denied bail. A bank teller accused of stealing $2,000, however, may be released with a low bail. Indigent defendants sometimes stay in jail for months while their cases are being considered because they are unable to post bail.

Defendants are assured that they will not face **double jeopardy**—the trying of a person a second time in the same jurisdiction for the same crime after having been found not guilty. Even new evidence cannot compel a defendant ruled innocent by a jury to be tried again in the same jurisdiction for that offense.

Equal Protection of the Law

Equal protection of the law is guaranteed by the Fourteenth Amendment to the U.S. Constitution, but its meaning binds the legal systems of many countries. It means that the law cannot discriminate because of class, race, sex, or religion. Equal protection has been used as a basis for extending civil rights to minority groups and even to majority groups when they have felt that they were being punished by being a member of a specific group. This right was the basis of racial integration rulings in housing, education, and voting in the United States. It was also the basis of rulings against racial quotas in university admissions, which had been established to promote the education of groups that were victims of previous discrimination.

HISTORICAL DEVELOPMENT OF RIGHTS

The idea that individuals have rights apart from the state is for the most part a modern concept stemming from the seventeenth century. In ancient Greece, in contrast, individuals were generally perceived to be a natural part of a political system with no private concerns outside of the state.

Although the prevailing political philosophies from ancient times to the seventeenth century had no concept of private rights, there were exceptions. Citizens in some Greek cities enjoyed freedom of speech and equality before the law. The Stoic philosophers of ancient Greece and Rome, moreover, argued that there are universal natural laws that belong to everyone regardless of laws made by humans. These laws, according to the Stoics, were superior to human law. Human beings

were supposed to be subservient to the natural law, with its notion of a "higher law." In medieval times some philosophers perceived natural law as part of God's law.

Not all early assertions of individual rights were derived from philosophical speculation. In England, for example, traditional practices guaranteeing some rights go back to before the thirteenth century. In this respect the English common law, which is judge-made law, revealed customary practices respecting rights, such as trial by jury and *habeas corpus*. The common law had its origins in the twelfth and thirteenth centuries, when royal judges traveled throughout England for the purpose of establishing what were the cases and customs of the local communities. **Common law** is the law that was "common" to the whole kingdom.

The idea of individual rights draws its modern origins from the social contract theorists of the seventeenth and eighteenth centuries, principally John Locke and Jean-Jacques Rousseau. Although there were great differences of interpretation between these theorists, both promoted the social contract—the notion that human beings had at some early time consented to form a state and had made a compact establishing a relationship between the government and the people (see Chapter 4).

The philosophical aspirations of individual liberty were enshrined in great documents, such as the English Bill of Rights (1689), the Declaration of Independence (1776), the Constitution of the United States (1787) and its Bill of Rights (1791), and the French Declaration of the Rights of Man and of the Citizen (1789). The rights in these documents were political rights and were adopted in constitutions in the nineteenth and twentieth centuries. In the twentieth century, particularly, rights have received a great prominence and have come to include even economic and social rights. The Universal Declaration of Human Rights, adopted by the United Nations in 1948 without a single dissent, established a universal acceptance of these rights—at least in principle. Even governments that violate human rights in practice pay lip service to human rights either by denying that they are in fact violating rights or by focusing on economic and social rather than political rights. In principle more than practice, then, the protection of human rights constitutes a norm of international behavior.[4]

JUSTIFICATION OF RIGHTS

The protection of human rights is based both on philosophical principles of natural law and on the practical benefits that accrue to a society revering human rights.

Natural Law

Philosophers justified human rights as being rooted in **natural law**. In the first century A.D., Cicero, the great Stoic philosopher, was one of the first to contend that universal laws are superior to human laws, which must be subservient to them. Later philosophers, like Thomas Aquinas and John Locke, asserted the superiority of higher over human or **positive law**.

Critics of natural rights argue that there is no such thing as "natural rights." They attack the idea that human rights must be defended in terms of a belief in absolute or inalienable rights that exist prior to the establishment of a community. They contend that there is no way to determine objectively what such absolute rights are and that the evaluation of rights must be made in terms of the consequences for society.[5]

Benefits to Society

According to some human rights' advocates, human rights are desirable because

[4] For a discussion of human rights as a goal of foreign policy, see Issue 10.

[5] Sidney Hook, *Heresy, Yes—Conspiracy, No* (New York: John Day, 1953), p. 19.

they protect individual liberty and allow a society to make decisions in a peaceful and rational manner. Many liberals justify their belief in human rights on the basis of their reverence for the dignity of the individual. Each individual, in their view, should be free to participate in political and social life as he or she deems fit. A society is just to the extent that it promotes human rights.

Advocates of human rights point also to the many other benefits involving peace and reason that accrue to a policy granting human rights. First, the society protects itself from becoming a police state in which the government cannot be challenged. Without civil rights and civil liberties, the state is free to suppress any opposition to its will, and human freedom is, consequently, destroyed.

Second, a system that reveres human rights allows for a rational mechanism to change laws peacefully. Without rights, the most powerful groups within and outside of government can prevent change through use of force and other means of coercion. Totalitarian dictatorship would be the most extreme result of such a society (see Chapter 3).

Third, a system that assures rights to all who accept the legitimacy of the system provides a vehicle for popular support of government. For government to maintain its legitimacy, it must adapt to changing economic and social conditions. If it suppresses groups demanding changes, a dissident element may be forced to operate outside of the system since its only means of protest is violence.

Fourth and perhaps most important, a system that reveres liberty allows the opportunity for intelligent decision making. The great English liberal John Stuart Mill argued in *On Liberty* (1859) that a society benefits when people are free to discuss issues openly. The truth, Mill claimed, is difficult to determine, and only in open discussion and debate can it be known. Oliver Wendell Holmes made a similar observation when he observed, "The test of truth is the power of thought to get itself accepted in the competition of the market."[6]

Critics of this justification of human rights have made many rejoinders. Marxists and communists have argued that political rights are fictional in a capitalist society because there can be no freedom without economic rights. Fascists have denounced rights either because they regard the state as superior to the individual or because they contend that certain racial groups (which they regard as inferior) should not be allowed to participate in the political process. Conservatives, while accepting constitutional principles granting rights, have emphasized the duties imposed on an individual who benefits from rights.

In spite of the criticisms leveled at human rights, today constitutions throughout the world openly proclaim a commitment to them. That rights are, in fact, violated in varying degrees from country to country is a reflection of the limitations of freedom in the world and not the denial of the norm that is almost universal.

[6]*Abrams v. United States*, 250 U.S. 616 at 630 (1919).

ISSUES

Even when human rights are accepted as a legitimate objective of society, they are not as "self-evident" as the Declaration of Independence asserts. One right sometimes conflicts with another right, for example. Does freedom of the press include the right to tape jury deliberations, or are the rights of defendants in criminal proceedings violated by such an act?

Often, the notion of rights is most complex near the point where rights reach their limits. Justification of civil disobedience is one case of such complexity. A debate on the justification of civil disobedience shows how difficult it is to set the legitimate limits of rights.

Even when there is agreement that the people who break the law in a democratic society should be punished, there is strong disagreement about how much punishment should be meted out to law breakers. One form of punishment inflicted in many societies is capital punishment. Many states have banned the death penalty for any offense. In some countries, such as South Africa, the People's Republic of China, and the United States, the death penalty is legal—although the crime for which a death penalty may result varies from country to country. In the People's Republic of China, economic crimes involving the theft of government property can bring a death penalty. In Iran and Iraq, political crimes can bring a similar punishment. In the United States, however, the death penalty is today reserved for those convicted of the most heinous murders.

The right of people to make bigoted remarks is a controversial matter. In reaction to insulting speech directed along racial, ethnic, and gender lines at some institutions of higher learning in the United States, a number of colleges, and universities adopted **hate-speech codes**—rules punishing speech that was deemed offensive to particular groups, such as minorities and women. Debates on the campuses considering the codes centered on the issue of whether the codes were in conflict with freedom of speech.

Racist incidents are on the increase at colleges and universities in the United States. At the University of Michigan, racist leaflets were distributed in dorms. At Northwest Missouri State University, white supremacists distributed flyers stating, "The Knights of the Ku Klux Klan Are Watching You." At Memphis State University bomb threats were made at the Jewish Student Union. At the University of Wisconsin, several racist incidents occurred, including a fraternity "slave auction" in which pledges in black face performed skits parodying black entertainers. At Stanford, a picture of Beethoven was portrayed with fuller lips and dark frizzy hair and then posted in a black studies dormitory.

Three debates are considered in this chapter: (1) Is civil disobedience justified in a representative democracy? (2) Should capital punishment be abolished? (3) Should hate-speech codes be adopted at public universities in the United States?

15/YES   IS CIVIL DISOBEDIENCE JUSTIFIED IN A REPRESENTATIVE DEMOCRACY?

Although laws must be obeyed in a democracy, common sense dictates that there are exceptions. An individual in a democracy has the option to dissent from the majoritarian point of view. No one who reveres democracy would challenge that point. The individual, however, has no right of resistance, because such behavior challenges the legitimacy of the system. If, however, an individual cannot in conscience accept the decisions of the majority because he or she regards them as unjust, that person may choose to engage in acts of civil disobedience. Democracies must allow for acts of civil disobedience.

Civil disobedience has been defined as the taking of a token action in defiance of the law for the purpose of changing the law. Civil disobedients take the act knowingly, lovingly, and above all peacefully. They are willing to accept punishment, such as fine or imprisonment, because they feel the issue of their concern is of such enormous significance that they are willing to sacrifice their freedom.

Civil disobedience is justified in a representative democracy because: (1) human laws are not valid when they violate higher laws of conscience; (2) civil disobedience reveres law; and (3) democracy is ultimately strengthened by accepting the principle of civil disobedience.

Higher Law. The term **higher law** refers to a universal law that transcends human law. For some, it has a religious connotation. Thomas Aquinas reflected this religious motivation when he commented, "And if a human law is at variance in any particular with the natural law, it is no longer legal, but rather a corruption of law."[7] Others identify the higher law with natural law, as expounded by John Locke and his philosophical descendants. Still others think of higher law in terms of abstract justice. No matter the source of the concept, what is important is that human law is subject to error or injustice, and there ought to be some legitimate means for an individual to show opposition to that law when it is in conflict with moral principles.

[7] Thomas Aquinas, *Summa Theologica*, Question 95, Article 2, in *Aquinas: Selected Political Writings*, ed. A. P. Entreves, trans. J. G. Dawson (Oxford, England: Basil Blackwell, 1965), p. 129.

The record shows many instances in which acts of civil disobedience have been justified. Some of the major cases have involved slavery, civil rights, national independence, and war.

When the Fugitive Slave Act of 1850 was passed in the United States, a major issue of conscience faced the opponents of slavery. The law stipulated that fugitive slaves be returned to their owners, even from the free states in the North. Some abolitionists refused to abide by the law. Some even went so far as to organize an "underground railroad" for the purpose of transporting slaves to Canada. These people believed they could not obey a law they believed wrong even though it had been duly enacted by an elected legislative body and declared constitutional by its judicial authority.

In the twentieth century, too, civil rights matters affecting black people and women have justified acts of civil disobedience. State and local ordinances in the South enforced segregation in public accommodations, such as hotels, transportation facilities, and restaurants. Sparked by leaders like Martin Luther King, Jr., many black people broke the segregation laws by sit-ins at lunch counters. White supporters joined southern blacks in "freedom rides" in efforts to integrate buses. King's policy of **direct action** (the taking of nonviolent measures, such as boycotts and sit-ins) was based on the moral necessity of violating unjust laws. Always he acted nonviolently. In Birmingham, Alabama, he willingly went to jail for his act of civil disobedience. King's actions were justified because racial segregation by law is morally reprehensible. Anyone devoted to human freedom in the United States had to oppose the acts of segregation, which treated black Americans as second-class citizens, and support those people—like King and his followers—who experienced imprisonment to end an immoral practice.

Women, too, have been victimized by laws that denied them the right to vote and equal opportunity to participate in the economy. In the United States, for example, the suffragists engaged in acts of civil disobedience, such as chaining themselves to buildings and tying up traffic. How else could they participate meaningfully in the political process since they were unable to vote in national elections? Ultimately in

1920, the Nineteenth Amendment granted women the suffrage.

Although slavery and civil rights have produced some major examples of civil disobedience, so, too, have independence and peace movements. Mohandas K. Gandhi, the Indian leader, was one of this century's great proponents of civil disobedience. His policy was one of **satyagraha** (literally, "firmness in the truth"), which many people (although not Gandhi) equated with passive resistance. He urged his partisans to take peaceful acts, such as marches and boycotts, to win rights for Indians in South Africa and to achieve the independence of India from British colonial rule. Gandhi became famous for his hunger strikes and for other acts of nonviolence. One of his tactics was to have his followers lie down on railroad tracks, thus preventing trains from moving. By taking such peaceful acts of civil disobedience, Gandhi contributed to the movement—both in India and in Great Britain—for the independence of his country.

Because of his close association with nonviolence, Gandhi became a hero to peace movements around the world. Even before Gandhi, civil disobedience was asserted as an antiwar device. Henry David Thoreau went to prison for his opposition to the war against Mexico (1846–48) and for his refusal to pay taxes. In 1849, he wrote the classic work on the subject, *Resistance to Civil Government*, which was republished after his death as *Civil Disobedience* (1866).[8] Thoreau went beyond mere civil disobedience, however, since he was opposed to all government, but he was most associated with civil disobedience in his opposition to war.

More recently, antiwar opponents resorted to acts of civil disobedience during the Vietnam War. Arguing that the United States was engaged in an immoral war, antiwar protesters went beyond dissent and took acts of civil disobedience. Quite rightly, many of them condemned the resisters who entered army draft

[8] According to the historian Lewis Perry, "Thoreau actually never spoke of *civil disobedience*, nor did anyone else use the term in print during his lifetime, so far as scholars can discover." Lewis Perry, "Civil Disobedience," in *Encyclopedia of American Political History: Studies of the Principal Movements and Ideas*, ed. Jack P. Greene (New York: Charles Scribner's Sons, 1984), 1:211.

board offices and ransacked the files or used explosives against government buildings. The truly civilly disobedient did not participate in acts of violence but refused to serve in the armed forces, or withheld part of their income taxes that they believed was devoted to the prosecution of the war, or tied up traffic for the purpose of protesting the war. In their view South Vietnam, the American ally, was a dictatorship and a war to prop it up in the face of a nationalist movement was immoral; the only recourse was to act in a civilly disobedient manner.

Reverence for Law. Those who act in a civilly disobedient manner revere legal processes. What they say is that they find a particular act of government to be so horrendous that they regretfully violate the law. It is not easy to take such an action. To burn a draft card, tie up traffic, chain oneself to a building, and refuse to pay taxes are acts regarded by many citizens as outrageous. To put oneself in a position as an outcast of the community requires a great deal of courage.

Some civil disobedients display a considerable amount of hypocrisy by their actions. They break the law as befits their conscience; but when an outraged mob attacks them, they clamor for protection as required by law.

Civil disobedients accept that criticism as much as they revere the law. What they hope, however, is that the majority will change its mind and come around to a different position. By their actions, they seek to bring public attention to their causes and enlist the majority to change the law. By suffering the loss of freedom and damage to reputation, they hope, eventually, that the law will reflect their judgment. The facts that for the United States racial segregation by law has been eliminated, women have the right to vote, and American participation in the war in Vietnam has ended are a tribute to the acts of civil disobedience that were unpopular at the time they were undertaken. Reverence for law has not been undermined because of acts of civil disobedience.

Democracy. Democracy is strengthened by a tolerance of civil disobedience. For a system to be democratic, it must have broad support among diverse elements of society. The processes of a representative democracy work slowly, and often groups become disenchanted with the slow responsiveness of government.

Groups subjected to discrimination or injustice cannot be expected to rely exclusively on constitutional processes that take years to institute remedies.

Faced with moral dilemmas deeply felt by a group, its leaders must have recourse to dissent or disobedience. In the 1960s, for example, black people felt that the processes of change, particularly social and economic change, were moving too slowly to produce tangible benefits. Most of them rejected extremist solutions as not suitable for democracy. Many saw in civil disobedience a remedy that would allow them to accept the legitimacy of the system. In some cases, they peacefully occupied schools to demonstrate that faculty in minority neighborhood schools should be more racially representative of the community. Like the civil rights activists, antiwar protesters acted nonviolently. They felt that the pace of bringing about peace was proceeding too slowly. Every day saw more people, Americans and Asians, maimed or dying in jungle warfare. By committing acts of civil disobedience, activists remained committed to the democratic ideal. Although not sanctified by law, the civil rights and peace activists strengthened democratic institutions because they channeled their energies in directions that a broader segment of the community would ultimately accept—racial justice and peace.

15/NO IS CIVIL DISOBEDIENCE JUSTIFIED IN A REPRESENTATIVE DEMOCRACY?

"Saints should always be judged guilty until proven innocent," the English political critic George Orwell once wrote in commenting about the saintly Mohandas Gandhi.[9] Orwell's warning should be applied to the many self-appointed saints in the civil disobedience community. Civil disobedience cannot be justified in a representative democracy because: (1) there are no higher laws than the laws that are constitutionally enacted; (2) laws must be respected; and (3) democracy is weakened to the extent that civil disobedient acts are committed.

Higher Law. In a representative democracy there are means whereby laws that the majority come to feel are wrong can be changed. The repeal of the Prohibition Amendment in 1933 is a notable example. So long as such means exist, there is no justification for appealing to a "higher law" and disobeying the laws that are duly enacted.

People who justify their actions in terms of the higher law appeal invariably to conscience as a guide to behavior. It is certainly true that conscience should guide the behavior of states and people. Respect for religious beliefs and philosophical commitments to justice or rights should be encouraged. The problem, however, is that there is no universal agreement about what constitutes principles of justice, rights, and natural law. The very idea that there are such universal principles of natural rights that reason can determine has been properly labeled "nonsense upon stilts" by Jeremy Bentham, an English writer of the late eighteenth and early nineteenth centuries.

Higher law is the justification for illegality by a variety of political partisans. We may well approve of the good intentions of the people who have spoken for the abolition of slavery, the expansion of civil rights, the establishment of national independence, and the promotion of peace; but we should understand that the methods used to attain those desirable goals are all important to liberty and order. It is not enough that the intentions of social critics are noble. We should remember the old saying that the path to hell is paved with good intentions.

Many *opponents* of these lofty principles have also asserted the principle of higher law. Segregationists, who resisted the desegregation rulings of the United States Supreme Court and the civil rights laws of Congress, also violated these laws with appeals to higher law. Even many young Nazis committed illegal acts in the 1920s, contending that the duly elected democratic government in Germany was corrupt and that they would not abide by the policies of such an immoral government. In more recent times

[9]George Orwell, "Reflections on Gandhi," in *The Collected Essays, Journalism and Letters of George Orwell,* ed. Sonia Orwell and Ian Angus (Harmondsworth, England: Penguin, 1968), 4:523. The essay was originally published in January 1949.

some of the people involved in the Watergate affair during the administration of Richard Nixon took illegal acts, such as breaking into offices, wiretapping, and burglarizing, because they felt that they were acting out of conscience against imagined enemies of the United States. If a legitimate democratic government permits individuals to determine for themselves what constitutes the higher law, there can never be a peaceful way to resolve differences of opinion.

The *Affirmative* cites cases of antislavery, civil rights for blacks and women, national independence, and peace as legitimate examples for justifying civil disobedience. We argue that in the first three matters, many of these acts cannot properly be considered examples of civil disobedience.

A system of slavery is one that excludes a group of people from participating in the political process. In the South, black people were not permitted to vote. Indeed, they were considered to be not human beings but property, which white slaveholders could buy and sell at will. Blacks, moreover, were not permitted the right to engage in open political activity; the punishment was imprisonment, beatings, and even death. It is wrong to use the civil disobedience application to such a case since civil disobedience is a concept that is by definition a process of a polity allowing legitimate means of political protest; and slaves had no political standing.

A similar case can be made for the sit-ins. Even after slavery was abolished, blacks were prevented from offering candidates in elections and from voting. If blacks had had the power to vote, the segregation laws would not have been on the books, as the later record of legislation attests. We argue that the sit-ins and freedom rides were justified because unless all people—except the young, criminals, and the insane—are assured the right to vote, they are permitted to take extraordinary, though nonviolent, measures. We would include the suffragists in this category.

Another point can be made in connection with the sit-ins and freedom rides. Often many of the people who engaged in these practices believed that the local and state statutes requiring segregation were in violation of First Amendment rights in the Constitution. They were *testing* the constitutionality of segregation by creating incidents requiring judicial deliberation. Testing a law is not an act of civil disobedience in the United States, since in the American judicial system a real case, rather than an advisory opinion, is essential before a court makes a judgment.

Acts of colonial peoples to achieve national independence, moreover, cannot be properly classified as civil disobedience. Gandhi as an Indian leader sought to end British authority over his homeland rather than force the British government to merely change a law.[10]

A clearer case in evaluating civil disobedience can be made for war resisters. Many countries, among them the United States, allow for a right of **conscientious objection** in which an individual may legally refuse to serve in the armed forces because of religious or deeply held philosophical beliefs against all wars. Conscientious objection is not the same as civil disobedience, however. In the Vietnam War, some partisans of civil disobedience did not have the religious or philosophical views against wars generally, but rather objected specifically to the war in Vietnam. These people often committed acts that we would classify as civilly disobedient.

We argue that their actions were both illegal and immoral. They had no right to substitute their judgment for that of the majority, as reflected in the laws. We contend that the historical record supports the assertion by some proponents of United States foreign policy that if South Vietnam went communist, a worse dictatorship would result. The fact that a totalitarian regime in Vietnam has been established under communist rule, complete with the taking of political prisoners, the suppression of religion, and the monolithic control over the media, education, and the economy, lends weight in retrospect to the soundness of their views. Even if this contention is not supported, however, the case of the wisdom or justice of American involvement in the Vietnam War was not so clear-cut as to justify acts of civil disobedience.

Reverence for Law. Those who act in a civilly disobedient manner have no respect for law. It is impossible to have a law that authorizes individuals to violate it. Respect for law is essential for any system to function. An effective system of law is possible only when appeals cannot be made to principles outside the legal system.

Civil disobedients determine for themselves what laws to obey and what laws to violate. Without law, there will only be chaos as each individual and group decides unilaterally what is right. "Like law itself," the legal scholar Alexander M.

---

[10]Carl Cohen, *Civil Disobedience: Conscience, Tactics, and the Law* (New York: Columbia University Press, 1971), pp. 46–47.

Bickel notes, "civil disobedience is habit-forming, and the habit it forms is destructive of the legal order."[11] The victims in such a lawless society will probably be many of the very same people who argue so adamantly for the right of civil disobedience, namely, the advocates of civil rights, social justice, and peace. If one group can decide for itself which laws to obey, so, too, will other groups. A system of law protects all groups in society. Without it, discussion ceases and violence begins.

Democracy. Civil disobedience in a democracy undermines the basis of the democratic order. A democracy by definition allows for many forms of protest activity to win the support of the majority. People are free to picket, publish articles and books supportive of their views, and petition their elected representatives. What civil disobedients do by their acts is to substitute their voice for the majority, and there is no justification for that kind of behavior in a democracy. So long as a democratic system allows for peaceful channels to register protest, civil disobedience cannot be justified.

[11] Alexander M. Bickel, *The Morality of Consent* (New Haven: Yale University Press, 1975), p. 119.

Totalitarian systems have no ethical constraints in coping with civil disobedients. As George Orwell observes, a Gandhi could engage in passive resistance because the British treated him forbearingly, and his appeals for justice could always command public attention. "It is difficult to see," Orwell writes, "how Gandhi's methods could be applied in a country where opponents of the régime disappear in the middle of the night and are never heard of again."[12] Orwell's point deals with an individual seeking to undermine foreign authority in his country, but it is also insightful in the context of civil disobedience. Democracies are vulnerable to civil disobedients because of their tolerance for heretics and dissenters. Too many acts of civil disobedience, however, and the basis of a democratic order is undermined.

If one group is entitled to substitute its will for that of the majority, then why not others? Before much time has passed, the basic underpinnings of a democracy are eroded, and the system can collapse by too many appeals of civil disobedience. If democracy is to be maintained, then all who disagree with the prevailing laws or policies must use the legitimate means of redress, lest they discover that they lose both the specific goal they seek and their fundamental freedoms.

[12] Orwell, "Reflections on Gandhi," p. 529.

16/YES   SHOULD CAPITAL PUNISHMENT BE ABOLISHED?

The uncivilized practice of capital punishment should be outlawed. Capital punishment is bad because: (1) it does not serve as a deterrent to killings; (2) it signifies a disrespect for life; (3) it makes a mockery of the law; (4) it is cruel and unusual punishment; and (5) it cannot bring back to life innocent people who were unjustly put to death.

Deterrence. Supporters of capital punishment have been moved to frenzy by gruesome stories of murders and other violent acts. They have incorrectly concluded that the safety of their families, their friends, and themselves would be more assured if the death penalty were imposed on the most violent criminals.

Although popular revulsion at murders is understandable, there is no conclusive evidence that capital punishment serves as a deterrent to murder. In the United States, for example, some

states have permitted capital punishment and others have not. An examination of the homicide rate in different states does not reveal that capital punishment is linked to a lower homicide rate. States that have reinstituted the death penalty have not experienced a decline in the murder rate. Many of the social science studies dealing with the subject suggest that the death penalty does not lower a homicide rate. At best, the evidence is inconclusive.

It is important to keep in mind that many kinds of homicides will clearly not be prevented when capital punishment is legal. Crimes of passion are a case in point. People who have severe psychological problems caused by brutalizing formative experiences, moreover, will not be deterred from murdering because they may be incapable of making rational decisions to thwart their violent impulses. The kind of person like Jeffrey L. Dahmer, who killed 15 young men and boys by luring his victims to his home, drugging them, murdering them, and dismembering them, is obviously a deranged human being. Anyone who would commit a crime like that has to be deranged. A death penalty on the law books would not serve as a deterrent to the Jeffrey L. Dahmers of the world.

If, as the advocates of capital punishment contend, capital punishment serves as a deterrent, then they should favor maximizing publicity generated by capital punishment through such spectacles as public hangings in city parks or electric-chair executions live and in color on national television. In that way, most people would be made more aware of what the consequences are to murder. In fact, death penalty advocates do not call for such a display of perverse taste.

Although proponents of the death penalty say that capital punishment saves lives, there is some evidence that capital punishment may cause homicides. In this regard psychologists have noted that there are some people who wish to take their own lives but are afraid to commit suicide. By causing murders, these people will feel assured that someone else—government— will execute them by punishing them with the death penalty.[13] However rare such people are in society, they constitute a refutation of the view asserted by the supporters of capital punishment about the lifesaving feature of capital punishment.

To be sure, the imposition of the ultimate sanction on a murderer ensures that *that* murderer will take no more lives. Few released murderers kill again in any event. One major study of eight American states, including California, New York, Ohio, and Connecticut, found that only half of 1 percent of murderers paroled or serving time were ever guilty of another homicide.[14]

Disrespect for Life. The act of taking a life through the imposition of the death penalty makes the point to society that life is of no value. Some years ago opponents of the death penalty in Canada put it aptly when they said, "Why do we kill people who kill people in order to teach that killing people is wrong?"[15]

There are sanctions other than the death penalty that should be imposed against violent criminals. Society should send a message to criminals and would-be criminals that they will be punished. As important as sending a message to the violator of the law, however, is a message that society sends itself. That message should be: Life is important, and we should not take another life when one already has been taken.

Disrespect for the Law. Supporters of the death penalty cite the need for the ultimate sanction in order to uphold law and order. In the way that the death penalty is actually implemented, however, an irreverence and disrespect for the law are revealed. The imposition of capital punishment is arbitrary and capricious and is often the result of racial or economic discrimination.

In most countries that have the death penalty, but in the United States in particular, being put to death for a specific offense is not universally mandated by the law. Some states in the American federal system have the death penalty for a particular offense, and other states do not. Some juries and judges are more severe than others, moreover. A legal system in a free society purports to be unbiased and impartial. Yet the application of the death penalty to one person instead of another is often an arbitrary decision.

Capital punishment is also disrespectful of law because the principal losers in the system are the poor and members of minority groups. Rarely is someone in the middle or upper classes executed for a capital offense. Often these people can obtain excellent lawyers who can plea bargain their cases. In **plea bargaining**, a defendant admits guilt to a lesser charge than the prosecuting attorney prepares to bring so as to avoid a more severe punishment.

In the United States, moreover, minority group members are disproportionately represented on death row. Forty percent of prisoners awaiting execution in the United States as of December 31, 1990 were black, according to statistics released by the U.S. Justice Department's Bureau of Statistics, although blacks con-

[13] Statement of Hugo Adam Bedau, professor of philosophy at Tufts University, in U.S. Congress, Senate, Committee on the Judiciary, *Capital Punishment,* Hearings, 97th Congress, 1st Sess., 1981, p. 521.

[14] Judith Marciano, "Death Penalty—No!" *New York Times* August 14, 1982, p. 23.

[15] Quoted by Henry Schwarzchild in U.S. Congress, House, Committee on the Judiciary, Subcommittee on Criminal Justice, *Federal Criminal Law Revision,* Hearings, 97th Congress, 1st and 2d Sess., 1981 and 1982, pt. 2, p. 1181.

stitute 12.1 percent of the U.S. population.[16] The evidence indicates that a black offender who kills a white person is more likely to get the death penalty than a black person who kills a black person or a white person who kills a black person.[17] There is much wrong with a system that is so arbitrary and capricious as to victimize one important segment of the population merely because of race or economic condition.

Cruel and Unusual Punishment. Inflicting the punishment of death upon law breakers is a practice with roots in ancient times. In the past some methods of death have been particularly depraved, such as boiling people alive, dismembering them, drawing and quartering, and impaling.

The standards of universal decency have changed. Many civilized people now believe it is not humane to kill anyone—even under the sanction of law—by hanging, the guillotine, electric chair, gas, or even lethal injection. Amnesty International has justly called for the abolition of the death penalty. Every Western democratic country has banned this practice except the United States.

Standards of punishment are not immutable. In earlier centuries the death penalty was inflicted for all kinds of offenses, and particularly for any form of murder. About two centuries ago, distinctions were drawn between first- and second-degree murder on the basis of the callousness of the act. Subsequent efforts have been made to further delineate different degrees of punishment for different kinds of crimes. Among these include distinctions between intentional and unintentional murders, and planned and unpremeditated killings. The psychological condition of the person who commits a harsh crime has been a mitigating factor in sentencing, moreover.

It would seem, then, that capital punishment should be abolished in those countries that revere civil liberties and civil rights. To say that capital punishment should be abolished does not mean to say that criminals who commit vicious crimes should go unpunished. A life sentence in a penal institution is a horrible sentence for anyone to experience. It is sometimes said that being in some prisons is worse than a sentence of death because of the prisoner's loss of freedom and, in some cases, lack of personal safety.

A purpose of punishment is to inflict suffering and deprivation of liberty on law breakers. Prisons safeguard the community from law breakers, and they provide sufficient retribution to those who commit horrible crimes on other members of the community.

Legal Mistakes. The possibility of making mistakes about a person accused of committing a horrible crime is another argument for abolishing the death sentence. Who can say if some of the more than 2,600 condemned people on death row in the United States are in fact innocent? No system of criminal justice is perfect. In the past innocent people have been unjustly sent to prison for crimes that they did not commit. When people are in prison, they can still be set free if evidence emerges of their innocence. Once they are put to death, however, the truth will not benefit them at all.

The death penalty is barbaric. It does not deter criminals from committing violent crimes, and it does not strengthen respect for life and law. It allows for no corrections of mistakes in the criminal justice system, and it should, consequently, be abolished.

[16] As cited in "Capital Punishment," *Facts on File* 51 (September 26, 1991: 741.

[17] Bedau, statement in *Capital Punishment*, p. 203.

16/NO   SHOULD CAPITAL PUNISHMENT BE ABOLISHED?

Let those who want to abolish capital punishment hear the horror stories of people whose loved ones have been murdered, maimed, or crippled, and perhaps even their sensitivity will be touched for the victim rather than the perpetrator of uncivilized behavior. Only then will they be likely to see the merits of capital punishment.

Capital punishment is a necessary form of punishment in a civilized society because: (1) it serves as a deterrent to killings; (2) it signifies a respect for life; (3) it affirms the principle of the rule of law; (4) it is a fitting punishment for certain kinds of crimes; and (5) it is for the most part likely to hurt the guilty rather than the innocent.

Deterrence. It is difficult to prove that capital punishment prevents people from killing. Clearly, some murderers will not be deterred by capital punishment. Some of these would include people who commit crimes of passion or insane acts. The law recognizes distinctions in the different kinds of murders that are committed, although, to be sure, the victims are dead no matter what the mental state of assailant. Many murders are committed, however, because the killers feel that they can get away with their crimes.

In the United States, for example, only three out of one hundred felonies ever lead to imprisonment. In New York, as the conservative writer Ernest van den Haag points out, "Such offenses as car theft, minor muggings, and minor burglaries have been *de facto* decriminalized."[18] This is to say that people are hardly ever punished for committing those offenses. In many respects crime pays when there is no effective punishment.

Although the evidence is sketchy, it is reasonable to assume that there is a relationship between the kind of punishment meted out and an offense. With more stringent enforcement of laws against drunken drivers, for example, people are probably less likely to drive under the influence of alcohol. It is reasonable to assume that the greater the penalty, the less likely an individual will be to commit a felony.

Some social scientists have provided evidence that capital punishment serves as a deterrent, although there is much controversy on this point. Isaac Erlich, an econometrician at the University of Chicago, argues that capital punishment prevents more murders than do prison sentences. Admittedly, it is impossible to speak scientifically on the subject since, as the political scientist James Q. Wilson notes: "To study behavior that does not occur is all but impossible."[19]

Many criminals act in a rational manner. They are not likely to commit crimes in locations where the police are out in high numbers. They make cost-benefit analyses based on an evaluation of risk to gains. If they feel that they can get away with murder, they will murder. A system that provides prompt and effective implementation of the death penalty would, consequently, be calculated into their cost-benefit assessments. If crime pays, there is no practical deterrent to people lacking moral values. If crime is punished, the immoral people will more likely be deterred.

In the United States, there has been an increase in the number of murders at the same time that there has been a decrease in the number of people legally executed for committing capital offenses. In 1950, 82 convicted felons were executed, many of whom were convicted for homicide. During the same year, 7,020 homicides were reported. In 1960, the number of legal executions dropped to 56, and the number of criminal homicides rose to 9,140. In the 1960s, there was a steady increase in the number of homicides, with 14,590 reported in 1969.[20] In 1990 there were 23,000 criminal homicides and only 23 executions.[21]

Reverence for Life. Critics of capital punishment berate proponents of this form of punishment because it shows a disrespect for life. That is not the case. Capital punishment signifies a reverence for life.

In Western societies more people are killed than are punished in violent crimes. In the United States the bloodbath is in homicides. The media report the daily toll: A six-year-old child abducted, tortured, and dismembered; a housewife raped and brutalized; an elderly retiree robbed and hammered to death; a skid-row derelict beaten to death. So common has murder become in the United States that reports of multiple killings are no longer considered to be important news items and wind up in the middle of a newspaper or at the end of a newscast—just more incidents in the life of a big city. Let us then fight fire with fire and show our respect for life

[18]Ernest van den Haag, "Thinking about Crime Again," *Commentary* 76 (December 1983): 74.

[19]James Q. Wilson, "Thinking about Crime," *Atlantic Monthly* 252 (September 1983): 76

[20]These figures are drawn from a statement by Norman Darwick, executive director of the International Association of Chiefs of Police, in *Capital Punishment*, pp. 116–17.

[21]Susan Okie, "Violent Crimes Up 10.0% Last Year," *Washington Post*, April 29, 1991, p. A6.

by punishing the perpetrator of violent crime in a manner befitting the crime.

Opponents of the death penalty like to point to the horrors of the death penalty—how the criminal suffered during the execution by electric chair or through lethal injection. What they ignore, however, are the sufferings of the innocent victims of the assailants who commit murders and rapes. Even from their graves, the victims cry out for justice.

Respect for the Law. Capital punishment demonstrates a reverence for law. In free societies law constitutes what a society regards as permissible or impermissible. A purpose of law is to permit people to abide by rules peacefully without resorting to violent means. In this sense, law is essential in a civilized society.

Most basic to a system of law is that human life is to be protected. Legal systems that do not at the minimum guarantee that principle will lose a sense of authority and legitimacy, which is essential to the stability of any political community.

Punishment should reflect the outrage of a community when illegal acts are committed beyond the pale of civilized behavior. The Nuremberg trials that were held after World War II to bring Nazi leaders to justice for their violations of international law were an apt demonstration of the outrage of the world community over Nazi acts. So, too, does capital punishment reflect the outrage of communities for extremely vicious crimes. Preserving the life of vicious criminals is too great a price to pay when the sanctity of the law is in jeopardy.

Nor is it relevant that members of minorities are disproportionately represented on death row. Statistics may be misleading in matters of the death penalty. The former Supreme Court Justice Lewis Powell has pointed out that, according to one study, only 4 percent of black homicide defendants got the death penalty, as opposed to 7 percent of white defendants. The conservative writer William F. Buckley, Jr., comments from Powell's observation, "So, a case can be made that capital punishment discriminates against whites."[22]

Moreover, whatever disparity exists along racial lines in this matter is irrelevant to the debate at issue. As the psychologist David Lester notes:

This is not an argument against the death penalty. It is an argument against discrimination. For example, discrimination in public transport or housing or restaurants did not lead to the elimination of buses, houses, or restaurants. It led to efforts to eliminate the discrimination.[23]

Fitting Punishment. Capital punishment is an appropriate punishment for the people who commit crimes that are so gruesome as to warrant the most supreme penalty that society can inflict. It is not true that the death penalty is "cruel and unusual" punishment.

The death penalty is an ancient form of punishment. The men who forbade "cruel and unusual punishments" in the Eighth Amendment of the Constitution did not mean to exclude capital punishment. What they had in mind was that certain methods of inflicting the death penalty, such as burning, drawing and quartering, and impaling, be eliminated. Criminals were put to death before and after the Bill of Rights was adopted, and it is clear that the Framers supported the principle of the death penalty. It is true that the Supreme Court in *Furman v. Georgia* outlawed the death penalty under certain conditions in 1972, but that was only because of the wording of the death penalty statutes in certain states. In *Gregg v. Georgia* the Court in 1976 upheld the principle of the death penalty for certain kinds of punishment.

To be sure, because we support the death penalty does not mean that it should be applied in all cases. We do not justify the death penalty for economic crimes, as was the practice in the past in many communist countries. Nor do we justify the death penalty for offenses that are accidental, unpremeditated, or committed as a result of mental disorders. But the death penalty should be applied for certain criminal offenses so horrible as to require that supreme penalty.

When society puts a killer to death, it is paying him or her back in kind for the atrocity that that individual has committed. It is retribution pure and simple. Retribution must be paid in kind for the offense committed. By not instituting this kind of penalty, the people who abide by the law are being punished. That betrayal of people who obey the law is a travesty to any just legal system.

---

[22] William F. Buckley, Jr., "The Bench and the Chair," *National Review* 39 (May 22, 1987): 15.

[23] David Lester, *The Death Penalty: Issues and Answers* (Springfield, Ill.: Charles C. Thomas, 1987), p. 61.

Legal Mistakes. To eliminate capital punishment because of the possibility of mistakes is not a justification for doing away with the death penalty. If a mistake is the criterion, then we ought to wipe all penalties off the books because of the possibility of mistakes.

It is, of course, true that there always exists the possibility of mistakes. In Western democratic systems, however, that danger is remote. Cases involving capital punishment are subject to review at different levels of the courts. In the United States the trying of the case and the cumbersome appeals process result in a delay of several years before all legal methods are exhausted.

It should also be recognized that there is much more professionalism in law enforcement than used to be the case. Police departments often demand that their police officials have academic credentials that are relevant to the work they are doing. Law enforcement agencies, consequently, are more likely than ever before to include expert criminologists, medical technicians, and intelligent police officers, so that the risk of punishing the innocent person by mistake is not likely.

Capital punishment, then, should not be abolished. It helps deter certain kinds of crime; it saves lives; it upholds the law; it is the appropriate punishment for certain kinds of offenses; and it is more likely to be applied carefully than ever before.

17/YES SHOULD HATE-SPEECH CODES BE ADOPTED AT PUBLIC UNIVERSITIES IN THE UNITED STATES?

To respond to incidents and insults directed primarily at racial and religious groups and to women, more than two hundred private and public institutions of higher learning have either revised their student codes or enacted new ones. Through such codes, colleges and universities hope to prevent offensive statements on race, sex, religion, national origin, or sexual preference. Discipline for violating the codes ranges from a reprimand to suspension and even expulsion.

The speech code adopted by the Board of Regents at the University of Wisconsin in 1989 is one example. It barred slurs or epithets that were based on a person's race, sex, religion, sexual orientation, disability, or ethnic origin. According to the code, students would be penalized if the slurs create a "hostile learning environment" for someone.[24]

Although a federal district judge struck down the Wisconsin code in 1991 on the grounds that it violated students' First Amendment rights, it is to be hoped that the wording of the code can be redrafted to meet a constitutional challenge. Courts have the authority to invalidate codes at public colleges and universities because they are creatures of the state. Private colleges and universities for the most part are free from judicial interference in such a matter.

Hate-speech codes at colleges and universities are desirable because: (1) the First Amendment does not guarantee an absolute right of freedom of speech, and hate speech falls into the category of a legitimate restriction on free speech; (2) hate speech is particularly offensive because of the harm it causes its targets; (3) hate-speech codes protect the atmosphere of learning important to universities; and (4) codes can be written in a manner assuring that freedom of speech will not be curtailed.

First Amendment Rights. The First Amendment appears to be precise and absolute. It states in part: "Congress shall make no law . . . abridging the freedom of speech." But few people argue that freedom of speech under the First Amendment is absolute. During periods of war and national emergency, courts have limited freedom to speak views that were dangerous to the war effort. However difficult it is for individuals and courts to define pornography, courts have said that governments can ban it. Courts have allowed government to restrict freedom of speech and the press in public elementary schools under certain conditions. Government restrictions on commercial speech, such as advertisements for liquor and tobacco, have been upheld. Laws have been enacted, moreover, to

[24] Michele Collison, "Hate-Speech Code at U. of Wisconsin Voided by Court," *Chronicle of Higher Education* 38 (October 23, 1991): A1.

allow civil damages to a person who has been defamed.

One way that the Supreme Court has curtailed speech is through the "fighting words" doctrine as asserted in *Chaplinsky v. New Hampshire*[25] and modified in other cases. According to this doctrine, a verbal attack targeting a particular individual in a direct confrontational manner that might produce a violent reaction may be penalized.

Courts have also sustained a restriction on freedom of speech when it interferes with the special goals of an institution. Freedom of speech, consequently, is regulated at a military base because the military requires unquestioned response to orders. Freedom of speech is restricted at schools and prisons because of their special functions.

Hate-speech codes at universities are not, therefore, establishing a precedent in the limitation of free speech. One can be a champion of the First Amendment and still favor hate-speech codes at colleges and universities. Such codes allow colleges and universities to perform their mission in society as a place where rational discussion aids the search for truth.

But even if one accepts a purist notion of the First Amendment, one could still support hate-speech codes. Advocates of free speech in a society explain that through the clash of ideas, people can make rational judgments about the best policies that will serve society. But epithets, insults, and racist and sexist symbols are not ideas; they are irrational speech. Irrational speech does not serve the cause of public discourse but promotes instead only irrational stereotyping deserving of no special protection.

Harm. Quite obviously, one must have a justification for restricting speech. As Oliver Wendell Holmes explained, one does not have the free speech right to falsely shout "fire" in a crowded theater because many people might be killed or injured while rushing to the exits.

And so, too, hate speech causes serious injury. Racial epithets against African-Americans are a case in point. Racist epithets tell African-Americans that they are second-class citizens, not worthy of the rights afforded to other Americans. Moreover, the epithets demean them not for anything that they have done but for who

they are. Such epithets also often imply physical threats.

It is sometimes said that hate speech will not end racism or sexism but will drive it underground. Even if such a view is accepted, it is irrelevant. For racism is an evil that causes harm to people just as a gun in the hands of a criminal can cause harm.

It is also said that the First Amendment has historically benefited minorities and others advocating unpopular ideas. But that is not always the case. First, the First Amendment coexisted with the institution of slavery. And even after the Civil War brought slavery to an end, violence and discrimination against African-Americans continued.

Second, we should be aware that when racism is allowed to be expressed, it can and will be strengthened. To permit racism the opportunity to take root through First Amendment protection creates a greater danger to society—to oppressed groups and to freedom itself—than would be the case if racist speech were punished.

Atmosphere of Learning. The issue under discussion is not hate-speech laws everywhere but hate-speech codes at universities. Universities are special places in a free society that must protect freedom of speech. The tradition of academic freedom in a university is based on respect for differing views; academic freedom is based in the belief that truth can be reached through the free exchange of ideas.

But hate speech stifles participation by students who are the objects of insults. Those who speak hate will cause minorities and women to refrain from participating in the dialogue that searches for truth. The purpose of racist epithets is to alienate the subjects of attack rather than engage them in dialogue. Hate-speech codes, in contrast, will strengthen participation by all members of a college and university community by making certain that no one is alienated from that community.

Hate speech often implies physical threats. When symbols of the Ku Klux Klan (KKK) are written on the walls of a black-student fraternity, they bring to mind the terror of the KKK, including the memory of lynchings that made the KKK a symbol of hate. The effect of this reminder is intimidation. And so, if the First Amendment absolutists have their way, racists might freely express the ideas, while their victims would be

[25]*Chaplinsky V. New Hampshire*, 315 U.S. 568 (1942).

stifled. As James T. Laney, the president of Emory University, says: "People do not feel free to speak when they are bullied—when the message they hear is not 'I disagree with you' but 'I wish you didn't exist.'"[26]

And so, hate-speech codes are valid because without them classes of people who have experienced injustice will be discouraged from speaking out.

Insults vs. Ideas. The courts have thrown out a number of university codes on the ground that they were restrictions on students' First Amendment rights. The hate-speech codes at the University of Michigan and the University of Wisconsin, for example, were ruled unconstitutional. But hate-speech codes can be written more precisely so as to be constitutional.

It is important to recognize that hate-speech codes are designed to deal with insults and not with ideas. They should not be written in a manner that discourages different points of view. And so, if a graduate student is pursuing research that shows ethnic or racial differences in I.Q., a code would not interfere with that research. Nor would it impede the work of someone who opposes affirmative action. And if someone openly expressed opinions taking issue with the opinions of civil rights or feminist groups, then he or she could proceed without fear of university interference—so long as the opinions were in the realm of ideas and not insults. Thinking is advanced through the conflict of ideas, but racist insults have nothing to do with the quest for truth.

Courts have already made some useful dis-

[26] James T. Laney, "Why Tolerate Campus Bigots?" *New York Times*, April 6, 1990, p. A35.

tinctions in matters of rights. The fact that it is difficult to make distinctions does not mean that distinctions cannot be made. While terms such as *obscenity* and *invasion of privacy* are difficult to define or to apply to concrete situations, courts have recognized that distinctions in these areas must be made to have legal consequences.

Courts have distinguished speech from action. Courts have held that people are free to speak out against the government but not free to incite a crowd to violence against an immediate target. KKK members are permitted to march in parades, but they are not allowed to wear hoods over their faces. Following this line of reasoning, universities may adopt codes to prevent epithets from being publicly uttered.

We should not fear that the existence of hate-speech codes in colleges and universities will lead us down a slippery slope toward dictatorship. Countries that revere civil liberties, such as Great Britain and Canada, have adopted group libel laws penalizing speech that defames ethnic and racial groups, and they have not experienced an erosion of civil liberties or free speech. We assert that the adoption of less-restrictive rules applying to public colleges and universities would not endanger freedom in the United States either.

It is essential that hate-speech codes be adopted at public colleges and universities. They are needed for their refinements to the First Amendment, their ability to prevent harm to students, the benefits that suit them to the learning atmosphere of colleges and universities, and the potential of drafting them to be in accord with the Constitution.

17/NO SHOULD HATE-SPEECH CODES BE ADOPTED AT PUBLIC UNIVERSITIES IN THE UNITED STATES?

Although college campuses in the United States have experienced increasing racism and sexism, hate-speech codes are not the appropriate remedy. Speech that is harmful to individual groups, such as minorities and women, must be condemned, but hate-speech codes simply replace one evil—group hatred—with another—the suppression of freedom of speech.

Hate-speech codes should not be adopted at public universities because: (1) they are a violation of the First Amendment; (2) more harm

than good will result from such restrictions; (3) universities require even more freedom of speech than is permitted in other segments of society; and (4) hate-speech codes are usually vague, and their vagueness promotes even greater erosion of liberty.

First Amendment Rights. The first Amendment provides a legal basis for free speech in the United States. It guarantees that individuals have the right to speak their opinions however much the opinions conflict with majority viewpoints.

The American constitutional system recognizes a distinction between acts and words. A white person who draws swastikas or KKK symbols on a black student's door can be charged with defacing property. A gang of thugs who assault a woman face legal penalties. These examples are acts, not words.

In protecting free speech, however, government must be neutral. It must not take a position favoring one individual's right to speak over another's but must act to preserve the freedom of both the majority and the dissenters.

Free speech must protect even obnoxious opinions. If the freedom of one group is compromised, the freedom of all groups is threatened. Thus, as has frequently been pointed out, the protection of free speech must often be most vigorously defended for people who are not nice: fascists, communists, pornographers, and even professional criminals. The only way to assure that our freedoms are maintained is to protect other peoples' freedom.

If today, students can be disciplined for wearing a sexist T-shirt, writing a racial parody, or displaying a Confederate flag—real offenses that have been the target of the hate-speech codes—then tomorrow, when the political atmosphere is different, advocates of civil rights and feminism can be denied freedom of speech. And so, we must allow people who disagree with us to have their say, no matter how obnoxious their viewpoints.

Harm. However well-intentioned the proponents of hate-speech codes may be, the codes would do more harm than good. First, denying people the freedom to openly express their views for fear of punishment does not mean that people abandon their positions, as the experience of communism attests. In communist tyrannies, people were forbidden to express views in disagreement with the prevailing communist ideology. But still they quietly hated communism. Once the communist system began to collapse, people poured into the streets to show their contempt for communism and the results of decades of communist government. The communist collapse in Europe, consequently, was swift.

All hate-speech codes accomplish is to drive hate speech underground. They do not eliminate it. And suppressed bigotry is more difficult to locate and confront. The codes may lead people to believe that bigotry had disappeared when in fact it continues to exist.

Moreover, the kind of bigotry that would appear above ground would change in form but not in substance. If bigots find that certain words are banned at a university, they will invent others as polite substitutes that will be more difficult to ban because superficially, at least, they are accepted as civil discourse. One cannot prevent an idea from being thought or an opinion from being held merely because one forbids the public utterance of words and ideas that are unpleasant.

Second, people who want to ban speech have a simplistic notion about the consequences. Prohibitionists thought that if alcohol were banned people would not drink. Health advocates believe that the banning of tobacco advertisements on television will decrease the number of smokers. And religious fundamentalists and some feminists hold that banning pornography will decrease sexual indulgence. Similarly, hate-speech code advocates think that banning bigoted speech will eliminate bigotry.

Third, hate-speech codes do not prepare students for living in the world outside of a college or university. These consequences can be harmful to those supposedly protected by the codes. Black students can be lulled into a false sense of security if they do not encounter the kinds of expressions they are going to hear in the real world. If universities become genteel places that suppress unpopular speech, young black people will graduate unprepared.

In this regard, Alan Keyes, a conservative African-American who served as a member of the U.S. delegation to the United Nations, says he would feel cheated if he were denied contact with white racist views. He added that under those conditions, if he got into a debate with a white racist who called him a nasty name, he would lose his mind.[27]

Fourth, hate-speech codes are condescending to minority and other students whom the codes are supposed to benefit. These codes assume that minority students are so incapable of expressing their own views and of dealing with bigots that they have to be protected from unpleasant words. In fact, minority students are familiar with the arguments and epithets mouthed by bigots and can be trusted to respond rationally and intelligently when they are the subjects of verbal attack.

[27] Steve France, "Hate Goes to College," *ABA Journal* 76 (July 1990), p. 49.

Fifth, it is important to keep in mind that minorities and representatives of unpopular causes have benefited from First Amendment protection. Abolitionists in the 1840s, organized labor in the 1920s and 1930s, civil rights protesters in the 1950s and 1960s, and war protesters in the 1960s and 1970s were aided by their free-speech right. Whereas today most college and university administrations are responsive to minority and women's concerns, in the future they may not be. It is essential, consequently, to strengthen the fundamental right of freedom of speech for all points of view if we want to have our own points of view heard when they are unpopular.

Atmosphere of Learning. Universities are special places, but they are still subject to the rights accorded to all Americans. The danger in the American system of rights is that too many groups seek to suppress freedom of speech when they regard a subject as a "special case" deserving an extraordinary exception to the principle of free speech. And so, conservatives have opposed the freedom of a protester burning the American flag in protest, tried to get an exhibit of homoerotic pictures of the artist Robert Mapplethorpe from being exhibited at a gallery in Cincinnati, and sought to ban offensive rap song tapes from being sold at stores. Some liberals favored banning an American Nazi march in Skokie in a predominantly Jewish neighborhood, imposing penalties on writers and photographers for creating pornographic works, and punishing people who tell sex jokes in the workplace. Many of those who would ban speech say that they believe in free speech but not in this particular case. But permitting too many "special cases" will nibble the principle away. The banning of hate speech on a campus should not be argued on a special case basis.

Universities are special places in American society—places that ought to allow for greater freedom than even the rest of society. The mission of a university is the search for truth. Universities are forums for discussion and debate based on reason. They are particularly able to respond to hateful ideas through the use of reason and to show those hateful ideas to be without foundation.

Why do some administrators, faculty, and students feel that the university community cannot handle hate speech? Codes make no sense when there are better ways to fight bigotry. When faced with racial or gender epithets, the university community can organize meetings to show opposition. The community can show by words and deeds that it is committed to fairness and equality for all its members.

Insults versus Ideas. A problem with codes is that they are inherently ambiguous, blurring the line between epithets and ideas. It is difficult to frame a code so that it is sufficiently restrictive and still constitutional. How many categories should be included in the scope of hate-speech codes? The University of Michigan code forbade not only any "behavior, verbal or physical, that stigmatizes or victimizes an individual on the basis of race, ethnicity, religion, sex, sexual orientation, creed, national origin [and] ancestry." It also protected "age, marital status, handicap, or Vietnam-era veteran status."[28] Such an all-encompassing code was appropriately declared by a court to be in conflict with the First Amendment.

Moreover, a major problem with these codes is that they give license to people to broaden their scope to include ideas as well as epithets and even to embrace trivial matters. It is one thing to discipline a student for an act he or she has taken, such as defacing someone's property or directly harassing an individual. There are legitimate penalties for such offenses that do not conflict with the First Amendment.

But hate-speech codes have been adopted that threaten to punish students for wearing T-shirts with offensive slogans, or printing cartoons in university newspapers, or hanging Confederate flags outside of a dormitory, or even hanging an American flag outside a dormitory.

Some declared offenses have been borderline cases, pursued because administrators find it easier to bring disciplinary action against insults than to ignore them as bad ideas. Is putting a Confederate flag outside of a dorm worthy of reprimand? It is in some codes. Are suggestions for "white studies" programs an insult or an idea? At one campus even "inappropriate laughter" could produce a reprimand if the laughter could be interpreted as tinged with racism or sexism. The vagueness of these codes suggest that they are a bad idea.

Hate-speech codes are contrary to the First Amendment, cause more harm than good, are ill-suited to the purposes of a university, and are too ambiguous. They have no place in public college and university communities.

[28]*Doe v. University of Michigan*, 721 F. Supp. 852, 866 (E.D. Mich. 1989).

KEY TERMS

Bail
Blasphemy
Capital punishment
Civil disobedience
Civil liberties
Civil rights
"Clear and present danger"
Common law
Conscientious objection
Direct action
Dissent
Double jeopardy
Due process of law
Economic and social rights
Equal protection of the law
Ex post facto law
Freedom of assembly
Freedom of petition
Freedom of religion
Freedom of speech
Freedom of the press

Grand jury
Habeas corpus
Hate-speech codes
Higher law
Natural law
Obscenity
Plea bargaining
Police state
Political rights
Positive law
Prior restraint
Resistance
Right
Right to confront one's accusers
Right to counsel
Right to trial by impartial jury
Satyagraha
Sedition
Self-incrimination
Slander
Warrant

QUESTIONS

Civil Liberties and Civil Rights

1. Are human rights meaningful if defined exclusively in political terms? Why?
2. Should a suspect go free merely because a police officer committed a technical violation of the law in securing evidence? Why?
3. What role should government play in regulating pornography? Why?
4. How would you reconcile freedom of the press with the rights of the accused in criminal proceedings?
5. What effect do constitutional rights protecting persons accused of committing a crime have on crime?
6. What is the meaning of equality in civil rights?
7. What criteria should be used in determining whether a particular group in a country is the subject of discrimination? Why do you select these criteria?

Civil Disobedience

1. Is resistance ever justified? Why?
2. Is there a higher law that takes precedence over human law? Explain.
3. What effect does civil disobedience have on strengthening a respect for law?
4. What effect do acts of civil disobedience have on popular support for the views that civil disobedients favor?
5. Should a democracy tolerate civil disobedience? Why?

Capital Punishment

1. What criteria should be used in determining whether capital punishment constitutes "cruel and unusual punishment"?
2. What effect would evidence indicating that capital punishment is inflicted disproportionately on minority and poor members of

society have on your opinion of the issue? What are the reasons for your answer?

3. What is the relationship between capital punishment and crime deterrence?

4. What kinds of crimes should warrant a sentence of capital punishment? What are the reasons for your answer?

5. What methods should be used in carrying out the death penalty? Are these methods humane? Does it matter whether they are humane or not? Why?

Hate-Speech Codes

1. What effect does a hate-speech code have on a campus?

2. What criteria should be used in evaluating whether a remark or event calls for a disciplinary action?

3. Who should determine whether a remark or event is in violation of a hate-speech code?

4. What criteria should be used to determine whether insults other than racial should be covered by hate-speech codes?

5. Is a hate-speech code consistent with the First Amendment? What are the reasons for your answer?

6. Should a law providing for hate-speech codes on private colleges and universities be adopted? What are the reasons for your answer?

RECOMMENDED READINGS

ABRAM, MORRIS B. "What Constitutes a Civil Right?" *New York Times Magazine,* June 10, 1984, pp. 52–54, 58, 60, 62, 64, 66. An analysis of the meaning of civil rights.

ALBERT, PETER J., and RONALD HOFFMAN, eds. *We Shall Overcome: Martin Luther King, Jr., and the Black Freedom Struggle.* New York: Pantheon Books, 1990. A collection of essays about the civil rights leader.

BARKER, LUCIUS J., and TWILEY W. BARKER, JR. *Civil Liberties and the Constitution: Cases and Commentaries.* 6th ed. Englewood Cliffs, N.J.: Prentice Hall, 1990. A casebook on the Constitution.

BICKEL, ALEXANDER M. *The Morality of Consent.* New Haven: Yale University Press, 1975. An argument that the morality of consent to law is essential to a free and civilized society.

BUNCH, CHARLOTTE. "Women's Rights as Human Rights: Toward a Re-Vision of Human Rights." *Human Rights Quarterly* 12 (November 1990): 486–98. A case for considering women's rights as part of human rights.

CRANSTON, MAURICE. *What Are Human Rights?* New York: Taplinger, 1973. Clarification by a political philosopher of the assumptions underlying human rights.

DONNELLY, JACK. *Universal Human Rights in Theory and Practice.* Ithaca, N.Y.: Cornell University Press, 1989. A broad treatment of the subject.

DONOHUE, WILLIAM A. "The New Agenda of the ACLU." *Society* 28 (January/February 1991): 5–13. A critique of the ACLU.

HENKIN, LOUIS. *The Age of Rights.* New York: Columbia University Press, 1990. An analysis of international human rights and the rights of the United States.

HOOK, SIDNEY. *Heresy, Yes—Conspiracy, No.* New York: John Day, 1953. An argument that the liberal has a commitment to protect heresies defined as unpopular ideas, but not conspiracies that would destroy fundamental liberties.

KARST, KENNETH L. *Belonging to America: Equal Citizenship and the Constitution.* New Haven: Yale University Press, 1989. A legal analysis of equality in the United States.

LAQUEUR, WALTER, and BARRY RUBIN, eds. *Human Rights Reader.* Rev. ed. New York: New American Library, 1989. A collection of major documents and articles on human rights.

RENTELN, ALISON DUNDES. *International Human Rights: Universalism Versus Relativism.* Newbury Park, Calif.: Sage Publications, 1990. A consideration of whether there is any such thing as universal human rights.

WALKER, SAMUEL. *In Defense of American Liberties: A History of the ACLU.* New York: Oxford University Press, 1990. A study of the role of a civil liberties organization in the U.S. political system.

Civil Disobedience

BAY, CHRISTIAN. "Civil Disobedience." *International Encyclopaedia of the Social Sciences* (1968), 2:473–87.

COHEN, CARL. *Civil Disobedience: Conscience, Tactics, and the Law.* New York: Columbia University Press, 1971. A general theory of civil disobedience.

FISCHER, LOUIS. *The Life of Mahatma Gandhi.* New York: Harper, 1950. A biography of a leading advocate of passive resistance.

HARRIS, PAUL, ed. *Civil Disobedience.* Lanham, Md.: University Press of America, 1989. A collection of essays on the subject.

HOOK, SIDNEY. "Neither Blind Obedience Nor Uncivil Disobedience." *New York Times Magazine,* June 5, 1966, pp. 52–53, 122, 124, 126, 128. A discussion of the limits of civil disobedience.

"Militant Morality: Civil Disobedience and Bioethics." *Hastings Center Report,* 19 (November/December 1989): 23–45. Articles on civil disobedience and bioethical issues, such as abortion, AIDS research, and animal rights.

"On Civil Disobedience, 1967." *New York Times Magazine,* November 26, 1967, pp. 27–29, 122, 124, 126, 128–32. A symposium dealing with the limits of civil disobedience including articles by William F. Buckley, Jr., Noam Chomsky, John Cogley, John Dollard, James T. Farrell, Lewis S. Feuer, Paul Goodman, Sidney Hook, Herbert S. Kelman, Irving Kristol, Dwight Macdonald, Richard Rovere, and Bayard Rustin.

Capital Punishment

AMNESTY INTERNATIONAL. *United States of America: The Death Penalty.* London: Amnesty International Publications, 1987. An analysis and critique of the death penalty in the United States.

BALDUS, DAVID C., GEORGE WOODWORTH, and CHARLES A. PULASKI, JR. *Equal Justice and the Death Penalty: A Legal and Empirical Analysis.* Boston: Northeastern University Press, 1990. A study of equal justice in death sentencing in the United States between 1972 and 1987.

BEDAU, HUGO ADAM. *Death Is Different: Studies in the Morality, Law, and Politics of Capital Punishment.* Boston: Northeastern University Press, 1987. A critique of capital punishment.

BERGER, RAOUL. *Death Penalties: The Supreme Court's Obstacle Course.* Cambridge, Mass.: Harvard University Press, 1982. An analysis of how the Supreme Court has dealt with capital punishment.

BERNS, WALTER. *For Capital Punishment: Crime and the Morality of the Death Penalty.* New York: Basic Books, 1979. A case for the death penalty.

BLACK, CHARLES L., JR. *Capital Punishment: The Inevitability of Caprice and Mistake.* 2d ed. New York: Norton, 1981. A case against the death penalty.

BOHM, ROBERT M., ed. *The Death Penalty in America: Current Research.* Cincinnati: Anderson Publishing Co., 1991. Eight articles of up-to-date research on the subject.

GOLDBERG, STEPHEN. "So What If the Death Penalty Deters?" *National Review* 41 (June 30, 1989): 42, 44. A defense of the death penalty.

GRAY, IAN, and MOIRA STANLEY, eds. *A Punishment in Search of a Crime: Americans Speak Out against the Death Penalty.* New York: Avon Books, 1989. The views of opponents of the death penalty.

HORGAN, JOHN. "The Death Penalty: Most Americans Favor It, But What Purpose Does It Serve?" *Scientific American* 263 (July 1990): 17–18, 20. An argument against the death penalty.

Hate-Speech Codes

BARRINGER, FELICITY. "Campus Speech Pits Freedom of Speech against Racial Slurs." *New York Times,* April 25, 1989, pp. A1, A25. A description of the issues centering on hate-speech codes.

FLEISCHMAN, LISA M. "Banning Racist Speech Begs the Real Questions of Curbing Racism." *Los Angeles Times,* October 14, 1990, p. M5. Banning racist speech does not end racism.

FRANCE, STEVE. "Hate Goes to College." *ABA Journal* 76 (July 1990): 44–46, 48–49. An overview of the subject.

GALE, MARY ELLEN. "Reimagining the First Amendment: Racist Speech and Equal Liberty." *St. John's Law Review* 65 (Winter 1991):

119–85. The First Amendment should be interpreted so as to deter racism, sexism, and similar prejudices on university campuses.

HENTOFF, NAT. "Free Speech on the Campus." *Progressive* 53 (May 1989): 12–13. A criticism of the way universities are curbing freedom of speech.

LANEY, JAMES T. "Why Tolerate Campus Bigots?" *New York Times*, April 6, 1990, p. A35. A defense of special codes against racial speech at universities by the president of Emory University.

LAWRENCE, CHARLES R., III. "If He Hollers Let Him Go: Regulating Racist Speech on Campus." *Duke Law Journal* 1990 (June 1990): 431–83. A case defending the regulation of speech on university campuses.

RIEFF, DAVID. "The Case against Sensitivity." *Esquire* 114 (November 1990): 120–24, 127–28, 130, 132. An argument that efforts to strengthen sensitivity toward racial and ethnic ideas pose a threat to the First Amendment and to education.

ROSENBERG, DAVID. "Racist Speech, the First Amendment, and Public Universities: Taking a Stand on Neutrality." *Cornell Law Review* 76 (January 1991): 549–88. An argument that attempts to legislate against hate speech at public universities is hostile to the First Amendment commitment to free speech.

SCHMIDT, BENNO C., JR. "Universities Must Defend Free Speech." *Wall Street Journal*, May 6, 1991, p. A16. A defense of free speech against attempts to limit it at universities.

SELEGUE, SETH M. "Campus Anti-Slur Regulations: Speakers, Victims, and the First Amendment." *California Law Review* 79 (May 1991): 919–70. A defense of regulations.

chapter 8

Political parties and elections

When in the summer of 1992, delegates of the Democratic party assembled in a national convention and nominated Bill Clinton for president, and delegates of the Republican party selected George Bush as their standard bearer, they were acting out an important role in a democratic system: the choosing of candidates by political parties to compete in meaningful electoral contests for the right to run the government. In democratic countries, members of legislative and top executive offices are subject to some form of electoral competition, whether directly or indirectly chosen by the people, and political parties often play an important part in deciding who will occupy those positions.

Although the term *political party* in the United States is often associated first with Democrats and Republicans, it is used as a label for many different kinds of associations. Parties are found in dictatorships, too. In Adolf Hitler's Germany the Nazi (National Socialist) party and in Joseph Sta-

lin's Soviet Union the Communist party monopolized party rule. Critics labeled those parties as totalitarian (see Chapter 3). Political parties, moreover, are a feature of some developing states in Africa and other Third World countries and are different from either the totalitarian parties or the competitive parties found in many Western countries.

Although many studies have been made of political parties, students of the subject differ considerably in defining them. We will define a **political party** in its democratic context as an organization formed to contest elections by selecting candidates to run under its own party label. Since political parties in democracies are diverse in composition, objectives, and relationships to government, we recognize that such a definition does not adequately describe all democratic political parties. It certainly does not define political parties in undemocratic countries, where elections are a sham.

To understand political parties, we shall examine first the origin of political parties, the functions they perform in political systems, party systems, and the debate over the possible decline of political parties. We shall then study the different kinds of electoral systems in which competitive parties operate in democratic systems before concluding with an evaluation of two prominent electoral methods that influence the character of political parties.

ORIGIN OF POLITICAL PARTIES

If the term *political party* lacks precision in definition today, it is in part due to the varied organizations called political parties over the centuries. The term *political party* was used to describe groups of nobles and their followers in ancient times. From then until the seventeenth century, it connoted "faction" or "interest."[1] With the development of parliamentary bodies in eighteenth-century England, groups of leaders acting collectively in Parliament were sometimes called "parties." Parties in the modern sense are a development of the nineteenth century and arose from the need to mobilize the electorate, which increased in size as population and suffrage expanded. Because the United States was the first country to grant the suffrage broadly, it became the first to have modern political parties. Some scholars date the formation of parties to 1800, when Jeffersonian Republicans achieved electoral success over the ruling Federalists, but others trace it to the 1830s, when white manhood suffrage became widespread. In Great Britain, modern parties were propelled by the Reform Acts of 1832 and 1867, which expanded the suffrage. It was in the 1860s,

[1]See Austin Ranney, "The Concept of 'Party,' " in *Political Research and Political Theory*, ed. Oliver Garceau (Cambridge, Mass.: Harvard University Press, 1968), p. 145.

however, that the British electorate became big enough for parties to engage in organizational activities. Many Western European nations, moreover, developed parties in about the middle of the nineteenth century. Modern political parties, then, originated in a democratic context: namely, the need to organize voters in competitive elections.

FUNCTIONS OF PARTIES

Political parties developed in the Western democracies, but they have become a feature of most political systems in the twentieth century. Although the functions of political parties vary among and within political systems, some of their more essential functions may be highlighted. These are aggregating interests, formulating programs, nominating candidates to contest elections, running government, and strengthening ties between the government and the people.

Aggregating Interests

An important function that some political parties perform is to bring together a variety of interest groups under a single organization. Such a process is known as **interest aggregation**. Particularly in countries that have two major political parties, such as the United States and Great Britain, each party consists of followers from a wide spectrum of economic, social, racial, and ethnic groups. It is usually the case that the differences separating the parties are not as great in two-party systems as they are in multiparty systems, such as exist in some Western European democracies. In developing countries, parties are often devices for uniting populations into a national identity, transcending local, tribal, or regional loyalties.

Political parties are not the only organizations that aggregate interests. Government agencies and interest groups themselves perform a similar function. In Western democracies, however, parties have often served an important role in uniting different interests. A key distinction between interest groups and political parties, in fact, is that generally the political parties play a greater role in interest aggregation.

Formulating Programs

Political parties prepare programs for consideration by the public. Parties serve to organize opinion that is often otherwise unclear and undirected, so that voters can make rational judgments about policies and candidates. The **party platform**, which is a statement of party objectives and promises, announces to the people what the party stands for. The platform itself results from the reconciliation of conflicts and the assertion of common principles by the different segments of the party. Without such reconciliation, party splits become likely.

Party programs and platforms are important features of what is called **party government**. This is a system (usually consisting of two parties) in which each party presents a clear program for government action. In such a structure, the electorate decides on the party and its platform in periodic electoral contests. The victorious party then assumes control of government and puts its program into action. The British party system is often the model used by advocates of party government (see Chapter 11).

Nominating Candidates

The recruitment of political leaders is one of the most prominent party functions. Selection processes vary considerably. In Israel, for example, a small group of party leaders determines who will be the party's designees in an election. In other countries, the nominating system may be highly de-

centralized. In the United States, **primary elections**, in which ordinary members of a political party decide who will be the party's candidate in an election, constitute one method of selecting candidates. Sometimes only people who have preregistered for a political party may vote in that primary, and such a contest is known as a **closed primary**. When any registered voter can vote in any party's primary, it is known as an **open primary**. Other methods of selection in the United States involve district conventions, state conventions, and state committees. To choose a candidate for the presidency, a national convention is called every four years in which the delegates selected on a statewide basis designate a party nominee. Much variation in the selection process prevails in different countries, but the recruitment of candidates is an important feature of political parties in both democratic and undemocratic political systems.

Running the Government

Parties nominate candidates and contest elections for the purpose of controlling government. The term of office for controlling the government varies from country to country. In democratic systems electoral contests are the recognized manner of transferring power from one group of leaders to another. In some democratic countries the elected officials in the executive branch can bring into office thousands of political appointees to help run the vast bureaucracy. In other systems, however, the number of political appointees is kept small (see Chapter 12). The relationship between the political party members in a legislature and the extraparliamentary party organizations varies among many political systems as well.

Government and the People

Political parties often serve as an important link between government and people because of the character of the electoral process and the legitimizing functions of elections. During periods of elections, masses of people become mobilized to engage in political activity to a greater extent than at other times. They listen to debates about policy issues, and they consider candidates expressing their views. Such activity educates voters about politics.

By engaging in electoral contests directed by political parties in a democracy, ordinary citizens tend to accept the rules underlying the democratic system as well as the electoral outcomes. Political parties, then, constitute the legitimizing function of government in those instances in which the masses of people accept the way in which political leaders are selected to run the government.

Many parties do not perform all these functions. Some parties, for example, are organized along narrow ideological lines and do not attempt to aggregate interests. Still other parties have no concern in running a government but act as a kind of interest group to attract national attention. In developing countries, moreover, political parties play a greater role in modernization and economic development than they do in developed countries.

PARTY SYSTEMS

A **party system** is the pattern of party relationships that exists within a political unit. Party systems are often compared in terms of their number, objectives, strength, structure, and sources of support.

Number

In the past, party systems used to be described in terms of whether they were one-party, two-party, or multiparty systems. Many writers today, however, regard such distinctions as inadequate because the patterns of parties are much too diverse within each category.

One-Party Systems. Some scholars contend that the notion of a *one-party system* is a contradiction in terms. A party is derived from "a part," they argue, and more than one party is required to make up a party system. Other scholars note, however, that the expression *one-party system* has empirical utility. They distinguish different kinds of one-party systems, moreover, and we shall consider these variations here. One-party systems include not only totalitarian parties in dictatorships but also dominant parties in democracies. The party systems of some developing countries, moreover, may be considered in the one-party category.

The one-party totalitarian system characterized Germany under Hitler and the Soviet Union under Stalin. Both the Nazi party and the Communist party constituted an elite group concerned with the transformation of society. Totalitarian parties seek to promote their political control over all sectors of society, and ideological considerations play an important role in their behavior (see Chapters 3, 4, and 5). Beginning in 1989, Eastern European governments previously under communist rule replaced their largely one-party systems with multiparty systems.

A **dominant political party system** is one in which, although parties are free to compete in electoral contests, one party wins elections and rules all the time. Southern states in the United States, for example, used to be dominated by the Democratic party. The dominance has been challenged by the Republicans with some success—particularly in presidential contests—in the past few decades. In some countries outside the United States, such as Mexico and Singapore, one party wins all the time. In 1988, however, the dominant party in Mexico declined in voting strength, and it is an open question whether the Mexican party system is undergoing systemic change.

One-party rule has also appeared in some of the developing countries. In Tanzania and Kenya, for example, the one-party systems are not the same as the totalitarian model. They consist of different social, economic, and ideological segments of the countries, and competition within the party is greater than in communist systems. An all-embracing ideology is not a feature of such a one-party system, moreover. The justification for that kind of system is often that the needs of economic development and political integration for a new country require a measure of unity that only the one-party system can generate.

One-party rule in Africa is coming under increased attack. By 1991, Cape Verde, Côte d'Ivoire, Gabon, and São Tomé and Príncipe had scrapped their one-party systems. And other African countries show signs of adopting multiparty systems in the 1990s.

Two-Party Systems. Two-party systems are found in the United States and Great Britain and also in most countries settled in part by British emigrants. A two-party system is one in which two major political parties are the principal contenders for power, and there is alternation of office between them at periodic intervals. The Democratic party and the Republican party in the United States, and the Labour party and the Conservative party in Great Britain, are the major parties in those countries.

Although the British and American examples are often used to illustrate two-party systems, both systems generally have more than two parties. In the United States, third parties, such as the Progressive party of Henry Wallace in 1948 and the American Independent party of George Wallace in 1968, appear periodically. In Great Britain, minor parties have played an important role since the nineteenth century. Such parties as the Liberal Unionists, the Irish Nationalists, the early Labour party, and the Liberal Democratic party today are cases in point.

Minor parties have played important roles in both Great Britain and the United States. They have served as parties of economic protest, and their rising strength has influenced one or both of the major political parties to alter their party programs. When minor parties have formed by seceding from major parties, they have influenced the prospects for electoral success of the major parties. Minor parties also bring new issues to the attention of the nation. In Great Britain, minor party support of the larger major party has been a prerequisite for forming a government in many instances.

Multiparty Systems. Multiparty systems, consisting by definition of more than two parties, are found in many countries, most notably in Western European states. In the Scandinavian countries, Belgium, Holland, and Italy, for example, no one party is strong enough to win control of parliament. Instead, after an election is conducted, a government is set up, composed of different political parties. In other words, the cabinet contains members from a coalition of parties. In fact, every Western European state has been governed by a coalition for at least some time in the twentieth century.

No Parties. Although most countries possess political parties, some countries have none. Traditional monarchical systems existing mostly in the Middle East and parts of Asia, for example, have no parties and rule on the basis of traditional ethnic ties. Saudi Arabia and Jordan are cases in point. Military regimes, which are found mostly in developing countries, also often rule without political parties. On occasion, the military rule is replaced by party rule when the military finds it essential to broaden its base of support.

Objectives

Political parties vary in terms of their goals. The terms *doctrinaire* and *broker* are used to contrast two parties with different kinds of objectives. A **doctrinaire party** is one which is concerned with promoting an ideological objective. In that sense, communist and socialist parties at their inception were doctrinaire parties, since they were devoted to establishing a political system based on strict adherence to communist and socialist ideologies, respectively. A **broker party**, in contrast, is one that mediates among diverse interest groups and avoids narrow ideological goals. Broker parties are said to be pragmatic, since they are willing to make adjustments to include ever larger numbers of voters. The Democratic and Republican parties in the United States are both broker parties, as are most socialist parties in Western Europe today.

Other classifications are also used, and a complete list of categories would be long. Among the most important, however, is the **revolutionary party**, which seeks to undermine the existing political system. Political parties formed in Third World areas at the time of colonial rule were often revolutionary as they sought to rid their country of colonial authority.

Strength

The strength of political parties varies. In dictatorships the strength of an illegal political party may be based on its elite character, conspiratorial activities, and unity. The Communist party in czarist Russia is a case in point. In democracies, however, strength is usually measured in terms of both the votes a party receives in an election and the number of seats it is able to win in the legislature. A major party usually can count on winning some districts nearly all the time. These are safe districts. Other districts, however, often swing from one party to another.

As we shall see, the percentage of votes that a party receives is often not directly transferred to a proportionate share of legislative seats. In Great Britain, for example, the Alliance (of Liberals and Social Democrats) won 25.4 percent of the vote in the general election of 1983 but obtained only

3.5 percent of the parliamentary seats. The Liberal Democrats won 18 percent of the vote in the general election of 1992 but only 3 percent of the parliamentary seats.

Structure

Parties vary in terms of relationships between the few party members who rule the party, or party elite, and the masses of party members; between parliamentary and extraparliamentary organizations; and between national and regional party units.

In **cadre parties** a small group of *notables,* to use the sociologist Max Weber's term, dominates party decisions, such as securing nominations and dispensing **patronage** (jobs given to political favorites). In the early development of political parties in the United States and Great Britain, for example, cadre parties played an important role. The Communist party of the Soviet Union was a recent cadre party.

Mass parties are those in which large numbers of the electorate are members of the party, which is usually led by a small group of professional leaders. The mass party is organized nationally into branches, with power ultimately at the national headquarters. The mass party has a program and provides a method for members to state policy preferences, select leaders, choose candidates for public office, and participate generally in the political process. The mass party arose from the expansion of the suffrage and political participation—features that have evolved most notably since the middle of the nineteenth century. European socialist parties are examples of mass parties in which millions of dues-paying members are organized.

The relationship between the parliamentary party and the extraparliamentary party differs among political systems. In Great Britain, for example, the parliamentary party has often resisted the demands of the party conference—the organization of the party outside of Parliament. Other political systems show a much stronger influence of the extraparliamentary party on the parliamentary party.

Parties differ, too, on the relationship between the national party organization and the regional party organizations. In the United States, political parties are largely decentralized. The power to nominate legislative candidates is often determined by a decision among party members at the state or local level. In other parties, such as the communist parties in Western democracies, power is more centralized at the national headquarters. There are noncommunist parties, too, that are more powerful at the center than in the regions of the country.

Sources of Support

Political parties vary in the kinds of membership they contain, their socioeconomic composition, and their sources of finance. In some systems the party may deliberately be kept small. The Communist party of the Soviet Union began as an illegal party that had to operate in a secret manner. It retained its elite status until the reforms of the Gorbachev era. Becoming a member of the Communist party used to be a far more meaningful event in a communist country than is registering as a Democrat or Republican in the United States. In the latter case, party membership is even difficult to determine, since often it consists of registering for a party at election and not engaging in any other political activity except voting in the general election.

Members of a political party can be distinguished in several ways. One method is to distinguish among **voters**, who merely cast their ballots for a party's candidate; **supporters**, who give some time to getting the party's candidates elected: **activists**, who devote a considerable amount of their time and energy to party affairs; and the elite, who rule.

Another way to consider party support is by examining the party's social composition. Some parties are composed of broad segments of society. Both the Democratic party and the Republican party in the United States, for example, consist of people from broadly based economic classes, ethnic groups, and social organizations. Other parties may consist of a more narrow element of society.

The social composition of a party is often influenced by the way a person becomes a party member. In some systems, becoming a party member consists of making an individual choice to do so. In others, an individual automatically becomes a member of a party merely by being a member of a particular group. When the Labour party was formed in Great Britain, for example, there was a close association between the party and the trade unions. Part of that association consisted of financing campaigns of Labour party candidates for Parliament. Today an individual trade union member can **contract out** (that is to say, make a formal refusal to contribute to a political party), however, but most members do not. In effect, then, the Labour party consists of many trade union members. Still, many of the members are free to vote for another political party and often do so.

Financial support varies among parties. In some countries the government provides money to candidates to run for office. In many democratic countries, however, money is raised from private sources. Laws regulating the amount of contributions and the manner of making donations influence the amount of money that a particular party can raise.

DECLINE OF PARTIES?

In Western democracies political parties have been declining in power in the twentieth century, although the extent of the decline is in dispute. The decline may be seen by examining some of the principal functions that parties are supposed to perform.

The role of the party in interest aggregation has diminished, as evidence in different countries attests. In describing the civil rights movement of the 1960s in the United States, the efforts of the British government to gain entry into the European Community, and the upheaval in France in 1968, the political scientist Anthony King concludes, "To the extent that political integration and mobilization took place, they occurred in structures largely set apart from the parties."[2] The antiwar movement and the environmental protection campaigns were formed by institutions outside of the parties, too.

Parties in democracies no longer set forth meaningful programs; nor do they initiate discussion of major issues. Often, party platforms consist of vague generalities, carefully crafted to avoid offending a significant segment of the electorate. Issues are put forward by other actors in the political process, such as interest groups, individual politicians, the media, civil servants, and academics.

The selection of candidates in some Western democracies is no longer dominated by party organizations. In the United States many candidates emphasize their "independence" from parties. Primaries have weakened the parties' ability to select candidates. Candidates seeking public office secure their own independent sources of finance through political action committees and voluntary contributions by citizens. The media, particularly television, have allowed candidates to appeal to voters directly rather than through the parties.

The rise of the civil service has diminished the ability of the political party to run the government. The number of posts of an appointive nature make up a smaller percentage of government employees than was the case in the nineteenth century. The party, consequently, has lost much of its patronage opportunities.

The decline of parties is not only a feature of Western democracies. In newly independent African countries, the power of political parties eroded until recently. In Third World countries generally, political parties have often been the victims of revolutionary movements or military coups.[3]

Some writers argue that the decline of political parties in democracies is bad for the future of democracy. In their view the rise of the political party and the rise of democracy go hand in hand. Without political parties to perform their traditional functions, these writers contend, other organizations, such as the media and single-interest groups, will do so. Such a development will lead to a loss of accountability in government and an erosion of national unity, they conclude.

Other writers take issue with this evaluation. As societies become more complex, they say, interests become diverse and differentiated. Parties in such a modern setting do not wither away, but they must share functions that they used to perform with other associations, according to this viewpoint.

Recent scholarship challenges the view of the decline of political parties. The argument put forward is that political parties are not declining but rather are in a transitional period. Some writers of this viewpoint assert that some national party organizations have adopted new functions to meet the needs of the contemporary political environment. In the United States, for example, national party organizations

---

[2] Anthony King, "Political Parties in Western Democracies: Some Sceptical Reflections," *Polity* 2 (Winter 1969): 117–18.

[3] Richard L. McCormick, ed., introd. to his *Political Parties and the Modern State* (New Brunswick, N.J.: Rutgers University Press, 1984), p. 12.

are playing an active part in getting candidates to run for national, state, and local offices. They are providing candidates with campaign services, including training sessions, survey data, and media assistance. Some political action committees, moreover, are taking cues from the political parties in deciding where to dispense campaign contributions.[4] Party bureaucracies are larger than in the past. And more than two of three citizens continue to think of themselves as Democrats or Republicans, during presidential elections.[5] Many people still make their voting decisions based on party considerations, moreover.

Another example of party resurgence is found in France. In 1980, French political parties were stronger than they had been at any time since the immediate postwar years. According to the political scientist Frank L. Wilson, the French political parties adopted new political approaches and strategies; public confidence in political parties was restored; party organizations were more active than they had been before 1980; they became a significant part of the political process; and parties fulfilled more capably their linkage to the people.[6] The evidence indicates that party activism continues in the early 1990s.

Political parties are for the most part a development of the nineteenth century. It is an open question whether the political party is in a permanent state of decline or whether it is going through a period of transition.

ELECTORAL SYSTEMS

Political parties in democracies devote most of their attention to contesting elections. Their prospects of electoral success depend in part on the electoral methods used that are sanctioned by law. These methods are rarely neutral in the sense that they are created for an objective registering of popular will through the ballot box. Rather, they are shaped by diverse historical traditions and social and political forces. We shall consider here some of the principal electoral systems of representation to show how the structure of electoral contests can affect voting outcomes.

Among the principal electoral methods are those based on territorial, functional, and proportional representation.

Territorial Representation

One of the most important electoral rules governs the size of the **constituency**, or electoral unit. In only a few countries is an entire country considered as the single unit for selecting legislative members. As indicated above, Israel is one case in point. In most countries, however, the unit for designating candidates is the electoral district.

The population and the shape of a district depend upon many factors. Sometimes the shape of a district is determined by constitutional features, such as in the federal system in the United States (see Chapter 10). Districts, however, may be unequally represented. In England, for example, a system of **rotten boroughs** existed from the sixteenth through the eighteenth centuries in which a member of Parliament could be elected by only a small number of people, while another member would have a constituency of millions. The situation of

---

[4] For a discussion, see Peter Hain, *Proportional Misrepresentation: The Case against PR in Britain* (Aldershot, England: Wildwood House, 1986), pp. 590–91.

[5] Martin P. Wattenberg, *The Rise of Candidate-Centered Politics: Presidential Elections in the 1980s* (Cambridge, Mass.: Harvard University Press, 1991), p. 40.

[6] Frank L. Wilson, "When Parties Refuse to Fail: The Case of France," in *When Parties Fail: Emerging Alternative Organizations*, ed. Kay Lawson and Peter H. Merkl (Princeton, N.J.: Princeton University Press, 1988), p. 506.

voting districts being unequal in population is known as **malapportionment**.

The shape of a district is a matter of concern to all elected public officials. A variation in the district boundaries that would reduce or enlarge the size of a group—whether economic, racial, or ethnic—can have a decisive impact on the prospects of a candidate from that district. The drawing of district lines to secure a political advantage is known as a **gerrymander**, named after Governor Elbridge Gerry of Massachusetts, who introduced the practice in the United States in 1812. As a result of redistricting, Gerry's party secured twenty-nine state senators with 50,164 votes, while the opposition party obtained only eleven members with 51,766 votes. The practice of gerrymandering continues in the United States, although the Supreme Court has restricted its use in certain extreme cases.

The apportionment of voting districts and the drawing of district lines influence the prospects of success for different political parties and candidates. Another influence is the number of officials selected from each voting unit. In Great Britain and the United States, the single-member district is the method used for selecting legislators. In a **single-member district**, only one person is chosen for an office from that district.

The method used for selecting legislators in the British House of Commons and the American House of Representatives is the **plurality system**, or **first-past-the-post system**. Whoever gets the largest number of votes is the winner. It is possible in a three-way contest for the winning candidate to receive less than a majority if more than half the votes are split among the losing candidates. In some countries, and even in some primary elections in the United States, a **majority system** is required, in which a candidate must win more than 50 percent of the votes. In that event the two candidates receiving the largest number of votes face each other in a second election, or **run-off**, to determine who the victor will be. The president of France is elected in this manner.

Although the principal method of legislative elections in the United States and Great Britain consists of voting within the single-member constituency, many countries and some localities vote for more than one candidate in a constituency. In such **multiple-member districts**, a voter is permitted to cast a ballot for more than one person. In a municipal contest in which five members of a city council are to be selected, for example, a voter may vote for five candidates.

Functional Representation

Representation based on territorial considerations is not the only electoral method; some systems employ functional representation, that is, representation by economic or social groups. Such a method is both ancient and modern. In ancient times representation was based on class and status. In medieval England the great estates were represented in Parliament. As early as the thirteenth century, representatives of the clergy, the nobility, and the burgesses constituted the Parliament.

Functional representation has also been used in the twentieth century. In fascist Italy, for example, a corporate state was established in which the legislature was composed of groups from different economic and social segments of society. The legislature in fascist Italy did not have the power of a legislature in a democratic society, but the corporate character of representation constituted a form of representation that, the fascist leaders believed, would lend legitimacy to their government.

Proportional Representation

More common as an electoral system is the system of **proportional representation** (PR). PR is a system in which candidates of political parties are elected in proportion to their voting support. This is the dominant system in Western countries and has also been used in many American cities. There are hundreds of variations in the PR system. The two most prominent, however, are the list system and the Hare system.

In the simple form of the **list system**, each political party nominates as many candidates as there are seats to be filled in that constituency. National list systems operate in Guyana, Israel, and Turkey. Israel is perhaps the best example of a country that has adopted the list system. In the Israeli parliament, called the Knesset, there are 120 seats. Each party nominates 120 candidates. Each party determines for itself who is ranked from first to 120th position. The voter has no choice of individual candidates but votes for a party. When all the votes are counted, each party receives the percentage of parliamentary seats equal to the percentage of votes that it has secured at the polls. Usually, in countries that have adopted the list system, no single political party obtains a majority of the vote. A **coalition government** (an alliance of parties that generally constitutes a majority) is formed. In a coalition government, most often the cabinet is composed of members from each of the elements of the coalition, but this does not have to be the case. Sometimes minor parties are more concerned with having particular policies adopted than with staffing cabinet positions.

In the **Hare system** the voter ranks his or her choices of candidates as first, second, third, and so on. When a candidate achieves a quota of votes set on the basis of

law or calculated from a formula of seats in that constituency, that candidate is elected. Then the candidate's surplus votes are given to the candidate to whom his or her supporters gave their second preference. If enough candidates still have not reached the quota, the weakest candidates are eliminated, and the second preferences of the voters who cast their ballots for them are counted until the victorious candidates have been elected. The idea of the system is to transfer votes until the number of seats is filled.

Since there are hundreds of different PR systems, it is often difficult to make generalizations about such systems. In a number of countries with the PR system a party must have a minimum percentage of the total vote to be accorded any seats in the legislature. In only a few PR countries do voters cast their ballots in a system in which the country forms one large multimember electoral district. Most PR countries have a number of multimember electoral districts with each district electing a particular number of representatives through PR. In the Norwegian Storting, each of 19 districts elects from 11 to 13 representatives according to the population to fill that 155-seat legislative body.

One unusual electoral form is that of Germany, which has a "**topping-up**" system. Half of the members of the Bundestag are chosen from individual constituencies on the first-past-the-post basis. The rest are selected from political parties participating in the election, so that the overall balance in the Bundestag constitutes the national distribution of the party vote.

ISSUE

Particular electoral systems have their supporters and critics. For more than a century one of the most discussed electoral issues is the relative merits of the majority or the plurality system and the proportional system of representation—a subject that is debated below.

18/YES   ARE MAJORITY OR PLURALITY SYSTEMS BETTER THAN PROPORTIONAL SYSTEMS OF REPRESENTATION?

Although proportional representation has its partisans in every democratic country, it is not nearly as good a system as majority and plurality systems. The case for the first-past-the-post system rests on: (1) the two-party system it encourages; (2) the democratic processes it strengthens; and (3) the political stability it enhances.

Party Systems. The first-past-the-post system encourages the formation of two-party systems. The experience of Great Britain and the United States, each possessing two major parties, confirms that fact. The voter in a system of two parties who seriously considers casting his or her ballot for a third party is often deterred from doing so by a realization that the vote will be "wasted"—that is, it will have no direct impact on deciding which of the candidates of the two major parties will win.

Although there are only two parties, the voters are presented with a real choice. Since each party offers an alternative candidate and an alternative program, the voter knows in advance that if his or her party wins, the victorious candidates will run the government. The voter also knows in advance what the policy of government is supposed to be. This is particularly true for the British system, but is also true for the American system in those instances when the executive and legislative branches are controlled by the same party (see Chapter 11). Of course, the government need not implement the program it professes, but then it can be held accountable for its omissions in the next general election. Often, party pledges are kept. The political scientist Gerald M. Pomper concludes from his analysis of 1,400 platform pledges over a period of twenty years (1944–64) that in the United States the political parties do pay attention to their platforms and do enact a good deal of their platforms into law.[7]

A PR system, in contrast, promotes a multiparty system. The voter does not even know before the election is conducted what the composition of the government will be if his or her party does well in gathering votes because no single party in a multiparty system is likely to achieve a clear-cut victory. A voter, moreover, cannot know what a coalition government (composed of cabinet members from different political parties) will do. The existence of the coalition government, then, means that the voter has decided very little as far as policy is concerned.

Democracy. Democracy is strengthened from the first-past-the-post system in many ways. Because the system encourages the electoral competition of two big parties, each party must seek the support of a broad spectrum of social, economic, and cultural groups in order to achieve electoral success. In the United States, for example, both the Democratic party and the Republican party have some support in all segments of American society.

Under a two-party system, the majority, in effect, constitutes a collection of many minorities. Since the margin of difference between the two parties is frequently under 5 percent, it is essential that neither party slight minority groups. To do so would mean a loss of significant electoral support. Party leaders are so concerned about minority support that it is not uncommon for the top candidates in statewide elections to come from different social backgrounds.

Advocates of PR argue that PR offers more opportunities than first-past-the-post systems for women and minority members to be elected to legislative posts. What they often fail to note, however, is the variation in the percentage of women or minority members in the legislative systems using the same PR electoral processes. Peter Hain concludes from his study of countries with similar list systems that Finland has four times greater a representation of women than Israel.[8] The political scientist Wilma Rule asserts that in party list systems in twenty-three democracies in 1980–82, women's parliamentary representation varied from a high of 28 percent in Sweden to a low of 4 percent in Greece.[9] In

[7] Gerald M. Pomper, *Elections in America: Control and Influence in Democratic Politics* (New York: Dodd, Mead, 1971), p. 178.

[8] Hain, *Proportional Misrepresentation*, p. 69.

[9] Wilma Rule, "Electoral Systems, Contextual Factors and Women's Opportunity for Election to Parliament in Twenty-Three Democracies," *Western Political Quarterly* 40 (September 1987): 483.

Hain's view, political culture, the strength of feminist ideas and social attitudes, as well as economic circumstances all play their part, and the exact role of the electoral system is not obvious.[10] Some of the same factors affect minority-group representation as well. So it is wrong to hold electoral forms exclusively responsible for the amount of female and minority representation in the legislature.

Democracy, too, benefits from the diversity of views that are reflected within the two parties in the legislature. In this regard, proponents of PR have an inaccurate conception of what a legislature is supposed to be. They regard a legislature as a place that represents the electorate in some sort of mirror image. In fact, however, all that is essential is that the legislature should reflect popular sentiment *in some general way*. The historical record reveals much evidence of this proposition from British and American experience. Catholic emancipation in Britain was approved by Parliament at a time when no Catholics were members of Parliament. Women were granted the suffrage in the United States, moreover, at a time when few women held elective posts. What was essential in each case was that the legislators advocating such positions were freely able to convince their colleagues of the wisdom of changing policy.

PR systems hurt democracy by often giving undue influence to small parties. Israel is a case in point. Because of the nearly equal strength of the Labor party and the Likud party, the balance of power has often been held by small religious parties that have been able to impose their orthodox religious views on what is primarily a secular society.

Finally, PR supporters argue that first-past-the-post systems are undemocratic because they produce electoral distortions favoring one or another party. PR districts can be and have been drawn to favor one or another political party, as is also the case in plurality systems. If electoral rules can be manipulated in both systems, it makes neither system more virtuous as far as democracy is concerned.

Stability. First-past-the-post systems are likely to produce more stable political systems,

as the British and American experience attests. Political parties must appeal to broad segments of the electorate and avoid becoming parties of the extreme ends of the political spectrum if they are to win elections. The major parties, consequently, reach toward the center of the political spectrum. They adopt somewhat similar programs lest they lose sizable segments of support. Such a practice encourages moderation in policy. Minor political parties that cater to extremist views cannot secure enough electoral support to become serious challengers to government power, and so the first-past-the-post system aids stability.

In contrast, PR encourages sharp divisiveness in government and society. All the political party must do to gain a foothold in the legislature is to gather a small percentage of the vote. The system of PR that existed in the Weimar Republic after World War I allowed the Nazi party to gain some seats in the German legislature, the Reichstag. Both the Nazi party and the Communist party were aided by PR. Extremist groups with limited support prefer PR because it allows them a certain measure of legitimacy through legislative representation. Political parties committed to destroying democracy should not be permitted to gain a foothold in parliamentary government—a prospect made likely by PR.

Not only do political systems become unstable because of the strength given to extremist groups through PR, but the very essence of a multiparty system—namely, coalition government—is inherently unstable. One can cite many examples, the most prominent of which was the Fourth Republic in France. France went through twenty-six governments in fourteen years. The average government lasted less than six months, and such instability in government made it difficult for France to provide coherent rule. Italy since World War II has also suffered from political instability caused by small parties withdrawing from the coalition constituting the government. Such weak government has had its impact on society, as the random and reckless acts of terrorist groups in Italy attest. First-past-the-post systems, in contrast, give a government time to rule, which is a measure for stability.

[10] Hain, *Proportional Misrepresentation*, p. 69.

18/NO ARE MAJORITY OR PLURALITY SYSTEMS BETTER THAN PROPORTIONAL SYSTEMS OF REPRESENTATION?

Proportional representation is the major electoral system of the continental European democracies. PR is better than first-past-the-post systems because it: (1) encourages a multiparty system; (2) is more democratic; and (3) is more stable.

Party Systems. Most students of political parties agree that the existence of PR encourages a multiparty system. They differ, however, about whether this is a good thing. We contend that two parties are too few to reflect the interests of mass democracies, with their differing economic, social, and ethnic elements. In addition, we argue that the multiparty system offers as much responsible government as does the two-party system.

Advocates of a two-party system praise a model of party government that bears no resemblance to the real world. First, the British experience reveals that one-party majority rule is the exception rather than the rule. The political scientist Harry Eckstein notes that "in the 77 years between 1885 and 1962, the era of modern parties and elections, Britain has had only 43 years of straightforward one-party majority rule."[11] British governments, then, ruled as a result of one or more small parties supporting a big one.

Second, the notion that in first-past-the-post systems party platforms and politicians' promises are meaningful is questionable because the platforms and pledges are often ambiguous and often violated. In the electoral campaign of 1932, for example, Franklin Roosevelt promised that if he were elected, he would balance the budget. Jimmy Carter promised in 1976, moreover, that he would reduce defense spending. And at the Republican national convention in 1988, the Republican presidential candidate, George Bush, said: "My opponent [Michael Dukakis] won't rule out raising taxes. But I will and the Congress will push me to raise taxes, and I'll say no, and they'll

push, and I'll say no, and they'll push again. And I'll say to them, read my lips, no new taxes."[12] Neither Roosevelt, nor Carter, nor Bush lived up to his promise, and they were not unique as politicians in two-party systems either.

One further point needs to be noted about the relationship between electoral systems and the number of parties. The assertion that simple majority voting leads to a two-party system with alternation in power is valid in some cases, such as Great Britain and the United States. It is not true in others, such as Belgium before 1894, Sweden before 1911, Denmark before 1920, and contemporary Canada.[13] With such different results in the number of parties, it is difficult even to generalize about the first-past-the-post system.

Democracy. Proportional representation serves the interests of democracy in many ways. The individual voter can be assured that he or she will not have to cast a ballot for a candidate he or she does not like. In proportional systems, there will be many narrowly defined parties, so a voter can feel confident that his or her interests are being represented by at least one of them.

Minorities, too, benefit from such a system. Minorities, who felt that they would be better protected by such a system, were an important influence in bringing about PR in the period before World War I. Countries containing ethnically diverse groups were the first to adopt PR: Denmark in 1885, the Swiss cantons in 1891, Belgium in 1899, Moravia in 1905, and Finland in 1906.[14]

PR would aid minorities and women in another way. Minority members and women are more likely to hold parliamentary seats in PR systems than in first-past-the-post systems. In Great Britain, for example, there has been no black or Asian MP from the 1920s until recently,

---

[11] Harry Eckstein, "Parties, Political: Party Systems," *International Encyclopaedia of the Social Sciences* (1968): 11:440.

[12] George Bush, "Transcript of Bush Speech Accepting Presidential Nomination," *New York Times*, August 18, 1988, p. A14.

[13] Eckstein, "Parties, Political," p. 448.

[14] Stein Rokkan, "Elections: Electoral Systems," *International Encyclopaedia of the Social Sciences* (1968), 5:12.

yet blacks and Asians constitute about 4 percent of the total British population. Only five minority members—three blacks and two Asians—won parliamentary seats in the general election of 1992. And so, they received less than 1 percent of the seats. Although women constitute more than half the population of Great Britain, they have never won even 10 percent of the seats in the House of Commons. In this regard a party will often feel that it should include minority members on a list system to show that its appeal extends to all sectors of the constituency. In the first-past-the-post system, in contrast, the party would be more likely to feel that the selection of a minority member may offend many voters and, consequently, cost the party votes.[15] Wilma Rule concludes from her study of twenty-three democracies that the party list system of PR provides the most political opportunity for women.[16]

A democracy, moreover, requires that a legislature represent its people. Representation means that the legislature should be a mirror image of the society. PR assures the proper form of representation as befits a democracy.

Democracy is further strengthened by avoiding the electoral manipulations of a plurality system. Such manipulations can lead to major distortions of voters' preferences. In the 1983 general election in Great Britain, the Liberal/Social Democratic Party Alliance won 25.4 percent of the popular vote but gained only 3.5 percent of the seats in the House of Commons. And in the 1992 general election, the Liberal Democrats won 18 percent of the vote but held only 3 percent of the seats.

First-past-the-post systems are usually based on territorial districting. Gerrymandering is often used by the party in power to redraw district lines for an electoral advantage. Historically, too, districts under plurality systems have not been composed of an equal number of people, thus giving an advantage to one of the major parties. PR can do away with many of the partisan advantages that in effect diminish the influence of many voters.

It is important to keep in mind that majority rule—an essential component of democracy—is often the exception in two-party systems. In Great Britain, for example, the ruling government has rarely won a majority of the votes. It usually has a plurality, which means that more than half of the people preferred some other parties. PR would be more democratic, as the coalition formed would be based on the political preferences of the majority.

Stability. Proportional representation produces stable political systems. A multiparty system need not be synonymous with "instability." The Scandinavian countries, for example, have experienced a great degree of political stability through coalition governments. And the Federal Republic of Germany, Luxembourg, and Austria were ruled more or less continually since World War II by stable coalition administrations. If the British and American systems are stable, it is because of the social harmony that exists among the people and the mutual trust the people have for their two major parties, and not because of the particular electoral system they employ.

Opponents of PR like to point to the experience of France in the Fourth Republic and to Germany in the Weimar Republic. Those examples are not valid because they ignore the underlying social, economic, and political forces that operated in both those societies. France experimented with eight different kinds of electoral systems in the past century, yet each system produced a multiparty structure. No system was adequate to prevent the sharp cleavages of French society from producing political instability. Given the nature of post–World War I problems faced by the Weimar government, moreover, even a different electoral system would not have been able to resist the Nazi onslaught. It is essential to recall that in 1932, a majority of the German people voted for political parties (such as the Nazi and the Communist) that were committed to the destruction of democracy. A two-party system could not have stemmed that tide. The political scientist Enid Lakeman notes that under the almost exact same electoral system in Weimar Germany, Czechoslovakia in the period between the world

[15]Vernon Bogdanor, *What Is Proportional Representation? A Guide to the Issues* (Oxford, England: Martin Robertson, 1984), pp. 113–15. See also Enid Lakeman, *Power to Elect: The Case for Proportional Representation* (London: Heinemann, 1982), pp. 134–38.

[16]Rule, "Electoral Systems," pp. 477–98.

wars produced the most stable and successful democracy in Eastern Europe.[17]

Stability in the political system is further aided by the character of coalition governments brought on by PR. An election in a multiparty system does not produce a brand new government. Ordinarily, it produces at most a shift of a few seats and cabinet posts to reflect changing popular sentiment. Continuity, consequently, is preserved. In the winner-take-all situation that arises from plurality systems, an entirely new government can bring about major policy shifts that may be a source of political instability.

In the decades since the adoption of the Ital- ian Constitution of 1948, Italian parliamentary regimes lasted an average of ten months. *But* there was much stability, as many party leaders attained office, lost office, and returned to office. As Joseph LaPalombara observes, "Since the war, five men—Christian Democrats Alcide de Gasperi, Amintore Fanfani, Aldo Moro, Mariano Rumor, and Giulio Andreotti—have served as prime minister five or more times. That they headed, all told, 29 different governments is almost irrelevant."[18]

PR systems, then, are superior to first-past-the-post systems.

[17]Enid Lakeman, *How Democracies Vote: A Study of Electoral Systems*, 4th ed. (London: Faber and Faber, 1974), p. 212.

[18]Joseph LaPalombara, "Partitocrazia," *Wilson Quarterly* 12 (Spring 1988): 104.

KEY TERMS

Activists
Broker party
Cadre party
Closed primary
Coalition government
Constituency
Contract out
Doctrinaire party
Dominant political party system
First-past-the-post system
Gerrymander
Hare system
Interest aggregation
List system
Majority system
Malapportionment
Mass parties

Multiple-member district
Open primary
Party government
Party platform
Party system
Patronage
Plurality system
Political party
Primary elections
Proportional representation (PR)
Revolutionary party
Rotten boroughs
Run-off
Single-member district
Supporters (political parties)
"Topping-up" system
Voters

QUESTIONS

1. If in fact political parties in Western democracies are declining, is this a desirable trend? What are the reasons for your answer?

2. What are the strengths and weaknesses of a two-party over a multiparty system?

3. What do elections decide?

4. What is the value of party platforms?

5. If the United States were to adopt a system of proportional representation, what would be its consequences to the American political system?

RECOMMENDED READINGS

BOGDANOR, VERNON. *What Is Proportional Representation? A Guide to the Issues.* Oxford, England: Martin Robertson, 1984. A case for PR in Great Britain.

BUDGE, IAN, and HANS KEMAN. *Parties and Democracy: Coalition Formation and Government Functioning in Twenty States.* New York: Oxford University Press, 1990. A study of party governments in the parliamentary systems of twenty democracies.

COLE, ALISTAIR, and PETER CAMPBELL. *French Electoral Systems and Elections since 1789.* Aldershot, England: Gower Publishing Co., 1989. An analysis of French electoral systems.

DUVERGER, MAURICE. *Political Parties: Their Organization and Activity in the Modern State,* trans. Barbara and Robert North. 2d ed. London: Methuen and Co., 1962. A classic study of political parties.

ELLIS, TOM, ROSALEEN HUGHES, and PHILIP WHITEHEAD. *Electoral Reform.* Fabian Tract 483. London: Fabian Society, 1982. A debate on PR.

GINSBERG, BENJAMIN, and MARTIN SHEFTER. *Politics by Other Means: The Declining Importance of Elections in America.* New York: Basic Books, 1990. An argument that American politics is being transformed by the declining importance of elections.

HAIN, PETER. *Proportional Misrepresentation: The Case against PR in Britain.* Aldershot, England: Wildwood House, 1986. A case against PR.

HERMENS, FERDINAND A. *Democracy or Anarchy? A Study of Proportional Representation.* Notre Dame, Ind.: University of Notre Dame, 1941. A classic critique of PR.

HERTZBERG, HENDRIK. "Let's Get Representative." *New Republic,* 196 (June 29, 1987): 15–18. A case for the adoption of a modified Hare system of electing Congress.

HOAG, CLARENCE GILBERT, and GEORGE HARVEY, JR. *Proportional Representation.* New York: Macmillan, 1926. A major work in defense of PR.

INGLE, STEPHEN. *The British Party System.* 2d ed. Cambridge, Mass.: Basil Blackwell, 1989. An account of British political parties within the context of the functions they are generally supposed to fulfill.

KEEFE, WILLIAM J. *Parties, Politics, and Public Policy in America.* 6th ed. Washington, D.C.: CQ Press, 1991. A study of how and why U.S. political parties function as they do.

KING, ANTHONY. "Political Parties in Western Democracies: Some Sceptical Reflections." *Polity* 2 (Winter 1969): 111–41. A questioning of the role attributed to political parties in Western democracies.

LAKEMAN, ENID. *Power to Elect: The Case for Proportional Representation.* London: Heinemann, 1982. A case for the single-transferable vote system.

LAVER, MICHAEL, and NORMAN SCHOFIELD. *Multiparty Government: The Politics of Coalition in Europe.* New York: Oxford University Press, 1990. A study of the politics of coalition government.

LAWSON, KAY, and PETER H. MERKL, eds. *When Parties Fail: Emerging Alternative Organizations.* Princeton, N.J.: Princeton University Press, 1988. A collection of essays on the subject.

MAIR, PETER, and GORDON SMITH, eds. "Special Issue on Understanding Party System Change in Western Europe." *West European Politics* 12 (October 1989): 1–191. Studies of political parties in Western Europe.

PEMPEL, T. J., ed. *Uncommon Democracies: The One-Party Dominant Regimes.* Ithaca, N.Y.: Cornell University Press, 1990. Studies of one-party dominant regimes in modern democratic systems.

RAE, DOUGLAS W. *The Political Consequences of Electoral Laws.* New Haven: Yale University Press, 1967. A major study of electoral systems.

SARTORI, GIOVANNI. *Parties and Party Systems: A Framework for Analysis.* Vol. 1. Cambridge, England: Cambridge University Press, 1976. A general theory of party-based politics.

TOLZ, VERA. *The USSR's Emerging Multiparty System.* New York: Praeger, 1990. A description of unofficial groups and a multiparty system in the Soviet Union since Mikhail Gorbachev.

WARE, ALAN. *Citizens, Parties and the State: A Reappraisal.* Princeton, N.J.: Princeton University Press, 1988. An analysis of the role of parties in the advancement of democracy.

WHITE, STEPHEN. "Democratizing Eastern Europe: The Elections of 1990." *Electoral Studies* (Guildford, England) 9 (December 1990): 277–87. An analysis of elections in countries previously under communist rule.

chapter 9

Interest groups

- Thousands of antiabortion activists assemble on the Mall to demonstrate in opposition to abortion.
- A computer bank prepares to process messages to members of the National Rifle Association (NRA). The messages will alert NRA members to a gun control bill being considered by Congress.
- A representative from Common Cause appears before a congressional committee and asks the members to approve legislation that would provide for government financing of congressional elections.

Scenes such as these are representative of a form of political participation common in Washington, D.C., and in other cities of the country where political decisions are made. These are the kinds of actions that interest groups take. An **interest group** may be defined as an association of individuals who have common goals and who interact to achieve those goals. An interest group is sometimes called a **voluntary association** or a **pressure group**,[1] and the people who represent the interest group in its dealings with government officials are known as **lobbyists**.[2]

Interest groups in one form or another have been in existence for centuries. They

[1] Some writers object to the term *pressure group* because of its sinister connotations and often because the work of political interest groups does not consist of applying pressure but rather of making a case for a particular point of view.

[2] According to one view, the term *lobbyist* had its origin in 1829 when *lobby-agent* was used to refer to those who sought special privileges at the Capitol in Albany, New York. Journalists shortened the word to *lobbyist*. See Karl Schriftgiesser, *The Lobbyists: The Art and Business of Influencing Lawmakers* (Boston: Little, Brown, 1951), p. 5. Another view traces the term *lobby* to mid-seventeenth-century England, when *lobby-agents* approached members of Parliament for special favors. *The Washington Lobby*, 2d ed. (Washington, D.C.: Congressional Quarterly, 1974), preface.

have, however, become stronger and more varied with the rise of both a complex industrial society and big government. It is in the United States that interest groups have emerged in greatest abundance and variety. It is in the United States, too, that the study of interest groups has received the most prominent attention from political scientists, although literature about interest groups in other countries is growing.

Because of the prominence of the American experience, most of the discussion that follows will deal with different groups in the United States. An examination of the different kinds of interest groups, why they were formed, and how they work in the United States will be made before a consideration of interest groups in other countries is undertaken.

VARIETIES OF INTEREST GROUPS

Interest groups may be classified in many ways. We may distinguish between multiple-issue groups that are organizations with diverse objectives, such as trade unions, and **single-issue groups**. In the latter case, the group is formed to deal with only one issue, such as abortion, gun control, and disarmament. Interest groups created to promote a variety of objectives include economic, professional, civil rights, public interest, religious, and government associations.

Economic groups consist largely of business, union, and farm associations. Business associations include such large organizations as the Chamber of Commerce and the National Association of Manufacturers; trade associations, such as the American Petroleum Institute and the American Bankers Association; and individual corporations, such as Exxon and General Dynamics.

Business groups may seek a variety of goals. They may be interested in keeping to a minimum the general level of government spending because of its potential in-

flationary impact on the economy. They may be concerned about specific areas of policy, such as tariffs and import quotas. They may favor government regulation to reduce the level of competition, or they may oppose government regulation because they find it meddlesome and costly. They may seek government subsidies or government contracts.

Unions have their own agenda. They have sought government protection to organize workers into trade unions. When it serves their purposes, they support industries in their pursuit of government contracts, as the quest for military contracts attests. They may also favor the enactment of rules requiring government agencies to purchase only from those firms who employ trade union members. They may seek broad objectives, such as welfare legislation, because they perceive that the principal beneficiaries will be their own members.

Farm groups are deeply involved in influencing government. Vast government subsidies have been given to some farmers to make certain that they are assured a basic minimum income for their efforts. Farmers have received many other benefits from the government, including weather information, grants for agricultural research, and low-interest loans. Farm groups have sought U.S. government support in eliminating trade barriers in other countries, so that U.S. agricultural products can have bigger foreign markets.

Professional groups seek to influence government. The American Medical Association (AMA) wants government regulations assuring that only qualified physicians can practice medicine. When malpractice insurance rates skyrocketed in the 1980s and 1990s, the AMA turned to government to help deal with the problem. The national and regional bar associations are concerned with matters of interest to the legal profession, such as qualifications for practicing law and appointments to the courts. University professors have organizations that are concerned not only with educational matters but with employment conditions, such as salaries and tenure, as well.

Civil rights organizations are active participants in the political process. The National Association for the Advancement of Colored People (NAACP) and the National Organization for Women (NOW) are cases in point. Such organizations devote their efforts to eliminating the barriers to equality brought on by discrimination based on race and gender.

For the most part, economic, professional, and civil rights associations are formed to achieve direct benefits for their members. In the 1970s, another type of group emerged in influence—the **public interest group** (PIG). This group may be defined as an association concerned with the improvement of the economic, social, and political environment without any immediate direct tangible gain to its members. Consumer and environmental groups fall into this category. So, too, does an organization like the American Civil Liberties Union (ACLU), which is primarily concerned with the protection of civil liberties and civil rights.

Religious groups have been particularly active in the United States in the 1980s and 1990s. Their concerns are not only spiritual. Issues of moral and practical interest have occupied their attention, such as abortion, pornography, prayer in schools, and tuition tax credits.

Government has interest groups, too. Lobbies from state governments and some municipalities have offices in Washington, D.C. They attempt to influence policy makers in the federal government on programs beneficial to them, such as mass transit and education. Departments and agencies of the federal government make their case before executive and legislative officials in such matters as defense and welfare. The Department of Defense, for example, pleads with appropriate congressional committees not to cut what it deems to be vital weapons systems.

Interest groups vary because people have different incentives for joining groups. As Peter Clark and James Q. Wilson observe, these incentives may be classified as material, solidary, or purposive. **Material incentives** are primarily economic, such as wages and salaries. **Solidary incentives** are intangible rewards derived from belonging to an organization, such as a fraternity or a club, and include such rewards as congeniality and the status resulting from membership. **Purposive incentives** arise from advancing a particular cause or ideology and include goals that do not benefit the members in any direct or tangible way, such as the beautification of the countryside or the elimination of government inefficiency.[3]

WHY HAVE INTEREST GROUPS GROWN?

Interest groups have a long history in the United States. Even before the Constitution was adopted, differences arose between debtors and creditors, commercial and landed classes, and people who lived in coastal or outlying regions. The struggle over the adoption of the Constitution reflects some of the conflicts among these groups.

Various explanations have been offered for the growth of interest groups. The most prominent reasons include economic development, increased heterogeneity, social disruption, the rise of government, the constitutional system, and political culture.

As the United States moved from an agrarian to an industrial society, the division of labor became more complex. Economic differentiation resulted in new economic associations, many of which were concerned with specialized interests. And so, for example, specialized trade associations have been created representing such

[3] Peter Clark and James Q. Wilson, "Incentive Systems: A Theory of Organizations," *Administrative Science Quarterly* 6 (September 1961): 129–66; James Q. Wilson, *Political Organizations* (New York: Basic Books, 1973), pp. 30–51.

interests as the semiconductor industry and the magazine industry. An advanced industrial society, moreover, made it possible for national organizations to use modern means of communication and transportation, linking members with a central organization.

The opportunities presented by a burgeoning economy in the United States produced a vast influx of immigrants from many countries. The United States has been called the "melting pot" because it molded people of different ethnic, racial, and religious backgrounds into a single nation. Still, the citizenry remains diverse, and such diversity encouraged the formation of groups.

Groups do not arise spontaneously merely because of their economic and social specialization. As the political scientists Allan J. Cigler and Burdett A. Loomis note, "Farmers and a landed interest existed long before farm organizations first appeared; laborers and craftsmen were on the job prior to the formation of unions."[4] Periods of economic and social disturbance sparked group formation. Unions grew powerful as a response to the Great Depression of the 1930s, and civil rights organizations proliferated as the demand for racial equality became more widely asserted in the 1950s and 1960s.

Because government has grown so dramatically in the twentieth century, groups have been formed in an effort to influence government decisions. Government regulation of business in such matters as the formation of monopolies, the protection of trade unions, the requirement of safety standards for workers, the inspection of products for safety and health hazards, and the imposition of antidiscrimination standards in hiring has sparked the growth of business associations.

[4] Allan J. Cigler and Burdett A. Loomis, "Introduction: The Changing Nature of Interest Group Politics," in *Interest Group Politics*, ed. Allan J. Cigler and Burdett A. Loomis, 3d ed. (Washington, D.C.: CQ Press, 1991), p. 6.

Economic groups are not the only associations to form in response to government growth. As government has involved itself in so many different policy areas, such as racial discrimination, women's rights, environmental protection, consumer safeguards, commercial advertising, and human rights abroad, organizations have been formed to promote these causes.

Government itself has been responsible for the formation of some groups. It has sometimes mandated the establishment of advisory boards consisting of economic, professional, or community representation. It has often enacted legislation requiring some kinds of citizen participation.

The constitutional system provides a reason for the establishment and development of groups. The Constitution protects the rights of free speech and association—prerequisites for the uninhibited formation of groups. The separation of powers between the executive, legislative, and judicial branches of government and the division of power between the national and state governments offer groups an opportunity to influence government at many different points in the political process. The relative weakness of political parties in the United States also provides interest groups with opportunities to influence policy.

American political culture has been conducive to group growth. Alexis de Tocqueville noted in *Democracy in America* (1835) that Americans had a tendency to join groups. He attributed this inclination to a desire for individuality and personal achievement. The tendency for Americans to join groups has continued to this day.

WHAT DO POLITICAL INTEREST GROUPS DO?

Interest groups seek to obtain economic, social, or ideological goals. To achieve their aims, they often use similar techniques, including shaping public opinion, making alliances with other groups, working directly to influence government decisions, and supporting candidates in electoral contests.

The success of a group in achieving its objectives depends considerably upon its ability to equate its own interests with the public interest. If it is successful, it has legitimized its claims on society. Issue 19 focuses on the concept of the public interest. For the moment, however, the **public interest** is defined as the interest of all, or the common good.

To influence public opinion, interest groups rely on a variety of techniques. They take advertisements in national magazines and in other media outlets, such as radio and television. Military contractors publicize weapons for national security, for example. Some political interest groups organize peaceful protest marches, such as the March on Washington in 1963 that focused attention on civil rights. Other political interest groups may, however, engage in violent acts, such as those pursued by extremist groups like the Ku Klux Klan.

Not all attempts to influence public opinion are successful, of course. Publicity campaigns by one group are often challenged by similar campaigns of opposing groups. For example, after the early attempts by advocates of the Equal Rights Amendment succeeded in getting about half of the state legislatures to ratify the amendment within the first year after congressional approval, an opposition formed that was able to slow down and ultimately defeat ratification of that amendment.

Groups not only attempt to influence public opinion but also try to influence the president, the legislature, the judiciary, and political parties. At the national level, groups may urge the president to propose legislation favorable to them or to veto hostile bills. They may request that advisory boards composed of interest group leaders or representatives be consulted before an administrative decision is made.

Because legislative committees play such an important role in the American political system, interest groups concern themselves with the work of committees dealing with policy areas that involve them. Farm groups, consequently, seek to influence the agriculture committees of the House and the Senate. Defense contractors focus their attention on the armed services committees. In some cases, an interest group interlocks with a relevant congressional committee and executive agency concerned about a policy area of mutual interest to each. This kind of relationship is known as the **iron triangle**, in which decisions are made in a policy area of mutual concern by a self-contained political community.

Groups seek to influence the judiciary, too. They may bring cases before the court in the hope of striking down a law or in interpreting existing law in a different way. The NAACP has been active in bringing cases involving racial discrimination before the courts, for example. Some writers suggest that this avenue is used by groups that are unlikely to prevail in Congress, the executive branch, and public opinion.

An interest group may work within political parties. It may try to have its views adopted by the platform committee of the major parties at their national conventions. It may give its support to particular candidates who are friendly to their views. Walter Mondale was endorsed by the AFL-CIO even before the first Democratic primary was conducted in 1984. Union support for his candidacy helped him win the Democratic nomination for the presidency in that year.

Although interest groups may try to influence political parties in the United States, they act differently from political parties in the American political system. An interest group is generally concerned with achieving some specific objective for its members. The principal function of a political party in the United States is, however, to take public office by winning elections. Political parties, consequently, must be more broadly based than interest groups if they are to win votes from the many segments of the electorate. Interest groups are, of course, concerned with influencing political parties by supporting candidates favorable to their objectives, but this is merely a tactic to achieve their aims rather than a design to constitute a government. Although there is a clear difference between interest groups and political parties in the United States, the two associations are more closely tied in Western European political systems. In such systems, a party may represent an interest group and nothing else.

Since interest groups generally have a stake in the outcome of elections, they often contribute money in electoral contests. In the United States interest groups have formed **political action committees** (PACs) specifically to provide financial support to candidates for public office. These PACs are keen observers of the political behavior of elected public officials in public policy areas of concern to the committees.

PACs "grade" political candidates. A high grade on labor union matters is likely to result in campaign contributions from trade unions. Similarly, business, environmental, and medical PACs are likely to support their "friends." Since candidates need money to conduct campaigns, they are solicitous of PAC endorsements and financial support.

INTEREST GROUPS IN OTHER COUNTRIES

Interest groups are not a unique American phenomenon, and how they organize and behave politically varies from political system to political system. The American political system, with its fragmentation of power among legislative, executive, and judicial branches, and between the national government and the states, furnishes a battleground for interest groups that is quite different from the British political system,

for example. British interest groups pay more attention to the executive than to the legislature and, consequently, usually present their cases to cabinet ministers and ministry officials rather than to an ordinary member of Parliament. Unlike the American congressional committees, British parliamentary committees play a very limited role in legislation. British pressure groups, therefore, do not spend their time with these committees. Some commentators note, however, that British interest groups have been paying more attention to members of Parliament since 1970 because the MPs have been showing increased independence and because of other changes in legislative practices.[5]

How political interest groups behave differs in other countries, as well. In Canada and France lobbyists give their attention to the cabinet and bureaucracy rather than to the legislature. The locus of power varies from political system to political system. In this context the maxim of Professor Samuel H. Beer is valid: "Where the power is, there the pressure will be."

As indicated above, the relationship between pressure groups and political parties also varies from country to country. Although some groups are associated more with one political party, in the United States most groups tend to be nonpartisan. Some contribute money to both major political parties. American political parties are composed of so many elements that they must compromise group interests rather than speak for only one interest. In continental Europe, in contrast, the tendency is for a close association between pressure group and political party, especially in multiparty systems. In Japan, the relationship between interest group and parliamentary member is so strong that some legislative officials are often perceived to be represen-

[5] Cliff Grantham, "Parliament and Political Consultants," *Parliamentary Affairs* (London) 42 (October 1989): 506.

tatives of particular interest groups to the legislature.[6]

To this point, our discussion has centered on interest groups in democracies. Because democracies are open societies, the activities of political interest groups are often known and publicly reported. Dictatorships, in contrast, are closed societies, so that much of interest group behavior is unknown or relatively secret. Until recently, scholars tended to ignore interest groups in dictatorships, particularly totalitarian ones. Power was generally portrayed as centralized, with no evidence of the existence of autonomous interest groups. Two prominent scholars of totalitarianism recognize some independent sources of power, such as the churches and the technicians, but refer to them as "islands of separateness."[7]

With the passing of Adolf Hitler and Joseph Stalin and an easing of the harshness of the cold war, in which Soviet-American relations were marked by confrontation politics, scholars concerned themselves with interest group behavior in the Soviet Union prior to its collapse in 1991.[8] Some found that interests were put forward in the Soviet Union to the Communist party leadership and that the clusters of individuals who shared common attitudes resembled in many instances the standard definition of an interest group. They noted a key exception was that interest groups formed differently in the Soviet Union than they did in such Western countries as the United States and Great Britain. Professor H. Gordon Skilling contended that interest groups were not formally organized, but were "more often loose groupings of like-minded or like-interested persons."[9] He and others pointed to groups such as judges, the secret police, churches, scientists, and the army as clearly identifiable in the Soviet Union and other communist countries.

Because of the enormous changes in the communist world since 1985—most notably, the implementation of *glasnost* and *perestroika* in the Soviet Union and the ultimate breakup of the country, the unification of Germany, and the emergence of democratic government in Eastern Europe (see chapter 5)—interest groups are now forming in an open fashion. It is likely that interest groups will become vigorous participants in the political process in these countries.

Although many political scientists agree that interest groups exist in dictatorships—even in totalitarian ones—they also assert that public officials in a democracy are far more vulnerable to interest group pressure than are their counterparts in a dictatorship. Unlike democratic political leaders, dictators can refuse to listen to "lobbyists."[10] Dictators may also dominate private associations by insisting that group leaders show loyalty to the dictator.

[6] Peter P. Cheng, "Japanese Interest Group Politics: An Institutional Framework," *Asian Survey* 30 (February 1990): 255.

[7] Carl J. Friedrich and Zbigniew K. Brzezinski, *Totalitarian Dictatorship and Autocracy*, 2d ed., rev. by Carl J. Friedrich (New York: Praeger, 1965), chap. 6.

[8] H. Gordon Skilling and Franklyn Griffiths, eds., *Interest Groups in Soviet Politics* (Princeton, N.J.: Princeton University Press, 1971); H. Gordon Skilling, "Interest Groups and Communist Politics Revisited," *World Politics* 36 (October 1983): 1–27.

[9] H. Gordon Skilling, "Groups in Soviet Politics: Some Hypotheses," in *Interest Groups in Soviet Politics*, p. 29.

[10] Lester W. Milbrath, *The Washington Lobbyists* (Chicago, Ill.: Rand McNally, 1963), p. 12.

ISSUE

Political leaders frequently blame the "special interests," such as oil companies, armaments manufacturers, or labor unions, for the evils of high prices, war, and inflation. These same lead- ers call for the pursuit of the public interest. Such clamor gives rise to an important issue of the role of interest groups in society.

19/YES ARE POLITICAL INTEREST GROUPS DETRIMENTAL TO THE PUBLIC INTEREST?

As in the first section of this chapter, we shall focus our attention on the American experience. We can see, consequently, that political interest groups are harmful to good government. Our case is based on three arguments: (1) interest group power is strongest among the most privileged few in American society; (2) because of interest groups, government officials must respond to narrow interests in opposition to the public interest; and (3) interest groups are inherently undemocratic.

Privileged Few. Interest groups are powerful because they possess resources that allow them to form, lobby, and obtain their objectives. These resources include first and foremost money. Without money, a group cannot even organize, communicate with its members, hire researchers to watch government policies in a particular area, retain the services of high-priced lobbyists, or get its message across to the public.

Realtors, automobile manufacturers, liquor interests, medical doctors, and the oil industry have no difficulty in organizing and articulating interests before appropriate government officials. People of lower economic classes are less likely to participate in politics than are people with higher incomes. Government responds to pressure. The old adage that the wheel that squeaks the loudest gets the grease is applicable to the political process.

When the powerful are faced with economic difficulties, they are strong and rich enough to influence government. Savings and loan officials were able to engage in practices that were so unsavory that taxpayers had to pay their bill— estimated in 1992 to be at 130 billion dollars. Poor farmers facing bankruptcy because of declining agricultural prices and land values do not have the necessary clout to prevent foreclosure of their farms because they are unable to pay their debt. "Street people" exist because they do not have the political talent and financial resources to get government to do for them what it is willing to do for major economic interests— keep them off the street.

The Public Interest. The number and variety of interest groups in the United States have already been described. What has not been stressed, however, is that each of these groups is concerned with its own well-being at the expense of the public interest. Just as the Scottish economist Adam Smith was wrong when he posited a society in which each individual pursuing a selfish interest would promote the good of all, so, too, do modern interest-group partisans err when they support political interest groups along similar lines.

We can take an issue like inflation as a case in point to see how selfish interests harm the public good. A factor that contributes to inflation is the level of government expenditures and the prices that consumers must pay for goods. The growth of government expenditures has come about largely as a result of pressure group activity. Farm groups have demanded price supports to assure a "fair price" for their agricultural products. The effect of government price supports to farmers was not only to make life better for the farmers but also to raise the price of farm products for consumers. Business groups asked for government contracts to build such items as federal highways for transportation and military hardware for defense, both of which raised public costs.

Expenditures such as these contributed in the 1970s to inflationary pressures on the economy—pressures that drove up interest rates, weakened the value of the dollar on foreign exchange markets, increased unemployment, and moved the country into an era of double-digit inflation.

Besides asking for government funds, interest groups sought other objectives that also contributed to inflation. When business groups used their influence to have the government establish tariffs to prevent lower-priced goods from competing with American products, they, too, were promoting inflation. When unions insisted that American ships (rather than low-bid foreign carriers) transport American wheat to foreign countries in government foreign-aid programs, that action, too, drove up prices.

The point is not that the goals of a particular private interest group are necessarily harmful. There is much support for many of the actions mentioned on behalf of American business, labor, and the poor. Rather, the effect of each group pursuing its own selfish interests is to contribute to inflationary pressures that are detrimental to all. Inflation has a deleterious effect on most groups in American society: business, labor, and the poor, for example. Since government is unable to treat the entire problem but must respond to the different constituencies, the public interest is not served. Political leaders are unable to stand up to powerful interest groups and must, consequently, work against the public good.

The evils of interest groups have long been noted. Jean-Jacques Rousseau argued in *The Social Contract* (1762) that the sum of private interests may work against the common good. James Madison criticized factional interests as "adverse to the rights of other citizens or to the permanent and aggregate interests of the community."[11] Walter Lippmann echoed these voices by favoring the public interest, which he defined as "what men would choose if they saw clearly, thought rationally, acted disinterestedly and benevolently."[12]

Critics of the concept of the public interest contend that it is impossible to define. It may be true that the public interest has no *analytical* utility in that it cannot be defined precisely or its influence evaluated properly. It does, however,

possess an *ethical* meaning by which actions of individuals, groups, and government officials may be judged.[13] In its ethical sense, the concept may have merit in describing what policy should be according to a moral standard. The term *public interest*, then, may be viewed as "a spur to conscience and to deliberation"[14] and is a reminder that the interest of all is not equal to the sum of the interests of each group.

Democracy. If the strengthening of democracy is a desired goal, then political interest groups may be viewed as weakening that goal. We can support this assertion in three ways: (1) the groups themselves are run in an oligarchic way; (2) the groups are not responsible to the electorate in the same manner as are elected public officials; and (3) the emergence of special interest groups has resulted in a weakening of political parties.

Interest groups, like any large organizations, are run in an oligarchic manner in which only a few rule. The sociologist Robert Michels refers to this development as the **iron law of oligarchy**, in which there are only a few who rule—rather than the masses—in large organizations.[15] Adolf A. Berle, Jr. and Gardiner C. Means describe an example of this phenomenon in the corporate world. They conclude that the managers of corporations are the rulers of those corporations in contrast to the stockholders, who do not participate actively in corporate affairs.[16]

It does not matter whether the organization is a corporation, a trade union, or a professional association. The masses of members do not participate actively in the running of the group. And the consequences of this minimal degree of participation can be significant. The political analysts Norman J. Ornstein and Mark Schmitt note that in recent years the staffs of interest groups

[11] James Madison, *Federalist*, no. 10, in Alexander Hamilton, James Madison, and John Jay, *The Federalist Papers*, ed. Clinton Rossiter (New York: New American Library, 1961), p. 78.

[12] Walter Lippmann, *Essays in Public Philosophy* (Boston: Little, Brown, 1955), p. 42.

[13] C. W. Cassinelli, "The Public Interest in Political Ethics," in *The Public Interest*, ed. Carl J. Friedrich (New York: Atherton Press, 1962), p. 45.

[14] J. Roland Pennock, "The One and the Many: A Note on the Concept," in ibid., p. 182.

[15] Robert Michels, *Political Parties: A Sociological Study of the Oligarchical Tendencies of Modern Democracy* (New York: Free Press, 1962), p. 15. The book was first published in 1911.

[16] Adolf A. Berle, Jr., and Gardiner C. Means, *The Modern Corporation and Private Property* (New York: Macmillan, 1933), chap. 5.

have been gradually losing touch with their own membership. The authors see as a reason for this development the emphasis on "short-term tactics over long-term goals of the groups' members."[17]

Even public interest groups are ruled in an oligarchic manner. Jeffrey M. Berry, a leading scholar on public interest groups, observes that the staff of these organizations expend significant resources for communicating to the public interest group members, "but only a minority of the organizations give their members formal opportunities to communicate back." Berry adds that most of these groups do not even go through the "pretense of structuring their organization in a democratic mold so they would at least have the appearance of being open to constituency influence."[18] If public interest groups that are

[17] Norman J. Ornstein and Mark Schmitt, "The New World of Interest Politics," *American Enterprise* 1 (January/February 1990): 48.

[18] Jeffrey M. Berry, *Lobbying for the People: The Political Behavior of Public Interest Groups* (Princeton, N.J.: Princeton University Press, 1977), p. 210.

committed to strengthening and extending democracy do not have an adequate mechanism for popular control, then little more can be expected from other associations.

Interest groups undermine democracy in another way. These voluntary associations are not accountable to the public. Public officials deliberate in the open. Their activities and policies are investigated by government agencies, Congress, and the media. In contrast, private interest groups conduct much of their work in secret. In some cases, they even withhold the lists of their members from government authorities. If government attempts to impose controls on private associations, it subjects itself to the criticism of destroying a free society.

Finally, the rise of interest groups in the United States has developed as political parties have weakened. What is needed to strengthen democracy are strong political parties. The electorate must have an opportunity at election time to choose between different programs offered by competing parties. Interest groups contribute to the fragmentation of the American political process by weakening political parties and so diminishing the significance of the electoral process.

19/NO ARE POLITICAL INTEREST GROUPS DETRIMENTAL TO THE PUBLIC INTEREST?

Political interest groups have too often been described in derogatory terms, such as *pressure boys, influence peddlers*, or *special interests*. An unbiased analysis of their role in a democratic political system reveals that they are essential to a free society and that they perform important functions in the political process. Our case is based on three arguments: (1) interest groups provide representation for all groups, not just the privileged few; (2) to the extent that there is such an identifiable object as the public interest, it is best served through the free play of interest groups seeking to achieve their objectives; and (3) political interest groups are essential for democracy regardless of their internal character.

Representation. American history offers many examples of disadvantaged individuals improving their condition as a result of the formation of interest groups. Poor farmers facing threats from monopolists and the railroads orga-

nized groups and successfully fought these powerful interests through government legislation. Labor unions emerged in response to oppressive and arbitrary actions by capitalists to exploit the working class.

If the system is rigged so that only the privileged few benefit, then how does the *Affirmative* account for the major programs of social reform enacted after vigorous opposition by the privileged in American society? Such social reform legislation includes social security, worker's compensation, Medicare, minimum wages, welfare assistance to the poor, and government aid to education.

Many of the disadvantaged in American society have surrogates who organize interest groups, known as public interest groups. It is they who lobby before government officials on such matters as health care, nutrition, environmental protection, and legal defense. Such organizations do not have the financial resources of their adversaries, but money is not the only component of influence—knowledge and status are important, too. The American Civil Liberties Union, Public Citizen, and Common Cause have had influence in getting government to meet the needs of the less privileged in society.

The Public Interest. Many social scientists are skeptical about using the term *public interest* or similar concepts such as *national interest* or *public good.* The historian Charles A. Beard studied how the term *national interest* has been used in American history and found a close relationship between the claims of special interests and the definition of the public interest.[19] The political scientist Glendon Schubert concludes much the same in his study of the public interest.[20]

The term *public interest* is used by all political interest groups to justify their demands on society. When business groups seek high profits, they argue that it is in the public interest. They support their case by contending that higher profits mean more investment for management, jobs for employees, and dividends for stockholders. When labor unions demand more benefits, or environmentalists ask for greater controls against pollution, or teachers seek better working conditions, or defense contractors urge more government expenditures for national security, they justify their claims by referring to the public interest or to the good of all. There is scarcely any issue that everyone agrees is consistent with the public interest—outside of survival. Even war, which is often supposed to symbolize national unity, finds pacifists and war resisters in opposition.

If anything, the public interest, then, may best be understood not in terms of some identifiable policy prescription but rather as the *process* by which political interest groups are free to compete within the context of democratic procedures, or "rules of the game" as they are sometimes called. Unless a philosopher-king furnishes a universally accepted grand design of a program covering all aspects of life, then

what government does is best justified by free group interplay.

Viewed in this light, we can see that political interest groups serve three vital functions in the political process: advice, acquiescence, and approval.[21] Even big government with its large and specialized bureaucracy needs to gather information and advice from interest groups. Any effort to evaluate why a particular type of aircraft crashed requires investigators to question representatives of the airlines and the manufacturers. If government is to have a health program, it must get information about health problems from the medical associations.

Government needs interest groups to acquiesce in programs, moreover. In a free society laws are often obeyed because people feel that the laws are just, not only because of fear of the penalty for violating the laws. If political interest groups are consulted rather than ignored in the framing or administration of the laws, their members are more likely to accept the outcome.

In addition to advice and acquiescence, interest groups are needed for the approval of government decisions. A government that passes laws without taking into account the groups involved may find itself having to cope with strikes, slowdowns, or even sabotage. The police, for example, can show their disapproval of a mayor's action by ticketing violators of the most minor traffic offense for the purpose of creating popular dissatisfaction with the mayor.

We can well imagine the difficulty that government would face in governing without the help of interest groups. The "public interest" would not be served well without these groups actively working in the political arena.

Democracy. Interest groups are essential to a democracy because they are evidence of a free society, and they are subject to effective political controls. We can argue the case of free-

[19] Charles A. Beard and G. H. E. Smith, *The Idea of the National Interest* (New York: Macmillan, 1934).

[20] Glendon Schubert, *The Public Interest: A Critique of the Theory of a Political Concept* (Glencoe, Ill.: Free Press, 1960).

[21] For a discussion, see Robert J. Lieber, "Interest Groups and Political Integration: British Entry into Europe," in *Pressure Groups in Britain: A Reader,* ed. Richard Kimber and J. J Richardson (London: Dent, 1974), p. 28; S. E. Finer, *Anonymous Empire: A Study of the Lobby in Great Britain,* 2d ed., (London: Pall Mall Press, 1966), pp. 30–31; Graham K. Wilson, *Interest Groups* (Oxford, England: Basil Blackwell, 1990), pp. 82–84.

dom although we accept the *Affirmative*'s contention that there is little democracy *within* interest groups in the sense of mass participation in elections and the overall working of the organization.[22]

The right of groups to form freely is a prerequisite of a free society. In the United States, the legal right is assured by the First Amendment to the Constitution, which forbids Congress from making any law abridging freedom of speech, press, peaceable assembly, and the right to petition the government for redress of grievances. The courts have properly been hesitant to restrict the right of groups to form so long as they abide by the "rules of the game."

There is another way in which freedom is protected by interest groups. The notion that voluntary associations are legitimate—that is, that any number of individuals displeased with the policies of government may form groups to bring about change—is inherently hostile to the totalitarian ideal. Totalitarianism assumes a uniformity of purpose, an integration of society under some ideology. To the extent that groups are permitted in totalitarian societies, they must be "harmonized" with that ideology, unless in practice they are so powerful as to defy control. In totalitarian systems, interest group leaders are appointed by or controlled by the ruling party. One of the first actions of totalitarian leaders upon coming to power is to destroy the autonomy of interest groups. For example, when the Bolsheviks came to power in Russia in 1917, they sought to make the Russian Orthodox church subservient to the communist regime.

A free polity assumes a distinction between state and society. The practice that groups may arise when necessary and act to change government policy serves as an impediment to totalitarian rule.

[22] Grant McConnell, *Private Power and American Democracy* New York: Knopf, 1967), pp. 122–23.

We can also argue that interest groups are subjected to a variety of constraints that limit their power. Because of these constraints, groups must act according to democratic practices. There are laws that make it a crime for individuals and groups to bribe public officials to achieve their objectives. To be sure, these rules are violated, but often the violators are subjected to criminal punishment.

In addition to the constraints imposed by law, interest groups are limited by other interest groups and by political parties and elections. Business must confront labor. Environmental groups must face business associations. Conflicts such as these give policy makers some discretion in making policy.

Other institutions, such as political parties, must work to aggregate the many interests that are asserted in the political arena, thus limiting the power of any single interest group. Elections continue to make a difference in the outcome of public policies. The interest group beneficiaries in the administration of Ronald Reagan were different in many cases from the beneficiaries under Jimmy Carter. Interests representing the military, business, and social conservatives were more likely to see their goals realized under Reagan than under Carter. Even with the declining strength of political parties, as the presidential elections of 1980, 1984, and 1988 indicate, elections continue to have significance in an interest-group state. Democracy in the United States continues to remain strong, consequently.

Although James Madison warned about the dangers of factions, he recognized that factions are inherent in the "nature of man." He realized that factions could not and should not be eliminated. He hoped that the system of American government with its dispersion of power would prevent any one interest or group of interests from controlling American society. The past two centuries have shown Madison to be right.

KEY TERMS

Interest group
Iron law of oligarchy
Iron triangle
Lobbyists
Material incentives
Political action committees
Pressure group

Public interest
Public interest group
Purposive incentives
Single-issue groups
Solidary incentives
Voluntary association

QUESTIONS

1. How would you compare interest groups in democracies with interest groups in dictatorships?
2. How do political interest groups differ from political parties?
3. Do public interest groups serve the public interest? What are the reasons for your answer?
4. What restrictions should be placed on interest groups in a democracy?
5. If there is a public interest, how would you describe it in policy terms?
6. In a democratic society in which interest groups are important, what types of interests are most likely to be unrepresented? What, if anything, can be done to guard against this?

RECOMMENDED READINGS

ABRAMSON, ALAN J., and RUDOLPH G. PENNER. "Special Interests, Public Opinion, and Public Policy." *American Enterprise* 1 (September/October 1990): 79–80. An argument that special interest power over spending in the United States is limited by public opinion.

BERRY, JEFFREY M. *Lobbying for the People: The Political Behavior of Public Interest Groups*. Princeton, N.J.: Princeton University Press, 1977. A scholarly account of public interest groups.

CHENG, PETER P. "Japanese Interest Group Politics: An Institutional Framework." *Asian Survey* 30 (February 1990): 251–65. An analysis of the interaction between state and society as it takes place between interest groups and government policy makers in Japan.

CIGLER, ALLAN J., and BURDETT A. LOOMIS, eds. *Interest Group Politics*. 3d ed. Washington, D.C.: CQ Press, 1991. Essays on group politics in the United States.

COCHRAN, CLARKE E. "Political Science and 'The Public Interest.'" *Journal of Politics* 36 (May 1974): 327–55. An evaluation of contemporary theories dealing with the concept of the public interest.

COXALL, W. N. *Parties and Pressure Groups*. 2d ed. London: Longman, 1986. A study of parties and pressure groups in Great Britain and their roles in the political system.

DREZON-TEPLER, MARCIA. *Interest Groups and Political Change in Israel*. Albany, N.Y.: State University of New York Press, 1990. A study of interest groups in Israel's political system.

ETZIONI, AMITAI. *Capital Corruption: The New Attack on American Democracy*. New Brunswick, N.J.: Transaction Books, 1988. A critique of political action committees.

FRIEDRICH, CARL J., ed. *The Public Interest*. New York: Atherton Press, 1962. A collection of essays on the public interest.

GAMSON, WILLIAM. *The Strategy of Social Protest*. 2d ed. Belmont, Calif.: Wadsworth Publishing Co., 1990. An examination of social protest groups that challenged some aspect of the *status quo* in the United States.

GRANTHAM, CLIFF. "Parliament and Political Consultants." *Parliamentary Affairs* (London) 42 (October 1989): 503–18. A discussion of the politics of British consultants.

HREBENAR, RONALD J., and RUTH K. SCOTT. *Interest Group Politics in America*. 2d ed. Englewood Cliffs, N.J.: Prentice Hall, 1990. A study of interest groups in the United States.

JORDAN, A. G., and J. J. RICHARDSON. *Government and Pressure Groups in Britain*. Oxford, England: Clarendon Press, 1987. A study of British interest groups.

LIPPMANN, WALTER. *Essays in the Public Philosophy*. Boston: Little, Brown, 1955. An argument that mass democracies have weakened the executive and exerted influence contrary to the public interest.

LONG, NORTON E. "Conceptual Notes on the Public Interest for Public Administration and Policy Analysts." *Administration and Society* 22 (August 1990): 170–81. An argument that the fields of political science, public administration, and policy analysis need the standard of the public interest to evaluate outcomes, management structures and processes, programs, and policies.

MAHOOD, H. R. *Interest Group Politics in America: A New Intensity*. Englewood Cliffs, N.J.: Prentice-Hall, 1990. A study of interest groups in the United States.

MALVERN, PAUL. *Persuaders: Influence Peddling, Lobbying and Political Corruption in Canada*.

Toronto: Methuen, 1985. A critical look at Canadian interest groups.

MILLER, CHARLES. *Lobbying: Understanding and Influencing the Corridors of Power.* 2d ed. Cambridge, Mass.: B. Blackwell, 1990. A practical guide for interest group officials in dealing with British government.

OLSON, MANCUR. *The Rise and Decline of Nations: Economic Growth, Stagflation, and Social Rigidities.* New Haven: Yale University Press, 1982. An explanation of the decline of states in terms of the rise of interest groups.

ORNSTEIN, NORMAN J., and MARK SCHMITT. "The New World of Interest Politics." *American Enterprise* 1 (January/February 1990): 47–51. An argument that U.S. interest groups are losing touch with their members.

PERTSCHUK, MICHAEL. *Giant Killers.* New York: W. W. Norton, 1986. An insider's account of public interest lobbying.

PETERSON, PAUL E. "The Rise and Fall of Special Interest Politics." *Political Science Quarterly* 105 (Winter 1990–91): 539–56. An argument that the power of the special interests in the United States has been in decline during the Reagan and Bush administrations.

RASKIN, MARCUS G. *The Common Good: Its Politics, Policies and Philosophy.* New York: Routledge and Kegan Paul, 1987. A plea for a social reconstruction to preserve the common good.

SCHUBERT, GLENDON. *The Public Interest: A Critique of the Theory of a Political Concept.* Glencoe, Ill.: Free Press, 1960. A critique of the concept of the public interest in theories of political behavior.

WILSON, FRANK L. *Interest-Group Politics in France.* Cambridge, England: Cambridge University Press, 1987. A study of interest groups in France.

WILSON, GRAHAM K. *Interest Groups.* Oxford, England: Basil Blackwell, 1990. A study of interest group politics from a comparative perspective.

part V

GOVERNMENT INSTITUTIONS

Politics involves the making of public choices. Government is the agency of making those choices (see Chapter 1). How the machinery of government is organized affects the policies of government and the responsiveness of government to different groups and individuals. A government that is structured so that power is fragmented, for example, may make economic and social change difficult to achieve.

For years, as a case in point, the cumbersome process of enacting laws in the United States delayed the realization of civil rights of black Americans. Dilatory tactics of southern legislators in Congress and southern governors in the states impeded change and prevented black people from participating equally in the political process.

How government is organized, then, has an important bearing on political life. The next three chapters deal with some of the major government institutions, how government structure has an impact on public policy, and the character of political systems. First, the relationship between central and regional institutions of government is considered in Chapter 10. Then, Chapter 11 describes the three principal institutions of government: legislatures, executives, and judiciaries. Chapter 12 deals with the role of the bureaucracy.

chapter 10

Federalism

In every political system government must have some way to relate its central governing units to smaller territorial divisions of the state. What that relationship is may have an impact on individual freedom, economic and social development, and political stability. Two principal institutional forms that have different links between central and regional governments are federal and unitary systems.

Six of the largest countries in the world—Argentina, Australia, Brazil, Canada, India, and the United States—are organized on a federal basis. Other federal countries are Austria, Germany, Malaysia, Mexico, Nigeria, Switzerland, and Venezuela.

As a concept, the term *federalism* has attained a widespread respectability, not nearly as much as the term *democracy* but nonetheless significant. Like democracy, federalism is difficult to define. It is derived from the Latin word *foedus*, which means

"contract," or "alliance," or "covenant." Throughout past centuries, however, *federal* has been used as a synonym for such words as *national, league,* or *decentralized.* Even in *The Federalist*, a collection of essays by three supporters of the ratification of the U.S. Constitution—Alexander Hamilton, John Jay, and James Madison—the term is used with different connotations.

If the past is cloudy about federalism, the present is even more so. Countries with varying political systems are today characterized as federal. From 1922 until 1991 the Soviet Union was officially classified as a **federation**—that is, a federal system. The United States, which has a political system quite different from the former Soviet Union, is also a federation.

Political scientists, moreover, are as much in disagreement about what constitutes a federal system as are government leaders and the general public. Some observers refer to federal and its related terms even to describe private associations, such as the American Federation of Teachers (AFT) in the United States.

One useful standard definition of **federalism**, however, is a political system organized on a territorial basis in which power is divided between two units—a central government (sometimes referred to as the national government or the federal government) and regional governments (sometimes known as states, provinces, cantons, republics, or *Länder*). In such a system both the regional units and the central government derive their authority from a written constitution. Generally speaking, in a federal system the regional units are fixed and can be changed only with their consent.

Examples of a federal system are plentiful. The United States is composed of fifty states. Canada has ten provinces. The former Soviet Union included fifteen republics. Each, however, has a central government, and the relationship between the central government and its federal units varies considerably from case to case in spite of their federal status.

A federal system may be more clearly understood if compared to two alternative systems of organizing government territorially: a confederation and a unitary system. A **confederation** is a loose association of regional units in which sovereign power is retained by the regional units rather than residing in the central government. The central government has no direct jurisdiction over individuals, consequently. Prior to the adoption of the Constitution, for example, the United States was governed as a confederation. Its constitutional authority was in fact named the Articles of Confederation. In that system states retained sovereignty, and the Articles of Confederation could be amended only with the unanimous consent of the states. To a considerable extent, the United Nations may be classified as a confederation today, since power and sovereignty are retained by the countries that make up its membership

rather than residing in the international organization itself. And the Commonwealth of Independent States—composed of twelve of the republics that made up the old Soviet Union—is the most recent example of a confederation.

In a **unitary system** sovereign power is retained in the central government and regional units are changed at will. All governmental authority is exercised directly over the citizens by the central government, except in those areas of responsibility delegated to regional or local authorities. In unitary systems, the territorial subdivisions are not permanently fixed. In 1974, for example, the British government reorganized the regional governing units, merging some, eliminating others, and enlarging or reducing districts as it deemed appropriate. Such an act is forbidden in the American Constitution as far as states are concerned, and the boundary lines of the states remain intact.[1]

Most of the countries of the world have unitary systems. These systems include a variety of political systems, among which are democratic, authoritarian, imperial, and totalitarian forms. In addition to France and Great Britain, countries that have unitary systems are Nicaragua, Zimbabwe, Japan, the People's Republic of China, Poland, and many others.

Federal and unitary systems are sometimes difficult to distinguish because all central governments have some links with regional units. A unitary system may, in fact, grant power to regional units so that those units have more power than even states or similar political entities possess in federal systems. Some writers contend that both unitary systems that give power to a regional unit by legislation and central governments that must share power with a regional unit are examples of **decentraliza-**

---

[1] One exception is West Virginia. That state was created out of the Commonwealth of Virginia as a Civil War measure and has continued to retain its separate identity.

tion—the allocation of power from higher to lower units.

Daniel J. Elazar, a leading scholar on federalism, and others challenge this contention. They point to the major distinction of a federal system: namely, that there is an agreement to share power between central and regional units. In a decentralized system the central authorities may decide to take that power back from a regional unit. In a federal system the central government is impeded from taking power back because of constitutional arrangements. In that sense a federal system is *noncentralized* rather than *decentralized*.[2]

CHARACTERISTICS OF FEDERAL SYSTEMS

Because of the variety of federal systems in the world today, it is difficult to use the term *federalism* in a precise manner. Varieties of federal systems are described below. In general, federal systems are characterized by: a division of powers, a written constitution, constitutional interpretation, and agreement to share responsibility.

Division of Powers

In a federal system, power is divided between a central government and regional governments. In the United States federalism has been perceived to be a system in which certain areas of public policy are dealt with by the national government and others by the states. The national government plays a preponderant role in foreign policy, defense, and interstate commerce. The states have primary responsibility in education, civil and criminal law, police power, and public order. This arrangement in the United States has been de-

scribed as **dual federalism**—a system in which each sphere, the national and state, has distinct powers. According to the political scientist David C. Nice, "Dual federalism is a fairly accurate portrayal of the early years of our governmental system, although perhaps not totally accurate."[3] Within the past two centuries, however, the role of the central government has grown with respect to the states, and many of the powers of the national and state governments now overlap and are shared. All that the principle of federalism requires is that there be a division of powers and some guarantee of the autonomy of each government in its own sphere.[4]

Written Constitution

The American federal system, like most federal systems, has a written constitution that sets forth the basic powers of both the central government and the states. To be sure, constitutional development depends not only on the specific statements of the Constitution but also on statutory laws, judicial interpretation, custom, and political practice; but the fact that there is a written constitution helps to solidify the federal character of the system.

The constitutional stipulations about federalism vary from country to country. The U.S. Constitution specifies the powers belonging to the federal government. The Tenth Amendment provides that those powers not delegated to the central government are reserved to the states or to the people. The Canadian Constitution, in contrast, specifies the powers of the provincial governments, and the residual powers belonging to the national government. A written constitution of a federal system as-

[2] Daniel J. Elazar, "The Role of Federalism in Political Integration," in *Federalism and Political Integration*, ed. Daniel J. Elazar (Lanham, Md.: University Press of America, 1984, p. 14.

[3] David C. Nice, *Federalism: The Politics of Intergovernmental Relations* (New York: St. Martin's Press, 1987), p. 5.

[4] William H. Riker, *Federalism: Origin, Operation, Significance* (Boston: Little, Brown, 1964), p. 11.

serts that each governing unit is given permanent recognition.

Constitutional Interpretation

Because in constitutional theory and practice conflicts arise between regional governments and the central government, some institution is essential to act as an umpire. In the United States the Supreme Court has this function. Similar courts exist in other countries.

At certain times the Supreme Court has decided in favor of the national government and at other times in favor of the states. Relying in part upon the national **supremacy clause** of the Constitution that declares that the Constitution, national laws, and treaties, "shall be the supreme Law of the Land," the U.S. Supreme Court has struck down as invalid many state statutes that were in conflict with that clause. In the early period of the American republic, critics of national government supremacy asserted that the states had a right to nullify a national law. The defeat of the South in the American Civil War settled the matter in favor of the national government.

Agreement to Share Responsibility

Federalism is more than just a legal compact to divide powers. It represents an agreement to share responsibility for governing between national and regional leaders. The U.S. Constitution, for example, offers formal legal devices in which this kind of cooperation is essential, such as in the amendment process (requiring action at the national and state government levels) and in the method of selecting senators by state legislatures (changed to popular election by the Seventeenth Amendment in 1913). The sharing has also become part of the developing historical process as national and state governments work together, often in a cooperative way, to make laws. Matching grants, in which the central government and state governments jointly fund programs in such areas as transportation, health, and education, serve as one example. Many federal government programs, moreover, are administered by state governments.

The political scientist Morton Grodzins points out that most people think of federalism in the United States as a three-layer cake, with national on top, state in the middle, and local at the bottom. A better way to describe the federal government–state government relationship, he argues, is by seeing it as a "marble-cake" pattern, in which the political and legal relationships are so mixed as to make it difficult to clearly distinguish between the responsibility of state and national governments. Thus, any place one "cuts into" the cake, one finds a mixture of powers.[5] Similar sharing occurs in the politics of other federal systems. Such a pattern has been described as **cooperative federalism**.

HISTORICAL EVOLUTION OF FEDERAL SYSTEMS

Federalism is generally regarded as an American invention. Ancient writers did not discuss this concept. Some political scientists date the precursors of federalism back to the ancient Jews, but the early attempts at federalism were more alliances and leagues than true federal systems in the modern sense. In the thirteenth century B.C. the Israelites sought to maintain national unity by linking their several tribes. Ancient Greek city-states established leagues, mostly for purposes of defense. The Achaean League (280–146 B.C.) was one of its notable examples. These, however, were more like confederations than federal systems. So, too, were the leagues of medieval commercial towns in Central

[5] Morton Grodzins, *The American System: A New View of Government in the United States*, ed. Daniel J. Elazar (Chicago: Rand McNally, 1966), pp. 7–10.

Europe, which were established for purposes of military defense. In 1291, the Swiss cantons organized a confederation to promote security. That confederation has gone through many changes and ultimately became, in the nineteenth century, a federation (although it retained the title of Swiss Confederation). Scholars differ about whether the government of the Netherlands in the sixteenth century could be called a federal system, although clearly it was not federal in the same sense as the American political system established in Philadelphia in 1787.

The U.S. Constitution was a landmark in the development of federalism. Before the American Revolutionary War, each of the thirteen North American colonies was individually linked to Great Britain. The war for independence required a greater degree of unity and, consequently, the revolutionary Continental Congress served as an instrument of unity. Members of Congress, however, served as delegates of their states rather than as national legislators.

The weakness of the confederation became apparent in the postwar period. Amendments to its constitution required unanimous agreement by the states. Important legislative matters required the consent of at least nine of the thirteen states. The Articles of Confederation provided for a weak executive and no federal judiciary. In the important area of national defense, the Confederation Congress was dependent upon the contributions of the states.

The convention called at Philadelphia to revise the Articles of Confederation led to the writing of the Constitution with federal features. This federal form of government, as the political scientist Carl J. Friedrich notes, was a "novel, unprecedented concept."[6]

The American practice of federalism in-

[6] Carl J. Friedrich, *Trends of Federalism in Theory and Practice* (New York: Praeger, 1968), p. 17.

fluenced other countries concerned with promoting unity while at the same time allowing for some regional autonomy. Canada particularly shows a strong influence from the American system. Its Constitution, which was framed in the British Parliament in 1867, is the eighth oldest of a federal nature. Paradoxically, Great Britain, which has a unitary system, served as one of the principal forces of federalism in the world by encouraging federal systems in its former colonies. In 1901, consequently, Australia was established as a federal system. In 1947 both India and Pakistan were created as independent countries with federal systems. Other former British colonies to become federal systems were Malaya (later Malaysia), Nigeria, and Cameroon. One notable failure was the British West Indian Federation, which had sought in 1958 to unite within one legal framework the ten British island colonies in the Caribbean. That federation lasted for only four years before it broke up.

The American model also influenced many Latin American countries in the nineteenth century. Argentina, Brazil, Mexico, and Venezuela continue to be federal systems at least in name. Many Latin American federal systems are more nominal than real, however.

In the mid-nineteenth century Switzerland adopted a federal constitution. Today the Swiss federal system, comprising different ethnic groups, flourishes. About 70 percent of Swiss people speak German, 19 percent speak French, and less than 10 percent speak Italian. The indigenous language, Romansch, is spoken by only a small minority. In the post–World War II period many nations composed of diverse ethnic groups followed the Swiss model in the hope of providing unity amid diversity.

The Constitution of the German Empire of 1871–1918 is sometimes described as federal. Some scholars contend, however, that the overwhelming influence of one of its constituent units—namely, Prussia—

was so great as to make Germany a poor example of a federal system.[7] The Austro-Hungarian Constitution of 1867—the Dual Monarchy, or *Ausgleich*—is sometimes cited as an example of a federal system. Under this structure Austria was centralized under German domination and Hungary centralized under Magyar authority. None of the other nationalities in Austria-Hungary, however, had representation. In effect, Austria-Hungary was not really a federal system.

Federal systems have become popular in the post–World War II period. Several countries in Africa and Asia have looked upon the federal system as a mechanism to allow for modernization while at the same time preserving diverse ethnic identities. Federal crises, in which secessionist movements emerged, have revealed, however, that the political form of federalism is not necessarily a strong unifying element. The case of the Biafran civil war in Nigeria in the late 1960s is perhaps the major example of the failure of a federal system. Even in an old established federal system like Canada, the secessionist movement by the French-speaking province of Quebec has had significant strength. Today—after the failure of accords that sought to revise the federal arrangements underlying the Canadian constitution—some French Canadians are committed to the independence of Quebec.

The federal idea also has been prominent in international institutions since the end of World War II. The European Community is one illustration. Another example, but one that failed, is the East African Community, linking Kenya, Uganda, and Tanzania. The United Nations may also be viewed as a confederation. The World Federalists Association (formerly the United World Federalists) supports the idea that the federal principle could be used to unite

the nations of the world into a global community in the manner that the thirteen American states became one nation with the establishment of the U.S. Constitution.

VARIETIES OF FEDERALISM

The character of federal systems varies widely. In fact, federalism is but one form of dividing power along territorial lines. In this respect a unitary system that allows for considerable power to be exercised on a regional or local basis may have more in common with, say, the federal system in the United States than it does with other unitary countries. Similarly, countries that have federal constitutions may in fact have unitary governments in spite of the federal label.

Federal systems, consequently, vary in terms of the division of powers, the underlying social composition of the federal units, and the degree to which the sharing of power is nominal rather than real.

Division of Powers

As indicated above, the formal constitutional provisions of federal systems vary. The constitutions of Canada and Australia enumerate powers of the regional governments and reserve power to the central government. In India, in contrast, the powers of both governments are enumerated. How much should belong to the regional units and how much to the central government? That is a question that has been answered in different ways at different times.

In the early years of the American republic, advocates of states' rights argued for at least coordinate state powers. Thomas Jefferson and John C. Calhoun became spokesmen for this point of view. In contrast, John Marshall and Andrew Jackson became leading proponents of national supremacy. The federal government–state government conflicts continue to the present day. Generally, the conflicts

---

[7] Kenneth C. Wheare, *Federal Government*, 4th ed. (New York: Oxford University Press, 1963), p. 50.

are muted in an age of cooperative federalism.

Power can be divided in other ways. In the American and Canadian pattern the major issue has involved the exercise of all components of power—legislative, executive, judicial, and administrative in policy areas—although the sharing of power has become prominent in the twentieth century. In Germany and Switzerland, however, administrative power is largely in the hands of regional units. Even in these countries, some functions, such as foreign affairs and defense, are handled at the national level.

Social Composition

The districts that separate one regional unit from another may or may not have homogeneous population. In Canada, the province of Quebec is predominantly French-Canadian. In Switzerland, the cantonal divisions are based principally on ethnic configurations. Switzerland was the first modern federation organized to bind indigenous ethnic and linguistic regions. India and Nigeria have reorganized their federal boundary lines to take into account new ethnic demands.

In the United States, however, the "melting pot" ideal, the historic origin of states based on colonial rather than ethnic considerations, and the mobile character of the American people have all contributed to the heterogeneous composition of most states. Certain ethnic communities have at times been centered in particular states: the Chinese in California, Irish in Massachusetts, and Jews in New York. But no entire state has become as distinct ethnically as, say, Quebec is in Canada.

Nominal or Real?

Scholars of federalism differ about the proper application of the word *federal* to specific countries. The political scientist Kenneth C. Wheare views the United

States, Australia, and Switzerland as the best examples of federal systems. Wheare includes Canada with the qualification that the Canadian Constitution is "quasi-federal."[8] He and others, however, perceived the Soviet federal system as a sham. Critics of the Soviet federal system contended that the Soviet Constitution may in fact have provided for a federal system, but principal components of such a system—such as an independent judiciary and a real independent regional power as a check upon the authority of the central governing unit (in this case dominated by the central Communist party)—were lacking. The critics' views would be in accord with Marxist theory, which looks at federalism as a temporary expedient in some cases until a unitary communist system can be imposed.

With the decline of the power of the Communist party in the Soviet Union brought on by *glasnost* and *perestroika* (see chapter 5), a number of Soviet commentators advocated a real—rather than a nominal—federal arrangement in their country. The problem for Soviet leaders, however, was that all the Soviet republics advocated independence from Soviet control.[9] Ultimately, Mikhail Gorbachev's hope of establishing an effective federal system failed, and the Soviet Union broke apart into its constituent republics.

Because of the variation of systems, it might be best to view federalism as a continuum rather than as something precise and fixed. Professor William H. Riker suggests that the range of possibilities between regional and national governments in a federal system may best be described in such a manner. Riker sets as a minimum condition that "the ruler(s) of the federation can make decisions in only one narrowly restricted category of action without

[8] Ibid., p. 20.

[9] For a discussion of federalism in the Soviet Union, see Stephan Kux, "Soviet Federalism," *Problems of Communism* 39 (March/April 1990): 1–20.

obtaining the approval of the rulers of the constituent units." The maximum condition, according to Riker, is that "the ruler(s) of the federation can make decisions without consulting the rulers of the member governments in all but one narrowly restricted category of action."[10]

MOTIVATING FACTORS OF FEDERALISM

In the past century an increasing number of countries have adopted federal systems, sometimes by choice of national leaders and at other times under the influence of foreign powers. Federalism arises from a political decision by the ruling elites to establish such a system. Several factors other than political ones have contributed to the establishment of federal states, and these may be best classified as military, economic, historical, ideological, social, and opportunistic.

Military

Professor William H. Riker asserts that federalism "is a bargain between prospective leaders and officials of constituent governments for the purpose of aggregating territory." According to Riker, the parties are predisposed to accept this bargain by "the expansion condition" and "the military condition." By *expansion condition*, Riker means that the politicians want territorial control either to meet an external military or diplomatic threat or to prepare for military or diplomatic aggression and aggrandizement. By *military condition*, Riker refers to the willingness of politicians to give up some of their independence because of the external military threat or opportunity.[11]

The American experience of the eighteenth century is a prime example of military and diplomatic factors playing a role in producing a federal system. Another example is Canada, since some of the Canadian provinces felt compelled to join the Canadian union in 1867 out of fear of an encroaching neighbor from the south.

Economic

Interdependent economies and the expectation of economic benefits contribute to a working federal relationship. The economic difficulties existing in the period immediately after the American Revolutionary War encouraged a federal system that would promote commerce. The fact that economic integration linked the economies of West Europe after World War II has been a major force in the strengthening of the European Community.

The inability of economic factors to link the units of the short-lived West Indian Federation in the post–World War II period was a cause of its demise. Lack of economic integration also played a role in the Biafran secessionist movement against the Nigerian federation in the 1960s, and in the secession of East Pakistan from Pakistan in 1971.

Historical

A long period of close association among territorial entities is often a contributory factor in enabling federalism to take hold. British colonial rule over the thirteen American colonies for more than a century before the Revolutionary War established a common legal system and a basis for unity. The association of the thirteen states during that war helped to promote a sense of unity. Australia and Canada also had a history of existing territorial units out of which a federal system could be constructed.

Ideological

For federalism to work, there must be a commitment on the part of the leaders of

---

[10] Riker, *Federalism*, pp. 5–6.
[11] Ibid., pp. 12–13.

the federation to make it work. Such has been the case with federal countries like the United States and Australia. One scholar, analyzing why four federations in the Third World failed in the post–World War II period, concluded that in all four federations a commitment to the "primary political ideal of federation itself" was lacking.[12]

Social

A federal system can work only if the people who constitute it can get along with each other. In the 1930s, when an independent federal India was first discussed, it was projected to include many ethnic and religious groups. By 1940, the Muslims, constituting a minority of the Indian subcontinent, rejected a federal solution for India and sought an independent Muslim country, which in 1947 became Pakistan. In cases in which subnational feeling is strong, federalism will not work. In the United States of the eighteenth century a feeling of such divisive subnationalism did not characterize the individual thirteen states, and a federal arrangement, consequently, became practical.

The Swiss experience is somewhat similar to that of the Americans. When the Swiss federation was established in 1848, the different nationalities of the country already had a long period of alliance or confederation. In the words of Kenneth C. Wheare, "They had come to think of themselves not only as German or French or Italian but also as Swiss."[13]

Opportunistic

As indicated above, many observers contended that the federalism of the Soviet Union was a sham because power was centralized in the ruling Communist party. Federalism is an un-Marxist idea. Neither Karl Marx and Friedrich Engels nor V. I. Lenin favored the federal form of government. Lenin adopted federalism in the hope that the many nationalities would look at communist rule in the Soviet Union as a vehicle of national self-determination rather than side with anticommunist or nationalist forces. He assured the nationalities, moreover, that their republics had the right of secession.[14] In practice, however, the Soviet system was unitary.

None of these motivating factors guarantee that a federal system must evolves. The national principle may be more powerful than the federal principle in some cases, and secessionist movements may emerge. Nor is it essential to have all of these factors present before a federal system is constituted. Over the past few centuries, however, these factors have in most cases played a role in building federalism.

[12] Thomas M. Franck, "Why Federations Fail," in *Why Federations Fail: An Inquiry into the Requisites for Successful Federalism*, ed. Thomas M. Franck (New York: New York University Press, 1968), pp. 196–97. For a discussion of the reasons why federations fail and succeed, see Daniel J. Elazar, *Exploring Federalism* (Tuscaloosa, Ala.: University of Alabama Press, 1987), pp. 240–48.

[13] Kenneth C. Wheare, "Federalism and the Making of Nations," in *Federalism: Mature and Emergent*, ed. Arthur W. MacMahon (Garden City, N.Y.: Doubleday, 1955), p. 34.

[14] Ivo D. Duchacek, *Comparative Federalism: The Territorial Dimension of Politics* (New York: Holt, Rinehart and Winston, 1970), pp. 137–38.

ISSUE

The federal system has a modern history of two centuries. Federalism is sometimes seen as a problem and at other times a solution to achieving political order and individual liberty. The debate below considers the pros and cons of federalism.

20/YES   IS FEDERALISM BENEFICIAL TO SOCIETY?

The widespread adoption of federalism throughout the world suggests that this institutional device serves a broad range of purposes. Among the most significant benefits of federalism are that it: (1) promotes freedom, (2) helps solve economic and social problems, and (3) strengthens the ability of government to cope with political problems of change and stability.

Freedom. The need to reconcile individual liberty with public order is a central concern of many political thinkers. In the past few centuries the historical record shows that federalism is well suited to encourage human freedom. Central to this view is the notion that individual freedom is strengthened when government power is fragmented. As the British political observer James Bryce notes, "Federalism prevents the rise of a despotic central government, absorbing other powers, and menacing the private liberties of the citizen."[15] In fact, Bryce's fear of despotic central government echoes the views of early supporters of federalism. The Framers of the U.S. Constitution, for example, hailed the establishment of federalism (along with the separation of powers) because they feared a strong, centralized, and despotic government.

A totalitarian system is centralized, and all elements of society are subordinated to the ruling government. A free society is hostile to such a system. A basic element of federalism—division of powers—is inherently opposed to the totalitarian ideal. Nelson Rockefeller, who served as governor of New York State, asserted this point when he noted that the federal idea "is a pluralistic idea. It gives scope to many energies, many beliefs, many initiatives."[16]

Federalism can protect individual liberty even against the attempts of the majority to constrain it. Professor William S. Livingston notes, "By its very nature federalism is anti-majoritarian."[17]

[15] James Bryce, *The American Commonwealth*, rev. ed. (New York: Macmillan, 1931), 1:351.

[16] Nelson A. Rockefeller, *The Future of Federalism* (Cambridge, Mass.: Harvard University Press, 1962), p. 9.

[17] William S. Livingston, *Federalism and Constitutional Change* (Oxford, England: Clarendon Press, 1956), p. 310.

When majorities become tyrannical, they may destroy or weaken liberty. Federalism serves, consequently, as a bulwark of freedom. As forces of centralization in economic and social areas of life become stronger, the regional units can serve as a counter to uniform rule imposed by the central government. If the central government attempts to establish more and more rules over areas of policy previously outside government activity, such as who should be hired for a job, who should be admitted to a university graduate program, who should have access to an individual's private financial information, or what kinds of products can appear on the market, then the states may serve as bastions of freedom in opposition to the encroachments of "the new despotism," even when the despots are the majority.

In this regard most federal systems have constitutional checks so that mere majorities may be prevented from acting capriciously. In the United States constitutional amendments, requiring ratification by three-fourths of the state legislatures or by special ratifying conventions in three-fourths of the states, serve as one example of a check on national majorities. In Switzerland constitutional amendments must receive a majority not only of total popular votes in a referendum but also a majority approval of the cantons. The power of less populated cantons, consequently, is made disproportionately strong. Such amendment procedures as exist in the United States and Switzerland, therefore, serve as a bulwark of freedom because they protect against the "tyranny of the majority," to use the expression of the French political philosopher Alexis de Tocqueville.

Federalism offers real opportunities for protecting individual liberty. If the national government adopts laws, policies, and rulings that impede individual liberty, individuals and groups adversely affected can turn to state institutions for help. In the past many American conservatives championed the cause of states' rights to protect property rights over human rights. American liberals have now begun to see that states' rights may serve their cause, too.

This may be seen particularly in matters pertaining to the Supreme Court. During the years when the Supreme Court was led by Earl Warren, liberals looked to the Supreme Court to protect political liberties because the Court was making historic liberal decisions. In the conservative Court led by Warren's successors, Warren Burger and William H. Rehnquist, liberals have not been able to expect the same kind of rulings. Many liberals, consequently, directed their energies to state courts. Some decisions of the state courts—notably California, Alaska, and Hawaii—have been most supportive of civil liberties.

Economic and Social Problems. The portrait of federalism as a reactionary force in society is inconsistent with the economic and social development of federal states. In practice, federalism has not been made obsolete by modern economic development, nor has it impeded social reform.

It is certainly true that the economies of countries have transcended regional boundaries, but federalism has adapted to changing economic needs. Federal systems, for example, have not let the giant corporations rule at the expense of the rest of society. With the approval of many states, the central government has adopted national institutions to cope with economic development. In the United States a Federal Reserve Board monitors interest rates and influences the money supply.

State boundary lines, moreover, have not inhibited creative patterns of relationships that transcend the state boundary lines. The Tennessee Valley Authority, for example, is a regional enterprise concerned with treating the Tennessee Valley region as an economic and developmental unit. The Port of New York Authority, which was organized to develop not only the New York metropolitan areas but also sections of New Jersey that are really part of the New York port area, is yet another example of creative federalism.[18]

Federalism, then, has not become antiquated because of a changing economy. Nor has it served to inhibit social reform. In the United States the states have not only pioneered in legislation of social reform, such as child labor and workmen's compensation laws, but have also demonstrated that they are willing to raise the money for welfare programs. Much of state reve-

nues is devoted to the welfare sector—particularly education, welfare assistance to the poor, health, and housing.

Former Canadian Prime Minister Pierre Trudeau contends that federalism is consistent with socialism, which, to some observers at least, is synonymous with social reform. Coming from French-speaking Quebec province, he strongly opposed the movement toward Quebec secessionism. He argued even before he was prime minister that federalism should be "welcomed as a valuable tool which permits dynamic parties to plant socialist governments in certain provinces, from which the seed of radicalism can slowly spread."[19] For Trudeau, each province of Canada is not at the same stage of social development, and federalism could allow for change at the proper time. The fact that the states in the American union responded to social reform programs at different times supports Trudeau's assessment and, consequently, demonstrates the vitality of federalism in our time.

Political Problems. Federalism is ideally suited to cope with political problems of change and stability. James Bryce was one among many writers who saw the political benefits of the federal principle. Two major points he made in this connection are: (1) federalism allows for experimentation on a limited scale before a new program is adopted nationally; and (2) federalism minimizes the risks involved in any political system.

With respect to experimentation, states have been in the forefront of the movement toward social reform. As Bryce asserts, "Federalism enables a people to try experiments in legislation and administration which would not be safely tried in a large centralized country."[20]

Many examples illustrate this point. About a half century before American women were given the right to vote in national elections, the state of Wyoming became the first to enact woman suffrage. Before the Twenty-sixth Amendment reduced the voting age to eighteen, Georgia had allowed eighteen-year-olds to vote. In the United States, government inspection of factories appeared first in Massachusetts in 1879, old age pensions originated in Alaska in 1915 even be-

---

[18] Since 1972 the agency has been known as the Port Authority of New York and New Jersey.

[19] Pierre Elliott Trudeau, *Federalism and the French Canadians*, introd. John T. Saywell (New York: St. Martin's Press, 1968), p. 127.

[20] Bryce, *American Commonwealth*, 1:353.

fore it was a separate state, child labor legislation started in Massachusetts as early as 1842, and unemployment insurance began in Wisconsin in 1932.[21] Many of the New Deal programs had their experimental origins in the period in which Franklin D. Roosevelt was governor of New York. Since the end of World War II, moreover, states have pioneered in legislation on fair housing and air pollution.

Many lessons were learned from these state programs, which helped to improve legislation when finally enacted on the national level. Bryce observes that a state finds it easier than the central government to make laws and correct mistakes. A state also finds it profitable to observe the outcome of laws of an experimental nature.[22]

In addition to the benefits of experimentation, federalism minimizes risks in the governance of a large and diverse nation. Bryce compares federalism to a ship built with watertight compartments: "When a leak is sprung in one compartment, the cargo stored there may be damaged, but the other compartments remain dry and keep the ship afloat." So, too, does federalism prevent social discord from "tainting the nation at large."[23]

If the United States had a unitary system, many of the policies currently decided on the state and local level would become national issues. Educational matters would, consequently, be decided in Washington rather than in the states. Some of the more volatile issues, such as which textbooks should be used in the schools, could easily become national points of contention, dividing religious and ethnic groups. These issues could, consequently, cause serious discord on a national level in a way they do not on a state level. By taking the pressure off Washington, conflict may occur at the state level and act in the way described by Bryce to keep the ship afloat.

[21] Rockefeller, *Future of Federalism*, p. 16.
[22] Bryce, *American Commonwealth*, 1:353.

[23] Ibid.

20/NO IS FEDERALISM BENEFICIAL TO SOCIETY?

The arguments for federalism on the grounds of freedom, economic and social change, and political consequences are without foundation. Closer evaluation of federalism reveals that these goals are better attained in unitary systems.

Freedom. The notion that federalism is essential to freedom is based on two false assumptions: (1) that federalism promotes weak government, and weak government leads to freedom; and (2) that the central government is more dangerous to liberty than are regional units.

Those who support the first assertion, that weak government promotes freedom, ignore the lessons of history. The British system of government with its unitary structure has a better record on the protection of civil liberties than does the federal United States. Latin American countries that adopted federal systems in the nineteenth and twentieth centuries succumbed in many cases to dictatorships rather than serving as protectors of freedom. The federal system of pre-Hitler Weimar Germany, moreover, did not function as a bulwark of freedom. Instead, Hitler was able to use one of the states—Bavaria—to gain a foothold for nazism in Germany. V. I Lenin's acceptance of federalism in the Soviet Union was tactical and did not promote freedom in his time and certainly not in the days of his successor, Joseph Stalin.

The second false assumption is that the central government is more dangerous to liberty than are the regional units. In the words of one political scientist, "Sin is no monopoly of the center nor virtue of the localities."[24] Long after a national majority sought to remove the barriers of racial discrimination and segregation in the United States, it was frustrated because of the acts of regional majorities in the states. For years segregationists who oppressed black people were the principal beneficiaries of federalism. Were it not for the acts of the national government in protecting blacks to obtain their rights to

[24] Leslie Lipson, *The Great Issues of Politics: An Introduction to Political Science*, 8th ed. (Englewood Cliffs, N.J.: Prentice Hall, 1989), p. 291.

vote and to participate in a racially integrated United States, freedom would have been thwarted.

Federalism may, in fact, have protected some minorities in Canada, most notably the French Canadians. In the past, however, it has been of little benefit to the Chinese in British Columbia, Hutterites in Alberta, or Jehovah's Witnesses in Quebec. When these groups were unpopular, the provincial governments were more support- ive of hostile sentiments directed against them than was the central government in Ottawa. "Had Canada been a unitary state," writes the political scientist Garth Stevenson, "these groups might have benefited."[25]

Regional units have often impeded liberty in other matters through censorship of books and films, through the banning of peaceful protest meetings, and through the denial of academic freedom. Professor Franz L. Neumann is correct when he comments that "the federal system may have speeded up inroads into the civil liberties of the United States rather than have protected them."[26]

One additional point about human freedom should be made. Those who argue that federal- ism promotes freedom because regional gov- ernments and the central government check each other often assume that each will restrain the other's authority in public policy areas. In fact, however, the pattern in federations, such as exist in the United States, Canada, Australia, and Switzerland, is such that *both* the central and regional authorities are expanding their power. The liberty of ordinary citizens is the vic- tim of increased government authority.

The record of the many areas of encroach- ment is generally known. States have enlarged their taxing power. Regulation at the state level has brought with it an army of state bureaucrats inspecting labor codes, building regulations, banks, hospitals, schools, businesses, and even private clubs. The argument that federalism will protect freedom is false in view of the expansion of government power at both the state and na- tional levels.

[25] Garth Stevenson, *Unfulfilled Union: Cana- dian Federalism and National Unity*, rev. ed. (To- ronto: Gage, 1982), p. 17.

[26] Franz L. Neumann, "Federalism and Free- dom: A Critique," in *Federalism: Mature and Emergent*, p. 48.

Economic and Social Problems. At a less complex period in the economic and social de- velopment of countries, the federal ideal was useful in coping with the major problems of soci- ety. In the age of capitalism weak government allowed for creative energy of entrepreneurs to utilize their skills for industrial development. Even Karl Marx approved of the resourcefulness of the capitalists (although not of the social chaos they produced) who went everywhere in the world in quest of profits.

In the twentieth century, however, federalism is more then irrelevant; it is an obstacle to eco- nomic and social progress. Let us look first at economic considerations.

The economic problems of the world have become more complex than in earlier centuries. As the preindustrial era has given way to indus- trial and postindustrial times, the arbitrary boundary lines that were used to set up regional political entities in federal systems have ceased to have any practical economic significance. In the United States, for example, the Tennessee Valley is located in several states, and it is im- possible to solve developmental problems in that area without transcending the state bound- aries. Similarly, as a national economy has ex- panded, so, too, has the need for a *national* transportation system. If each state or province engages in planning exclusively along regional boundary lines, then the needs of a modern economy will not be served.

In this context the British socialist Harold J. Laski is one of the foremost critics of federalism, and his views reflect a classical criticism based on economic considerations. According to Laski, federalism is "a luxury" in modern indus- trial society. Laski criticizes its weaknesses: It is insufficiently positive in character; it does not allow for rapid enough action; it inhibits the emer- gence of necessary standards of uniformity; it requires too many compromises that waste time; and it is reactionary.[27]

Laski's criticism, written in 1939, remains valid today. How can federalism cope with an organization like General Motors, with its many divisions scattered not only throughout the United States but overseas as well, and with its revenues in excess of those of most govern- ments of the world? It can be seen that federal- ism cannot deal effectively with the problems of

[27] Harold J. Laski, "The Obsolescence of Fed- eralism," *New Republic* 98 (May 3, 1939): 367.

a complex capitalism, such as unemployment and economic growth. Only a unitary system with a strong central government can handle giant industry.

The very character of the economy has brought with it many changes. In advanced economies, markets have become national— even global. Communication and transportation systems span continents. Even the labor force is no longer regional. Fifty individual states in the United States or ten provinces in Canada are not structured to solve the needs of such economies.

In addition to being obsolete in dealing with economic matters, federalism inhibits the search for solutions to the major social problems afflicting modern societies. The welfare state— with its demand for greater government involvement in health, education, and housing—has been adopted in nearly every country in the world. Regional institutions are incapable of coping with the clamor for an ever greater capacity and will to impose sufficient taxes to finance the welfare state.

In matters of economic and social reform, the national government in the United States has made notable achievements through legislation such as the Clayton Antitrust Act of 1914, the La Follette Seamen's Act of 1915, the Civilian Conservation Corps Act of 1933, the National Labor Relations Act of 1935, the Social Security Act of 1935, and the Fair Labor Standards Act of 1938. As the historian Henry Steele Commager notes, "These laws did more to establish social justice than the whole corpus of state labor legislation since the Civil War."[28]

Environmental problems, too, have required national solutions. The Mississippi River runs through several states, and problems of pollution require national rather than state action in keeping that body of water clean. Corporations manufacturing insecticides, moreover, are national in scope, and only the resources of the government in Washington are sufficiently strong to regulate the chemical industry and its far-ranging empire. The awareness of the need for a strong central government is seen everywhere. In Germany, the Constitution has been altered to give the central government more powers to legislate and supervise ecological matters. We can see, then, the irrelevance of federalism.

Political Problems. Federalism generates political problems, most notably problems of centralization, experimentation, and accountability. Federalism has not served as a barrier to centralized government either in dictatorships or in democracies. In the Soviet Union, the federal system established by Lenin remained federal in name only, since power was in the hands of the ruling Communist party. Even in democracies, the power of the central governments has grown with respect to regional governments in nearly every federal system. Policy previously thought to be within the exclusive jurisdiction of the regional governments, such as education and transportation, has now become strongly influenced by the center.

In the United States the central government has threatened to use its power to withhold funds from states that do not comply with equal opportunity employment laws in order to force adherence to national standards on the hiring of women and minority group members. State control over transportation policy, moreover, has been influenced in a similar manner. When some state legislatures in the United States sought to increase a nationally imposed maximum automobile speed limit of 55 miles per hour, national transportation authorities threatened to cut off highway funds, the loss of which would be a severe blow to highway construction. The state legislatures, consequently, backed away from their intended confrontation with the central government in the interest of economics and retained the 55-mph speed limit. They hoped, however, that Congress would enact legislation allowing them to raise the speed limit, which it ultimately did in 1987 for rural areas.

What is true for centralization in the United States is true for nearly all federal systems. Even the Confederacy of the southern states, which went to war in 1861 on the issue of states' rights, centralized powers in the Confederate central government at the expense of the states. The federalism scholar S. Rufus Davis insightfully describes the emergence of the central government in federal systems "as leader, financier, director, promoter, coordinator, guide, stimulator, pacifier, aggressor, pace-setter, equalizer; the most prestigious, the most influential, the political superior and most effective manipulator of all the parts, singly or collectively."[29]

---

[28] Henry Steele Commager, "Tocqueville's Mistake," *Harper's* 269 (August 1984): 73.

[29] S. Rufus Davis, *The Federal Principle: A Journey through Time in Quest of Meaning* (Berkeley: University of California Press, 1978), p. 148.

The increased powers of the center can be seen in many ways. The status of national figures is generally higher than that of regional leaders. Media attention is directed more to national than to regional matters. In free societies, more people vote in national than in regional elections. The irresistible move toward centralization is clear in nearly every political system.

Supporters of federalism, moreover, make too much of a claim for the role of experimentation and risk limitation in federal systems to meet the needs of diversity in large and complex societies. The advantages of experimentation and risk limitation are not exclusive to federal systems. Unitary systems allow for diversity, too. In Great Britain, for example, a long tradition of local self-government allows for initiative and variation by local authorities. The powers given to a Northern Ireland parliament between 1920 and 1972 also served to decentralize power to allow for regional decision making. Special provisions in Parliament for Scottish and Welsh affairs allow recognition of the different "nations" that constitute the United Kingdom.

Since unitary systems can support diversity and autonomy, the merits of federalism in this regard are not noteworthy. The crucial point for diversity, as William H. Riker observes, has much to do with whether local officials are elected by or are in some other way responsive to local citizens. Federalism, consequently, hardly makes any difference in the way people are governed.[30]

Finally, federalism poses problems of accountability in a democracy. The American federal system offers an example. In an era of cooperative federalism, where the relationships among national, state, and local institutions are so complex, it is often difficult to hold accountable public officials at different levels.

Today, national and state governments play important roles in education, health, safety in the workplace, public welfare assistance, and environmental protection. The ordinary citizen cannot know whom to hold accountable for government actions. Democracy requires accountability so that citizens can make rational judgments at election time. With power fragmented in a federal system, however, an important support of democratic rule is undermined.

Too much has been made of federalism. In sum, federalism has been a threat to freedom, inhibited economic development and social reform, and created unnecessary political problems.

[30] William H. Riker, "Six Books in Search of a Subject, or Does Federalism Exist and Does It Matter?" *Comparative Politics* 2 (October 1969): 139, 145.

KEY TERMS

Confederation
Cooperative federalism
Decentralization
Dual federalism

Federalism
Federation
Supremacy clause
Unitary system

QUESTIONS

1. Which is closer to the people: the regional governments or the national government? What are the reasons for your answer?

2. If the United States had adopted a unitary system of government in 1787, how would history have been different?

3. Can a dictatorship have a federal system? What are the reasons for your answer?

4. What effect does federalism have on economic development?

5. Is federalism a stepping-stone to world peace? Why?

6. Would a federal solution help in solving problems posed by ethnic and religious differences, such as in Northern Ireland, Israel, and Lebanon? Why?

7. What are the prospects of the European Community becoming a strong federation? What are the reasons for your answer?

RECOMMENDED READINGS

AMLUND, CURTIS ARTHUR. *Federalism in the Southern Confederacy.* Washington, D.C.: Public Affairs Press, 1966. An argument that during the course of the American Civil War, the Confederate government resembled the federal system of the Union.

BERGER, RAOUL. *Federalism: The Founders' Design.* Norman, Okla.: University of Oklahoma Press, 1987. An examination of Framers' intent by a legal scholar.

BOWMAN, ANN O'M., and RICHARD C. KEARNEY. *The Resurgence of the States.* Englewood Cliffs, N.J.: Prentice Hall, 1986. An argument that the states are responsive, responsible, and progressive political actors in this scheme of U.S. federalism and intergovernmental relations.

BRYCE, JAMES. *The American Commonwealth.* Rev. ed. New York: Macmillan, 1931. Vol. 1. An analysis of federalism in the United States.

BURGESS, MICHAEL, ed. *Federalism and Federation in Western Europe.* London: Croom Helm, 1986. A study of European federations.

COMMAGER, HENRY STEELE. "Tocqueville's Mistake." *Harper's* 269 (August 1984): 70–74. A defense of strong central governments.

DAVIS, S. RUFUS. *The Federal Principle: A Journey through Time in Quest of Meaning.* Berkeley: University of California Press, 1978. A historical treatment of federalism with an evaluation of its etymological, theoretical, and empirical merits.

DUTT, R. C., ed. *Centralism and Devolution of Power.* New Delhi: Lancer, 1990. A study of federalism in India.

DYE, THOMAS R. *American Federalism: Competition among Governments.* Lexington, Mass.: Lexington Books, 1990. A theory arguing that federalism can be seen as a competitive system among state and local governments.

ELAZAR, DANIEL J. *Exploring Federalism.* Tuscaloosa, Ala.: University of Alabama Press, 1987. A comprehensive analysis of federalism.

———, ed. *Federalism and Political Integration.* Lanham, Md.: University Press of America, 1984. Articles on the role of federalism in political integration throughout the world.

FERRELL, THOMAS H. "What If There Were a Unitary Rather Than a Federal System?" In *What If the American Political System Were Different?*, ed. Herbert M. Levine. Armonk, N.Y.: M. E. Sharpe, 1992. Chap. 2. A speculation about federalism.

GALLIGAN, BRIAN, and CLIFF WALSH. "Australian Federalism: Developments and Prospects." *Publius* 20 (Fall 1990): 1–17. A survey of recent developments in Australian federalism.

JANIGAN, MARY. "In Search of a Nation's Heart." *Maclean's* (Toronto) 103 (June 11, 1990): 19–23, 26–28. An overview of the history of Canadian federalism.

KOVACEVIC, ZIVORAD. "Ethnic Tensions in the Yugoslav Federation: Implications for the Region." *Mediterranean Quarterly* 2 (Winter 1991): 78–87. A discussion of the implications of a breakup of the Yugoslav federation to the republics of Yugoslavia and neighboring countries.

KRAUTHAMMER, CHARLES. "Blest Be the Ties That Bind." *Time* 136 (August 13, 1990): 76. An argument that federalism is the wave of the future, but only if freedom is permitted.

LASKI, HAROLD J. "The Obsolescence of Federalism." *New Republic* 98 (May 3, 1939): 367–69. A critique of federalism.

LIVINGSTON, WILLIAM S. *Federalism and Constitutional Change.* Oxford, England: Clarendon Press, 1956. A study of the process whereby diversified elements in a federal state integrate and compromise their differences.

MORLEY, FELIX. *Freedom and Federalism.* Chicago: Henry Regnery, 1959. An assessment of the impact of centralized government on individual liberty.

RIKER, WILLIAM H. *Federalism: Origin, Operation, Significance.* Boston: Little, Brown, 1964. A major work on federalism.

———. "Six Books in Search of a Subject, or Does Federalism Exist and Does It Matter?" *Comparative Politics* 2 (October 1969): 135–46. The author answers, "Hardly at all."

ROBERTSON, DENNIS BRIAN, and DENNIS R. JUDD. *The Development of American Public Policy: The Structure of Policy Restraint.* Glenview, Ill.: Scott, Foresman, 1989. An argument that a biased, conservative political structure and distribution of power have both fragmented and limited the development of fair and effective public policy in the United States.

SIMEON, RICHARD, and IAN ROBINSON. *State, Society, and the Development of Canadian Federalism*, Toronto: University of Toronto Press, 1990. An overview of Canadian federalism.

SIMPSON, JEFFREY. "The Two Canadas." *Foreign Policy*, no. 81 (Winter 1990–91): 71–86. A discussion of recent developments in Canadian federalism.

WHEARE, KENNETH C. *Federal Government*. 4th ed. New York: Oxford University Press, 1963. A classic work surveying federal systems in Australia, Canada, Switzerland, and the United States.

chapter 11

Parliamentary and presidential systems

With the principal exceptions of anarchists and libertarians, most people today accept the inevitability of the state—and particularly government—in any modern complex society. Even Adam Smith, the advocate of a *laissez-faire* philosophy, regarded government to be essential in satisfying at least the minimum needs of national security and police protection. Modern liberals, socialists, and communists clearly accept the existence of government, although they differ about what it should do.

Given the widespread acceptance of government, one problem has been how it should be organized. Those who hold the view that government can be a force for good and can promote economic prosperity, maintain national security, and provide the benefits of the welfare state have tended to support a centralized institutional device capable of allowing government leaders to achieve those goals easily. The political systems of Great Britain and the People's Republic of China, although differing enormously, are similar in at least

one respect: Both are organized to allow for centralized governmental control.

Not everyone, however, is certain that government should be organized in a centralized manner. Even among those who accept the necessity of government, there are many who fear that a government in which power is too centralized can be both dangerous to individual liberty and responsible for policies that are either poorly conceived or unnecessary.

The American political system was founded on the principle that government is dangerous to individual liberty. Based on the theories of the French philosopher Baron de Montesquieu, it adopted an institutional structure in which power was divided not only at the national level among different units of government but also at the regional level between national and regional governments.[1]

[1] The division of powers between national and regional governments is discussed in Chapter 10.

Since Montesquieu's formulations in the eighteenth century, many writers have used his classifications of government into legislative, executive, and judicial power to describe the organization of government. In this scheme, legislative power is the making of laws, executive is the implementation of laws, and judicial is the interpretation of laws or the determination of whether acts of governments or individuals are in compliance with the laws.

Since the eighteenth century, distinctions have been made between legislative, executive, and judicial *functions* and the formal *institutions* of government that were set up ostensibly to pursue those functions. Although in theory, legislatures carry out legislative functions, executives carry out executive functions, and the judiciary carries out judicial functions, often each of these institutions performs not only its traditional functions but also roles normally attributed to the other branches of government. As we shall see, for example, when in the United States the judicial branch—the U.S. Supreme Court—declares a statute duly enacted by Congress to be unconstitutional, it is in fact performing a legislative function. Because of the ways in which institutions have developed, some scholars use terms other than *legislative, executive* and *judicial* to describe functions of government. They prefer, for example, to speak of *rule-making, rule-application,* and *rule-adjudication,*[2] terms that allow them to classify government functions and institutions in a more intelligible manner. We shall use the traditional classification of executive, legislative, and judicial, however, since these provide a more familiar basis of understanding government organization.

LEGISLATURES

Legislatures are representative assemblies that enact laws. Not all legislatures are pow-

[2] See particularly Gabriel A. Almond and G. Bingham Powell, Jr., *Comparative Politics: A Developmental Approach* (Boston: Little, Brown, 1966), chap. 6.

erful institutions in law making; some are mere showcase institutions without any actual power in public policy. As we shall see, legislatures perform functions other than law making.

Legislatures are known by different names in different countries. In the United States the legislature is known as Congress; in Great Britain, it is Parliament. Senate, Diet, Assembly, and Knesset are also used in different countries to signify legislative bodies.

Organization

Legislatures are either **unicameral** (one chamber), as in Finland, Sweden, and Norway; or **bicameral** (two chambers), as in the United States, Great Britain, and Germany. In bicameral legislatures, the first, or lower, chamber consists of popularly elected representatives. The second, or upper, chamber often consists of representatives who may be chosen by popular vote or selected on the basis of other considerations, such as geography, birth, or economic classification. United States senators are elected by direct popular vote, but until 1913 they were chosen by the state legislatures. The British House of Lords has been constituted primarily on the basis of inherited rank. Fascist Italy organized its legislature according to economic classifications.

Legislatures are generally too large to conduct the vast amount of government business before all their members. They carry on legislative tasks through committees. In some countries **standing committees** serve as permanent committees that handle specialized matters for the term of the legislature. An appropriations committee investigates matters involving government spending, for example, and a foreign affairs committee considers legislation pertaining to international relations. These committees can play an important role in the political process. In other countries standing committees are not differentiated according to function and consider any measure sent to them from the point of view of technical legal correctness. Still another form of committee is the **select committee**, which is a temporary committee that handles one problem and then disbands. **Joint committees** are found in bicameral systems and include members from each chamber. A **conference committee** is a committee composed of legislators from different legislative chambers whose purpose is to adjust differences between the chambers on a particular bill.

The committee system is one manner in which a legislature is organized. Still another is by political party (see Chapter 8). In some legislatures party organization is strong, which means that the party members in the legislature generally vote along party lines on important issues. A political party may be strong enough to prevent legislators from securing renomination for election on their party labels if they vote against legislation proposed by their parties, and such discipline helps party unity. In other legislative systems parties are weak, and the legislators are dependent on their home constituencies rather than on the central party organization for their renomination on the party labels. Great Britain is an example of a strong and centralized party system. The United States is an example of a weak and decentralized party system. In some countries, such as Italy and France throughout most of their modern history, moreover, the legislature is composed of many party groupings. Great Britain and the United States, in contrast, each have two dominant parties.

Origins

Legislative institutions existed in ancient Greece and Rome. They evolved gradually in the medieval period out of the advisers to the monarch. Great Britain, the Mother of Parliaments, experienced the gradual development of representative legislatures. As early as the thirteenth century the king relied on representatives from the different estates—nobility, the church, and the burgesses (townsmen)—to provide advice and furnish money. For the most part European legislatures slowly grew in power at the expense of the ruling monarch. At first, legislative chambers were organized and dominated by the landed aristocracy, but gradually their power was diminished by representatives chosen first by the middle classes and later by all elements of society.

Functions

Because the power of legislatures differs greatly throughout the world, it is difficult to generalize about them. Historically, however, the major functions of legislatures have been to make laws, to tax and spend money, to debate issues, to oversee administration, to legitimize the rules that a government proclaims, and to recruit political leaders of government and socialize political elites. Some legislatures are powerful and perform all or most of these functions; some are weak and perform a few of these functions; and others are mere window dressing and perform none of these functions.

Legislation. Legislatures today as in the past deal with **legislation**—laws that are binding on the community. In the nineteenth century legislatures played a forceful role in introducing proposals for legislative action (**bills**). In many countries today bills are prepared in the executive branch of government, although they may be formally introduced in the legislature.

Taxes. A major function of legislatures is to authorize the raising of taxes and the appropriation of money. Most laws are not self-implementing but need government agencies to carry them out. Consequently, if a legislature decides to destroy a government program, it can reduce or deny appropriations to it. Historically, the principle that parliamentary approval is essential for the executive to tax goes back to the Magna Carta (1215).

Debate. One important role of legislatures is to serve as a forum where issues are debated publicly. According to the liberal English philosopher John Stuart Mill, Parliament is "at once the nation's Committee of Grievances and its Congress of Opinions" through which every segment of society and every eminent individual it contains can argue a point of view.[3] In Great Britain the principle that public debate is essential in a free society is a fundamental component of the political system. It is institutionalized through the establishment of the loyal opposition in which the minority in Parliament is recognized as having the duty to oppose the government without fear that its opposition will be regarded as subversion. One of the major advances of a free society was the creation of a **loyal opposition**—a group of minority-party members whose criticism of the government was regarded as legitimate rather than as an act of treason.

Administration. Legislators play a role in overseeing the administration of government. They may conduct formal investigations of the behavior of particular government agencies to make certain that these agencies are carrying out the laws in the manner prescribed by the legislature. For example, a special congressional committee was formed in 1987 to investigate the actions of officials during the administration of Ronald Reagan who sold arms to Iran in exchange for the release of U.S. hostages held captive in Beirut and used profits from the sales to finance guerrilla forces (or Contras, as they were called) fighting against the Marxist government in Nicaragua.

In Great Britain the **question hour** is the formal device by which cabinet members are asked questions directly by members of Parliament about any matter pertaining to the conduct of government. The ability of a cabinet member to respond intelligently and forcefully to the questions contributes to the reputation of the member within his or her party.

To oversee government agencies some legislators have designated an **ombudsman**—an official whose job is to make certain that government officials apply the law and regulations as legislatively prescribed. The ombudsman conducts investigations of public officials when complaints are made by citizens. Although originated in Sweden, the office of ombudsman has been established in other countries, including Norway, Denmark, and Israel.

Legitimization. A major function of a legislature is to legitimize the rules of a society. Legislatures are regarded as institutions that in some manner represent the people of a political system. John Stuart Mill commented on the legitimizing function in observing that when Parliament allows all diverse points of view to be expressed, those whose opinion is overruled shall "feel satisfied that it is heard, and set aside not by a mere act of will, but for what are thought superior reasons, and commend themselves as such to the representatives of the majority of the nation."[4]

As mentioned above, some legislatures may in reality have no power and serve as mere showcases. The fact that many dictatorships establish powerless legislatures with representatives from different regions, classes, religions, and racial groupings reveals the legitimizing role of legislative institutions that nearly every government attempts to secure.[5]

[3] John Stuart Mill, *Representative Government*, in his *Utilitarianism, Liberty, and Representative Government* (New York: Dutton, 1951), p. 321. The book was originally published in 1861.

[4] Ibid.

[5] For a study of the relationship between legislatures and political stability, see William Mishler and Anne Hildreth, "Legislatures and Political Stability: An Exploratory Analysis," *Journal of Politics* 46 (February 1984): 25–29.

Political Recruitment and Socialization of Political Elites. Legislatures serve to recruit leaders for membership in the political elite of the nation and to socialize them into the political system. In some political systems executives frequently consult with legislators and make concessions to them in order to get support.

Legislators, moreover, have been a source of candidates for executive office. Such is the case in the United States today, but it has also been true for Chile and the Philippines in the past. John F. Kennedy and Lyndon Johnson served as senators and established national reputations for their work in the Senate before they became president. Chile's last four freely elected presidents—Salvador Allende, Eduardo Frei, Jorge Alessandri, and Patricio Aylwin—were senators before they became president. In the Philippines every president except four has risen to that position from the senate.[6]

In addition to recruiting new members into the political elite, legislatures play a role in socializing the political elite. Legislatures often become a place where members acquire shared political values and institutional attachments. When such attachments are strong, legislators manage conflict through government bargaining so as to prevent or minimize violence. The effect of such cooperative efforts is to strengthen political stability. Not all legislators, however, develop such shared values, and legislatures may become institutions in which conflict is heightened.

Other. Legislatures may act as courts and try officials for misconduct in office. In the United States, for example, the House of Representatives has the responsibility for **impeachment**—an indictment of high officials for malfeasance in office. The

[6]See Michael L. Mezey, *Comparative Legislatures* (Durham, N.C.: Duke University Press, 1979), p. 226.

Senate actually tries the official if he or she is impeached. In some systems, moreover, legislatures appoint the chief executive. How extensive and diverse are the powers of the legislature depend on tradition and political relationships underlying different political systems.

EXECUTIVES

The **executive** branch of government consists of an individual or small group that executes the law. It, too, is known by different names in different countries. In the United States the executive is known as the president. In other countries the titles include king, prime minister, premier, president, chancellor, and even emperor.

Organization

A major distinction in the organization of executives is between chief of state and head of government. A **chief of state** is usually a figurehead or ceremonial leader—someone who symbolizes the nation. Usually, this person exercises no major political power, although on occasions he or she may play some role. In Great Britain, Holland, and Sweden, the king or queen is the chief of state. In other countries, such as Germany, India, and Israel, the chief of state is known as the president.

The **head of government** is the political leader of the nation who conducts the actual management of government. In parliamentary systems (see below), the political leader is known generally as either prime minister, premier, or chancellor. In the United States the president is both the head of government and the chief of state.

The executive branch of government refers often to the top leaders of the government. In parliamentary systems the executive consists primarily of the prime minister and cabinet. The **cabinet** is a group of top ministers who direct the departments of government.[7] To speak of "The Government" in Great Britain, for example, means the prime minister, cabinet, and other ministers. British cabinet members are in both the executive and the legislative branches since they continue to serve as members of Parliament. In many countries the executive branch includes not only the cabinet of the head of government but others on his or her staff who are close advisers although they do not direct departments of government.

Different methods are used to select chief executives. The chief of state is sometimes chosen through inheritance, as in Great Britain, Holland, and Sweden; or through the direct election by the people, as in France.

Functions

The principal functions of the executive are to serve as a symbolic national leader, to formulate policy, to enforce the law, and to direct the administration of the law. Executives, however, perform other functions, which, as is the case with legislatures, vary among political systems.

Ceremonial. The executive is regarded as the ceremonial leader of all the people. When the executive makes speeches on national holidays or travels on state visits to other countries, he or she is the symbol of the diverse groupings that constitute the state. Because most democratic countries have chiefs of state who are primarily figureheads and generally out of range of partisan criticism, the chiefs of state can perform their ceremonial functions more easily than can the leader of a country who combines in his or her person the titles of head of government and chief of state.

[7] The term *cabinet* comes from the seventeenth-century use of the word in France, meaning a small, private apartment, or *closet*, in which the king met privately with his close advisers.

Policy Making. The executive's powers are not merely ceremonial. Policy making is one of the most important executive tasks. Executives play important roles in foreign policy, national security, and the presentation of legislation generally.

As chief diplomat, the head of government is charged with the responsibility for conducting a foreign policy designed to serve national interests abroad. The head of government is expected, moreover, to provide a military establishment commensurate with those interests.

Chief executives have expanded greatly their role in legislation. Proposals for new laws may be introduced formally in the legislature by elected legislators, but often they are drafted by the head of government, cabinet, and staff officials. The heads of government in many countries, moreover, can influence the prospects for success of a bill in granting or withholding their support.

Law Enforcement and Administration. Chief executives, too, enforce the law through supervision of the *bureaucracy*—the executive agencies of the government (see Chapter 12). As the bureaucracies of countries throughout the world continue to grow, the chief executives continue to be held accountable for the actions of the many and varied government agencies. It is the heads of government who often appoint the top layer of political officials supervising the agencies of government. It is the heads of government, moreover, who are held responsible for acts of misconduct that go on under their formal supervision.

Other. Executives serve other functions besides formulating policy and directing administration. They play roles in judicial matters by nominating judges for positions in the courts. They may issue pardons to those convicted of crimes. They also serve as party leaders.

JUDICIARY

The **judiciary** is that branch of government concerned with the administration of justice. In democratic political systems the independence of the judiciary is regarded as an essential prerequisite of a free society.

Organization

In many countries there is a hierarchy by which courts are structured. Lower courts—**courts of original jurisdiction**— hear cases when first presented. An **appellate court** hears cases on appeal from the lower courts. The highest courts deal with the most important judicial questions. The Supreme Court is the highest court in the United States and hears cases on appeal, but it is also authorized to have original jurisdiction in certain kinds of cases, such as those to which a state is a party.

In some systems special courts exist to deal with such matters as tariffs, taxes, and juveniles. Often, however, the rulings of these courts may be appealed to higher courts.

Justices are selected in different ways. They are often appointed by the executive with the approval of the legislature. In the United States, for example, a federal judge is nominated by the president and confirmed by the Senate. In some countries judges are elected directly by the people, as in Switzerland and in some states of the United States.

The term of the judges varies. In some cases judges sit for life and can be removed only for misconduct in office. Some judges, however, are appointed for fixed terms. Still others must run in elections at intervals.

In general in democratic societies, even in systems that do not operate under the separation of powers principle, the independence of judges is assured. The suppression of a judiciary is often regarded as a step toward dictatorship. Efforts to influence judges on specific cases from outside the courtroom are regarded as either illegal or violations of judicial propriety.

Functions

The principal functions of the judiciary include the interpretation of the law, the application of the law to concrete cases, the settlement of disputes among individuals, and, in some political systems, the determination of the constitutionality of the law.

Courts interpret laws, for not every law is clear on particular details. Some laws, moreover, may conflict with other laws, and the courts must determine which have validity in particular cases.

Courts apply the law to concrete cases. Conflicts arise among different segments of the government and between government and individuals, and the courts determine the outcome of these cases based on their interpretation of the law.

Courts perform a role in settling disputes among individuals. Private contractual obligations, for example, are often brought before a court when one of the parties feels that the provisions of the contract are not being carried out by the other party.

In some countries, such as the United States, Australia, and Canada, the court has special powers of *judicial review,* which is the power of a court to declare unconstitutional any act of the executive or legislative branches of the government (see Chapter 3).

PARLIAMENTARY AND PRESIDENTIAL SYSTEMS

Two principal forms of government in democratic societies are the parliamentary and the presidential systems of government. Great Britain is the leading example of a *parliamentary system*, and the United States is the major representative of the *presidential* (sometimes called the *congressional) system*. Other countries have some similarities with each of these systems, although their different traditions and political forces have brought about significant variations from the British and American models in terms of the number of major political parties, the method of electing legislators, and the relationship between the central and regional governments.

Great Britain

The main features of the British **parliamentary system** are: the supremacy of Parliament; the fusion of the executive and legislative branches; the existence of party government; and the heavy reliance on traditional practices rather than a written constitution.

Supremacy of Parliament. The British Parliament may pass any law, on any subject, and the law of Parliament is the supreme law of the land. A British Parliament can, if it so chooses, suppress civil liberties or suspend elections without fear that its acts are unconstitutional. No court can declare an act of Parliament to be null and void since the power of judicial review simply does not exist in Great Britain.

Fusion of Executive and Legislative Branches. The legislature in Britain consists of the House of Lords and the House of Commons. In the twentieth century the power of the House of Lords has been reduced to a minimal level. The House of Commons is the central legislative unit and consists of 650 members. The House of Lords contains nearly 1,200 members, whose tenure in office is variously based on hereditary privilege, appointment for life, and religious or judicial leadership. The executive branch of government consists of the monarch, whose role is mostly that of a figurehead, and the prime minister and cabinet, who are the political leaders of the country. Each cabinet member heads a ministry that directs the government bureaucracy. The prime minister and cabinet are not separately elected but rather are members of the House of Commons and retain their executive positions until such time as an election is called and their party is defeated or they lose a vote of confidence.[8] (When a member of Parliament resigns or dies, a **by-election**, or special election, is held in the member's constituency.) A **vote of confidence** is approval of a government's major proposals. In the event that the government loses such a vote, the prime minister must go to the monarch, who by tradition accepts the call for a general election. Under such a fusion of power, a paralysis of government brought on by conflict between the executive and the legislature cannot occur.

The British cabinet is said to abide by the principle of **collective responsibility**, by which all members of the cabinet are held accountable for the acts of any single cabinet member. If a cabinet member cannot support the decisions of the government, then he or she is expected to resign.

Cabinet members are people who usually have had extensive experience in parliamentary affairs. They have usually risen from the ranks after proving themselves in different government positions. The prime minister is the head of the cabinet and a person who has widespread support in his or her own party. The prime minister must keep that support or risk being replaced without a general election but merely by a decision of his or her own party in Parliament to choose another person from the party to head the government.

Party Government. The British parliamentary system of government is characterized by strong party government. Two

---

[8] But even in these cases, the prime minister and cabinet members retain their seats in the House of Commons so long as they are reelected in their individual constituencies.

major parties, Conservative and Labour, dominate the legislature. At times, however, minor parties can hold votes that are necessary for a party with the largest number of legislators to rule. In Great Britain party leaders enforce discipline among their members. Although members of a party are free to debate issues, in most cases they vote the way that their party decides on major issues. There are cases, however, in which a free vote is permitted. Party members can vote their conscience in a **free vote**. On these matters, a vote of confidence is not at issue.

Members of Parliament vote as their party determines. If they vote against the party that constitutes the government, then they increase the prospects that the government will not receive its vote of confidence and all the members of the Parliament will have to "stand" for election. The central party organization can deny renomination to any of its recalcitrant members, and the evidence indicates that a member of Parliament once denied the party label has difficulty being re-elected. Since the 1970s, however, members of Parliament have been showing a greater independence from party control than ever before. Members of Parliament are not required to come from the constituencies that elect them to office.

Tradition. The British system of government is not based on a written constitution in the manner of the U.S. Constitution. Instead, the British constitution is said to be made up of some major documents, such as Magna Carta, the English Bill of Rights, and the Reform Act of 1832, and traditions that have evolved over the centuries. One of these traditions is that elections are called by the prime minister when he or she deems the time is right. A maximum "term" of five years is permitted, but the prime minister may call an election before that. In 1974, for example, Labour Prime Minister Harold Wilson called an election only several months after the British people had voted his party into office. He hoped to increase the size of the Labour majority in the House of Commons and succeeded in doing just that. This power to choose an election date is one that maximizes the prospects of reelection by the party controlling the government.

By tradition, also, the minority party is regarded as the loyal opposition. A **shadow cabinet** of opposition minority party members sits opposite the government cabinet members in the House of Commons, ready to challenge the government and replace it should the government lose a vote of confidence and the subsequent election.

Theoretically, the British system of government could be regarded as tailor-made for a future dictator, since the British system would assure a majority party the right to outlaw the minority party, destroy the free press, and imprison critics of the government. The fact that the system of government is not used in this way reflects the reverence for dissent that is part of the British political culture.

Other Parliamentary Systems

The British parliamentary system is regarded as one model of a parliamentary system, and a stable one at that. A strong two-party system and the fusion of executive and legislative branches have assured that government can rule and be responsible. Other parliamentary systems are not so stable, however.

France has had many different types of government in the past two centuries. It has experienced republics, monarchies, and empires. Frequent changes have established a revolutionary tradition in French politics.

The political instability of France has been pronounced in this century. The Fourth Republic (1946–58) was a particularly unstable parliamentary system characterized by a multiparty rather than two-party system. The people who formed a government, consequently, had to assemble a coalition of disparate elements to win a vote of confidence. Government tenure was brief in such a system, as the support of one or more parties was frequently withdrawn. Between November 1945 and September 1958, France had six national elections and twenty-six different governments. It was because of such instability in government and the continuous crises that resulted that a different system was established in the Fifth Republic under Charles de Gaulle in 1958. The new Constitution retained only some of the elements of the parliamentary system. A president is now separately and directly elected by the people. Unlike the situation for British ministers, the French ministers are prohibited from being members of the National Assembly.

The political systems of Western European governments are parliamentary. They are also multiparty in that no single party gathers enough electoral support to constitute a majority. After the election results are in, a coalition government—composed of elements of two or more parties—is formed.

United States

The political system of the United States is the principal example of the presidential system of government. The main features of the American **presidential system** at the national level are: separation of powers and checks and balances; decentralization of political parties; a written constitution; and judicial review.

Separation of Powers and Checks and Balances. Unlike the British parliamentary system, the American form of national government is based on separate spheres of power. The creation of distinct branches of government—Congress, the president, and the Supreme Court—is the product of a philosophy of **separation of powers**, with its assumption that concentrated power is dangerous to liberty. In the words of James

Madison, a strong supporter of the Constitution, "The accumulation of all powers legislative, executive, and judiciary in the same hands . . . may justly be pronounced the very definition of tyranny."[9]

Congress has primary legislative power, the president primary executive power, and the Supreme Court primary judicial power. A system of **checks and balances** in which each branch of government has some powers of the other two encourages the fragmentation of power. Because of checks and balances, Congress has some executive power (such as the power of the Senate to confirm appointments by the president) and some judicial power (such as the power to create new courts and to enlarge the size of the Supreme Court membership). The president has legislative power (such as the power to veto bills passed by Congress) and judicial power (such as the power to nominate justices to the federal courts). The Supreme Court has legislative power (such as the power to declare a statute unconstitutional) and executive power (such as the power to administer court rulings). By establishing a system of checks and balances, the Framers deliberately made government cumbersome.

The president is at the center of the system. Originally, the president was supposed to be elected by the electoral college, a group chosen by the state legislatures, insulated from popular control. In practice today, however, the electoral college generally reflects the popular vote. The president and cabinet are constitutionally prevented from holding simultaneously both their executive offices and seats in Congress. Unlike the British system, the president may never have even served in the legislature but rather may have moved up from another position, such as military officer, governor, or even private citizen.

[9] James Madison, *Federalist*, no. 47, in Alexander Hamilton, James Madison, and John Jay, *The Federalist Papers*, ed. Clinton Rossiter (New York: New American Library, 1961), p. 301.

The president is elected for a fixed four-year term. With the exception of Richard Nixon, no president has resigned his office. The president's cabinet consists of men and women whom he appoints with the consent of the Senate. They are not members of the legislature but head executive departments.

Congress includes the House of Representatives and the Senate. The House consists of 435 members. The number of House seats from each state depends upon population. By tradition, the representatives are chosen from *single-member districts*, in which only one member is elected from each district. Also by tradition, House members reside in the constituencies that elect them. Members of the House must face election every two years. The work of the House of Representatives is done mostly by committees, with leadership of those committees based on seniority and party considerations. At times, however, the seniority principle has fallen when the rank-and-file members of the majority party on the committee so decide. Party leadership plays a role in the organization of the House, but the party does not have the unity that exists in the British House of Commons. The House has real power to deal with all bills and has the special power of originating revenue bills.

The Senate is composed of two members from each state. Senators are elected for six-year terms, but only one-third of them are elected every two years. Originally senators were chosen by the state legislatures, but since the Seventeenth Amendment was ratified in 1913, they have been elected directly by the people. The Senate's work, too, is conducted mostly in committees along the lines of seniority and party influence that characterize the House committees. Unlike the upper chamber in Britain, the Senate has real power to deal with all bills. A bill does not become a law until it has the approval of both the House and the Senate. In addition, the Senate has special powers of "advice and consent" to confirm presidential appointments and to approve treaties. Senators reside in the constituencies that elect them.

The Supreme Court of the United States stands at the apex of the nation's court system. Today it consists of nine members, although originally in 1789 it had only five justices. Supreme Court justices receive their office by presidential appointment with confirmation by the Senate. They retain their office for life or until they resign and can be dismissed only by impeachment by the House of Representatives and conviction by the Senate. As mentioned above, the Supreme Court has the power of judicial review. The Supreme Court, moreover, must deal with real cases and does not give advisory opinions.

Decentralization of Parties. Party organization is decentralized in the American political system. The national party organization cannot discipline legislators as their British counterparts may do. A representative secures the nomination for Congress from a regional constituency. If he or she fails to get support from that constituency, then the person will not secure the nomination of the party.

Party organization in the legislature is at its strongest at the time that each chamber is organized. By custom, the committee assignments for each chamber are determined by party designation. By tradition, the chair of the committee is the member of the majority party on the committee with the longest seniority on the committee. Also by tradition, the minority party has representation on each committee.

Because of the decentralization of political parties and the separate election of president and Congress, party government does not exist in the United States. It is even possible to have a president of one political party, and both the House and Senate of another. Such was the case in the presidential administrations of Richard Nixon, Gerald Ford, and George Bush. Republican president Ronald Reagan faced a Republican Senate and a Democratic House in his first term, and a Democratic

Senate and House in his second term. Unlike the British system, moreover, the president does not have to confront a vote of confidence. Proposals that his administration puts forward may be voted down without any consequence to the continuation of the president in office until the fixed four-year term has ended.

Written Constitution. The American political system is governed by a written constitution. The Constitution embodies the fundamental principles and political structure underlying the political system. Since the first ten amendments were ratified in 1791, only sixteen additional amendments have become the law of the land.

The Constitution sets out certain government requirements that have lasted for two centuries, such as the fixed term of office for president and Congress and the system of federalism. It has been flexible enough, however, to allow for change either through amendment, statute, custom, or judicial interpretation.

Judicial Review. The question of whether the Framers intended that the Supreme Court should have the power of judicial review is still debated among students of the Constitution. Since John Marshall formally asserted this right in *Marbury v. Madison* in 1803, the Court has played an important role in the legislative process. It is clear that the Framers intended that the Supreme Court should have the power to declare state laws unconstitutional, however. The Court has often exercised that power against state laws that were in conflict with legislation of the national government.

TRENDS IN EXECUTIVE-LEGISLATIVE RELATIONSHIPS

Governments throughout the world vary in terms of the relationships among the legislature, executive, and judiciary.

In dictatorships power is centralized, and dictators sometimes govern without even the fig leaf of legislatures to legitimize their claims to rule. In other dictatorships, however, legislatures are created but exercise either no or greatly limited power.

In previously authoritarian countries, however, legislatures have gained new power. Russia and the countries of Eastern Europe are examples. Although their degree of power varies, these legislatures are newly independent and their assertive role in the political life of a country is regarded as a barometer of freedom.

In democracies, on the other hand, executives have generally expanded power at the expense of legislatures. The reasons are varied: the requirements of foreign policy, the growth of domestic government programs, the inability of legislatures to act swiftly, and the important role of the media.

Considerations of foreign policy have played a prominent role in the growth of executive power. Particularly in the twentieth century—the age of intercontinental ballistic missiles and jet aircraft—the necessity of taking swift action has enhanced the power of the executive. Wars, too, have played their part, as often legislatures are willing to delegate powers to the chief executive in times of national peril.

Domestic government programs have also worked to increase the power of the chief executive. In the nineteenth century much of the work of the legislature could be handled within a short period of time each year. With the appearance of the welfare state and the regulatory state in the twentieth century, however, even diligent legislators have found it difficult to keep up with complicated details about such diverse subjects as education, health, transportation, and employment. Legislators, consequently, often delegate much of their authority to the bureaucracy that is administered by the executive branch of government.

The sheer variety and complexity of legislative committees and interests make cumbersome legislative action. In many democratic systems, before a bill becomes a law it must go through a long process of "touching bases" with interest groups and legislative power brokers. The chief executive, consequently, is in a much better position to present unified programs and take decisive action.

Finally, the media have focused public awareness on chief executives. The president of the United States, for example, commands the attention of newspapers, magazines, and television. Television particularly has brought the presidential personality to the attention of American citizens nearly every day. What is true of the American president is also true of chief executives in other countries.

Although the power of legislatures has diminished in democracies, it is clear that legislative institutions remain effective in influencing the course of legislation and the course of the political process itself. As the experience of Richard Nixon in the Watergate affair and Ronald Reagan in the Iran-Contra affair indicate, legislatures are capable of checking chief executives when their power exceeds constitutional bounds.

Legislatures in democracies, moreover, are more representative today than they have ever been before. Elections for legislative office are more honest, and constituency boundaries are being drawn with greater fairness. As political scientist Yves Mény notes: "Parliaments remain the forums of political life *par excellence* and, seen from this point of view, their audience, far from shrinking, has increased, thanks to the Press, television, and radio, all of which are mediators and broadcasters of the parliamentary debate."[10] Legislatures remain important actors in democratic governments.

[10] Yves Mény, *Government and Politics in Western Europe: Britain, France, Italy, West Germany,* trans. Janet Lloyd (New York: Oxford University Press, 1990), p. 193.

ISSUE

The American presidential and the British parliamentary systems of government constitute two of the oldest democracies in the world. Each has survived wars and depressions. Each, moreover, has its champions arguing the virtues of the one or the other. When the subject of institutional reform arises in the United States, it often centers on the question of whether the United States should learn from British experience.

21/YES — SHOULD THE UNITED STATES ADOPT THE BRITISH PARLIAMENTARY SYSTEM OF GOVERNMENT?

Throughout this century many writers, including such notables as the political scientist and president Woodrow Wilson and the journalist Walter Lippmann, have called for major structural changes in the American political system so that it will more closely resemble British parliamentary government. We concur with this position and contend that the American system should be restructured so as to allow for the designation of two separate officials: a chief of state who would be a ceremonial leader, and a prime minister who would be a member of the legislative body. We would also eliminate the system of federalism and put government power completely into the hands of a newly formed Congress. That Congress would be unicameral and would select the prime minister and cabinet. The American prime minister would have much the same powers that his or her British counterpart possesses today. A strong, centralized, two-party system would assure party discipline, and the loss of a vote of confidence in Congress would bring on a general election. The American prime minister could be dismissed by his or her party without the necessity of going through a general election. The prime minister's cabinet would be composed of members of Congress. Each cabinet member would be in charge of an executive department. The Supreme Court would no longer have its power of judicial review, although it could interpret the law as enacted by Congress.

Such structural changes are essential in the American political system. With such alterations, the system would achieve the following advantages: (1) government would become more accountable and democratic; (2) government would become more efficient; and (3) traditional powers, presently assumed by the executive, would be restored to the legislature. We would then have a government that would be streamlined enough to carry us through to the twenty-first century.

Accountability and Democracy. Representative democracy has been defined in Chapter 3 as a system of government in which elected public officials represent the people. Advocates of democracy differ as to the particular character of the representative. Some view the representative as a **delegate**—a person who must represent the interests of his or her constituency whether or not he or she agrees with those interests. Others view the representative as a **trustee**—a person who votes on the basis of conscience in legislative considerations for those principles in which he or she believes. Either theory, however, implies that representatives must in some way be accountable to the people who elect them.

If a Labour government is in power in Great Britain, then Labour is held accountable for what happens to the society. If the inflation rates rise rapidly or foreign policy setbacks are experienced, then it is Labour's fault. Accountability is clear in a system in which the legislative and executive power are fused.

In the United States, however, power and authority are dispersed. "The splitting of sovereignty into many parts amounts to there being no sovereign," the nineteenth-century British writer Walter Bagehot observed.[11] Particularly in situations in which the president belongs to one party and the Congress to another, responsibility is claimed only for good news and not for bad. When Republican Gerald Ford was president, he blamed the Democratic Congress for inflation because of its spending policies. It was difficult for voters to hold elected public officials accountable in such a diffused system. Democracy requires accountability, and parliamentary reforms in the American political process along British lines would provide for that accountability.

Efficiency. The American political system of government is a highly inefficient way to rule. The U.S. Constitution was created in the late eighteenth century at a time when the population of the United States totaled only about 3 million people who lived mostly in eastern coastal states. At that time, the American economy was dominated by agriculture. Moreover, the United States was a country on the periphery of power politics dominated by the big European powers.

The Constitution of 1787 created an inefficient government because government was regarded by many eighteenth-century Americans as a necessary evil. Today, strong government is necessary but not possible, given the constitutional constraints imposed by a document written for the needs of two centuries ago. "The separation of powers between the legislative and executive branches, whatever its merits in 1793," writes the Washington attorney Lloyd Cutler, "has become a structure that almost guarantees stalemate today."[12]

Today, the United States needs a structure that can provide positive government to meet the needs of a modern industrial society. The rapidly changing global economic situation makes necessary decisive action that only a unified government can provide. The position of the United States as a superpower, moreover, requires the country to speak with one voice rather than having the executive trying to move in one direction and the legislature trying to get the executive to move in another. A parliamentary system based on the British model, then, would allow for the positive and efficient government that our system currently lacks.

Efficiency in government would be helped by putting people with long experience in govern-

[11] Walter Bagehot, *The English Constitution*, 2d ed. (London: Oxford University Press, 1952), p. 201. The study was originally published in 1867.

[12] Lloyd Cutler, "To Form a Government," *Foreign Affairs* 59 (Fall 1980): 127.

ment into positions of responsibility. To become a minister requires many years of working one's way up through party ranks and developing a knowledge about government. By the time an individual becomes a prime minister in Britain, he or she has learned how to get things done in government.

The separate election of president and Congress, in contrast, means that an individual can come to the presidency with little or no experience in dealing with the Congress. Walter Bagehot commented in 1867 about the low quality of executive talent recruited to the presidency. He regarded this situation as caused by the separation of powers. He did indicate that Abraham Lincoln was an able president but noted aptly that "success in a lottery is no argument for lotteries."[13] In more modern times individuals attaining the presidency from outside the legislative branch have had to "learn on the job" while the country was being impaired by the president's inexperience.

The parliamentary system, moreover, would assure that the most talented members of Congress would retain their seats and not be ejected from the legislature because of electoral defeat. Good people could be given **safe seats** from which members of their party are nearly always elected so as to assure their making a continuing contribution to the government. The country benefits when it retains legislators of talent as active participants in the political process.

Legislative Assertion. In 1885 Woodrow Wilson published a study of the American system of government entitled *Congressional Government,* which reflected where power resided at that time. In the twentieth century, however, the executive branch of government has come to play a more prominent role in government decision making.

The examples are varied and include foreign policy, national security, and domestic matters. In foreign policy *executive agreements* (which require merely the approval of the president) have increasingly been used instead of treaties requiring Senate approval. In national security matters, moreover, the president has used his powers as commander-in-chief to involve the country in acts of war. The Constitution specifically indicates that Congress shall have the power to declare war, but American involvement

[13]Bagehot, *English Constitution,* p. 28.

in Korea in the 1950s, in Vietnam in the 1960s and 1970s, and in the Persian Gulf in the 1990s did not come about by formal declarations of war. American casualties in the first two wars were high, and the mere fact that war was not declared did not alter the high price the country paid for executive action.

Domestic matters, too, have experienced executive encroachment, as presidents have authorized government snooping, wiretapping, and surveillance of private individuals without congressional authority. Executives also have expanded their powers in the management of the economy, determining at times such matters as price and wage controls and import-export restrictions.

The high point of executive power came during the Watergate affair, when power became wrongdoing. For a period of more than a year, President Richard Nixon and his top aides struggled to ward off investigations by Congress and the courts. The conduct of government was slowed down by the struggle. Ultimately, Richard Nixon resigned. No American president had been previously thrown out of office before his term expired, and none had previously resigned. The fixed period of four years made it impossible to remove the president without a grave constitutional crisis.

Had the United States been governed by a parliamentary system, it would not have had to go through such an agonizing experience. In 1940, Prime Minister Neville Chamberlain was replaced by Winston Churchill when Chamberlain's policy of appeasement against Adolf Hitler became discredited. In 1956, moreover, Anthony Eden resigned over the failure of his policy on the Suez Canal, and he was replaced by Harold Macmillan. Both Churchill and Macmillan came to power without a constitutional crisis and without a general election. It would have been possible, and much more sensible, to remove Richard Nixon in the same way that Chamberlain and Eden were removed had the United States been governed by a parliamentary system.

The same parliamentary system would be desirable even if a president has not been guilty of wrongdoing. When Herbert Hoover was elected president in 1928, he was a popular figure. The Great Depression beginning in 1929, however, diminished his popularity. In spite of the extended period of economic devastation, Hoover remained in the White House until 1933, when Franklin D. Roosevelt came to power and promised the American people a "New Deal" to get the country out of its economic difficulties.

As the nation moves toward the twenty-first century, it must streamline its government to meet the even more complex challenges ahead. A parliamentary system would allow for government to be accountable, efficient, and responsive to popular demands.

21/NO SHOULD THE UNITED STATES ADOPT THE BRITISH PARLIAMENTARY SYSTEM OF GOVERNMENT?

The argument that the United States would have better government if it adopted the British parliamentary system should be dismissed after a close examination is made of both the current British political system and the American political system. We shall leave aside for argument's sake the practical contention that such a reshuffling of powers and institutions would not be possible to implement in the United States. Even Walter Bagehot contended that the parliamentary system worked best in a limited area with uniform standards of wealth and education. He felt that it could not work for the entire American political system.

Let us take the *Affirmative*'s points of accountability and democracy, efficiency, and legislative assertion to justify our case.

Accountability and Democracy. It is true that power is fragmented in the American political system. It is false, however, that government is not held accountable because of the system of separation of powers. In Great Britain the voter has little choice but to cast a ballot for a particular candidate with a party designation. In the United States, by contrast, the voter can hold a variety of public officials accountable for their actions since the voter casts a ballot separately for a representative, a senator, and the president. As the political scientist Don K. Price notes, the presidential system provides the voters with a "double-check on their government" through their president and other elected officials. Price adds that however poorly the president and Congress are carrying out their responsibilities, the voters "are not kept from exercising their controls by a system of mutual deference that results from the fear of disturbing each other's [president and Congress] tenure of office."[14]

[14] Don K. Price, "The Parliamentary and Presidential Systems," *Public Administration Review* 3 (Autumn 1943): 327.

The American system of separation of powers is in fact more accountable than the British parliamentary system, as the evidence reveals. Because of the separation of powers, the system assures an independent legislature capable of challenging the actions of the executive. The legislature may subpoena civil servants to disclose executive actions in the American system, a practice denied in the British political system. There is much more disclosure about what government is doing in the American political system than in the British system. This feature is explained in part by the fact that the laws of press freedom allow more discretion to American journalists than to their British counterparts. Another important reason for the disclosure of so much information, however, is that legislators do not have to fear that their careers will be ruined if they either vote against or organize opposition to the president, who is also a member of their political party. A people who are able to have access to vast amounts of information are in a far better position to hold government accountable for its acts, as befits a democracy.

Efficiency. The American political system is far more efficient than its detractors would have us believe. Although the Constitution is nearly two centuries old, it has been a document that has not put the political system into a cast-iron mold. Not only have amendments changed the Constitution to meet the needs of the times, but custom, political practices, statutes, and judicial interpretation have all contributed to the continuing success of the political system.

Even with an "antiquated" Constitution, the nation has been able to adapt to its foreign policy, national security, and domestic needs. In foreign affairs the small power of the eighteenth century has become the superpower of the twentieth century, with its orientation moving from an isolationist to an internationalist perspective. In national security matters, moreover, the country has been able to maintain its institutions and way of life in spite of threats from enemies abroad. In domestic matters the separation of powers did not prevent the growth of the welfare state, the regulation of big industry, and the protection of the environment.

The key to the success is that although the system of checks and balances may seem, on paper at least, to thwart action by government, it does not prevent patterns of cooperation between the executive and legislative branches of government. Such cooperation may be seen in foreign policy. The Senate has approved nearly a thousand treaties and turned down about twenty, and only five in the twentieth century. "In general," writes the political scientist James Q. Wilson, "the Senate tends to go along."[15]

Often we pay attention to the major conflicts between the branches in such highly dramatic cases as the defeat of the Versailles Treaty by the United States Senate in 1919, the confrontation of President Franklin D. Roosevelt and Congress over the size of the Supreme Court, and the congressional and executive conflicts in the Watergate affair; but these cases are the exceptions rather than the rule of government. In point of fact, cooperation often characterizes the relationships of the two branches of government; if it did not, then it would be impossible for American government to function.

There is no clear case to indicate that a parliamentary system would be more or less efficient to meet the problems of the day. British governments, too, have not always coped well with their problems, as the lack of preparation for World War II and the inflationary spiral of the 1970s testify. More than mere government structure accounts for efficiency in government.

There is no assurance, moreover, that if the United States were to try to adopt a British-type parliamentary system to replace the current presidential system it would retain a two-party system. The experience of France under the Fourth Republic shows that a multiparty parliamentary system may be highly unstable and inefficient. It is wrong to tinker with the Constitution when we do not know what greater problems might result.

Efficiency in government depends, too, upon the quality of the personnel in government. The evidence does not indicate that American presidents have been unqualified to rule. Men such as Thomas Jefferson, Abraham Lincoln, Theodore Roosevelt, Woodrow Wilson, and Franklin D. Roosevelt were outstanding chief executives. Though assuming the office of president from outside the ranks of the legislature, moreover, they did not lack political experience. Wilson and both Roosevelts, for example, were state governors, and their activities at the state level provided them with sound executive experience.

The American system, moreover, allows for clearer political direction of the bureaucracy than does the British system. When a new president is elected, he brings to the administration not only cabinet secretaries but thousands of undersecretaries and other executives. Often, these are people with great experience outside government who inject fresh ideas into government so it operates more effectively. In the realm of defense, for example, Elihu Root was regarded as a superior secretary of war, and James Forrestal as an outstanding secretary of defense, although these men came to their positions from law and banking, respectively. Cabinet members, moreover, can be selected on the basis of their administrative competence, which may be tested outside of government, rather than from their skill at debate, a characteristic emphasized in the parliamentary system.

In the matter of personnel many able legislators are reelected for several terms in Congress under the current decentralized system of primaries and elections. Even if an able legislator is defeated in an election, however, that person may continue to have an influence on policy. At times, defeated legislators may be given cabinet positions or be taken into the administration as advisers to the president. The defeated legislators can run again for election. Their influence would be strong, moreover, if they merely concerned themselves with events and wrote occasional articles and books about subjects of national importance. Defeated candidates do not have to become "nonpersons" in the manner of out-of-favor political figures in totalitarian dictatorships.

Legislative Assertion. It is certainly true that legislative power has declined with respect to executive power. Congress, however, has expanded its power with respect to the entire system. In years past Congress met annually for

---

[15] James Q. Wilson, "Does the Separation of Powers Still Work?" *Public Interest*, no. 86 (Winter 1987): 48.

only a few months. Now its work is so vast that it is usually in session for most of the year. As government operations have expanded, so, too, has the scope of congressional activities. The enlargement of the congressional staff, moreover, has given legislators the opportunity to oversee executive actions.

Although legislative power has declined with respect to the executive throughout the world, there is no evidence to indicate that the parliamentary system is any more successful in reversing the trend toward executive dominance. When Woodrow Wilson wrote *Congressional Government*, moreover, he was critical of the undue influence of Congress on legislation and felt that a parliamentary system would strengthen the president. In fact, the British parliamentary system has experienced an increasing amount of centralized control. Some British commentators have argued that the British prime minister's power has become comparable to that of the American president. In this regard the British prime minister has the authority to make appointments to office, conclude treaties, and declare war—all without securing parliamentary consent. Geoffrey Smith observes that one dissatisfaction of British legislators is that "Parliament is thought to be merely a rubber stamp for the decisions of government."[16]

The British parliamentary system encourages a more quiescent legislature and a strong executive. When a political party is in power, the leaders of the party enforce discipline so its members do not vote against the government and thus throw the entire legislature into general elections. The legislator votes the way the party dictates as determined by the executive if he or she is the prime minister and of the same party. The point, however, should not be overstated, since party leaders take into consideration the interests of the different elements of their party. Nonetheless, the party's ability to discipline recalcitrant members of Parliament is a deterrent to "rocking the boat."

In fact, the no-confidence vote has for the most part lost any real effectiveness as an instrument of legislative control of the executive. Not since 1885 has a government commanding a majority by one party in the House of Commons been overthrown by a no-confidence vote. Governments have been toppled through no-confidence votes since then, but in those cases the government did not have majority control and needed the support of members of Parliament from other parties.

The question hour, moreover, is another overstated institution of check on the executive. As the political scientist James L. Sundquist notes, "One of the first things learned by a rising politician in a democracy is how to artfully avoid giving information he does not want to give."[17] The question hour may test the oratorical abilities of government leaders, but it is not really as significant for revealing information as its advocates pretend.

The American system of separation of powers has allowed for legislative assertion when the executive has exceeded his authority. The decade of the 1970s witnessed such legislative activity. A War Powers Act limited the power of the chief executive in the conduct of foreign policy. The Freedom of Information Act assured many Americans unprecedented access to government documents. Scholars have even relied on such previously classified documents to publish devastating indictments of executive actions.[18] Other laws of the 1970s included limitations on campaign expenditures for presidential campaigns and congressional reforms of the budgetary process. The increasing role of Congress in budgetary matters is, in fact, one of the most significant post-Watergate reforms. The entire Watergate story with its televised hearings and forced disclosures of private, taped presidential conversations in the Oval Office of the White House was revealed to the public. Watergate showed that the existing system works to deal with executive usurpation of constitutional authority. The congressional investigation of the Iran-Contra affair, moreover, again demonstrated the power of Congress to hold the president to account for illegal administration activities.

[16] Geoffrey Smith, "Parliamentary Change in Britain," in *The Role of the Legislature in Western Democracies*, ed. Norman J. Ornstein, (Washington, D.C.: American Enterprise Institute for Public Policy Research, 1981), p. 37.

[17] James L. Sundquist, "Parliamentary Government and Ours," *New Republic* 171 (October 26, 1974): 14.

[18] For example, see William Shawcross, *Sideshow: Kissinger, Nixon and the Destruction of Cambodia* (New York: Simon and Schuster, 1979).

A fixed system of holding office may seem to have some drawbacks, as the cases of Herbert Hoover and Richard Nixon attest. There is, however, another side to the story. A president who is assured of the post for four years is more encouraged to take strong action and disregard the clamor from Congress. The historian Arthur Schlesinger, Jr., observes that John Adams resisted congressional agitation for war with France during his administration as president, and President Harry Truman fought the explosion of congressional wrath when he fired General Douglas MacArthur as supreme allied commander of United States forces in Korea.

"Yet in retrospect," Schlesinger notes, "these two doughty Presidents never had finer hours."[19]

The case for the adoption of a parliamentary system has not been proven. It is well to heed the words of John Kennedy, who said in another context, "If it is not necessary to change, it is necessary not to change." It is, consequently, not necessary to change a system that has worked for two centuries.

[19] Arthur Schlesinger, Jr., "Parliamentary Government," *New Republic* 171 (August 31, 1974): 14.

KEY TERMS

Appellate court
Bicameral legislature
Bills
By-election
Cabinet
Checks and balances
Chief of state
Collective responsibility
Conference committee
Courts of original jurisdiction
Delegate theory
Executive
Free vote
Head of government
Impeachment
Joint committee

Judiciary
Legislature
Legislation
Loyal opposition
Ombudsman
Parliamentary system
Presidential system
Question hour
Safe seats
Select committee
Separation of powers
Shadow cabinet
Standing committee
Trustee theory
Unicameral legislature
Vote of confidence

QUESTIONS

Parliamentary and Presidential Systems

1. What effect does judicial review have on democratic processes?
2. What effect does the decline of legislative power and the strengthening of executive power have in democracies?
3. Is it possible today to strengthen legislatures in democracies? If so, how? If not, why not?
4. To what extent does political culture rather than government structure affect political

stability? What are the reasons for your answer?
5. What are the advantages and disadvantages of a fixed term of office for the head of government?

An American Parliament?

1. If a "Watergate" had happened in Great Britain, would the British parliament have handled the situation differently from the way it was handled by the U.S. Congress? What are the reasons for your answer?

2. What are the obstacles in the Constitution that prevent the United States from adopting a parliamentary system of government?
3. Which system—parliamentary or presidential—is likely to have a stronger legislature? Why?
4. How has the caliber of leaders of American

presidents compared to that of British prime ministers?
5. Had the U.S. Constitution of 1787 established a parliamentary system, what difference would that have made to the course of American history? What are the reasons for your answer?

RECOMMENDED READINGS

Parliamentary and Presidential Systems

ABRAHAM, HENRY J. *The Judicial Process: An Introductory Analysis of the Courts of the United States, England, and France*. New York: Oxford University Press, 1986. A selective comparative introduction to the judicial process.

BAILEY, CHRISTOPHER J. *The U.S. Congress*. New York: Basil Blackwell, 1989. A study of Congress.

BARILLEAUX, RYAN J. *The Post-Modern Presidency: The Office after Ronald Reagan*. New York: Praeger, 1988. A contention that the office of the presidency under Ronald Reagan and his successors is fundamentally different from that of his predecessors.

BLONDEL, JEAN. *The Organization of Government: A Comparative Analysis of Governmental Structures*. Beverly Hills, Calif.: Sage, 1982. A study of the main characteristics of government in the world.

CURTIS, MICHAEL, ed. *Introduction to Comparative Government*. 2d ed. New York: Harper and Row, 1990. A survey.

DRAGNICH, ALEX N., JORGEN S. RASMUSSEN, and JOEL C. MOSES. *Major European Governments*. 8th ed. Pacific Grove, Calif.: Brooks/Cole Publishing Co., 1991. An introduction to the subject.

GATES, JOHN B., and CHARLES A. JOHNSON, eds. *The American Courts: A Critical Assessment*. Washington, D.C.: CQ Press, 1991. A collection of articles on the U.S. judicial system.

GOLDMAN, STUART D. "The New Soviet Legislative Branch." *Congressional Research Service Review* 11 (March/April 1990): 20–22. The Soviet legislature in the Gorbachev era.

HAMILTON, ALEXANDER, JAMES MADISON, and JOHN JAY. *The Federalist Papers*, ed. Clinton Rossiter. New York: New American Library, 1961. Papers, originally published in 1788 in support of the ratification of the Constitution, that remain a classic work on government.

LAUNDY, PHILIP. *Parliaments in the Modern World*. Brookfield, Vt.: Gower Publishing Co., 1989. A survey of the organization and work of parliaments throughout the world.

LUNEY, PERCY R., JR., ed. "The Constitution of Japan: The Fifth Decade." *Law and Contemporary Problems* 53 (Winter and Spring 1990): entire issue. Articles on Japan's constitutional and political development.

MEZEY, MICHAEL L. *Comparative Legislatures*. Durham, N.C.: Duke University Press, 1979. A comparative analysis of legislatures.

———. *Congress, the President and Public Policy*. Boulder, Colo.: Westview Press, 1989. A plea for changes in executive-legislative relations in the United States.

NORTON, PHILIP. *The British Polity*. 2d ed. New York: Longman, 1991. An overview of the British political system.

———, ed. *Legislatures*. New York: Oxford University Press, 1990. A collection of articles on legislatures.

———, ed. "Special Issue on Parliaments in Western Europe." *West European Politics* (London) 13 (July 1990): entire issue. A study of the relationship between legislatures and executives between 1970 and 1990 in seven Western European countries.

An American Parliament

BAGEHOT, WALTER. *The English Constitution*. 2d ed. London: Oxford University Press, 1952. A classic work on British government originally published in 1867.

CUTLER, LLOYD. "To Form a Government." *Foreign Affairs* 59 (Fall 1980): 126–43. A criticism of the separation of powers and a plea that the United States move toward a parliamentary system.

ESBEREY, JOY. "What If There Were a Parliamentary System?" In *What If The American Political System were Different?*, ed. Herbert M. Levine. Armonk, N.Y.: M. E. Sharpe, 1992. Chap. 5. An essay speculating about a U.S. parliamentary history.

GOLDWIN, ROBERT A., and ART KAUFMAN, eds. *Separation of Powers: Does It Still Work?* Washington, D.C.: American Enterprise Institute for Public Policy Research, 1986. Essays on the subject.

LIVINGSTON, WILLIAM E. "Britain and America: The Institutionalization of Accountability." *Journal of Politics* 38 (November 1976): 879–94. An argument against the establishment of a parliamentary system of government in the United States.

MILKIS, SIDNEY M., and MICHAEL NELSON. *The American Presidency: Origins and Development, 1776–1990.* Washington, D.C.: CQ Press, 1990. A comprehensive history of the presidency.

PRICE, DON K. "The Parliamentary and Presidential Systems." *Public Administration Review*, 3 (Autumn 1943): 317–34. A case that the United States should not adopt a parliamentary system.

ROBINSON, DONALD L. "Adjustments Are Needed in the System of Checks and Balances." *Polity* 19 (Summer 1987): 660–66. A call for changes in the U.S. constitutional system.

————, ed. *Reforming American Government: The Bicentennial Papers of the Committee on the Constitutional System.* Boulder, Colo.: Westview Press, 1985. A reprint of many articles and book excerpts dealing with constitutional reform in the United States.

SCARROW, HOWARD A. "Parliamentary and Presidential Government Compared." *Current History* 66 (June 1974): 264–67, 272. An evaluation of the pros and cons of each system.

SCHLESINGER, ARTHUR, JR. "Parliamentary Government." *New Republic* 171 (August 31, 1974): 13–15. A case against the adoption of a parliamentary system in the United States.

SUNDQUIST, JAMES L. *Constitutional Reform and Effective Government.* Washington, D.C.: Brookings Institution, 1986. An analysis of the weaknesses of the U.S. constitutional system and a plea for reform.

SUNDQUIST, PAUL S. "Congress and Parliaments." *Congressional Research Service Review* 10 (March 1989): 31–32. A comparison of the two legislative institutions.

U.S. CONGRESS, JOINT ECONOMIC COMMITTEE. *Political Economy and Constitutional Reform.* Hearings, 97th Congress, 2d Sess., 1982. Testimony and reprinted articles on structural reforms in the American political system, with attention to the parliamentary system of government.

WILSON, JAMES Q. "Does the Separation of Powers Still Work?" *Public Interest*, no. 86 (Winter 1987): 36–52. The author says Yes.

chapter 12

Bureaucracy

Big government is a feature of contemporary society in spite of popular complaints about its size and performance. Today's conservatives complain about the inefficiencies of government and the failures of government social programs but support bigger government in the form of law enforcement and armed forces. Today's liberals point to the dangers of government intruding upon the civil liberties of the people but call for increased government spending on education, health, and social programs.

Concern with big government is not unique to the United States. Nearly every country in the world—regardless of whether it is democratic or dictatorial—has experienced an increase in the number of people who staff government and an expansion in the functions of government. Because of its size and scope, there is little doubt that bureaucracy plays a prominent role in public policy and in influencing the character of political systems. To evaluate the power and role of the bureaucracy in one political system—a democracy—it is first essential to examine the central features of a bureaucracy. We shall then study what it does, why it has grown, how it is organized, and how it is composed.

WHAT IS BUREAUCRACY?

The term *bureaucracy*, like the terms *democracy* and *socialism*, lacks a definition that is universally accepted. *Bureaucracy* is sometimes used in a disparaging manner to mean bumbling, unimaginative, rigid, and inefficient government administrators. Many social scientists, however, describe bureaucracy in a neutral way to mean a specific form of social organization involved in administrative efforts, and it is this latter meaning that will be applied in this chapter. Specifically, we shall use the term **bureaucracy** to mean a government organization, established in departments, agencies, and bureaus, that carries out government activities according to fixed rules.

The first person to study bureaucracy in a systematic fashion was the German social scientist Max Weber. In his book *Wirtschaft und Gesellschaft* (Economy and Society), published in 1922, Weber described an ideal-type bureaucracy as one characterized by:

1. officials organized in fixed jurisdictional areas,
2. a hierarchical arrangement of offices (organized in a pyramidlike structure with each lower office under the control of a higher one),
3. written documents ("the files") that contain the rules to be applied in every case,
4. full-time employment by experts in administration,
5. impersonality in applying rules uniformly.[1]

Weber's use of an ideal type was not a description of how bureaucracy actually works. It was, rather, a model highlighting features that would allow for a systematic study of comparative social organizations. In Weber's view, bureaucratic organization was the most efficient form of social organization the world had experienced. The West, according to Weber, had a compulsive cultural drive to rationalize social and economic processes. By *rationalize*, Weber meant to have the ability to control the material and social world in terms of cause-and-effect relationships rather than through religious or mystical explanations.

Weber described bureaucracy as the central feature of modern society. His analysis of bureaucracy included not only government organization but also the administration of large private organizations. Since Weber, social scientists have concerned themselves with further analyses of the management of large organizations at both the government and private organizational levels.

In many respects large private organizations and government organizations have similarities. If the government's United States Postal Service and private corporation's United Parcel Service are taken as examples, it can be seen that the basic work of these two organizations is the same. Parcels must be sent to a depot; rates must be set based on such factors as weight, size, and destination; a distribution center must sort the parcels by destination; and freight vehicles must transport the parcels to their ultimate receivers. A hierarchy of offices of each organization indicates the responsibility of each official in those organizations.

Although administration has similar characteristics in the public and private sectors, as the example of the transportation of parcels indicates, the differences are vast. First, government organizations pursue a wider range of activities than do private organizations. Second, the kinds of services that government undertakes, such as police protection, education, and welfare, cannot generally be measured in terms of profit-and-loss figures of the private association. Third, government agencies are often required to achieve more goals than comparable private organizations. A private corporation, for example, may seek the most efficient means to secure profits; whereas a comparable government organization may be required to make decisions based not only on efficiency but on fairness, justice, and external political factors. Fourth, public employees are generally more secure in their jobs and their promotion steps are more stable than employees in the private sector. Fifth and last, since government agencies are held to more public scrutiny and accountability, they must be able to document every administrative act; hence, public agencies pay more attention to the rules, necessitating enormous paperwork and red tape. These differences do not apply in each case, and

---

[1] Max Weber, "Bureaucracy," in *From Max Weber: Essays in Sociology*, ed. H. H. Gerth and C. Wright Mills (New York: Oxford University Press, 1946), pp. 196–98.

exceptions are widespread. In general, these differences distinguish the public from the private sector.

WHAT THE BUREAUCRACY DOES

The bureaucracy plays an active role in the political process of most countries, and it engages in many activities. Among its most important efforts are the implementation of laws, preparation of proposed legislation, regulation of the economy, licensing in economic and professional matters, and the providing of welfare services.

Implementation of Laws

Government agencies are established and conduct their activities on the basis of specific legislative authorization. In the justification of its actions, government officials indicate that they are involved in the **administration**, or carrying out, of the law. The distinction between what they do and the legal authorization of their acts was first made in a systematic manner by Woodrow Wilson in 1887 and Frank Goodnow in 1900.[2] For them, politics in a democracy reflected the political values expressed through public opinion, political parties, and interest groups. Elected public officials, they argued, should be concerned with responding to these political forces. In their view, administrators were supposed to be politically neutral, acting only to implement the policies of duly elected officials.

To some extent, the politics-administration distinction is valid. The legislature enacts a law and appropriates money for specific purposes, such as tax collection and

[2]Woodrow Wilson, "The Study of Administration," *Political Science Quarterly* 2 (June 1887): 197–222; Frank Goodnow, *Politics and Administration* (New York: Crowell-Collier and Macmillan, 1900).

coal mine inspection, and the government agencies involved use those funds as directed. Most government agencies do what is mandated to them by constitutional authorities lest they be called to account for avoiding their legal responsibilities.

Many students of government, however, challenge the politics-administration model, calling attention to the prominent role that bureaucracy plays in the political process. Studies of government agencies show that agencies are not merely value-free administrative organizations but are, rather, active participants in all areas of policy.

In fact, some social scientists contend that bureaucracies actually legislate. They argue that legislation is often drafted in a vague or general manner, and it is left to the government agencies and bureaus to interpret the legislative mandate as best they can. Agencies may use this discretion to act in an aggressive or passive way depending upon such factors as whether the agencies support the legislation or the legislation diminishes the power of the bureaucratic organization. In the United States, for example, civil rights agencies in the administrations of Presidents Richard Nixon, Gerald Ford, and Jimmy Carter were accused by conservatives of applying the civil rights laws in ways in which Congress did not intend. Specifically, conservatives condemned executive actions in affirmative action and in busing. In the administration of Ronald Reagan, in contrast, civil rights agencies were accused by liberals of failing to implement civil rights laws or of moving too slowly in combating racial and gender discrimination.

The power of the bureaucracy is enhanced not only by the imprecision and incompleteness of legislation but also by the expertise that government agencies possess, permitting bureaucrats to direct policy as they deem fit. Elected public officials, in contrast, often lack this technical information to pursue investigations of government agencies to force them to act in accordance with legislative direction. In effect, then, the bureaucracy legislates.

Preparation of Legislation

Because of its expertise, the bureaucracy plays a role in the preparation of legislation. Although bills are formally introduced by legislative members, they are, in fact, drafted by government agencies most concerned with their content. Members of the bureaucracy are often called to give their view openly or privately about the proposed legislation before legislative bodies.

Democracies differ in how open a role the bureaucracy plays in legislation. In the United States the civil servants actually appear before congressional committees when directed to do so. In Great Britain legislative committees are generally not important in shaping legislation, and the influence of the professional bureaucracy is exerted primarily through the ministry and the executive branch.

Regulation

Government agencies play a regulatory role in political systems. They regulate some industries by such methods as determining rate structures and defining the character of competition. In the United States, for example, the regulatory commissions, such as the Federal Communications Commission and the Securities and Exchange Commission, regulate activities of the communications and securities industries, respectively. Other countries have similar agencies that deal with these and other matters. Some countries even nationalize the kinds of industries that are private but regulated in the United States.

Licensing

One form of regulation is licensing, and agencies use their powers of licensing to influence the behavior of private organiza-

tions. Licensing may occur on a national scale or on a local or regional one. Licensing to fly aircraft along specified routes is an example of a national license activity. A license may be given locally for permission to sell alcoholic beverages or to dispense prescription medicines. Doctors, lawyers, and dentists are required to have licenses to practice so as to assure standards of professional competence by these specialists.

Welfare Services

Many government services today are in the welfare sector. In principle, teachers in public institutions are part of the welfare bureaucracy. So, too, are welfare workers who look after the poor and the sick. Today, the welfare sector has expanded to include the arts, so some music, theater, and dance programs receive government funds to help them survive. Social security, unemployment compensation, veterans' benefits, and public medical care assistance have all generated vast bureaucracies that have contributed to the growth of government personnel and expenditures.

THE GROWTH OF GOVERNMENT

Early historical documents disclose that bureaucracy has roots going back to ancient Egypt and China. Whenever large projects require the recruitment of many people possessing different skills, bureaucracy is necessary to plan the project, organize the personnel and matériel, and coordinate its diverse components. For ancient Egypt, a bureaucracy was needed to develop the Nile River. In more modern times a bureaucracy was essential to produce the atom bomb.

The major growth in the bureaucracy, however, has been in the past two centuries. To a large extent, it is the product of an increasingly complicated economy. The industrial revolution, with its specialization of labor, consumption of many raw materials from distant countries, and use of technicians skilled in engineering, chemistry, mathematics, and physics, required a greater talent in managerial skills than called for in a less-developed economic system. Modern capitalism, then, was a major factor in requiring administrative skills. Later, however, government played a more positive role in the bureaucratization of the world.

The past two centuries have been marked by a growth in government, both in expenditures and in the number of people employed by government. There has been variation in expenditures and in the size of the bureaucracy within specific periods, but the trend has generally been upward in both elements. We should note, however, that it is not necessarily the case that an increase in government expenditures automatically means a corresponding increase in the size of the bureaucracy, since some government programs require minimal administrative needs.

Government has grown for many reasons. Most important have been the demands of the economy, the role of national security, the claims of the welfare state, and the pressures exerted by the bureaucracy itself.

Economy

To many capitalists, the essence of the good society is one in which government plays only a small role (see Chapter 5). The leading proponent of free enterprise, Adam Smith, attacked government and principally the mercantile system, which involved massive government intervention in the economy.

Some capitalists remained true to the faith by advocating weak government. Others, however, called for government intervention to protect and strengthen economic expansion. As United States secretary of the treasury, Alexander Hamilton proposed a system of tariffs to protect American industry, for example. In fact, customs officials constituted a large bureaucratic unit in the first century of the American republic. Capitalism, too, received government assistance in building railroads and digging canals. Government subsidies were given to capitalists in the eighteenth century to encourage inventions and to stimulate industry.

In the twentieth century, government growth has been further stimulated by the appeals of capitalists in many areas. Subsidies are demanded and given to those in the agricultural sector, representing not the yeoman farmer but rather big corporations. Tariffs rise and fall depending upon the effects of competition from items produced in different countries. Technical assistance is provided to business interests through direct grants for research or through the provision of government services.

Government growth can be explained only in part by the demands of the capitalists for protection from competition and for other commercial purposes. The complexity of the economy led to government expansion. Air transport and communications are two of many examples of government intervention. In the United States private airline companies were formed during the early days of air transport. The need for air safety and the desire by the established airline companies to avoid competition in prices encouraged the development of government agencies that could achieve both goals. Traffic had to be regulated to avoid midair collisions, and aircraft had to be made airworthy.

In communications government agencies were established to control airwave frequencies. Radio stations, and later television stations, were given licenses to operate over specific frequencies so that they would not experience interference from other broadcasters.

Not only was the increased complexity of the economy a factor in government expansion, but so, too, were the demands from those whose interests were harmed by the rising power of industrial corporations, such as consumer and labor groups. In the nineteenth century, capitalism experienced the consolidation of firms and the rise of **monopolies** (in which one company controls the market for a product or service) and **oligopolies** (in which that power is held by a few companies). Demands were made to break up the giant industries so competitive forces would prevail. New government agencies were formed to achieve that goal.

Consumers in the twentieth century have been active in promoting government inspection of goods that have been produced by industry. To be sure, many companies in pursuing their own self-interest were concerned with producing high-quality products, but often companies were preoccupied with cutting costs—a factor that created hazards of safety and health. In more recent times, consumer groups have grown stronger in many countries and have spurred the growth of consumer-protection agencies for the purpose of securing credit opportunities and more rights for the consumer.

In addition to consumer demands, the rise of labor unions as a power in the political arena contributed to government growth. In the economic sector labor unions sought the protection of government to organize and to serve as collective bargaining agents. In the United States the National Labor Relations Board (NLRB) was established in 1935 to give labor those rights. Today, the NLRB deals with many cases involving disputes between labor and management. Labor also played an important role in the expansion of government in the welfare sector.

National Security

Protection of the country from external attack is an important element of government growth. Geographical location—a fixed component of international relations—permitted both the United States and Great Britain, as insular powers, centuries of low-level expenditures on military defense.

Some observers say that war is the most important reason for government growth. Modern war is a vast industrial operation requiring the centralized allocation of scarce resources for military purposes. During wartime, governments establish or enlarge agencies for organizing military conscription, determining military priorities, and instituting price and wage controls. Countries often spend more on veterans' benefits than they do for the actual conduct of the wars for which the veterans fought.[3]

In the twentieth century, billions of dollars are spent each year on defense not only by the United States and Great Britain but also by other countries (see Chapter 14). The defense budget of the United States constitutes a large share of the federal government's bureaucracy, although its percentage of total government expenditures has been surpassed by the welfare sector in the past two decades. Totalitarian dictatorships often seek national security funds, moreover, to serve the needs of their large bureaucratic forces bent on control of other nations and people.

Welfare

In the twentieth century, the acceptance of the idea that the government has a responsibility to promote individual welfare through providing services in education, health, job security, and retirement assistance has contributed much to government growth. The welfare state is found in nearly every country in the world (see Chapter 5). In the United States it achieved

[3] Bruce D. Porter, "Parkinson's Law Revisited: War and the Growth of American Government," *Public Interest*, no. 60 (Summer 1980): 50–68.

its impetus from the New Deal programs of President Franklin D. Roosevelt in the 1930s. Welfare benefits have expanded in the United States during both Republican and Democratic administrations.

Today government is engaged in furnishing welfare services to people. Government provides education not only at the elementary school level but also in high schools and colleges. Hospital and health services are furnished to needy people. People who are infirm, elderly, or sick receive benefits such as grants and direct services.

One reason why it is difficult to cut government spending is that the beneficiaries of welfare programs regard them as **entitlements**—that is to say, permanent benefits that individuals should receive when they are legally qualified to obtain them. Social security, Medicare, unemployment compensation, and veterans' benefits are examples of entitlements. Entitlements plus other obligations of government, such as interest on the national debt, make about 80 percent of U.S. government spending "uncontrollable." Most other industrialized countries have even higher proportions of uncontrollable expenditures, because their social programs are more extensive than those of the United States.

Bureaucratic Pressures

Another cause of government growth is the government bureaucracy itself. Agencies tend to get bigger by promoting new programs and strengthening existing ones. Government agencies often seek to enlarge their size. The bigger an organization grows, the easier its chances for survival becomes. Opportunities for promotion are greater, moreover, as a government agency expands its budget. Even agencies whose original purposes seem forgotten tend to remain. In the words of a report of the Committee on Administrative Management in the administration of President Franklin D. Roosevelt, "There is among governmental agencies great need for a coroner to pronounce them dead, and for an undertaker to dispose of the remains."[4]

Often the size of a bureaucracy increases not because of the impetus of new programs and greater enforcement but because of a natural tendency of organizations to expand. Professor C. Northcote Parkinson suggests satirically that the reason for government growth can be explained in this manner. Parkinson analyzed the size of the British Colonial Office. He discovered that as the British Empire declined, the number of people employed in the British Colonial Office actually increased. He concludes from this and other data that **Parkinson's Law** applies to organizations, to wit: Work expands so as to fill the time available for its completion.[5] University professors have noted that Parkinson's Law applies in periods of declining student enrollment to university administrators and not to faculty members.

Some critics question the validity of Parkinson's Law. They note that although government agencies are resilient, some are not immortal.[6] They say that the size of some government organizations has been reduced, as was the case of the United States military establishment after World War II and the Vietnam War. They add that it is wrong to generalize based on superficial relationships. The British Colonial Office, for example, was given new tasks. It is no wonder, then, that it was increasing in size as Britain was losing its colonies.[7]

[4] *Administrative Management in the Government of the United States* (Washington, D.C.: Government Printing Office, 1937), p. 34.

[5] C. Northcote Parkinson, *Parkinson's Law and Other Studies in Administration* (Boston: Houghton Mifflin, 1957), p. 2.

[6] Herbert Kaufman, *Are Government Organizations Immortal?* (Washington, D.C: Brookings Institution, 1976).

[7] Porter, "Parkinson's Law Revisited," p. 53.

Government has grown, then, for many reasons. Although critics have complained about government growth, there is little likelihood that the size of the bureaucracy will decrease to any significant degree. Even many political leaders who are elected on a program of reducing government expenditures find that by the time their administrations have ended, government has grown bigger, not smaller. Ronald Reagan is a notable example. Bureaucracy seems to be a permanent feature of modern society.

HOW IS BUREAUCRACY ORGANIZED?

The huge and complex tasks of government require organization. Students of administration often refer to two different kinds of organization: formal and informal. **Formal organization** is the legal structure of a government unit. **Informal organization** is the unofficial arrangement of power that exists because of political or personal factors not related to the formal organizational structure.

Formal Organization

The principal classification of the administrative machinery of government is the department or ministry. The department is divided into agencies, bureaus, or divisions. At the top of the department are the political appointees, but the offices of the organization are staffed primarily by permanent public officials.

In describing organizations, some writers in administration make a distinction between line and staff agencies. **Line agencies** are organizations concerned with the direct performance of the functional goals of the administrative unit. **Staff agencies** are organizations that perform advisory functions. In the actual behavior of the agencies of government, however, it is difficult to distinguish the functions that line and staff agencies perform. Other kinds of agencies are **housekeeping** or **service agencies**, which engage in tasks that are common to a number of agencies, such as transportation, personnel, and purchasing functions.

From a formal organizational point of view, power is at the top. Subordinates are assigned tasks throughout the hierarchy or chain of command. Each subordinate has a specific job and is responsible to his or her immediate superior.

Informal Organization

In practice, few organizations actually function according to the power relationships suggested by a model of formal organization. Often bureaucrats lower down the chain of command have more influence than their superiors. For years, for example, J. Edgar Hoover, as director of the Federal Bureau of Investigation (FBI), had so much influence and such high prestige that his superiors—the men who served as attorney general in different administrations—were restrained in dealing with him.

Bureaucrats accumulate a vast expertise and important contacts over the years. Political appointees often hold their positions for a short period of time, but career government officials work in their departments in many cases for decades. If the rank-and-file members of a bureaucracy do not agree with the policies of their political leaders, they can sometimes circumvent those leaders through manipulating informal sources of influence. The administration of Richard Nixon complained, for example, that the bureaucracy was not responsive to the administration's political commands. Nixon, consequently, enlarged the staff of the Executive Office in an attempt to get the bureaucracy to respond to his will.

Because of the system of the separation of powers in the United States, the bureaucracy is often free to play off elected officials in the legislative and executive branches against each other in a manner calculated to enhance the interests of the bureaucracy. In the United States, however, the politics of the bureaucracy is often subjected to public observation. In other political systems bureaucratic politics frequently operates beyond scrutiny by the general public.

Bureaucracies, then, are part of the political process and are not the neutral administrators that Wilson and Goodnow described. The informal ties that have developed between the bureaucracy and political leaders have helped to strengthen the bureaucracy in different political systems and made it a permanent feature of modern political systems.

THE COMPOSITION OF THE BUREAUCRACY

Governments have used different methods to staff administrative offices. In prerevolutionary France, government offices were purchased and dispensed as private property. Another method of staffing government was used in the United States in the early nineteenth century: The victorious president and his party distributed government jobs to supporters. Under Andrew Jackson this system of political patronage became known as the **spoils system**. Jackson's partisans argued that the elected officials should be able to staff government departments with people committed to the principles of the victor. "To the victor belong the spoils" was the slogan of those supporting the Jacksonian method of recruiting personnel.

The systems of purchase and spoils had defects. Purchase did not provide for an equitable or effective means of administration. The spoils system made staffing too unstable, as new administrators replaced the old with the frequency of changeovers by electoral results. Both systems required no expertise for appointment, moreover.

The modern movement to create a trained professional public service, or **civil service**, began in eighteenth-century Prussia. The Napoleonic administrative reforms in France, moreover, became a model for reforms in other countries. The civil service in Prussia and France established the principles of a professional career in civil service with protection of the status and tenure of public employees.

In Great Britain, the Trevelyan-Northcote report of 1854 led in the following year to the formation of a Civil Service Commission that set the basis for civil service reform. By 1870, entrance in the Home Civil Service was established based on open competitive examinations.

In the United States, the movement for civil service reform intensified after the Civil War. Its objective was to curb the abuses of the political "machines" from public service. The Civil Service Reform Act was passed in 1883. A Civil Service Commission was created, and a system of competitive examinations was made the basis for hiring federal government employees. The law initially covered only 10.5 percent of all federal jobs, but was gradually expanded so that it now includes more than 90 percent of federal government employees. Some government units, such as the Federal Bureau of Investigation (FBI) and the Central Intelligence Agency (CIA), remain outside the jurisdiction of the Office of Personnel Management (a successor agency of the Civil Service Commission) and recruit directly through their own procedures, but these government organizations, too, use merit as a criterion for selection. Most state governments use comprehensive merit systems for selecting state employees.

The character of the civil service varies among countries. For example, the American and British systems, although based on merit, differ in some respects. The American system encourages specialized backgrounds and a career service open to a wide variety of talents, while the British system opts for generalists and a closed career service. In addition, the higher offices at the assistant secretary and undersecretary level in the United States are mostly political, rather than civil service, appointees. In Great Britain, however, the corresponding positions are held by civil servants. The higher civil service in Britain, moreover, is dominated by Oxford and Cambridge graduates, whereas the American civil service leadership has a broader recruitment base.

Other characteristics of the civil service vary among countries in socioeconomic composition, honesty, and professional training. In general, however, the features of a modern civil service system remain the same: a group of professional public servants gaining position on the basis of objective competitive examinations, promotion through seniority and merit, and protection from dismissal for party or personal considerations. This is the model that reformers have used in the past two centuries, although there are ample cases in which these standards are not applied.

ISSUE

The extent of government growth throughout the world cannot be denied. The significance of that growth and the evaluation of bureaucracy's power, however, have become controversial issues. A primary concern of students of bureaucracy is an appraisal of the effectiveness of democratic controls on the civil service.

22/YES CAN THE BUREAUCRACY BE CONTROLLED IN A DEMOCRACY?

Democracy, by definition, is a system of government based on popular rule. Democracy, in practice, provides sufficient safeguards against bureaucracies to make them accountable to the people. Among the most significant of these safeguards are: (1) elections; (2) constitutional and political constraints imposed by the legislative, executive, and judicial branches; (3) referendums; (4) the controls that the bureaucracy exerts on itself; and (5) the impact of nongovernmental actors in the political process, such as interest groups, the media, and political parties.

Elections. A major component of democracy is free elections based on the principle of majority rule. Particularly in parliamentary systems, but in presidential ones as well, candidates and political parties put forward programs that they intend to carry out if they are elected. If the electorate is unhappy with the actions of the governing officials, it can elect a new group of leaders who will redirect the bureaucracy.

Although the electorate may be displeased with the acts of particular bureaucrats, in general it has supported the expansion of government services. There is scarcely much political support for eliminating services required for public safety, such as fire and police protection. Public education programs also have popular support, as do social security and veterans' benefits. If the bureaucracy grows, it is because people basically approve of the government services they are receiving and elect political leaders who will assure the continuation of those services.

Constitutional and Political Constraints. Democratic political systems have many safeguards against bureaucratic usurpation. Legislative, executive, and judicial institutions act to provide political direction of the bureaucracy.

Legislative controls involve laws, appropriations, appointments, investigation, and supervision. Traditionally, legislatures enact laws that control government agencies. Some of these laws establish the jurisdiction of agencies. Legislatures have even passed legislation destroying particular government units.

The lifeblood of government agencies is appropriations. Legislatures can destroy the effectiveness of an agency by reducing the amount of money it has to operate. Legislatures assure that the funding of an agency depends on how well that bureaucratic unit serves the public.

Legislatures also play a role in appointments, and the political appointees who reach high-level positions greatly influence the behavior of the government agency involved. The legislature can use the power of confirming appointments to influence how a government agency will act.

Legislatures may also use their powers of investigation to influence bureaucratic behavior. When legislative units observe and investigate government agencies, they are performing the function of **oversight**. Investigations are sometimes conducted to uncover facts that bureaucrats may be reluctant to reveal. Often, however, investigations are designed to influence public opinion and to point out to the bureaucracy that it is not moving in the direction the legislature prefers.

Finally, the legislature has at its command some bureaucratic institutions that are directly accountable to it. In the United States, the General Accounting Office (GAO) is an agent of Congress that audits administrative expenditures. Such a custodian of the nation's purse serves as a watchdog against unauthorized use of funds appropriated to different government agencies. In addition, many countries have the office of ombudsman, in which a troubleshooter with direct access to the legislature is appointed to remove the obstacles of red tape created by the bureaucracies in their dealings with the public (see Chapter 11).

In many democratic systems the executives have power to control the bureaucracy. The executives direct overall policy, influence legislation, and make appointments to the political positions dominating the bureaucracy.

Heads of government normally have principal administrative power. They are at the helm of state and thus can direct policy. In the United States, for example, the president heads the cabinet; in turn, the cabinet dominates the bureaucracy. If the president decides to pursue a particular course in foreign policy, the State Department and Defense Department bureaucracy must provide support lest disciplinary measures be taken. When General Douglas MacArthur took unauthorized actions as United States military commander in South Korea during the Korean War, his commander-in-chief, President Harry Truman, fired him. Truman's action against an insubordinate official is typical of disciplinary measures that may be taken against bureaucrats in military and nonmilitary positions.

The power of the chief executives over policy is often revealed in their role in legislation. In a system of separation of powers, they may veto bills they do not like. American presidents have, moreover, increasingly developed centralized budgetary controls that influence bureaucratic behavior. In the United States, the Office of Management and Budget (OMB) gives the president powers in this manner, and similar institutions have been established in other countries.

Heads of government have powers of appointment. Not only do they designate officials to cabinet-level positions and fire them if they do not carry out their duties according to their policy goals, but they also use their own staffs to supervise the vast bureaucracy. Both the cabinet and staff members supervise the bureaucracy carefully so that the vast government apparatus conforms to political rule.

The courts are often the last resort for both citizens and elected officials when the bureaucracy acts in an irresponsible manner. An individual who feels that he or she has been subjected to unfair treatment by the bureaucracy is free to take a government agency to task for such unfairness.

Court records are filled with cases won by citizens against police officials who exceeded their authority, tax collectors who interpreted the tax law incorrectly, and inspectors who invaded people's privacy. The principle of the *rule of law* in which every act of an official must be taken according to a specific law must be obeyed by public officials if they expect their official actions to be sustained by judicial authority.

Referendums. Another important constraint on the bureaucracy is the use of the *referendum*—the putting of a public question to a vote (see Chapter 3). In some countries, the people can vote directly on matters that have a vital influence on the strength and policies of the bureaucracy. Voters have decided many issues in this way, including tax authorization for roads, schools, and libraries; the level of taxation in general; and the creation of police review boards. Although referendums do not exist in many parliamentary systems, they do offer a means of influencing bureaucratic behavior.

Self-Control. Although public officials are subject to legal controls, they often act in a responsible manner not because of those controls but rather because of their commitment to a code of behavior based on professional principles. The fire fighters who risk their lives to rescue invalids trapped in burning buildings, the public school teachers who zealously help their students to advance in their careers, the health officials who successfully locate the source of food poisoning—all are displaying pride in their work and the highest standards of professional conduct. Such codes of self-control often make the bureaucracy responsible as much as the more formal political controls.

Interest Groups, the Media, and Political Parties. In democracies, bureaucracies respond to pressure from interest groups, the media, and political parties. Political interest groups exert influence in all sectors of the political process (see Chapter 9). Since the bureaucracy is important in making policy, interest groups attempt to influence its political behavior. A steel manufacturer needing protection from imports, farmers pressing for subsidies, feminists demanding support by government for affirmative action programs, and veterans insisting on educational benefits—all these are examples of the sometimes successful pleadings of interest groups in their bids to get the bureaucracy to respond to their demands.

Interest groups are strengthened by their expertise, which can challenge the expertise of the bureaucracy. When Defense Department agencies vigorously defended President Reagan's "Star Wars" directives for building a space defense system, they were challenged by scientific organizations such as the Union of Concerned Scientists. This group, consisting of internationally renowned scientists, some of whom were Nobel laureates, argued that the program was expensive, destabilizing with respect to U.S.-Soviet military relationships, and unworkable. Their expertise gave them credibility with some members of Congress.

In addition to interest groups, the media have come to play an effective role in influencing the bureaucracy. Investigations by journalists from the print and electronic media have resulted in changes in bureaucratic behavior in such matters as the administration of prisons and mental health institutions.

Political parties, too, play a role. The people chosen to head cabinet-level positions are often prominent members of the victorious political party. Particularly in those countries in which political parties are strong, the appointment power is important. The political appointees of the bureaucracy influence the activities of the bureaucracy and make it responsive to popular pressure.

Because the public is accustomed to notice the violations of law by the bureaucracy, it sometimes neglects to recognize the many responsible actions of the bureaucracy. Democratic systems have created adequate political safeguards to prevent the bureaucracy from acting as a "state within the state." Codes of professional conduct, moreover, help the bureaucrats to keep within proper bounds.

Critics of bureaucracy tend to describe the bureaucracy as if it were some hideous unified organization. In fact, bureaucrats are more likely to be at odds with each other than they are with the elected public officials who direct them. Air force, army, and navy contend among themselves for missions and control of a larger share of the defense budget. State universities compete with each other for research funds. Regional and national bureaucracies vie for control over administration of different projects. Bureaucracies, then, are so divided among themselves in a democracy that they permit the political leaders to pick and choose among them and, consequently, provide political direction.

Bureaucracies are not out of control of democratic forces. They are the servants of democracy and not the masters.

22/NO CAN THE BUREAUCRACY BE CONTROLLED IN A DEMOCRACY?

Although democracies claim to have political control of the bureaucracy, in actual fact these controls are generally ineffectual. Bureaucracies are able to circumvent the ostensible controls imposed by: (1) elections; (2) constitutional and political constraints placed by the legislative, executive, and judicial branches; and (3) referendums. Moreover, (4) bureaucratic self-controls often work to impede political controls rather than to enhance them, and (5) the nongovernmental actors that might exercise controls have been kept in check by an increasingly big and powerful government.

Elections. Elections do not have the influence they are supposed to have according to their democratic proponents. In presidential systems the separate election of executive and legislature makes it difficult, if not impossible, to hold a single political group responsible for government action (see Chapter 11). Bureaucracies are, consequently, free to manipulate the two branches of government. In many parliamentary systems political leadership is exercised by an unstable coalition of political parties, and this situation results in enhanced power for the permanent bureaucracy. Even in a stable two-party parliamentary system, such as exists in Great Britain, the ruling leaders are enormously dependent upon the bureaucracy for their expertise and their support.

Constitutional and Political Constraints. Legislative powers to make laws, establish budgets, confirm appointments, conduct investigations, audit government expenditures, and serve as watchdogs over bureaucratic dealings with citizens are inadequate instruments of political control. This was not always the case. In the nineteenth century, legislatures in democracies were powerful, but that was at a time when the tasks of government were less complicated. In the twentieth century, however, Congress and the legislatures of other countries have lost much of their power, and the unelected bureaucracy has assumed many of the powers previously belonging to the legislatures.

Bureaucratic power has risen in part because of the sheer volume of bills that legislators must consider. Even industrious legislators do not have time to read every bill, let alone understand them. So complex are the subjects dealt with by law that legislators have often written legislation in the most general terms and have given discretion to government agencies to act within certain guidelines. The amount of discretion is great, unfortunately. Bureaucrats must themselves interpret legislative mandates. A law directing an agency to act "in the public interest" is a case in point. The concept of public interest is so am-

biguous as to allow agencies great leeway in acting. In making rules, consequently, many of the agencies are in fact legislating. Theoretically, there is a distinction between an administrative ruling and a law; in practice, however, agencies legislate.

The traditional power of legislatures over the budget has been much diminished, too. The influence of the executive branch has been strengthened in the preparation of the budget, and it is difficult for the legislative branch to present an alternative budget. Budget proposals are generally prepared by the bureaucracy itself, which seeks to preserve its prerogatives. The political scientist Aaron Wildavsky observes for the United States that the largest determining factor of the size and content of this year's budget is last year's budget.[8] The system of achieving steady increases in the funding of bureaucracies—or **incrementalism** as it is called—is actually written into the French budgetary process, in which items in the *services votés* are accepted unless there is an explicit challenge and only new items (*measures nouvelles*) are given careful examination.[9] This is to say that bureaucracies generally count on a certain amount of funding from year to year and then they can bargain for more. Legislators' actual influence to alter budgets in any significant manner (except in an upward direction) is minimal, as the record of continually rising government expenditures in democracies suggests in most cases.

In theory, the legislative power of confirmation over political appointments is important in controlling the bureaucracy. In some countries the legislature does not have that power, since the executive decides on appointments. In any event, the bureaucracy can influence the confirmation process in those systems that grant legislatures a formal veto over appointments. One can be sure, for example, that the bureaucracy in the Department of Agriculture would use its political influence to assure that someone friendly to agricultural interests is selected to be secretary of agriculture in the United States. Bureaucracies in other departments would act simi-

[8] Aaron Wildavsky, *The New Politics of the Budgetary Process* (Glenview, Ill.: Scott, Foresman, 1988), pp. 78–79.

[9] B. Guy Peters, *The Politics of Bureaucracy*, 2d ed. (New York: Longman, 1984), p. 214.

larly if confronted with the nomination of potentially unfriendly secretaries.

Legislative investigations are not effective safeguards against bureaucratic power. These investigations often attract public attention through the media, particularly television, but in fact they are limited in the influence they have on bureaucracies. Agencies may make cosmetic changes to get the spotlight of public attention off them for the moment. Soon, however, they are back to their old habits. In the aftermath of the Vietnam War and Watergate, for example, the Central Intelligence Agency (CIA) was subjected to severe scrutiny by congressional investigations. These inquests revealed major wrongdoing, and congressional efforts were successfully made to restrict the powers of the CIA in covert operations abroad and in domestic surveillance. By the early 1980s, however, the CIA was regaining much of its power in these areas. Political controls were not strong enough to keep the CIA in check.

Legislative powers in auditing are after-the-fact determinations, and they have minimal influence on the bureaucracy. Although considerable publicity is generated by close observation of how bureaucracies dispense funds, audits take a long time to complete. Promises to reform are often made when wrongdoing or foolish expenditures are uncovered, but there is no remedying past sins.

Finally, although the ombudsman has been somewhat helpful, such an institution has not been established in every country. Usually, moreover, the ombudsman's success depends upon voluntary compliance by the bureaucracy. The voluntary aspect leaves many areas of bureaucratic wrongdoing beyond the control of elected legislative officials.

The executive is even less influential in dealing with the bureaucracy than is the legislature. The powers of directing overall policy, influencing legislation, and making political appointments are not strong enough to budge the entrenched bureaucracy.

In directing overall policy, the head of government is often at a greater disadvantage than is the legislature. At least many members of the legislature are in office for long periods of time and consequently develop an expertise in particular areas of public policy that are of interest to them and their constituencies. Often, however, the head of government is not in power for a long period of time and does not possess the specialized knowledge necessary to master the intricate details in which the bureaucracy revels.

The bureaucracy can insulate itself from executive controls in many ways. It possesses information that it can release or withhold as it deems necessary to strengthen its political position. It can, moreover, call on interest groups in the private sector to rally around the government organization when threatened by the executive. When a chief executive decides to close down a military installation as an economy move, for example, the military bureaucracy is assisted by all those interest groups that gain economically from the existence of that military installation. The military bureaucracy carefully cultivates private associations, and its behavior in this regard is not unlike that of other segments of the bureaucracy. Similar dominance is achieved by the welfare bureaucracy, the educational bureaucracy, and other bureaucracies for control in their areas of public policy.

In addition to facing obstacles to directing overall policy, the head of government has difficulty in getting his or her legislation adopted. Much of the legislation is written by the bureaucracy itself, and it is no wonder that bureaucrats have a vested interest in maintaining their power and privileges.

The executive's power to make appointments is limited in controlling the bureaucracy. If the executive chooses someone hostile to the department he or she is to administer, the candidate may find it difficult either to be confirmed by the legislature or, if confirmed, to actually rule the department. Informal patterns of power are maintained by the bureaucracy with the legislature. Bureaucrats, moreover, can make the head of a government agency look bad and undermine the political base of support. A new reform police chief, for example, may find that too vigorous application of new rules leads to opposition by the rank-and-file members of the police department. The police have been able to undermine the political leadership through strict enforcement of the traffic laws, for example, leading to public frustration with the police chief.

Even efforts to increase the staff of the executive have not proven successful. The executive staff, often numbering in the hundreds and in some cases the low thousands, is no match for the bureaucracy in the government agencies. The staff lacks the numbers, expertise, and influence to challenge the entrenched bureaucracy.

The judicial power to control the bureaucracy is limited both as a practical matter and because of new developments within the bureaucracy. As a practical matter, the ordinary citizen does not possess the resources to challenge bureaucrats. It takes time and money to prove that a driver was not speeding, as a police official charges. It is much easier to pay the ticket. The old adage, "You can't fight City Hall," suggests the frustration that the ordinary citizen faces when dealing with the city bureaucracy.

Yet another limitation of the judiciary is the establishment of administrative tribunals. Although higher courts are often permitted to review decisions of an administrative tribunal, in practice the courts have often preferred to let the administrative rulings stand. Courts lack the necessary expertise to deal with the technical problems examined by specialized administrative tribunals. To the extent that bureaucracies can adjudicate conflicts, they retain the judicial function within their own power.

Referendums. Although referendums are sometimes used in efforts to influence bureaucratic behavior, they are not generally successful in achieving those results. The referendum is not a legal device in many political systems. It is sometimes used in a nonbinding manner nationally, although it is employed in a binding manner regionally and locally. Even in those instances when it is used, the referendum can be managed to suit the needs of the bureaucracy.

One way of circumventing the will of the people through a referendum is through the phrasing of a referendum question. A question may be asked in such an obscure way that wrangling will continue for years after the results are in. The scheduling of a referendum, moreover, can affect the outcome. A referendum can be made part of the general election, which will produce a large turnout of voters. Or a referendum can be conducted at vacation time when perhaps only a small percentage of the voters—those most organized by the bureaucracies—will turn out. The notion that referendums provide a popular check on the bureaucracy, then, is false.

Self-Control. It is certainly true that the overwhelming majority of bureaucrats are hardworking and honest. Many maintain strong professional standards in their work. We should not, however, confuse commitment to professionalism with political controls. For example, military officers who are committed to the professional standards of their services often act in ways to strengthen the military services rather than subject themselves and their military organization to political control. Self-control in this fashion is the very opposite of democratic control.

Interest Groups, the Media, and Political Parties. Neither interest groups, nor the media, nor political parties provide the necessary controls of the bureaucracy. In every industrial democratic country in the world, government has come to play a prominent role in the management of the economy. In some countries entire industries previously held in private hands are now dominated by the government. Government controls now extend in varying degrees of power to prices, wages, credit, and employment. Government subsidies to private businesses assure many a quiescent and supportive business interest group. In defense industries, in particular, government military managers direct the "private" industries.

Interest group subordination to government is not the case for economic associations alone; it also applies to other private associations. Government involvement in social equality, consumer protection, and welfare has also made "private" associations subservient to the dictates of the bureaucracy.

The media have been as ineffective as interest groups in moving the bureaucracy. Media interest is sporadic. The media do not have the resources to investigate the bureaucracy thoroughly. In some areas, particularly national security, bureaucrats are forbidden by law from passing along "classified" information to the media. In some democracies, moreover, government either owns, controls, or dominates the electronic media, particularly television.

It is true that **whistleblowers** (government employees who reveal wrongdoing by government organizations) do give information to the media about government wrongdoing. The media then provide the information to the general public. Often, however, the whistleblower whistles his or her career away, as fellow workers in the agency look on him or her as a traitor. Few whistleblowers are successful in moving up the career ladder in the government agencies for which they work.

Political parties, too, cease to have much influence—at least not the influence they once had. In the United States political parties are weak (see Chapter 8). A substantial amount of political patronage is no longer in the hands of political parties but has been transferred to civil service commissions. In nearly every Western democratic country, the civil service performs functions, such as providing jobs and dispensing social services, that were previously handled by political parties.

The bureaucracy, then, has appeared in democratic countries and has grown in power. In the United States, for example, the administration of government is scarcely noted in the Constitution. Yet the bureaucracy has risen here as elsewhere. Bureaucratic power has expanded throughout the world to a point beyond the mere carrying out of the laws. It has moved into executive, legislative, and judicial areas previously held by others. It has consequently made a mockery of democracy. In this regard, it is well to recall the warning of James Madison in the *Federalist Papers*: "The accumulation of all powers legislative, executive, and judiciary in the same hands . . . may justly be pronounced the very definition of tyranny."[10] The bureaucrats in "democracy," then, have achieved what Madison and others of his time feared: the concentration of power. Having concentrated their power, they put to disbelief the notion that the people in a democracy actually rule.

[10] James Madison, *Federalist*, no. 47, in Alexander Hamilton, James Madison, and John Jay, *The Federalist Papers*, ed. Clinton Rossiter (New York: New American Library, 1961), p. 301.

KEY TERMS

Administration
Bureaucracy
Civil service
Entitlements
Formal organization
Housekeeping agencies
Incrementalism
Informal organization
Line agencies

Monopolies
Oligopolies
Oversight
Parkinson's Law
Service agencies
Spoils system
Staff agencies
Whistleblowers

QUESTIONS

1. How would you assess the accuracy of Parkinson's Law in describing the size of the bureaucracy?
2. How would you compare the behavior of bureaucracy in democracies with its behavior in dictatorships?
3. What are the similarities and the differences between public and private bureaucracy?
4. How would you compare the behavior of the military bureaucracy with nonmilitary bureaucracies in a democracy?
5. Can government spending be cut? If Yes, how? If No, why not?
6. How can bureaucracy be made more accountable in a democracy?

RECOMMENDED READINGS

ABERBACH, JOEL D. *Keeping a Watchful Eye: The Politics of Congressional Oversight.* Washington, D.C.: Brookings Institution, 1990. An examination of the growth of congressional oversight of the federal bureaucracy.

BEETHAM, DAVID. *Bureaucracy.* Minneapolis: University of Minnesota Press, 1987. A brief analysis.

BLAU, PETER M., and MARSHALL W. MEYER. *Bureaucracy in Modern Society* 3d ed. New York:

Random House, 1987. A sociological study of organizations.

BURKE, JOHN P. *Bureaucratic Responsibility.* Baltimore: Johns Hopkins University Press, 1986. A theory of bureaucratic responsibility.

BURNHAM, JAMES. *The Managerial Revolution.* Bloomington: Indiana University Press, 1966. A major work predicting the rise and dominance of a managerial class.

FESLER, JAMES W., and DONALD F. KETTL. *The Politics of the Administrative Process.* Chatham, N.J.: Chatham House, 1991. A discussion of the practical issues and problems of the administrative process.

FRIEDEN, KARL. "Public Needs and Private Wants." *Dissent* 34 (Summer 1987): 317–25. A criticism of the argument that government is inefficient.

FRY, BRIAN R. *Mastering Public Administration: From Max Weber to Dwight Waldo.* Chatham, N.J.: Chatham House Publishers, 1989. The ideas of major scholars in public administration are explained.

GOODSELL, CHARLES T. *The Case for Bureaucracy: A Public Administration Polemic.* 2d ed. Chatham, N.J.: Chatham House, 1985. A defense of bureaucracy in the United States.

GORMLEY, WILLIAM T., JR. *Taming the Bureaucracy: Muscles, Prayers, and Other Strategies.* Princeton, N.J.: Princeton University Press, 1989. Proposals for solving the problems of bureaucracy.

JABBRA, JOSEPH G., and O. P. DWIVEDI, eds. *Public Service Accountability: A Comparative Perspective.* West Hartford, Conn.: Kumarian Press, 1988. A study of public accountability from a comparative perspective.

KAUFMAN, HERBERT. *Are Government Organizations Immortal?* Washington, D.C.: Brookings Institution, 1976. An argument that government organizations are enduring but not immortal.

KINGDOM, J. E. *The Civil Service and Liberal Democracies: An Introductory Survey.* London: Routledge, 1990. An introduction to the bureaucracies of nine countries.

MATEJKO, ALEXANDER J. *The Self-Defeating Organization: A Critique of Bureaucracy.* Westport, Conn.: Praeger, 1986. A plea for alternatives to bureaucracy.

PARKINSON, C. NORTHCOTE. *Parkinson's Law and Other Studies in Administration.* Boston: Houghton Mifflin, 1957. An explanation of bureaucratic expansion based not on societal needs but on the tendency of government agencies to expand.

ROSEN, BERNARD. *Holding Government Bureaucracies Accountable.* 2d ed. New York: Praeger, 1989. An analysis of accountability in the American administrative system.

VON MISES, LUDWIG. *Bureaucracy.* New Haven: Yale University Press, 1944. An indictment of bureaucracy as a form of tyranny.

WEBER, MAX. *From Max Weber: Essays in Sociology,* ed. H. H. Gerth and C. Wright Mills. New York: Oxford University Press, 1946. Chapter 8 contains Weber's classic work on bureaucracy.

WILDAVSKY, AARON. *The New Politics of the Budgetary Process.* Glenview, Ill.: Scott, Foresman, 1988. A comprehensive analysis of the budgetary process in the United States.

WILSON, JAMES Q. *Bureaucracy: What Government Agencies Do and Why They Do It.* New York: Basic Books, 1989. A study of bureaucratic behavior in the United States.

part VI

INTERNATIONAL POLITICS

Politics is the study of the allocation of values. In domestic politics the values may be economic, security, psychological, welfare, or ideological. International politics, which deals primarily with the relations among states, is also the study of the allocation of these values. International politics, however, is different from domestic politics because ordinarily, in the international arena, there is an expectation of violence rather than peace. The conditions essential for peace within a state—effective legal institutions, a constitutional consensus, and an expectation of justice—are lacking in a global context.

In international politics there is a greater anticipation of violence than in domestic politics, as may be seen from the size of military budgets. Despite the astonishing developments in the Soviet Union in the Gorbachev era, the loose commonwealth of states among twelve of the former Soviet republics, and the end of the cold war, the world still spends hundreds of billions of dollars each year for military purposes. Some of this money is used to maintain order at home. The bulk, however, is disbursed to protect the state against foreign enemies. To be sure, there is much intra-state violence in the world, as the conflicts between Catholics and Protestants in Northern Ireland, Sikhs and Hindus in India, and Azerbaijanis and Armenians in Azerbaijan demonstrate.

Fear of violence, then, sets the stage for international politics in a way that it generally does not in domestic politics. Another difference between the two types of political activity involves legal institutions. Politics within a state operates frequently within a context of effective national legal institutions. Executive, legislative, and judicial powers are spelled out in the state's constitutional documents. When a violation of the law occurs, as in the case of a mugging, a witness may call the police, who, in turn, try to protect or assist the victim and apprehend the assailant for subsequent trial. The legal institutions at the international level, however, are not powerful. International institutions, such as the General Assembly of the United Nations and the International Court of Justice (ICJ), depend upon the voluntary cooperation of the states. It is literally possible for states to get away with international murder because there is no effective international police force that possesses greater power than the military forces of the states.

A reason for the absence of such international legal institutions is that constitutional consensus is more likely to characterize the communities that constitute a state than the international political system. Although states that contain diverse and conflicting ethnic and economic divisions sometimes suffer from political instability, often they do not.

A consensus is often achieved domestically rather than internationally because people expect justice from the government and are willing to abide by its laws and policies. In the domestic context, people often respect laws that they oppose because they feel that, overall, the system is just. A similar feeling toward international institutions is usually absent or weak.

Because of these considerations dealing with violence, legal institutions, constitutional consensus, and justice, self-preservation or security becomes an important goal. The study of international politics, consequently, is dominated by the quest for security, although other factors play important roles in motivating states' behavior.

Chapter 13 discusses the participants in international relations, with a focus on states. It deals with the factors motivating states in their relations with other countries. An issue involving aid to poor countries is then considered.

Chapter 14 discusses power in world politics and the methods that states use in their relations with other states. Issues of the role of the United States in world politics, the effectiveness of economic sanctions, and the possibility of disarmament are considered.

chapter 13

International politics: motivations

Consider some of the major news stories in the 1980s and early 1990s:

- Iraq invades its neighboring country, Kuwait, making it a province of Iraq.
- Middle East rivals, most notably Israelis, Syrians, and Palestinians, begin peace negotiations seeking to resolve long-standing disputes involving territory and power.
- More countries than ever, most notably Iraq, Iran, Libya, Pakistan, North Korea, are seeking to acquire weapons of mass destruction, including nuclear, chemical, and biological weapons.
- Attempts by countries to reduce tariff barriers and other impediments to trade encounter domestic criticism.
- United Nations (U.N.) representatives successfully arrange for the release of Western hostages, long held captive in Lebanon.

Matters such as these that affect people of diverse locations across national or continental lines are often described as world politics. As the news stories indicate, world politics may involve war and peace, per-

sonal security, and economic well-being. When the cold war came to an end, countries as distant as Cuba and Syria had to adjust their policies toward other countries. When Iraq invaded Kuwait, not only neighboring countries but Western countries, too, were afraid that the conquest was the first stage in an attempt by Iraq's leader Saddam Hussein to control the oil fields of the entire Middle East. As support for protectionism increased in some quarters, those in other quarters began to fear that trade wars would result.

In this chapter we will study the actors who are engaged in world politics and why the principal actors behave the way they do.

THE ACTORS

Who They Are

States are the primary actors in world politics. The features of a state—people, territory, government, and sovereignty—

are described in Chapter 1. The world is composed of more than 185 states varying in power, objectives, and culture. Military power, for the most part, is dominated by the state. The state collects taxes to finance armies and organizes the defense of the political community.

The state is not the only actor in the global arena, however. Groups and international organizations are other actors in that arena, and they are playing a more important role in this century than they did in the last. Among groups affecting world politics, economic, religious, subnational or ethnic, and professional organizations play the most important roles.

In the twentieth century one of the prominent economic groups is the *multinational corporation* (MNC), which is defined in Chapter 2 as a large enterprise with offices and/or branches in numerous countries conducting business operations across state lines. Examples are International Telephone and Telegraph (ITT), International Business Machines (IBM), and Shell Oil Company. More than a century ago, Karl Marx noted the increasing interdependency of the global economy brought on by the rise of industrialism in the West. The twentieth-century form of that interdependency is sometimes seen in such MNCs.

Religious groups are also prominent global actors. When the pope speaks on matters of faith or politics, Catholics all over the world are interested in what he says. At times the interests of the Catholic church and the interests of the political leaders who govern Catholic countries conflict, as Poland in its years of communist rule attests. Other religious groups—Jews, Muslims, and Protestants, for example—also play important roles in global politics.

Subnational or ethnic associations are also actors. As Chapter 2 indicates, the populace in many states includes people of diverse ethnic backgrounds. Some ethnic groups challenge the validity of specific borders and organize paramilitary units that fight for an independent state. The Palestine Liberation Organization (PLO) is

a notable example. It seeks to establish a Palestinian homeland in the Middle East and engages in military and diplomatic efforts to achieve its objectives. It is recognized by many states although it is not a state. The PLO is one of many subnational actors. Other organizations seeking independence for Puerto Rico and Kurdistan have also achieved some notoriety.

Professional associations often reflect professional interests that transcend national barriers. International associations concerned with psychology or medicine, for example, have asserted the need to promote professional standards when those standards were in jeopardy in various places around the world. The effectiveness of these organizations varies from group to group, however, but they are not without influence.

International organizations are also actors in the global arena. There are different types of these organizations: general international organizations, regional organizations, functional agencies, and alliances.

General international organizations involve nearly all the countries of the world and deal with a variety of international problems. In this century the League of Nations and the United Nations are examples of general international organizations.

Regional organizations are international organizations that are concerned with a specific geographic region. The Organization of American States (OAS), whose members come from the Western hemisphere, is a regional organization concerned with hemispheric problems. The Arab League is another example of a regional organization.

Functional agencies are international organizations concerned with specific social, agricultural, or health policy. The World Health Organization (WHO), which deals with problems of health such as the eradication of smallpox and cholera, is a prominent example. The Food and Agricultural Organization (FAO) and the United Nations Educational, Scientific, and

Cultural Organization (UNESCO) are others.

Alliances are organizations of common defense among nations. The North Atlantic Treaty Organization (NATO), which is today composed of the United States and fifteen other countries, was established in 1949 for the purpose of mutual defense primarily against the Soviet Union. The Warsaw Pact, which was dissolved in 1991, consisted of the Soviet Union and six Eastern European allies. It was set up in 1955 as a counter to the inclusion of the Federal Republic of Germany in the NATO alliance.

The Declining Significance of the State?

Some writers argue that the state is declining in significance (see Chapter 2). They point to military, economic, and environmental factors as evidence.

The state was founded in part to provide for greater military security, which more local institutions could not furnish in the face of technological developments in weaponry. In the age of intercontinental ballistic missiles and nuclear weapons the state can no longer assure security because there is no defense against nuclear weapons at the present level of technology.

Economic security was another reason for the creation of the state. The world, however, has become interdependent. Decisions made in a country may affect economies of different countries. New actors, such as MNCs, have come to dominate states in economic matters. The annual income of Exxon, for example, is higher than the annual income of most countries in the world.

Environmental problems, such as water pollution, air pollution, and the decline of rain forests, are increasingly perceived as global problems requiring global solutions. For example, the people living in a state may pollute its waterways. Often, however, the pollution cannot be confined to that state but affects other states as well.

The view that states are declining is challenged. Some writers contend that the state is still the major provider of security, economic well-being, and environmental protection. Although there are problems that have transcended state boundaries, these writers say, the state has been able to solve them without relinquishing its authority.

Even most writers who see the state in decline do not regard it as extinct—like the dinosaur. Because of its preeminence, we shall focus our attention on the state in this and the next chapter. Here we shall concern ourselves with the factors motivating state behavior.

WHY DO STATES BEHAVE THE WAY THEY DO?

A psychiatrist may spend many hours, days, and months with a patient to piece together an explanation of why the patient behaves the way he or she does. Social scientists devote much more time analyzing state behavior. Because there are so many actors involved in international politics and because the historical record is always limited, the problems for social science investigation are enormous.

A variety of theories have been put forward to explain why states behave the way they do. Experts on **geopolitics**, for example, try to explain international behavior in terms of geographical relationships. Marxists have found economics to be the single motivating factor.

It is not the purpose here to analyze the validity of these or other one-cause theories. Instead, a variety of plausible explanations of state behavior are presented, including security, economics, nationalism, ideology, military considerations, prestige, and psychology.

Security

Security is one of the most important factors in explaining state behavior, as we have seen from our discussion about the difference between international politics and domestic politics. **Security** in the international context may be defined as a feeling that the territorial integrity, ruling government, or way of life of a country is safe from destruction by outsiders.

Many states live in fear of their neighbors and even of distant powers. Military forces watch warily on each side of the borders between Israel and Syria. The potential ability of countries such as Libya, Iraq, and Iran to produce weapons of mass destruction is a matter of concern not only to their neighbors but also to countries located thousands of miles away.

The fact that there is so much armament along borders and facing distant rivals should not suggest that insecurity always characterizes the relations of states. The boundary line between the United States and Canada, for example, is the largest unguarded border in the world. France and Germany, which for many generations viewed each other as a military threat, no longer think of each other in that way. Mexico and the United States still have differences, but the United States–Mexican border is marked by customs and immigration officers rather than brigades of armed forces. The feeling of security, then, varies from country to country and from period to period. It remains, however, one of the most important factors influencing the behavior of states.

Economics

Economic factors—some related to security and others not—motivate state behavior. A country may need water resources that are blocked by an adversary and take military measures to achieve access to those resources. Such an action may be considered, in part at least, as economic, since the entire economy would suffer from a loss of such a fundamental need as water. A country, too, may go to war to enhance its control over mineral wealth in some disputed territory, or to assure sources of raw materials, or to guarantee markets.

Often economic causes are associated with private groups concerned with their own well-being. In the nineteenth century, for example, economic adventurers sought the support of their governments in overseas investments. The history of U.S. intervention in Latin America and European interference in Africa and Asia reveals much about the connection between private investors and imperialism, although debate persists on which were dominant— the political institutions or the private corporations. In our contemporary period, similar theories have been put forward to explain the foreign policy of Western nations in general and the United States in particular. It was charged, for example, that the reason the United States went to war with Iraq in 1991 was because it feared that the price of oil would rise if Iraq's expansion into Kuwait went unchecked.

Nationalism

Nationalism is described in Chapter 2 as an ideology in which a people regardless of their race, class, or religion feel that they have more in common with each other than they do with other people and give their highest loyalty to a state or part of a state that may eventually become a separate state. Nationalism has been a factor in the enlargement of states, the contraction of states, and in the manipulations of big powers.[1]

Ideology

Nationalism is but one of many ideologies that have international significance. Liberalism, fascism, and communism are three principal ideologies with international ramifications.

Liberalism is a political philosophy that

---

[1] See Chapter 2 for a discussion of the impact of nationalism.

emphasizes individual liberty (see Chapter 4). In the twentieth century particularly, some political leaders—Woodrow Wilson and Jimmy Carter most notably—asserted the promotion of human rights as a foreign policy goal.[2].

Fascism, too, has its appeal. The alliance of fascist nations—Germany, Italy, and Japan—in World War II may be explained by ideological similarities, although other factors were involved.

Communism as an ideology, though today a spent force, used to be a factor in state behavior. For decades, a major political problem of students concerned with analyzing the political behavior of the Soviet Union was to determine to what extent Soviet foreign policy was dictated by the ideology of Marxism-Leninism and to what extent it was motivated by security interests. Some students contended that ideological considerations could be seen in the importance of communist doctrine to the Soviet political leadership. Others, however, argued that the doctrine was just a cloak for the security interests of the country.

Military Considerations

Military considerations have taken many forms. In the nineteenth century, for example, American naval leaders argued for the necessity of establishing overseas political control so that naval coaling stations could be assured to American naval vessels. With the advent of the *cold war* (that period immediately following World War II in which the Soviet Union and the United States had intense confrontations, mostly in nonmilitary matters), American military leaders called for the leasing of overseas military air force bases to assure American air superiority over the Soviet Union.

Students of World War I, moreover, have pointed to the way in which purely

[2]The issue of human rights and foreign policy is discussed in Issue 10.

military plans could influence political considerations. Conversations between British and French military authorities in the decade prior to the war linked their two countries in a way that made it likely that they would be allies in a war against Germany.

Another example of the impact of military plans on political decision making was the Schlieffen Plan, a German plan developed at the beginning of the twentieth century to defeat France in case of a war on two fronts. It involved invading France through neutral Belgium and, when implemented in 1914, assured that the war would involve those countries, such as England, that had given their pledge to support Belgian neutrality.

Prestige

Prestige is a country's reputation for power. Often, in international politics, states behave in certain ways because they wish to maintain their reputation for power. As a result of agreements entered into by the Allied Powers in World War II, for example, those powers were assured access to Berlin, which was located hundreds of miles inside the Soviet-dominated sector of Germany. The United States and its allies had to fend off many attempts by the Soviet Union and its allies to place all Berlin under communist control. At each point, however, the West resisted. An airlift in 1948 shipped food and supplies to the people of Berlin after Soviet officials had closed off ground transit, and the Soviets soon determined to end the surface blockade. In the 1950s and 1960s, moreover, American presidents responded with a show of military strength when they felt that Berlin was being threatened by the Soviet Union.

Political actions of this kind constitute one example of the role of prestige in foreign policy, but there are many others. The program announced by President John F. Kennedy in 1961 to put a man on the moon before the decade was out was an attempt to show that the reputation of the United States for technological leadership could be assured. In some respects the possession of nuclear weapons by an increasing number of nations is regarded by the newcomers to nuclear weapons as a symbol of prestige.

Psychology

Psychological factors play a role in explaining the behavior of states, although these are difficult to document. The term *state behavior* is, in truth, an abstraction. What is meant, really, is that the leaders of a state act in the name of a state. If the leaders are mad or incapable of perceiving accurately the correct condition of international political affairs, then clearly the fact that these individuals controlled the levels

of power at the time may be understood, at least in part, by psychological explanations. Can the foreign policy of Adolf Hitler be studied without making an attempt to understand the psychology of this one person, particularly his personal craving for power? There is no easy Yes or No answer to this question, but there is evidence that a psychological explanation is plausible.

Psychological factors play a role in group behavior. At times, some groups are ready to go to war and at other times they wish to remain at peace. Mass hysteria has been blamed for some kinds of international political behavior.

All the above factors, then, can be motivating factors behind foreign policy.

ISSUE

The great disparity in income between advanced industrial countries in the West and many impoverished countries in the Third World—the developing states of Africa, Asia, and Latin America—has given economic development a prominent position on the global agenda. The debate below considers whether the West should redistribute its wealth to the Third World to narrow the economic gap.

23/YES   SHOULD THE WEST REDISTRIBUTE ITS WEALTH TO THIRD WORLD COUNTRIES?

For more than half the people of the world, poverty is a way of life. Their poverty is a *permanent condition* in which the fundamental minimums of food, clothing, and shelter are not assured. The horrors of mass starvation, disease, and malnutrition are brought to the world's attention from television's reporting of such disasters as the drought that decimated sub-Saharan Africa in the 1970s and 1980s. The case of Ethiopia in 1984 and 1985 is perhaps the most grim example of the death produced by economic deprivation. The everyday misery of the poor in Third World countries, however, is often unnoticed except by the statisticians who record economic indices, the relief agencies that work to alleviate it, and the wretched masses who are its victims.

What many affluent people in the West take

for granted—balanced diet, decent homes, automobiles, jobs, and education—is not available to the vast majority of the world's population. The poor now demand attention, however. A **revolution of rising expectations** (in which people no longer expect a condition of poverty to be a permanent fixture of life but anticipate steady improvement in the quality of their lives) is taking hold in Third World countries. That revolution is shattering traditional institutions and even world order and is the central concern of Third World political leaders.

To understand the wide gaps between the rich and poor countries of the world, it is essential to compare the industrialized and nonindustrialized states. For the most part the rich countries of the world are racially white, while the poor are nonwhite. The rich consist of the advanced industrialized countries of the world. Since most of these countries are located in the northern latitudes—North America and Europe—they are often referred to as the **North**. The poor include the countries that have not made advances in industrialization. Since most of these countries are located in the southern latitudes—Latin America, Africa, and Asia— they are often referred to as the **South**. **North-South problems**, then, usually refer to the economic ties between the **haves** and **have-nots** (the wealthy countries and the poor).

Countries with a **gross national product** (GNP, the sum of goods and services produced by a nation in a year) of $4,300 or more per capita are often described as **developed. Developing countries** (or **less-developed countries**) are states with less than $4,300 per capita income that are seeking economic growth.[3]

The stark fact of poverty is there for all to see. The statistics, however, do not tell the story of the enormous problems facing developing countries in their quest for economic self-sufficiency. Their economic problems are often caused by high population growth, low per capita income, malnutrition, a weak ability to form capital for investment, poor health standards, illiteracy, dependence on agriculture, and cultural traditions that are hostile to economic development.

Because of the great disparity between the North and the South, the world's attention has been drawn to the necessity of raising the living standards of the South's impoverished population. A most noteworthy effort at popularizing the problem was the declaration on the establishment of a New International Economic Order (NIEO), which was adopted in May 1974 at the Sixth Special Session of the United Nations General Assembly. In that declaration a plea was made for the rich countries of the world to share their wealth with the developing countries.

Such a policy can only be beneficial to ending poverty in the Third World. Redistribution is not only essential as a matter of simple justice, but it is also owed to the Third World by the West because: (1) Western exploitation is historically responsible for Third World poverty; and (2)

Western economic ties with the Third World today continue to be exploitive.

Western Exploitation. The poverty of Third World countries is owing to Western exploitation. Although *imperialism*, which has been defined as the expansion of one country into another, existed long before the rise of the West, its dynamic modern record stems from nineteenth-century penetration by the West into Latin America, Asia, and Africa. Great Britain, France, the United States, Holland, Belgium, and Germany were the principal exploiters, and these countries, too, were the most developed as far as capitalism and industrialism were concerned. Other Western countries, such as Spain, Portugal, and Italy, also built up their existing colonies or opened up new areas of the world hitherto sheltered from Western "civilization."

The historical record of imperialism is one of political, social, and economic exploitation. Politically, the colonial masters often ruled without adequately preparing an infrastructure of local administrators and political leaders. The case of Mozambique under Portuguese rule is a notorious example. Socially, many colonialists looked down on their charges as inferior people. Racial discrimination was often the result of such an attitude.

In many cases economic exploitation had the greatest impact on the economies of both the advanced and underdeveloped areas of the world. The English liberal J. A. Hobson and the noted communist V. I. Lenin both argued that Western imperialism came about primarily from capitalist exploitation.[4] These and other writers revealed how the Western capitalists used colonies to acquire cheap raw materials and new markets for their goods. Because of such exploitation, the West achieved its economic ascendancy.

Rather than considering the needs of the peoples of Africa, Asia, and Latin America, the colonial masters distorted the Third World economies to serve Western interests. The principal instrument of that distortion was to make one or two primary products the essential element in each colony's economy. **Primary products** are crops, minerals, and fuels that are essentially taken from the earth with little pro-

---

[3] The figure of $4,300 is used by the World Bank to indicate the maximum per capita income a country may have (in 1990 dollars) beyond which the World Bank will no longer lend it money.

[4] J. A. Hobson, *Imperialism* (London: Allen and Unwin, 1938); V. I. Lenin, *Imperialism* (New York: International Publishers, 1939). Lenin's *Imperialism* was first published in 1916.

cessing involved. One-product economies—such as cocoa in the Gold Coast (now Ghana), rubber in Malaya, tin in Bolivia, and copper in Chile—became the economic norm for the Third World. The market for these products was in the West rather than in the Third World. The price of the commodity, consequently, was dependent upon what the West would pay, and that amount was low. Third World countries did not have the economic leverage to develop their own economies for their own needs. Not only were prices of primary products kept low, but these prices were subject to wildly fluctuating market conditions. Even after developing countries achieved their independence, they could not engage in making sound long-term plans because of such fluctuations.

Perpetuating Poverty. Imperialism has really not come to an end, although technically political rule has been transferred to local leaders. Economic dependency has been retained in the form of capital acquisition, commodity prices, and foreign aid.

With political independence, the new nations faced many of the economic problems that the West had solved at an earlier period. In order to create wealth the Third World had to increase productivity. Capital was essential to bring about this improved productivity. Much of that capital, however, was and is in private hands—in banks and big corporations. These capitalist institutions only invest in Third World countries if they are assured of enormous profits. Western capitalists, moreover, restrict credit for those economic activities that might interfere with the Western economies, and they also seek a fast and high return on investment.

Third World countries are no match for the power of these economic giants—multinational corporations with global interests. The revenues of General Motors alone exceed the gross national product of each of more than one hundred countries. The effect of such an imbalance is detrimental to the Third World. In the words of two leading scholars of multinationals, "The development track pursued by the global corporation in those years [the 1960s] contributed more to exacerbation of world poverty, world unemployment, and world inequality than to their solution."[5]

[5] Richard J. Barnet and Ronald E. Müller, *Global Reach: The Power of Multinational Corporations* (New York: Simon and Schuster, 1974), p. 151.

One mechanism of Western exploitation remains the control of prices of primary products. If these prices get too high, then Western consumers can switch to substitutes—tea for coffee, for example. In most cases, Third World countries have not been successful in forming **cartels** (organizations that can control the price and quantity of a product) to obtain high prices for their products.

The Organization of Petroleum Exporting Countries (OPEC) was the exception to the rule. In 1973, the price of oil began to rise as OPEC successfully wrested control of the oil price from the big private oil companies. In a period of several years the price of oil increased tenfold. Oil was, however, unique in not being able to be substituted. Cartels of other primary products, consequently, would not have the same leverage as OPEC. Even OPEC began to decline in influence in the 1980s, as conservation, increased exploration for energy resources, alternative energy sources, differences among OPEC members, and economic recession combined to push the world market price of oil down. By 1986, OPEC was regarded as a moribund organization, no longer able to determine the production levels and price of oil. By early 1992, it remained ineffective in setting world oil prices.

Foreign aid is another device of Western imperialism because of the way it is dispensed. Instead of considering aid as a moral obligation of the advanced industrial states resulting from the colonial legacy of oppression, the former colonial powers regard it either as charity or as a means for further exploitation. The advanced countries should follow the recommendation of the United Nations and apply a standard of 0.7 percent of national income for economic aid to the less-developed countries. None of the major industrial countries, however, has met this standard. The industrialized countries of North America, Western Europe, and Japan provide only 0.35 percent of GNP for aid—about half the recommended amount.

Aid is given in two forms: military and economic. Since the end of World War II, Western countries have armed the Third World to the detriment of the latter. The new countries have become dependent upon the West for their military security. Scarce resources that should be used for economic development, moreover, are now diverted to military purposes, thus slowing down the pace of economic development. Since the revolution in military technology consists of producing newer weapons that make the old weapons outmoded quickly, Third World countries find their expenses related to military aid constantly rising. Their dependence on the West thus becomes ever greater.

Economic aid is also designed to help the West. Domestic producers of farm products, for example, benefit when the West ships wheat and corn to Third World countries. Furthermore, aid is given only to projects that will not result in competition with Western industrialists.

Because of its bad historical record and its present exploitive actions, the West owes a debt to the Third World. Without the wealth derived from the exploitation of the nonwhite peoples of the world, the West would be poor today. Redistribution of income, according to the spirit of the New International Economic Order, is a proper way to compensate for past injustice and to promote equality among the peoples of the world.

23/NO SHOULD THE WEST REDISTRIBUTE ITS WEALTH TO THIRD WORLD COUNTRIES?

There is no gainsaying the fact that there is appalling poverty in Third World countries. Poverty is an evil, since most of us agree that "something should be done" to provide at least the necessities of life. What that "something" is, however, is the central issue. The *Affirmative* avoids considering the complexities of North-South relationships in its prescription of a New International Economic Order.

An analysis of North-South relationships must deal with two points: the character of the Third World and the method that should be used to eliminate poverty. On the first point, the Third World is not monolithic. Some of its countries have small populations and are rich; Kuwait and Saudi Arabia, with their immense oil resources, are cases in point. Others are large and poor: China and India, for example. Some countries are so poor that they have even been described as consisting of a special category—the **Fourth World**—in which the economic plight is almost without hope of salvation. Within Third World countries, moreover, there are rich people and poor, merchants and factory workers, aborigines and Western-educated professionals, and sheiks and peasants. To treat the Third World as a single entity, then, is to ignore an important fact necessary for analysis.

On the second point—the method used to eliminate poverty—we should stress that even if we recognize the problem, we need not agree on the solution. Transferring wealth from one group to another may lead to a waste of resources. Government programs that have been designed to transfer wealth from the affluent to the poor in the West have often been unsuccessful in achieving their objective of eliminating poverty.

Having made these initial comments, we can now present our case against the NIEO. The main points here are: (1) the West is not responsible for Third World poverty; and (2) it is not exploiting Third World countries today.

Western Exploitation. Western liberals take keen satisfaction in blaming Third World poverty on the dynamics of Western capitalism. In this appraisal, they are wrong. It is "do-gooders" who are guilty of inaccurate historical analysis. The West is not responsible for Third World economic decay but rather for its political, social, and economic progress.

Imperialism was not a necessary consequence of capitalism, as Leninists and some liberals would have us believe. Some of the most prosperous capitalist countries—Sweden and Switzerland—never acquired colonies during the nineteenth-century scramble. Portugal, which possessed a large empire, remains one of the poorest countries of Western Europe. Capitalists, moreover, often resisted the imperial ventures of political leaders.[6]

Politically, Western intervention often brought an end to tribal wars that had been going on for centuries. Colonial powers sought to maintain law and order in the territories under their control and, consequently, brought peace and stability instead of war and disorder. In some cases, moreover, they did establish an infrastructure of local government. The British, particularly, created local institutions of self-government and prepared the way for independence.

In social matters the racism of Western imperialists certainly was prevalent. It would be wrong

[6]See Raymond Aron, "The Leninist Myth of Imperialism," in his *The Century of Total War* (Boston: Beacon Press, 1954), chap. 3.

to conclude, however, that the West introduced racism to the Third World. Racial antagonism was endemic in many areas of the Third World long before nineteenth-century imperialism. Colonial governments often protected racial minorities. The fact that ethnic Chinese in Southeast Asia and Asians in East Africa have suffered discrimination in the past three decades is a reminder of the precolonial roots of racism.

Economically, the West brought more prosperity to the peoples of the Third World than they had experienced in the preceding centuries. The West had to establish an infrastructure—railroads, ports, highways, communication links—since these were prerequisites for industrial development. Karl Marx himself commented favorably on imperialism when he noted that Western imperialists were replacing feudalism with capitalism. Until the West took over, much of the Third World experienced grim poverty. The West brought science and technology, increased prosperity, eliminated endemic diseases, and often extended life expectancy.

Many of the people who criticize Western imperialism have a Leninist orientation on the world. They perceive capitalism as exploitation in any context, and especially in an imperial situation. They regard any profit as theft. The capitalists who invested in the Third World, however, often did so at great risk to their lives and capital. They created entire new industries. It is certainly true that they often built an economy based on a single product and that world market prices fluctuated. Had it not been for the West, however, these colonies would not have had a market to develop.[7] Western interests brought rubber to Malaya and tea to India. These products were not produced by those countries before the arrival of Westerners.

The charge that Western imperialism is responsible for Third World poverty can easily be dismissed when we note that those countries that were least linked to the West are among the poorest in the world. Some of the most economically underdeveloped countries, moreover, were never colonies (Afghanistan, Tibet, and Liberia). As the economist P. T. Bauer notes, the areas of the Third World in which the West made the most extensive contacts with the Third World are the most prosperous: "the cash-crop–producing areas and *entrepot* ports of Southeast Asia, West

Africa, and Latin America; the mineral-producing areas of Africa and the Middle East; and the cities and ports throughout Asia, Africa, the Caribbean, and Latin America."[8]

We cannot blame the West for Third World poverty, then, since without Western intervention poverty would be worse. To say that the colonies were essential for Western prosperity, moreover, is to ignore the fact that the West had achieved self-sustaining growth *before* it embarked on its major imperial adventures in the late nineteenth century.

Perpetuating Poverty. The West has an interest in making Third World countries politically stable and economically strong. It is a Marxist myth that economic relations constitute a **zero-sum game**, in which any gain from one player is automatically a loss for the other. Had American capitalists sought to maximize their economic advantages over war-torn Europe after World War II, they would never have supported a Marshall Plan (named after United States Secretary of State George C. Marshall) that rebuilt the European economies. As the Western European economies revived, they provided a market for American products. Today as in the past, trade ties are strongest among highly industrialized countries rather than between industrial countries and poor countries. The people of Bangladesh, one of the poorest countries in the world, cannot afford to purchase computers from the United States, but the people of Germany can.

Western countries are currently helping Third World countries on the path to development. The new states of the world benefit from Western private and government assistance. The multinational corporations that invest capital in Third World countries are engines of development and not instruments of exploitation. They tie the global economy together in a more meaningful way. Of course, they are only going to invest capital if they can be certain to make profits.

In engaging in their own business ventures, the multinationals risk their capital. The risk of investing in Third World countries is high because of wars, political instability, and potential nationalization of property. The multinationals must, then, seek high profits. Nevertheless, even with high profits, they bring new technology to the new countries; employ thousands of local personnel; stimulate the business of small, local

[7]P. T. Bauer, "Western Aid and Third World Poverty," *Commentary* 61 (January 1976): 32

[8]Ibid.

economic interests; and spread prosperity. Often, moreover, they set examples for local business interests to follow in labor-management relations. Those countries that have permitted Western capitalists to develop their economies have done rather well. South Korea and Taiwan, for example, have had two of the highest growth rates in the world, and both have opened themselves to capitalist investment.

The notion that countries that have great dependence upon a single product must be constantly in a servile condition and impoverished is certainly not true. The non-Western world, it should be remembered, is not the only place that produces primary products. Developed countries, too, are major primary-producers, and they benefit from high prices for their commodities. In the 1970s, there was a major increase in the world market price of many primary products— silver, copper, gold, and coffee, for example— and the price rise aided producers in both advanced and developing countries. Third World countries, however, have been wise to diversify their economies so that they will be less susceptible to wide fluctuations in world market prices.

Foreign aid, too, has been offered to help Third World countries. Military aid is designed not to make Third World countries dependent upon the West but rather to allow them to satisfy their legitimate security objectives. The fact that the costs of the new military technology are spiraling is a characteristic of the new technology that affects not only the Third World but developed countries as well.

International aid to Third World countries has had successes and failures. That aid, overall, has not been beneficial to Third World countries. Graham Hancock has observed that aid is often dangerous to the poor and inimical to their interests. Moreover, it has damaged the environment and ruined lives, supported and legitimized brutal tyrannies, facilitated the emergence of large and incompetent bureaucracies, sapped the initiative of ordinary people, turned potential entrepreneurs and intellectuals in the developing countries to engaging in nonproductive administrative activities, created a moral tone that avoids the difficult task of wealth creation, and encouraged government officials to suppress popular choice and individual freedom.[9] The lessons of aid suggest that a major redistribution of wealth from the West to the Third World would be economically disastrous to Third World economies themselves.

The aid that has been forthcoming by the West has been generous indeed. Restrictions imposed by the West to assure that the aid will be used for the purposes to which it has been designated, rather than "without strings," have been called exploitation. Anti-West critics prefer the disbursement of aid through international organizations that would exercise only weak and ineffectual controls. The record of foreign aid shows that any new international economic order could only be harmful to the people whom it is intended to benefit.

We should rid ourselves, then, of both the Leninist talk about Western guilt and the cant about redistribution of wealth. The West achieved its wealth before the age of imperialism. It owes its prosperity to its political system and to a culture that encourages economic development. The Third World, too, can reach out and even, in time, surpass the West, provided it creates the political and cultural setting for a similar advance. Such an advance will arise when development rather than redistribution becomes the main theme of Third World policy.

[9]Graham Hancock, *Lords of Poverty: The Power, Prestige, and Corruption of the International Aid Business* (New York: Atlantic Monthly Press, 1989), p. 189.

KEY TERMS

Alliances
Cartels
Developed countries
Developing countries
Fourth World
Functional agencies
General international organizations

Geopolitics
Gross national product (GNP)
Haves
Have-nots
Less-developed countries
North
North-South problems

Prestige
Primary products
Regional organizations
Revolution of rising expectations

Security
South
Zero-sum game

QUESTIONS

International Politics: Motivations

1. Should states resort to war to maintain their prestige? What are the reasons for your answer?

2. What effect does interdependence play in the ability of states to persist as viable actors in the global arena?

3. What are the legitimate security interests of the United States?

4. What role do economic considerations play in the conduct of U.S. foreign policy?

5. What alternatives are there to a global system of independent states? Would these alternatives produce a better world than the current system?

Third World

1. Is capitalist investment in Third World countries a form of imperialism? What are the reasons for your answer?

2. If capitalism is eliminated and replaced with socialist economies, would imperialism continue to exist? What are the reasons for your answer?

3. What responsibility do prosperous states have in redistributing their wealth for the benefit of the Third World?

4. Why have some Third World countries been successful in economic development and others been failures?

5. How should the West promote prosperity in the Third World?

RECOMMENDED READINGS

International Politics: Motivations

BEHRMAN, JACK N., and ROBERT E. GROSSE. *International Business and Governments: Issues and Institutions*. Columbia, S.C.: University of South Carolina Press, 1990. A study of the relationships between international business and governments.

BURTON, JOHN. *Conflict: Resolution and Provention*. New York: St. Martin's Press, 1990. A historical and theoretical perspective of conflict resolution and provention.

COLOUMBIS, THEODORE A., and JAMES H. WOLFE. *Introduction to International Relations: Power and Justice*. 4th ed. Englewood Cliffs, N.J.: Prentice Hall, 1990. An introduction to the subject.

HOLSTEIN, WILLIAM J. "The Stateless Corporation." *Business Week*, no. 3159 (May 14, 1990): 98–106. An assessment of the power of international corporations.

KOBER, STANLEY. "Idealpolitik." *Foreign Policy*, no. 79 (Summer 1990): 3–24. An analysis of idealism in foreign policy.

LIEBER, ROBERT J., ed. *No Common Power: Understanding International Relations*. 2d ed. New York: HarperCollins, 1991. An introduction to international relations.

LUARD, EVAN. *The Globalization of Politics: The Changed Focus of Political Action in the Modern World*. New York: New York University Press, 1990. An argument that the focus of global politics has shifted from the state to transnational political action.

MORGENTHAU, HANS J., and KENNETH W. THOMPSON. *Politics among Nations: The Struggle for Power and Peace*. 6th ed. New York: Knopf, 1985. A realist view of international politics.

NIEBUHR, REINHOLD. *Moral Man and Immoral Society: A Study in Ethics and Politics*. New York: Scribner's, 1932. A theologian looks at conflict.

RIEBER, ROBERT W., ed. *The Psychology of War and Peace: The Image of the Enemy*. New York: Plenum Press, 1991. Studies of the psychosocial foundations of war and peace, particularly emphasizing the importance of the making of enemies.

RYAN, STEPHEN. *Ethnic Conflict and International Relations*. Brookfield, Vt.: Dartmouth Publishing Co., 1990. An examination of the dangers and suffering associated with violent ethnic conflict, with particular attention to the interface of domestic and international politics.

WALTZ, KENNETH N. *Man, the State, and War*. New York: Columbia University Press, 1954. An analysis of theories of international relations.

Third World

BAUER, P. T. *Equality, the Third World and Economic Delusion*. Cambridge, Mass.: Harvard University Press, 1981. A critical assessment of liberal and socialist views on Third World economic development.

BISSELL, RICHARD E. "Who Killed the Third World?" *Washington Quarterly* 13 (Autumn 1990): 23–32. An argument that the Third World as a political movement has disintegrated.

BLACK, JAN KNIPPERS. *Development in Theory and Practice: Bridging the Gap*. Boulder, Colo.: Westview Press, 1991. An assessment of economic development.

BROWNE, STEPHEN. *Foreign Aid in Practice*. New York: New York University Press, 1990. An introduction to the history, forms, rationale, and functions of foreign aid.

ELFSTROM, GERARD. *Moral Issues and Multinational Corporations*. New York: St. Martin's Press, 1991. An assessment of the moral issues confronting multinational corporations.

FALCOFF, MARK. "First World, Third World, Which World?" *American Spectator* 1 (July/Au-

gust 1990): 11–12. An argument that the Third World has lost its power in the post–cold war era.

HANCOCK, GRAHAM. *Lords of Poverty: The Power, Prestige, and Corruption of the International Aid Business*. New York: Atlantic Monthly Press, 1989. A criticism of official aid organizations that are committed to assisting the Third World.

HAQ, MAHBUB UL. *The Poverty Curtain: Choices for the Third World*. New York: Columbia University Press, 1976. The case for a new international economic order.

HOBSON, J. A. *Imperialism*. London: Allen and Unwin, 1938. A major work that blames capitalism for nineteenth-century imperialism.

JIABOW, CHEN. "Third World's Role in International Affairs." *Beijing Review* 33 (January 22, 1990): 10–12. An argument that the Third World remains an important force in international politics.

LENIN, V. I. *Imperialism*. New York: International Publishers, 1939. A communist critique of imperialism. First published in 1916.

NAFZIGER, E. WAYNE. *The Economics of Developing Countries*. 2d ed. Englewood Cliffs, N.J.: Prentice Hall, 1990. An introduction to the subject.

NEWFARMER, RICHARD S. "Multinationals and Marketplace Magic in the 1980s." In *International Political Economy: Perspectives on Global Power and Wealth*, ed. Jeffrey A. Frieden and David A. Lake. 2d ed. New York: St. Martin's Press, 1991. pp. 192–207.

RUBNER, ALEX. *The Might of the Multinationals: The Rise and Fall of the Corporate Legend*. New York: Praeger, 1990. An assessment of multinational corporations.

SORMAN, GUY. *The New Wealth of Nations*. Stanford, Calif.: Hoover Institution Press, 1990. An argument that capitalism is the best means for economic development in the Third World.

chapter 14

International politics: instruments and constraints

In August 1990, Iraq invaded its neighboring country, Kuwait, and announced that it was incorporating Kuwait as a new province. The president of the United States pondered the options open to the United States—options ranging from making a formal protest to economic sanctions and even to war.

Although most foreign policy events are not as dramatic as this one, a question posed to decision makers in the conduct of foreign policy is: What method should be used in solving a problem? The choice of response depends upon the state's power and the wisdom of the state's leaders. This chapter considers the components of power, the methods that states use in their dealings with other countries, and the constraints on power. Issues of the future of American foreign policy, the effectiveness of economic sanctions, and the possibility of disarmament are then evaluated in debate.

POWER

Power is the ability to influence people to do things they may not want to do. In this sense a teacher has power over students, a bully has power over weak people, a banker has power over potential borrowers, and a prison guard has power over inmates. States, too, have power. That power varies from country to country and depends upon many factors. The most important of these factors are: geography, population, natural resources, industrial capacity, military strength, transportation, communications, diplomatic skills, intelligence, internal cohesion, government administration, and national character.

Geography

Geography—location, topography, and frontiers—is important in determining power. Where a country is located is one of the few fixed elements of power. In the nineteenth century the fact that Prussia (and later Germany) was situated in Central Europe, with potential powerful enemies on most of its borders, meant that it would have to finance a large standing army to protect its security. The geographical reality that the United States is located thousands of miles away from the European mainland meant that any European power would face difficulty in maintaining the logistical support for an extended war against the United States.

Topography plays a role in power, too. Since Vietnam possessed so much jungle, for example, the United States could not depend upon its leadership in military technology to defeat communist Vietnamese guerrillas. Since Yugoslavia, moreover, contained mountains that could be used by a well-trained, indigenous guerrilla army, Joseph Stalin may have hesitated to send troops to put down Josip Broz Tito, when that dissident Yugoslav communist leader stood up to the Soviet Union in 1948.

There is much variation also in the character of frontiers. The Pyrenees Mountains separating Spain from France served as a natural boundary and fortification for Spain for many centuries. The Alps, too, achieved the same purpose for Switzerland. The fact that Israel has few natural boundaries, such as mountains and rivers, is a source of insecurity to its policy makers and people.

Population

The power of a country does not necessarily depend upon the size of its population; if that were true, the two most powerful countries in the world would be India and China. Large populations may be, in fact, a drain on a country's economy. What is important for power in the international arena is the demographic structure of a population, particularly the age distribution. Also important from a power point of view is the character of the population: How many people are skilled? How many can be mobilized for foreign policy purposes?

Natural Resources

Possession of resources gives a country advantages in the conduct of foreign policy because in times of crisis it is not dependent upon foreign commodities that may be denied to it. The fact that the United States was so wealthy in fertile land, agricultural products, coal, and oil contributed to its becoming a big power.

The mere possession of resources is not a prerequisite for power. Japan, with practically no natural resources, became a world power because of its ability to secure these resources from overseas suppliers and because of its tremendous economic achievements in production and technological development. Even countries that control huge natural resources may not have the capital or technological know-how to develop them. For a long period of time, Brazil was an example of such a country, although at its current rate of growth Brazil could easily be a big power by the beginning of the twenty-first century.

Industrial Capacity

Since the industrial revolution, the power of states has been influenced by their industrial capacity. The fact that the major powers of the world over the past century have been industrial countries—the United States, the Soviet Union, Germany, Great Britain, and Japan, for example—reveals the significance of industrial power. Modern armed forces are mighty industrial machines requiring the services of people skilled in the industrial arts—engineers and scientists, for example. Countries that cannot obtain such skilled personnel are at a disadvantage in the conduct of foreign policy.

Technological achievements are also important. A country that is a leader in technology, such as communications and aircraft manufacturing, may be able to offset disadvantages of economy and population.

Military Strength

Military strength is dependent upon the quality of military leadership, the supply and excellence of armaments, and the character of troops. A military leadership that devises poor plans and uses outmoded tactics could cause a powerful country to experience defeat. The military leaders of Europe at the beginning of World War I, for example, prepared for a war of frontal assaults. Millions of casualties later, new tactics relying on the tank and mobility succeeded in breaking the stalemate of trench warfare.

The amount and quality of weapons is another important factor. No matter how brave the troops, an army must have up-to-date weapons as well as food, clothing, and medicine. Victory in battle does not always depend on which side spends more, but the kinds of weapons are often crucial.

Military strength is also influenced by the quality of an army. How well are the troops trained? How committed are they to the cause for which they are ostensibly fighting? Israeli forces, for example, have excellent *esprit de corps*. In contrast, the South Vietnamese forces contained many soldiers who deserted or who did not fight effectively, although there were many who did.

Transportation

From the point of view of international relations, a transportation system is good if it is set up in a way to assist the state's foreign policy and has adequate facilities. In the Franco-Prussian War, Prussia's railways allowed the Prussian general staff to move troops and supplies rapidly without wasting time on long, forced marches. The fact that the North had a developed railway system and the South did not contributed to the North's victory in the American Civil War. In modern times, air and sea transport are major transportation elements. The United States possesses enormous airlift resources in its commercial sector that can be diverted to military use in periods of national emergency.

Communications

Particularly in wartime, communications systems play a vital role. They permit commanders to keep in touch with fighting forces and to reshuffle troops and supplies as the combat situation requires. At present, the communications world has experienced a revolution, with communication satellites and high-speed computers involved in decision making. The development of such modern devices has allowed more centralized control over the armed forces.

Diplomatic Skills

Diplomacy is regarded as the brains of foreign policy. The ability of diplomats varies and depends on their education, their political freedom to report and evaluate the overseas diplomatic situation, and their wisdom. At certain times, superior diplomats have played crucial roles in the history of nations. At the time of the American Revolution and the immediate period thereafter, such outstanding diplomats as Thomas Jefferson, Benjamin Franklin, and John Adams helped the new United States. Certainly, the eminence of Otto von Bismarck in Prussia-Germany, Prince Metternich in Austria, and Lord Castlereagh in England contributed to successes in the foreign policy of their countries in the nineteenth century.

Intelligence

Intelligence is the information gathered about the capabilities and intentions of other states. Most countries engage in intelligence activities, ranging from collecting official published government reports and newspaper articles to the use of spies and espionage to gather information from friends and foes alike. Intelligence services have had successes and failures. The British writer Ian Fleming popularized British intelligence services with his depiction of the exploits of the fictional James Bond character. Most intelligence work is, however, of a scholarly nature. Knowing the military plans of an adversary is important; but in present-day conditions, knowledge about climate, agricultural production, and demographic factors is vital as well.

Internal Cohesion

If a country is at the brink of civil war or there is strong opposition to particular foreign policies, decision makers are less effective in exercising the power of the state. When the United States was engaged in a civil war from 1861 to 1865, it left itself vulnerable to foreign intervention and was lucky that no invasion occurred. France did interfere in the Western hemisphere, however, by creating a Mexican outpost for its empire and placing Maximilian on the throne.

All political leadership is vulnerable to internal divisiveness, and foreign policy may exacerbate the difficulties. The Russian government of Czar Nicholas II was toppled in part because of its losses in World War I. The conduct of foreign policy in the political administrations of Richard Nixon and Gerald Ford, moreover, was severely circumscribed because of opposition to the war in Indochina by a large segment of the American public. On the other hand, President George Bush used military force successfully against Iraq because he enjoyed popular support for this action.

Government Administration

The quality of bureaucratic administration is a variable in the conduct of foreign policy. An entire bureaucratic apparatus must be able to collect taxes and recruit troops in times of national emergency. A corrupt bureaucracy may instill great popular distrust in government. An efficient bureaucracy can expedite the prosecution of a war.

National Character

Some scholars have argued that there are some traits that characterize individual nations and permeate every class, region, and religion in that nation. These traits constitute what can be called the **national character**. For example, the Afghan people are believed to have a tradition that reveres independence—a quality that has led them to fight fiercely against foreign foes.

INSTRUMENTS OF POWER

States must choose from a variety of instruments of foreign policy to achieve their goals. Among the principal methods are alliances, balance of power, economic measures, military force, collective security, disarmament and arms control, diplomacy, international law, international organization, and intelligence.

Alliances

In the past few centuries, power has for the most part been distributed unevenly. States have often not been strong enough to provide for their own security. They have often, therefore, entered into alliances to better protect themselves. Sometimes alliances have been entered into for mutual expansion, as in the case of the German-Soviet Nonaggression Pact of 1939, in which Germany and the Soviet Union secretly discussed how they might divide Poland and the Baltic republics.

Grand alliances, in which the major powers have united into opposing factions, have often been formed after war has begun. The grand alliances that vanquished Napoleon in the nineteenth century and defeated Germany and Austria in World War I and World War II were of this variety. In both cases, however, the alliances came after the acts of aggression. The most prominent Western alliance, the North Atlantic Treaty Organization (NATO), was formed in 1949 as a deterrent to attack by the Soviet Union. According to NATO supporters, if the Soviet Union knew in advance that an attack on one NATO member would be viewed as an attack on all, the Soviets would leave all the NATO members alone. The Soviet Union established its military alliance, the Warsaw Pact, in 1955 with a warning to the West to respect the sovereignty of the Soviet Union and its allies. But the Warsaw Pact was disbanded in 1991 several months before the Soviet Union ceased to exist as an independent country. NATO continues to exist, but its future is uncertain.

Balance of Power

A key concept in international relations is the balance of power. Although it is used in different ways, **balance of power** generally implies a condition in which alliances balance each other off to maintain the peace and if one state or a group of states becomes too powerful, other states will unite to challenge the strong power. Balance of power assumes that the international political environment is always dangerous and states must take measures to preserve their security. Unless states take these measures, they risk great danger such as conquest or foreign domination.

Those who advocate the pursuit of balance of power politics advocate the approach of *Realpolitik*, or foreign policy realism, in which power considerations—as distinguished from moral ones—are the dominant factors of policy making. When British Prime Minister Winston Churchill said that to preserve the security of his country he would make a pact with the Devil, he was asserting this "realistic" view. Realists often distinguish themselves from idealists, who place moral considerations as primary objectives of foreign policy and seek radically new solutions to foreign policy problems (see Chapter 3 and Issue 10 in Chapter 4.)

In the eighteenth and nineteenth centuries balance of power experienced its heyday. At that time, there were several important powers that were, by themselves, not strong enough to dominate Europe or the world. One country—Great Britain—used its naval superiority against a power perceived to be upsetting the balance—France under Napoleon—and restored the balance of power with the support of its allies. It was widely believed that the balance of power helped to promote peace in the world.

In the nuclear age, however, the situation is different from past centuries. While the cold war simmered, the Soviet Union and the United States had extraordinary power. Each had enough nuclear weapons to destroy civilization. Under such circumstances, the balance of power did not operate as it had in earlier centuries, although it played a role in limited or regional conflicts. As more countries develop and produce nuclear weapons, balance of power becomes ever more complicated.

Economic Measures

States have at their disposal a variety of economic means to influence other nations. They may order an **embargo** on goods to or from an adversary—that is, exclude its nationals from trading with nationals of adversary countries. The raising and lowering of tariffs is another device of using economics as a weapon of foreign policy. Placing states on a *most-favored nation* list allows them to receive the lowest tariff schedules. Quota systems may restrict the amount or type of goods that are permitted to be imported into a state. States may also forbid or limit the amount of economic investment permitted by foreign nationals. During times of war, a state may take more stringent economic measures, such as freezing an enemy's assets under its control and thus preventing the enemy from using those assets.

Economic aid (the transfer of capital from one country to another) can be an instrument of foreign policy. The transfer may involve money, commodities, or goods. Foreign aid may consist of grants or loans. **Bilateral aid** is given directly from one state to another. A state may provide aid to an international organization, such as the United Nations, which would then dispense the aid to individual states. Such an "internationalization" of aid is called **multilateral aid**.

Relatively well-to-do countries have given aid for political or humanitarian purposes. When the goal is political, it is often designed to influence the policy choices of foreign decision makers. The United States has engaged actively both in political and humanitarian foreign aid. The **Marshall Plan**, which gave economic assistance to a war-ravaged Europe after World War II, was predominantly motivated by the political needs of the United States, which required a strong Western Europe as a counter to the Soviet Union. American disaster relief to the victims of earthquakes and wars is an example of humanitarian aid. It is often difficult, however, to distinguish between political and humanitarian uses of aid, since they are not necessarily mutually exclusive.

Military Force

War is an instrument of power, although not by any means the only one. At present,

different kinds of war may be distinguished: total nuclear war, limited nuclear war, general conventional war, limited conventional war, guerrilla warfare, and terrorism.

Total nuclear war is a war that involves the major nuclear powers who use nuclear weapons without limit against their adversary. During the cold war, only the United States and the Soviet Union could engage in such a war.

Limited nuclear war involves the use of some nuclear weapons in war. These weapons are, however, limited in size and perhaps in target area. It is unknown now whether limited nuclear war would escalate into total nuclear warfare or could be contained. Since the United States detonated atom bombs on Hiroshima and Nagasaki in Japan in World War II, no country has used nuclear weapons in war.

General conventional war is a World War II–type war in which the major powers would be involved but would not use nuclear weapons. It is unlikely that a general conventional war would take place in a world with nuclear weapons.

Limited conventional war is a war fought between two countries in which at least one of the belligerents does not use all the resources at its command. The Korean War of 1950–53 involved primarily the United States and South Korea on one side, and North Korea and China on the other. Although the United States possessed nuclear weapons, it did not use them, nor did it bomb sanctuaries in the People's Republic of China that were used as a conduit for supplies to North Korea.

Guerrilla warfare involves the use of unconventional warfare against an established government. Although guerrilla warfare has its roots in antiquity, in contemporary times it is most associated with communist Chinese leader Mao Zedong, who waged a successful guerrilla war against the Nationalist Government of Chiang Kai-shek. By relying on hit-and-run tactics and ambushes by peasant forces,

Mao was able to undermine confidence in the Nationalist Government and seize control of Mainland China in 1949. The Vietnamese communist leader Ho Chi Minh used similar tactics in the Vietnamese war against France in the 1950s and against the South Vietnam government and United States forces in the 1960s. Afghan guerrillas waged a similar type of warfare against Soviet armed forces in Afghanistan in the 1980s.

Terrorism is an instrument of warfare that is generally conducted not by states but rather by substate actors, such as ethnic or radical groups. Often, however, terrorism is assisted through training or equipment by states. **Terrorism** is the use of force against civilian populations and includes such activities as hijacking of aircraft, bank robberies, political assassinations, and the bombing of buildings and other property for the purpose of undermining the authority of a government and calling attention to a cause. It is sometimes known as **urban guerrilla warfare**.

Collective Security

Collective security is a system of organizing power in world politics in which all the states of the world join forces to repel acts of aggression by any state. Provisions of the Covenant of the League of Nations and the United Nations Charter establish the principle of collective security. The idea is to use either economic or ultimately military measures to prevent any act of aggression from succeeding.

Economic sanctions were used unsuccessfully, however, against Italy following its invasion of Ethiopia in 1935. The United Nations attempted to apply collective security in 1950 when North Korea invaded South Korea. Essentially, however, the Korean action was a United States cause, although many other states contributed troops and matériel to the United Nations campaign. The communist members of the U.N. never joined in collective security against North Korea. The war against Iraq in 1991 was another example of collective security since most countries sided with the U.N.-backed armed forces against Iraq.

Disarmament and Arms Control

Disarmament is the abolition of armed forces and weapons. **Arms control** is the regulation of armed power and weapons at a particular level to improve the security of states.

Attempts to eliminate or reduce armaments have been reflected in international agreements within the past century. Major concern with regulation, however, has been a consequence of the advent of nuclear weapons by the big powers and the proliferation of nuclear weapons to many countries.

Although states have entered into different kinds of agreements regulating armaments, such as the Partial Nuclear Test Ban Treaty of 1963 and the Nonproliferation Treaty of 1967, the amount of money spent for armaments remains high. Some states are reducing military expenditures because of the end of the cold war, but others continue to devote vast sums for military purposes.

Diplomacy

Diplomacy, according to one of the leading students of the subject, Harold G. Nicolson, is "the management of international relations by negotiation."[1] States send ambassadors to foreign countries to represent their interests and to ascertain the intentions of the leaders of those foreign countries. Diplomats engage in a variety of methods, the most notable of which is *negotiation*. Traditionally, negotiations have been undertaken in a secretive manner. In the twentieth century, however, with the rise of democracy, the expansion of new

---

[1] Harold G. Nicholson, *Diplomacy*, 3d ed. (London: Oxford University Press, 1963), p. 15.

forms of media, and a desire to win the support of public opinion throughout the world, diplomacy has been more open to public attention. In the past, moreover, diplomacy was mostly undertaken among ambassadors, foreign office officials, and political leaders. In the twentieth century international conferences and organizations provide for new forms of multinational diplomacy.

International Law

International law is a body of rules that states feel bound to obey. These rules have evolved over the past three centuries because of the growing interdependence of states and the need to avoid military conflict. International law has dealt with most subjects that have or could have resulted in military conflict, such as territorial jurisdiction, the law of the sea, the law of war, diplomatic protection, and the protection of nationals abroad.

International law is derived from many sources, such as customs, treaties, judicial agencies and scholars, and statutes of international organizations. Although much attention is given to the violations of international law on some of the more highly intense political issues, international law is widely accepted in many areas of policy. States do not cavalierly enter into international agreements for the purpose of violating them, and that is why they spend so much time in negotiating details.

Still, international law is not binding on most states, nor is the authority of the International Court of Justice (ICJ) supreme. States may give to the ICJ compulsory jurisdiction on some matters provided that the other party to the dispute grants the ICJ the same jurisdiction. In 1985, the United States withdrew its automatic consent to ICJ jurisdiction in some cases because the court was considering charges made by Nicaragua against the United States. No compulsion, however, exists that can force a state into presenting a case before the ICJ against its will or even accepting the decision of the court. Usually, however, once a party accepts the jurisdiction of the court, it is ready to accept the court's decision.

International Organization

International organizations are primarily a twentieth-century development. In the nineteenth century the Congress of Vienna in 1815, following the defeat of Napoleon, initiated the concert of Europe, or **concert system**. At the congress, representatives of the European powers met to redraw the map of Europe. Throughout the century thereafter, the powers convened to deal with specific matters, but their work was intermittent and they built no permanent organization.

Other early international organizations were the international unions. Some of the earliest were the European river commissions, which regulated the traffic on major rivers. The Universal Postal Union and the International Telegraphic Union were other important unions in the nineteenth century.

Finally, the Hague Peace Conferences— the first in 1899 and the second in 1907— established organizational precedents of lasting significance and dealt with some general topics of international law, such as disarmament.

The major international organizations of this century are the League of Nations and the United Nations. The League was created after World War I as a general international organization. Its hope of preventing a world war ended when Adolf Hitler attacked Poland in 1939.

The United Nations is the most prominent international organization today. In addition to the ICJ (described above), its major institutions are the Security Council, the General Assembly, the Secretariat, the Economic and Social Council, and the Trusteeship Council. Starting with a membership of 51 nations in 1945, it had 175 members, as of May 1992. The rise to independence of former Western colonies swelled the numbers of countries and altered the character of the organization.

States feel no compulsion to abide by the United Nations' wishes. The principal agency to act in matters pertaining to the maintenance of international peace and security is the Security Council, which consists of ten nonpermanent members and five permanent members—United States, Russia, Great Britain, France, and China. Each of the permanent members is permitted to cast a veto and, consequently, prevent a majority decision on important matters.

The General Assembly, consisting of representatives of every U.N. member, also plays a role in security matters but can only make nonbinding recommendations. With the rise of Third World states, much of the attention of the U.N. has shifted to the General Assembly.

The Secretariat, headed by the secretary general, is the executive arm of the U.N. Its duties include administration of the U.N. complex and the carrying out of resolutions approved by the other organs of the U.N., chiefly those of the Security Council and the General Assembly.

The Economic and Social Council concerns itself with economic and social matters, as its name suggests. The Trusteeship Council has dealt with issues pertaining to the administration of political entities under colonial rule.

Both the League of Nations and the United Nations have considered matters of the greatest concern to international security and peace, such as war, racism, and economic relations. The record of both those organizations shows, however, that there is nothing along the lines of a world government in sight in this century. Still, the U.N. has demonstrated a renewed vigor. U.N. resolutions against Iraq provided legal and moral justification for allied sanctions and military intervention. Secretary General Javier Perez de Cuellar played an important role in the release of Western hostages held captive in Iran and in achieving peace in a civil war long raging in El Salvador.

Other international organizations, such as regional associations and multinational alliances, also allow countries to present their views. Whether a state uses these or general international organizations—or even no international organizations—depends on its commitments to those organizations and its perception of the outcome of international deliberations in those units.

Intelligence

States must get as accurate information as possible about the intentions and capabilities of other states. In the 1920s, an American secretary of state forbade spying on the Japanese because, he said, gentlemen don't do that kind of thing. Today, however, the intelligence networks of most countries pay less heed to gentlemanly behavior.

Intelligence activities have been described above. To the extent that a state can get accurate information about its adversary, it can make better decisions to strengthen its security. A demoralized intelligence community or one torn asunder by political infighting can only harm the conduct of a country's foreign policy.

CONSTRAINTS ON POWER

States are not free to do what they wish in international politics. States feel constrained to act because of moral, legal, pragmatic, or political considerations.

Moral

An examination of international behavior shows considerable diversity under similar circumstances. The legacy of British imperialism of the late nineteenth and early twentieth centuries is more favorable than, say, the Belgian legacy. When the British departed from India, they had already provided the basis of local self-government and the rule of law. The Belgians, however, had plundered the Congo.

The American war in Vietnam, moreover, was marked by attention to protecting the lives of civilians. Atrocities did occur, as the My Lai massacre revealed. Because of moral considerations and media attention, United States military and political leaders felt constrained about the kind of military action they took. Critics of United States policy, however, pointed to the deaths of innocent civilians and the impossibility of distinguishing a "purely military" target in a guerrilla-type war. Still, it is clear that limitations were imposed on the military.

Legal

The role of international law has been discussed above as an instrument of power. It is also a constraint on power. States often feel bound to follow the rules of international law.

The protection of diplomats is a case in point. Even when states go to war against each other, diplomats are permitted to return to their home countries. Prisoners of war are protected from torture by international conventions. Commercial transactions are encouraged because of legal agreements covering business relationships. Even arms control agreements are for the most part followed.

Pragmatic

States are constrained from taking certain actions for pragmatic reasons. These constraints, for example, include military and political matters.

The nonuse of nuclear weapons since the end of World War II shows the impact of military constraints. Even when the United States had a monopoly of nuclear weapons from 1945 to 1949 and a superiority for more than a decade thereafter, it did not use these weapons. It accepted a *status quo* arrangement in Korea in 1954 rather than use nuclear weapons, and it withdrew from Vietnam rather than use them. Both the Soviet Union and the United States found these weapons too dangerous to use.

Political

States are also constrained from taking action because of political considerations. Countries possessing nuclear weapons oppose the proliferation of nuclear weapons to other countries. Although Israel destroyed a nuclear reactor under construction in Iraq in 1981 and the United States led a coalition that set back the Iraqi nuclear program, these cases are the exceptions rather than the rule.

ISSUES

The kind of foreign policy a state adopts depends on a variety of factors, including geographical location, perception of threats to its security, the values of the leadership and the people, and the instruments of power at its disposal. Three questions are considered in this chapter: (1) Should the United States adopt an isolationist foreign policy? (2) Are economic sanctions an effective instrument of foreign policy? (3) Is disarmament possible?

Until the twentieth century the United States pursued an isolationist foreign policy. Its role in the cold war made the country a truly global power. With the break-up of the Soviet Union, however, it is essential to appraise U.S. foreign policy anew.

Economic sanctions have been a traditional instrument of power. They were used recently against Iraq before the Gulf War of 1991 and continued thereafter. Are they effective?

Disarmament is a long-term hope of idealists who wish to eliminate the scourge of war. Is disarmament possible or is it unrealistic?

24/YES   SHOULD THE UNITED STATES ADOPT AN ISOLATIONIST FOREIGN POLICY?

Now that the United States and its allies have triumphed over their bitter rival the Soviet Union, it is time to return to a foreign policy of isolationism that marked its early history as an independent country. Such a policy is desirable because: (1) it is in the U.S. national interest; (2) the United States no longer has the economic resources to play an interventionist role; (3) the United States should allow other countries to solve their own problems; and (4) Americans need to concern themselves with domestic matters that have long been neglected.

National Interest. For more than a century after it was established, the United States pursued a policy of **isolationism**—a policy of abstention from international commitments in the belief that a country's security and well-being are best served by staying out of the affairs of distant states. The fact that the United States was separated from Europe and Asia by thousands of miles of ocean provided it with a certain measure of safety. The major powers in the eighteenth and nineteenth centuries were in Europe, and these powers were often in conflict with each other. Great Britain developed a naval strength that was perceived as sufficiently strong to maintain a balance of power by shifting sides.

The United States benefited from such an arrangement. Not having to keep an eye on Europe, it expanded westward from its eastern seaboard and become a continental power. It was blessed with rich resources, and its boundless opportunities attracted immigrants who used their talents as entrepreneurs, factory workers, and farmers to make the country into a major economic power. This expansion occurred before technological developments such as air power and then missiles made surprise attacks on the United States possible. Americans had plenty of time to develop internally and to prepare for war. And so, U.S. **national interest**—the core values that serve the security and well-being of a country's people—was best served by its policy of isolationism.

In foreign policy, the countries of this hemisphere were of primary concern to the United States. In 1823, the Monroe Doctrine (announced by President James Monroe) sought to prevent European powers from interfering in the Western hemisphere and served as a warning that the United States would protect its interests in North and South America.

The twentieth century marked a major shift in American foreign policy. When World War I broke out in 1914, the United States tried to remain neutral. But German submarine attacks on U.S. ships and Germany's threat to the balance of power in Europe brought the United States into the war. After the war was over, President Woodrow Wilson failed to get the United States involved in a permanent security arrangement with other countries through U.S. participation in the League of Nations. The United States returned to its policy of isolationism. But the rise of fascism in Germany, Italy, and Japan made American policy makers concerned over new prospects for war.

When World War II broke out in 1939, the United States again tried to remain neutral. But when the Japanese attacked Pearl Harbor in Hawaii in December 1941 and Germany immediately declared war on the United States, the country found itself again at war. It is clear that without the participation of the United States, the fascist powers would have conquered most of the world. American interventionism was necessary to preserve the country's security and restore independence to the victims of Axis aggression.

When World War II came to an end, Americans again hoped to return to their country's traditional policy of isolationism. This time, however, it faced a new enemy, the Soviet Union. Under the leadership of Joseph Stalin, the Soviet Union established communist regimes in Eastern Europe and sought to extend its influence throughout the world. And again, the United States became the leader of the coalition of forces that challenged a totalitarian power. It adopted a policy of **containment**—the thwarting of Soviet expansionism by political, military, or economic means. The policy, which remained intact for more than four decades, was successful in that the Soviet empire dissolved and communism as a viable ideology was discredited (see Chapter 5).

Today the United States is the only superpower. With the exception of ethnic and regional conflicts, the world is for the most part at peace. There is, moreover, no serious global threat facing the United States, no dangerous global challenger such as Nazi Germany or the Soviet Union.

Consequently, the United States ought to return to its traditional policy of isolationism. Such a policy means that the United States could bring most of its armed forces back from overseas, reduce defense expenditures, reshape its armed forces to protect its shores as well as its interests in this hemisphere, and use its wealth and resources for its own well-being rather than for people whose political systems, values, and interests are often at odds with its own.

Economic Resources. When World War II came to an end, the United States was the only belligerent whose economy was in good shape. European countries and Japan were devastated by the war in terms of both the loss of life and the collapse of basic industrial and agricultural production. In 1945, the United States owned two-thirds of the world's gold resources. It held a dominant industrial and agricultural position. It was the only country with nuclear weapons, and its military power was without equal.

The period since 1945 has seen the decline of U.S. economic strength. Today Western Europe's economy has recovered and it is a major economic force. In the Pacific Basin, Japan, South Korea, and Taiwan are making major economic gains. So impressive have the economic accomplishments of these countries been that the next hundred years have been forecast as the Pacific Century.

The economic decline of the United States has been steady over the past few decades and is reflected in many ways. U.S. manufactured goods are unable to compete as effectively as they did in the past. A number of business operations have moved offshore because of poor management, high labor costs, or low quality in production standards. The United States, the country that pioneered in television, no longer manufactures television sets. Japanese cars have made major inroads in the U.S. market. The dollar has lost ground to other currencies. Foreign companies have bought up some of the tangible economic resources held in the United States, including real estate, hotels, and publishing houses. Foreign corporations such as Toyota and Honda are building their own plants in the United States. In addition, the United States has amassed huge debts. By 1992, the national debt had reached more than $4 trillion.

Given the dismal economic condition of the United States, the country no longer has the luxury of being the world's policeman. The experience of the United States in the Persian Gulf war in 1991 demonstrated this weakness. Although the United States led the coalition that defeated Iraq's leader Saddam Hussein, it could not have done so by relying exclusively on its own economic resources. Instead, Operation Desert Storm (as the allied military operation was called) marked the first time in the twentieth century that the United States fought a war and financed it through funds from other countries.

One could well doubt that the American people would have been willing to engage in such an operation if they knew that their taxes would consequently go up. It is unlikely that international incidents will again unite so many other countries to foot the bill. The United States should recognize that it no longer has the resources to play the role of world policeman.

Our Problems and Their Problems. With the end of the cold war, some Americans proposed new ways to spend their countrymen's blood and money. One group would have the United States follow the prescription of Woodrow Wilson to make the world safe for democracy. And so, they think that it is the mission of the United States to assure that democracy is promoted in such countries as China and Saudi Arabia.

Wilson had hoped that the establishment of a League of Nations and the expansion of democratic government would be a prescription for peace. This democratic missionary impulse resonated in the speeches of presidents after Wilson. In enunciating the Truman Doctrine in 1947, President Harry Truman justified assistance to Greece and Turkey by asserting that the establishment of dictatorships is a threat to U.S. security. And in 1961, President John F. Kennedy said in his inaugural address: "Let every nation know, whether it wishes us well or ill, that we shall pay any price, bear any burden, meet any hardship, support any friend, oppose any foe to assure the survival and success of liberty."[2]

Whether these presidents were prepared to spend American lives and money to promote freedom everywhere is dubious. In the cold war, for example, the United States supported many dictators who were oppressing liberty in the name of opposing communism. In any case, there is no evidence that interventionism is necessary for U.S. security at costs the American people are prepared to accept.

As mentioned, the United States is now the only superpower. It should, however, adapt its foreign policy to the realities of the times. Otherwise it will bear unnecessary burdens and produce situations that will be harmful to its own national interest.

Moreover, many U.S. allies are now capable of providing for their own security. The European members of the North Atlantic Treaty Organization (NATO) are more populous and three times as wealthy as the fifteen republics that made up the old Soviet Union. Western Europe is capable of getting along without U.S. troops deployed on its shores. There was a time when the stationing of U.S. forces in Europe helped to convey to the Soviet Union a message that an attack on Western Europe would mean a U.S. response. Such assurance strengthened the resolve of U.S. allies and may have deterred the more adventurous elements of the Soviet leadership from aggression. But the Soviet threat has now disappeared. Similarly, there is no danger today that China is going to attack Japan or any of its other neighbors. And Japan is now rich enough to provide for its own security. The U.S. security guarantee to Japan has only allowed that country to devote its resources to its own economy. Consequently, it is now in a position to compete more effectively with the United States than it would have been able to do if it had had to provide for its own security.

To say that the United States should be isolationist does not mean that the country should disarm. On the contrary, the United States should remain strong. That strength should rely heavily on air and sea power to preserve the freedom of the seas. Given the proliferation of

nuclear weapons and ballistic missiles in unstable Third World countries, the United States should continue its research and development on its Strategic Defense Initiative (SDI) (an antiballistic missile defense system) to assure that no country with nuclear weapons could successfully attack it.

To be sure, there will continue to be regional disputes. But most of these disputes can be resolved by the regional powers on the scene. In the past, regional powers used and sometimes manipulated the United States by asserting that their security (which often meant the security of a dictatorial clique) was essential in the cold war against the Soviet Union and communism. But the cold war is over, and in most cases the United States can let regional disputes be solved by regional players. If one small Middle East country conquers another, well, that is too bad but not worth the blood of a single American.

In this regard, we should take as an example the U.S. experience in the Persian Gulf war. In August 1990, Iraq, led by the ruthless dictator Saddam Hussein, attacked its neighboring country, Kuwait, and annexed it. To be sure, the Persian Gulf area has a large deposit of the world's oil. Although the United States was right to oppose Saddam's move, it should not have gone to war.

First, Kuwait was ruled by a corrupt royal family that was never committed to democratic processes and freedoms. The United States was not fighting to protect democracy.

Second, even if Iraq succeeded in conquering Kuwait, it would not have controlled the world's oil. With Kuwait, it would have controlled 7 percent of world oil production; with Saudi Arabia, it would have controlled 15.7 percent. Such control would have allowed Saddam to raise prices somewhat, but he would not have been able to wreck the economies of the West.[3]

Third, at the minimum, the United States could have provided air and naval assistance to Saudi Arabia, the major oil producer in the region. The dispatching of U.S. air and sea power would have been sufficient to thwart any plans of Saddam for extending his power into Saudi Arabia.

Fourth, economic sanctions had been im-

[2] John F. Kennedy, Inaugural Address, January 20, 1961, in "Text of Kennedy's Inaugural, Outlining Policies on World Peace and Freedom," *New York Times*, January 21, 1961, p. 8.

[3] Ted Galen Carpenter, "Uncle Sam as the World's Policeman: Time for a Change?" *USA Today* (Magazine) 119 (January 1991): 21.

posed on Iraq. These sanctions were working, and the United Nations adopted resolutions supporting such moves. Iraq could not export its oil, and, consequently, was paying a big price for its aggression. Although some supplies were getting through across Jordan and Iran, the embargo was causing prices of commodities to skyrocket.

Fifth, since the United States took the lead in the Persian Gulf crisis, the regional powers opposed to Iraq did not have to make the sacrifices that they should have made to meet the challenge. The message they received from the United States was that when in trouble, they could always count on Uncle Sam to bail them out. That is a message other countries heard as well. When they are in trouble, they will also turn to the United States to solve problems that they should handle on their own.

Sixth, while one of the factors for U.S. intervention might have been to upset Saddam's quest to develop and produce instruments of mass destruction (such as nuclear and chemical weapons), at best the intervention was able to achieve some modest success. But the overall problem of proliferation of nuclear weapons and other weapons of mass destruction remains. At least six Third World countries are expected to possess intercontinental ballistic missiles before the year 2000, and eight others already have or are close to developing nuclear weapons.[4] The United States will not be able to prevent those states from achieving their goals. It shows no sign that it is willing to take preemptive strikes against some of these countries, most notably Iran and Libya.

Seventh, for all of the allied effort, Saddam remained in power after Kuwait was liberated. Iraq's Kurdish population is in worse economic condition than it was before the war started. The same is true of Iraq's Shiites. The continuing economic sanctions seem not to have hurt Saddam and the people close to him who are capable of getting whatever scarce goods they need but rather have punished the masses of ordinary

[4] Thomas L. Friedman, "Rethinking Foreign Affairs: Are They Still a U.S. Affair?" *New York Times*, February 7, 1992, p. A10.

people who had nothing to do with bringing on the war itself.

U.S. intervention was a consequence of failing to recognize that the world has changed. The United States should no longer assume the world policeman role and pursue instead its own national interest so that it does not get involved in any more Operation Desert Storms.

Domestic Needs. The United States has spent trillions on defense. As a consequence, it has neglected some of its own social and economic needs. There was a time when the United States was right to make sacrifices, especially when it took action against the totalitarian Nazi and Soviet dictatorships. But Americans now live in a new age.

The infrastructure of the United States is falling apart. Its mass transit facilities are in decay, and its roads and bridges need repair. The United States has lost its competitive advantages, and many of its industries are now offshore. The country used to be an economic superpower; it is no longer. The strength of its automobile and television production industries has deteriorated. The educational system is not producing students capable of succeeding in a highly sophisticated postindustrial economy.

More than 35 million Americans in 1992 were without any health insurance, and the rising costs of health insurance was threatening to deny still others the health care they used to take for granted. The homeless population is a sorry sight in every major American city as well as in rural areas. The drug problem continues to destroy minds and lives.

It is time, then, that the United States return to its traditional policy of isolationism. Such a policy does not mean lack of concern with overseas matters. Even in its earlier isolationist period, the United States never sought to close itself off from the rest of the world in the manner of Japan for so many centuries. It traded with other countries, and it involved itself in international matters. What the new isolationist policy would be, however, is a course of action based on the notion that the United States can come home to deal with its own pressing problems and let the world take care of itself.

24/NO   SHOULD THE UNITED STATES ADOPT AN ISOLATIONIST FOREIGN POLICY?

That the world has changed because of the end of the cold war cannot be denied. But those who yearn for a quieter, gentler U.S. foreign policy akin to that of the country's earlier history ignore the many changes that make a vigilant and active global role necessary. The United States should maintain a foreign policy of **internationalism**—a policy based on the belief that the interest of a state requires an active involvement in the affairs of other states. The United States, consequently, should reject isolationism because: (1) internationalism is in the national interest; (2) the country has sufficient economic resources to play an international role, and the well-being of the American economy depends on maintaining that role; (3) other countries lack the will or the resources to play a global role similar to that of the United States, and many of them would be unable to cope with regional threats without U.S. help; and (4) the solving of domestic and foreign policy problems has little to do with an internationalist policy.

National Interest. The national interest of a country has been defined as the core values that serve its security and well-being. In the last decade of the twentieth century, those values are different from what they were in the last decade of the eighteenth century.

We can begin with security. In the eighteenth century, the industrial revolution was only beginning to be applied to warfare. Today the weapons of war include instruments of mass destruction. These nuclear, chemical, and biological weapons can reach their targets within minutes and wipe out millions of people within seconds.

The proliferation of weapons of mass destruction is proceeding rapidly, and the ability to deliver them through ballistic missiles is increasing. Some of the countries that have sought these weapons, such as Iran and Iraq, have perceived the United States as their bitter foe. The United States can no more ignore dangers posed by these countries today than it could the threats made by the Soviet Union and its allies during the cold war.

The nuclear threat, moreover, continues in what was the Soviet Union. Although both the United States and the Soviet Union worked to reduce the number of strategic and tactical nuclear weapons at their disposal, there remains much uncertainty about how the nuclear story will play out among the republics that constitute the new Commonwealth of Independent States. Reports indicate that Russia alone will possess these weapons. But is there any assurance that in the years necessary for the weapons in the other republics to be destroyed or to be transferred to Russia, the other republics will not change their minds and choose to become nuclear powers?

And what about the thousands of nuclear scientists that used to work on nuclear weapons in the Soviet Union? There are reports that some of them are being sought for the nuclear programs of Third World countries hostile to the United States. Is the future work of these scientists not a matter of U.S. national interest?

The United States faces security problems from terrorists, too. At times, terrorists have state sponsors, but sometimes they act on their own. Americans are by now quite familiar with terrorist actions: the assassination of U.S. diplomats, the hijacking of aircraft, the taking of hostages, the targeting of U.S. businesses abroad, and the kidnapping of U.S. government officials and business representatives abroad. As terrorists gain more technical expertise, it is possible—some say probable—that they will acquire instruments of mass destruction that clearly pose a threat to the United States.

In the minds of many terrorists, the United States is the personification of evil. Some terrorists object to the United States as the preeminent capitalist country. Still others hate the United States for its support of Israel or its Western values and culture. From the point of view of U.S. foreign policy, it does not matter so much what attracts terrorists to anti-Americanism. What is important is that the United States must meet worldwide challenges posed by so many terrorist groups, with their agendas based on nationalism, socialism, anarchism, or nihilism. Consequently, the United States needs to cooperate with friendly countries to stop the terrorist threat to Americans at home and abroad.

The United States has reasons other than a concern for security for remaining internationalist. The country's economy has grown increasingly complex and integrated into the global economy. When the stock market in Japan falls, the United States is concerned that it will not be able to sell the bonds that cover the U.S. Treasury Department's borrowing. When the European Community imposes a tariff barrier against U.S. agricultural products, American farmers suffer.

Although the United States has vast resources, it still depends on foreign sources for some essential materials. Oil is one example; the United States imports 45 percent of its oil. Since oil is so vital to U.S. economic interests, should not the United States concern itself with protecting its lifeline to the world's energy producers?

The United States is, moreover, a major trading nation. Over the past few decades, foreign trade has tripled its share in the U.S. economy, from 5 to 15 percent of the gross national product.[5] Moreover, the United States cannot control capital markets—the places in which capital is raised for financing or expanding private or public enterprises—because of the growth of international monetary flows. Is it not in the U.S. national interest to protect its foreign trade when it is threatened by military action or by protectionism?

If the economic success of the United States depends upon events beyond its borders, the country faces problems that cannot be solved within itself, problems that were virtually nonexistent in the late eighteenth century. Environmental problems are a case in point. The ozone layer is disappearing, for example. According to credible scientific analysis, the destruction of the ozone layer is caused in part by the release of certain chemicals, principally in industrial countries. If the ozone layer disappears, the incidence of cancer will increase to possibly harm millions of people. To deal with the problem requires the action of many countries, not just the United States.

The explosion of the nuclear reactor at Chernobyl in the Soviet Union is another environmental example. Radioactive elements released from that accident struck not only the Soviet Union but distant countries as well, damaging crops and jeopardizing health.

Nor can the United States cope unilaterally

[5]Joseph S. Nye, Jr., "Why the Gulf War Serves the National Interest," *Atlantic Monthly* 268 (July 1991): 56.

with the drug problem. Illegal drugs are produced in many countries of South America, Asia, and Africa. The illegal drug trade is an international phenomenon, requiring the active intervention of the United States in countries producing and exporting these drugs.

And since national interest involves core values, it is essential to keep in mind that the core values of Americans today include a respect for human rights. Americans identified with the liberation of the people under communist rule and the expansion of freedom in Eastern Europe. When the Berlin Wall came tumbling down, Americans rejoiced. Americans, too, condemned the South African policy of *apartheid*, endorsed the economic sanctions that caused harm to the South African government, and praised the movement to allow the black majority's participation in South Africa's government. Americans also condemned the brutal actions of the Chinese government in the massacre at Tienanman Square in Beijing in 1989.

Like the isolationists, internationalists advocate that the United States should pursue the national interest. But the national interest today encompasses an internationalist foreign policy quite different from the narrow policy that perceives of that interest exclusively or primarily in local terms.

Economic Resources. The United States should not be written off as in decline. The percentage of its world GNP today is approximately what it has been throughout the twentieth century (between 22 and 26 percent), with the exception of the years immediately following World War II. For all the talk about the Pacific Century, the U.S. economy is twice the size of Japan's and is larger than that of the entire European Community. The U.S. standard of living is still the highest in the world. The United States is the largest exporter of manufactured goods.

The United States still maintains a dynamic system with many attractions for economic growth. It possesses vast natural resources. It has a people with entrepreneurial talents and managerial skills. The United States, moreover, continues to be a mecca for immigrants. Since the 1970s, the United States has accepted more legal immigrants than the rest of the world combined. About half the doctoral candidates in engineering at U.S. universities are foreigners. More than half of the foreign Ph.D's remain in the

United States. The U.S. economy clearly benefits from the country's immigration policy.

Whatever difficulties the U.S. economy is experiencing cannot be blamed on excessive military expenditures derived from its internationalist foreign policy. There is no clear case that high defense expenditures lead to economic decay. In the period of the most rapid U.S. growth—from 1948 to 1973—defense expenditures were a much larger fraction of GNP than they have been in the slow-growth period since 1973. South Korea and Taiwan spend a greater percentage of GNP on defense and have a higher growth rate than that of the United States. The defense expenditures of Great Britain as a percentage of its GNP declined in the years preceding 1978, at the same time that the British economy deteriorated.

Moreover, it is assumed that if the United States were to pursue an isolationist position, its defense bill would decline. That assumption, however, is not correct since one cannot be sure about the kind of force it would be necessary to build to meet the challenges newly created by the turning away of the United States from the problems of the world.

While one can make a case for the Strategic Defense Initiative, at best one can only say that it is still in the research and development stage. Few scientists would argue that it is a fail-safe system that could knock down every nuclear-tipped missile thrown at the United States. Its justification is for a limited attack from a country with only a few nuclear weapons. Still, it is impossible to assure that it will work or that terrorists would not be able to smuggle in nuclear weapons and detonate them in the United States.

Their Problems and Our Problems. It is not at all a foregone conclusion what the response of a country will be when faced with a threat or an act of aggression. Some countries fight back, but others surrender. Governments—particularly of militarily weak states—are often reluctant to act when they have no allies. If they can find someone to lead the way, however, they will be more likely to take risks.

Were it not for the leadership of the United States, Saddam Hussein would have been encouraged to intimidate his neighbors and expand, thus jeopardizing the oil resources so vital to the economies of advanced industrial states. The regional powers lacked the wherewithal or the will to challenge Saddam on their own.

The Persian Gulf is vital to U.S. security interests, as every president—Democrat and Republican—in the post–World War II period acknowledged. And contrary to the assertions of the isolationists, U.S. involvement in Operation Desert Storm was in the national interest for several reasons.

First, the United States is dependent upon oil. About 40 percent of the energy it uses comes from oil, and 45 percent of its oil is imported. It is true that the United States is dependent upon the Persian Gulf area for only 5 percent of its oil, but other countries are heavily dependent. It is likely that Saddam would have eventually raised the price of oil considerably. Moreover, if the supply of Persian Gulf oil were curtailed, the world market price of oil would have risen, thus affecting the price of oil in the United States, too. However sluggish its economy was in 1990 and 1991, the United States would have been in even worse economic condition as a result of inflation.

Second, as it is now known, Saddam's nuclear-weapon program was far more advanced than Western intelligence agencies had suspected. Saddam's goal was for Iraq to be the dominant power in the region, but fortunately his plans were upset by the U.S.-led coalition that brought his forces to defeat. Had he been allowed to proceed with his nuclear program, he would have posed a danger not only to his neighbors but to every advanced industrial country dependent upon oil. The additional revenues he would have acquired from oil would have financed his ambitious quest to obtain weapons of mass destruction.

Third, the dust has not settled following the cold war; we still cannot see the new world order clearly. The gulf war was, however, the first major international event in that new order. As such, it was an example of collective security and a major success for the United Nations, which sanctioned the economic and military measures taken by the United States and its allies. A precedent has been established in which collective action through the U.N. is regarded as a legitimate and effective means to thwart aggression in the world. Had the United States failed to act in support of the U.N., a major failure for collective security and the U.N. would have marred the new world order.

Fourth, the fact that the United States had the financial and military support of other countries in the war can serve as a precedent for limiting any attempt to make the United States a world policeman. The United States made a major effort to show that it acted with the support of the U.N., and this fact can be used by opponents of unilateral foreign policy actions by the United States in the future.

Fifth, for all of its obvious limitations, the United States is still the only country in the world that has the political, military, and economic strength to be the major player in any matter that is a serious risk to international peace and security. The fact that the United States acted quickly and galvanized the world into responding to the aggression in Iraq is a tribute to the immense political and military weight that the United States possesses. Had there been no U.S. response, there would have been no alliance response, and for that matter, no U.N. response.

Sixth, as the syndicated columnist Charles Krauthammer points out, the involvement of the United States abroad is in many ways an essential pillar of the American economy. He notes: "The United States is, like Britain before it, a commercial, maritime, trading nation that needs an open, stable world environment in which to thrive. In a world of Saddams, if the United States were to shed its unique superpower roles, its economy would be gravely wounded."[6]

The well-being of the United States economy, consequently, needs trading partners who feel secure, sea lanes that are safe to travel, and oil prices that are not inflated.

Domestic and Foreign Policy Needs. It is true that the United States has domestic problems. And it is correct to point to deficiencies in such matters as education, health, housing, and the like. But the solutions to these problems have little to do with foreign policy.

In this regard one does not know whether a policy of isolationism will lead to any savings in defense expenditures. Even the isolationists agree that the United States needs to have a strong military establishment. Moreover, the federal defense budget in 1992, constitutes only approximately 5.4 percent of gross national product.

[6] Charles Krauthammer, "The Unipolar Moment," *Foreign Affairs* 70, no. 1 (1990): 27.

So many of the social problems that the United States faces lack government solutions. When young people spend time before television sets rather than studying, there is little that the government can do to reverse that pattern. Besides, there is no relationship between the amount of money spent on a student's education and his or her educational accomplishments.

Similarly, it is not at all clear that government can do much more about some of the great social problems such as homelessness or the decline of the family. Indeed, there is a body of thought that argues that government programs worsen rather than improve solutions to social problems.

It can also be argued that the military helps rather than hinders solutions of some social problems. Take, for example, the social problem of racism. The U.S. military is more racially integrated than any other social institution. Opportunities for advancement for minorities are greater in the military than in the private sector. The military has done an excellent job of assuring that its people are drug free. The U.S. military is also a mechanism of social mobility.

Libertarians argue that the savings secured from abandoning an internationalist policy can be used to reduce taxes so that people can solve their own problems. But it is doubtful that the reductions will be so great as to significantly affect the lives of the people most in need. Liberals argue that the savings secured from abandoning an internationalist policy can be used to support government programs to solve social problems. But again it is doubtful that such support will significantly alter the quality of the lives for the people most in need.

And so, no benefits would accrue to the United States for pursuing an isolationist policy. Such a policy would harm the national interest because of the proliferation of weapons of mass destruction, the threats from terrorists, the interdependence of the global economy, and the need to promote U.S. values throughout the world. Isolationism would damage the U.S. economy. The problems of foreign states often affect the United States. There is no evidence, moreover, that a turning away from the world would make the United States capable of dealing with its domestic difficulties.

25/YES   ARE ECONOMIC SANCTIONS AN EFFECTIVE INSTRUMENT OF FOREIGN POLICY?

States and international organizations use a variety of methods in the conduct of foreign policy. Economic **sanctions**—punitive measures taken against a state by another state, group of states, or international organizations—have proven to be one such effective method. If seen in a proper and limited context, the case for sanctions is based on four principal considerations: (1) the historical evidence shows that sanctions can be successful; (2) efficient implementation of sanctions is possible; (3) sanctions can undermine the ability of targeted governments to maintain the support of their people; and (4) sanctions offer a useful instrument of diplomacy, particularly in the nuclear age.

Historical Evidence. Economic sanctions have a long history that can be traced back to ancient times. For the most part, however, sanctions have become a major means of influencing state behavior in the twentieth century. The United States has been a principal user of sanctions, as have countries that are allied with the United States. But sanctions have also been used by the Soviet Union, and even Third World countries have relied on them. International organizations, such as the League of Nations and the United Nations, have resorted to sanctions, too.

It is essential to mention at the outset that the label *success* in evaluating sanctions must be carefully circumscribed. Under optimum conditions, success means that sanctions get a target country to completely reverse course and, consequently, change policy. But success can also be minimally achieved if the target country is forced to pay a price for its behavior.

Because it is often difficult to isolate factors that contribute to a country's political behavior, one cannot say with absolute certainty that particular sanctions produce a particular result. In many cases, sanctions are an important contributory factor in bringing about a policy sought by the targeting country. A number of examples may be cited to prove the point.

The United States imposed sanctions on the Marxist government of Salvador Allende in Chile in the early 1970s. These sanctions helped to speed the economic decay that undermined the government and led to Allende's overthrow.

Countries institute sanctions not only against their enemies but also against their friends. In 1956, the United States threatened to impose economic sanctions against Great Britain and France during the Suez crisis in which those countries, along with Israel, went to war against Egypt. Both the British and the French withdrew their forces from the Sinai in part because of U.S. restrictions on oil deliveries and trade credits to Great Britain and France.

Sanctions by the United States against South Korea and Taiwan from 1975 to 1977 deterred those countries from building nuclear reprocessing plants, which might have made them capable of becoming nuclear-weapons states. President Jimmy Carter's use of sanctions against the regime of Anastasio Somoza in Nicaragua from 1977 to 1979 helped bring down that government.

In 1973 Arab oil-exporting countries imposed an embargo against the United States and Western Europe and threatened to extend that embargo to other countries that supported Israel. Israel's sovereignty and strength were not, as a consequence, impaired, but the embargo did achieve some important consequences. The very threat of the embargo helped to encourage hoarding of oil and drove up oil prices around the world, thus contributing to an inflationary spiral. Many governments in Europe and elsewhere adopted a more hostile policy toward Israel in response to the pressure of the embargo.

The United Nations instituted economic sanctions against the white-ruled government of Rhodesia in 1965 in the hope of undermining the government and allowing for black majority rule. These measures did help to undermine the economic strength of the Rhodesian government, which in 1980 transferred power to a black-majority government that renamed its country Zimbabwe.

Great Britain and other European Community countries imposed sanctions on Argentina when the British and Argentines went to war over control of the Falkland Islands in 1982. Had the war been inconclusive rather than a British victory, the sanctions would no doubt have contributed to disrupting the Argentinian economy.

Sanctions were imposed against South Africa for more than three decades in an effort to put an end to South Africa's policies of *apartheid*, or the separation of people on the basis of race. Sanctions were first applied following an incident in March 1960, when police fired on a crowd of unarmed blacks in Sharpeville, killing sixty-nine people. In 1963, the United Nations asked its members to voluntarily stop their arms trade with South Africa. The U.N. approved mandatory arms-trade sanctions in 1977. The Organization of Petroleum Exporting Countries stopped oil exports to South Africa in 1973. In 1985 and 1986, the United States, the European Community, and the Commonwealth countries (formerly the British Commonwealth) adopted further economic sanctions against South Africa.

The South African government began to change its policy. In 1990, Nelson Mandela, the leader of the African National Congress, (ANC) was released from prison after serving 27 years as a political prisoner. The ANC is the principal black group fighting to end white minority rule in South Africa. It was legally banned by the South African government for 30 years. In 1990, however, the ban was lifted. In 1991, the laws against *apartheid* were repealed, and South Africa moved to achieve democratic representation for its black majority. Sanctions, consequently, were ended with these changes. It is clear that sanctions played a role in bringing about the transformation of the South African political system.

The most notable recent application of sanctions was against Iraq following its invasion of Kuwait in August 1990. The United Nations voted sanctions against both Iraqi imports and exports. After the coalition war freeing Kuwait in early 1991, sanctions remained in force pending Iraq's compliance with U.N. resolutions requiring Iraq to: (1) dismantle its chemical, biological, nuclear, and ballistic missile capability; and (2) pay a large percentage of its oil revenue to Kuwait as war reparations.

Sanctions, then, have been effective instruments of foreign policy. The historical record shows major successes against such countries as Chile, Rhodesia, and South Africa.

Implementation. Critics of sanctions often point to the failure of sanctions to be comprehensive or to the inability of a targeting country, group of countries, or international organizations to win universal support for applying sanctions. To be sure, if sanctions are evaluated according to such extreme standards, then one could argue that they are not successful. But sanctions are more often designed to make the targeted country pay a price for its action, and often they do take a slow but steady toll.

After Soviet forces moved into Afghanistan in 1979, President Jimmy Carter imposed a partial grain embargo against the Soviet Union, which had a continuing problem producing enough agricultural products to meet its needs. It is true that Moscow sought and obtained alternative sources of grain from countries such as Argentina and Canada. Nevertheless, the Soviets could not make up shortfalls in feed-quality grains and, consequently, suffered a shortage of meat in 1979 and 1980.

U.S. economic sanctions against Poland were effective after the Polish government declared martial law and cracked down on Solidarity, the Polish trade union. The Reagan administration sanctions included a prohibition of U.S. loans and credits, U.S. opposition to Polish participation in the International Monetary Fund, and denial to Poland of *most-favored-nation* trade status. Sanctions were lifted in 1984 and 1985 when virtually all political prisoners were released and Poland moved toward democracy.

The Rhodesian government paid a price as a result of the sanctions imposed first by Great Britain and then by the United Nations. Ultimately, the white-ruled government gave way to the black majority.

Much attention has been given to the imposition of economic sanctions against South Africa because of its policies of *apartheid* and minority-white rule. It is true that South Africa was able to circumvent many of the penalties imposed from without. For example, it purchased arms from countries that did not comply with the U.N. resolutions. But it had to pay higher prices for black-listed items.

The cost for maintaining *apartheid* was high. Between the mid-1980s and 1991, about $10 billion in capital was taken out of South Africa. American assets in South Africa tumbled from $2.6 billion to $1.5 billion, and, according to a U.S. Chamber of Commerce estimate, an additional $2 billion was lost annually in bilateral trade and investment. Moreover, 197 American companies **divested**—disposed of their investments—leaving only 129 companies still operating in the country.[7]

[7]Christopher Wren, "South Africa Faces Lingering Wounds to Its Economy," *New York Times*, July 14, 1991, Sec. IV, p. E3.

"I don't know if [South African President F. W.] de Klerk would have moved as quickly, if ever, without sanctions," observes Robert Rotberg, a specialist in southern Africa. "Coupled with increasing unrest, sanctions made perpetual apartheid impossible."[8] And it is clear that the South African government was in a hurry to get sanctions removed after it ended *apartheid.*

Popular Support. Economic sanctions help undermine government support in targeted countries. They send a message to the government and people of the targeted state as well as to the rest of the world. When U.S. companies divested and the U.S. government imposed sanctions against South Africa, for example, the white voters of South Africa were singled out for condemnation as supporting a policy that was beyond the world's moral pale. The black majority of South Africa was, consequently, encouraged to carry on its struggle for freedom and equal political rights. Blacks in South Africa thus continued to engage in acts of protest, thereby requiring the South African government to expend more funds on maintaining law and order.

Moreover, foreign investors lost confidence in a country that had become a pariah state in the world community and was in social and economic turmoil. Their withdrawal undermined popular support even further. In Rhodesia in the 1960s and 1970s and South Africa in the 1980s, antigovernment guerrilla operations increased after international sanctions were imposed. In both countries, many white people left their homeland in search of physical safety and political stability. Sanctions, then, also took their toll in terms of undermining internal support for the government.

When the Chinese government ruthlessly suppressed a peaceful democratic protest in Tiananmen Square in Beijing in 1989, the Bush administration complained about the violation of human rights but imposed only minor sanctions against China. By not adopting strong sanctions, the administration sent a message of nonsupport to the democratic movement, thus encouraging the Chinese government to continue its policy of suppression.

Diplomacy. In the twentieth century, economic sanctions are not perceived as a cause of war and are therefore seen as safer than military means to obtain objectives. Considering the fact that the world lives in a nuclear age, many nuclear-weapons states regard military means as too dangerous, since wars can escalate beyond the intentions of the governing officials who make decisions of war and peace.

In a diplomatic sense, economic sanctions give a signal that a country regards an issue to be important. When the United States instituted the partial grain embargo against the Soviet Union in 1979, it gave a signal to Moscow that it was willing to bear the costs to an important U.S. industry to show its condemnation of the Soviet military move that placed Soviet forces closer to the Persian Gulf. When the United States imposed economic sanctions on Nicaragua in 1985, U.S. policy makers were very much aware that the immediate economic effect would not be significant. Still, the embargo served as a signal to Nicaragua and its major supporters—the Soviet Union and Cuba—that the United States regarded expansion of Nicaraguan military power into Central America as a threat to U.S. security.

In the case of Iraq, sanctions were never given a full chance to work. It is clear, though, that they were achieving great impact. In the few months before the coalition invasion of January 1991, 150,000 foreign workers left Iraq; the Iraqi government called up at least one in four of able-bodied men between the ages of fifteen and sixty; virtually all exports and imports (except imports of food and medicine) were stopped; and Iraq's gross national product was reduced by 40 percent.[9]

The embargo had a great chance of success. In no previous case in history did sanctions have the degree of international support they had in this instance. Moreover, such sanctions had never before been as comprehensive. What was required was patience—maybe a year. But President George Bush was too impatient and chose war to achieve the result that sanctions could have eventually produced—the liberation of Kuwait. Not surprisingly, the coalition victory took a heavy toll in Iraqi lives and property.

Economic sanctions offer an effective instrument of power to political leaders in another way. Particularly in democracies, leaders may be un-

[8] As quoted in George C. Moffitt III, "U.S. Sanctions Get Credit for Anti-Apartheid Role," *Christian Science Monitor,* July 2, 1991: 7.

[9] Testimony by Robert McNamara in U.S. Congress, Senate, Committee on Foreign Relations, *U.S. Policy in the Persian Gulf,* Hearings, 101st Congress, 2nd Sess., 1990, p. 5.

der popular pressure to take some kind of action. When military action may be deemed too dangerous, economic sanctions offer leaders a device that can give them some flexibility while retaining some political initiative. Such may have been the case with the partial grain embargo of 1979.

How and when economic sanctions are to be instituted is a matter of political judgment.

Effectiveness depends in part on the vulnerability of a country to such sanctions as well as the resolve of the government and people of a targeted country.

Though sanctions are often portrayed as a policy that cannot work, the record shows that states can achieve their foreign policy goals by using this important method.

25/NO ARE ECONOMIC SANCTIONS AN EFFECTIVE INSTRUMENT OF FOREIGN POLICY?

The case against using economic sanctions is based on many considerations. The most important are the following: (1) the historical evidence shows that sanctions are for the most part unsuccessful; (2) sanctions cannot be well implemented because they are rarely comprehensive and too easily circumvented; (3) they serve to unify the people behind the targeted government; and (4) they signify a failure of diplomacy.

Historical Evidence. For the most part, economic sanctions have not achieved their goals, and in some cases they have even been counterproductive. When the League of Nations imposed sanctions against Italy for its invasion of Ethiopia in 1935, Italy did not withdraw from that African country. In fact, the failure of sanctions against Italy accelerated the decline of the League because of a loss of prestige.

The Soviet Union was no more successful than the League of Nations when it imposed economic sanctions against Yugoslavia in 1948 to protest Yugoslavia's move for independence from Soviet domination. In spite of the fact that Yugoslavia was a communist country at the time that Joseph Stalin was the leader of both the Soviet Union and the world communist movement, Yugoslavia was able to continue on its independence course, redirecting its economic ties to Western countries and away from the Soviet Union and its allies.

Nor did the Arab oil boycott beginning in 1973 last long. None of the three goals set by the Arab members of the Organization of Petroleum Exporting Countries (Israeli withdrawal from territories seized in the Middle East War of 1967, self-determination for the Palestinians, and a change in the status of Jerusalem) was achieved. When seventeen Arab countries imposed sanctions

against Egypt after it made peace with Israel in 1978, the Egyptians did not renege on the peace achievements agreed to at Camp David in the United States.

Much has been made of the sanctions against Rhodesia and South Africa. The British imposed sanctions against Rhodesia in 1965 when the white-ruled Rhodesian colonial government announced it would become independent. British Prime Minister Harold Wilson said at the time that measures taken by his government would restore legality in Rhodesia "within a matter of weeks rather than months."[10] It took fifteen years and thirty thousand deaths before the white-ruled government of Rhodesia agreed to a peace settlement. Factors other than sanctions, such as guerrilla warfare and white emigration, contributed more significantly to the demise of the government than did sanctions.

When the United Nations decided on an arms embargo against South Africa in 1977, South Africa built its own arms industry. The country was already self-sufficient in food. What brought *apartheid* down was not a failure of the South African economy resulting from sanctions but rather a loss of political will by South Africa's white leaders.

The U.S. partial grain embargo against the Soviet Union in 1979 did not bring about the removal of Soviet forces in Afghanistan. The embargo, which became an issue in the presiden-

[10]Commonwealth Prime Ministers' Meeting in Lagos 1966: *Final Communique*, Cmnd. 2890 (London: HMSO, 1960), p. 5, as cited in Margaret P. Doxey, *International Sanctions in Contemporary Perspective* (Houndmills, England: Macmillan, 1987), p. 38.

tial election campaign of 1980, was ended by Ronald Reagan in April 1981. When Soviet forces began their withdrawal from Afghanistan in 1988, they were reacting to the casualties they had suffered as a result of continuing resistance by Afghan guerrilla forces—supplied in part by the United States—and reflecting the reassessment of Soviet foreign policy by Mikhail Gorbachev. They were not beaten by economic sanctions.

Another example of the failure of sanctions is Cuba. The United States imposed trade sanctions on Cuba in 1960 in the hope of toppling the communist government of Fidel Castro. The Cuban leader remained in power and became strongly tied to the Soviet Union in spite of the sanctions. Moreover, he played a role in aiding communist and anti-American forces in the Western hemisphere as well as in Africa.

Cuba's main problems resulted from Gorbachev's cut in support to Soviet client states. Castro's Cuba was given perhaps a mortal blow when the Soviet Union collapsed in December 1991. As of this writing Cuba is dependent on its own meager resources. Developments in the communist world rather than sanctions undermined Castro's support at home.

The historical evidence is conclusive: Economic sanctions do not work.

Implementation. Economic sanctions are easily circumvented. One reason for the facility at circumvention is that sanctions are rarely universal. Another reason is that targeted countries can easily take countermeasures to offset the penalties of sanctions.

The sanctions instituted by the League of Nations against Italy failed in part because not every country in the world was a member of that international organization. The League, moreover, refused to embargo vital raw materials or to cut communications with Italy. The U.S. grain embargo against the Soviet Union in 1979 did not have the support of many countries. The Soviet Union was able to purchase grain in large quantities from Argentina and Canada. And the embargo itself was only partial, since Washington agreed to meet its contractual obligations for grain shipments to the Soviet Union.

The oil embargo of 1973 provides another example of the difficulties countries experience in achieving universal support for sanctions. Non-Arab members of the Organization of Petroleum Exporting Countries did not join the em-

bargo. Major oil companies could still sell to countries that had been targeted for the oil ban. The Arabs, moreover, did not control the world supply of tankers or refineries.

Targeted countries can find many ways to circumvent sanctions. Their agricultural products and minerals, for example, can be exported to a country not complying with the sanctions and then transshipped as though not associated with the targeted country.

South Africa was particularly successful in finding ways to get around sanctions. It stockpiled vast supplies of oil. Private companies were set up in the West to serve as dummy corporations to buy what was necessary for ultimate South African destination and to sell South African products abroad. African countries that had been the most vocal critics of South Africa—Zimbabwe, Tanzania, and Mozambique—maintained a vigorous economic relationship with South Africa.

Indeed, South Africa took steps to become economically self-sufficient. It had a strong industrial capacity, vital food supplies, and rich minerals, and was able to find substitutes for some items that were in short supply because of sanctions.

It was not sanctions that ended *apartheid* and started democratization. Rather, it was other developments, most notably: (1) the coming to power of President F. W. de Klerk, a man with vision and new ideas for his country; (2) the civil unrest that the government found difficult to curtail; (3) the drying up of capital from private financial institutions as a result of the civil unrest; and (4) the disintegration of international communism, long regarded by proponents of the *status quo* as behind the movement to end *apartheid*.

Another method of circumventing sanctions is through the use of multinational corporations (MNCs). With offices in many countries, these organizations can make deals that a corporation based in one country may not be able to make because of a government's decision to impose sanctions. In 1982, President Ronald Reagan sought to prevent oil-pipeline machinery from being sold to the Soviet Union. Western European allies of the United States did not agree with the U.S.-imposed sanctions, however, and encouraged and even allowed MNCs with offices in Western Europe to sell that equipment to the Soviet Union.

In late 1990 sanctions against Iraq were having an impact on Iraq's economy and ability to wage war. Still, it continued to occupy Kuwait. President Bush believed that sanctions could not achieve the desired result. He recognized that Iraq was able to partially circumvent the sanctions by importing food and supplies from Jordan and Iran. No doubt he also worried that the longer it took for sanctions to be effective, the greater the likelihood that the coalition he had put together would fall apart.

Popular Support. The effect of economic sanctions is generally to rally people around the government in time of stress. Nationalism is so powerful a force that a leader of a targeted country can easily whip up nationalist feeling against an enemy.

Soviet sanctions against Yugoslavia brought the several nationality groups in that country together in their support of Yugoslav leader Marshal Josip Broz Tito. Castro was able to mobilize anti-American feeling in Cuba in part because of the sanctions.

In response to the taking of U.S. hostages from the American Embassy in Teheran, the United States instituted sanctions against Iran. Hostage taking was seen in many countries as a clear violation of international law. Nevertheless, the Iranian government was able to work Iranian public opinion into an anti-American frenzy.

Even after Saddam Hussein was defeated in 1991, sanctions against Iraq remained in effect. Saddam and his ruling officials had no difficulty in getting the goods and services they needed. But ordinary people were devastated by the continuation of the embargo. Saddam pointed to the Americans as responsible for the difficulties the Iraqi people were enduring and whipped up anti-American feeling.

One of the reasons that governments often become more popular when their countries are targeted for sanctions is that, ultimately, it is impossible to penalize a government without harming a people. The case of South Africa is particularly illustrative of this point.

The first group to be hurt by sanctions in South Africa is blacks. When U.S. college campuses rallied for the divestment of stocks in companies doing business with South Africa, enormous pressure was exerted for U.S. corporations with factories in South Africa to end their operations there. Many of those companies had the best records for hiring blacks and promoting them to top positions. Such action was taken in part in response to a movement headed by Leon Sullivan, a Baptist minister from Philadelphia. Once the U.S. companies withdrew from South Africa, their companies increasingly came under the control of white South Africans, who did not feel committed to abide by the Sullivan Principles, which improved conditions of blacks in these companies. The result of divestment meant that conditions for blacks became worse.

Diplomacy. Economic sanctions are a failure as a diplomatic tool. First, they do not work. Second, even if they could work, domestic opposition often forces a government to drop its sanction program. The U.S. grain embargo of the Soviet Union is a case in point. Wheat producers in the United States were hurt by the embargo, and Ronald Reagan championed their cause. When he became president, he ended the embargo.

Third, countries imposing sanctions often antagonize their allies, as allies do not always hold similar interests on every issue. The pipeline controversy of 1982, for example, opened a wedge between the United States and its Western European allies. Similar conflict occurred over U.S. sanctions on Cuba, Iran, and Nicaragua.

Fourth, the imposition of sanctions as a demonstration of support for human rights may undermine the foreign policy of the country imposing sanctions. In this regard, although China suppresses the human rights of its people, it is still important in world politics. It can produce and export ballistic missiles and nuclear weapons. If the United States imposes economic sanctions, the more hard-line elements of the Chinese leadership may seek to retaliate against the United States by selling such weapons to enemies of the United States, such as Iran and Iraq.

Support for sanctions has no ideological base. Many liberals called for sanctions against South Africa and for other countries that violated human rights. Many conservatives opposed sanctions against South Africa but favored them against communist countries, such as Cuba. Sanctions may make some people feel morally virtuous, but evidence indicates that they fail as an instrument of foreign policy.

26/YES   IS DISARMAMENT POSSIBLE?

Disarmament is at the forefront of the world agenda, and it is now possible because: (1) the world has already experienced examples of disarmament; (2) the world is more aware of the danger of nuclear war than ever before; (3) a number of technological developments are working to promote disarmament; and (4) the collapse of one superpower—the Soviet Union—and the end of the cold war have increased the prospects for peace.

Historical Experience. The world has known both war and peace. It is wrong to think that the history of the world is a history of war alone. The problem for those concerned with the well-being of humanity is how to eliminate war. The way to do that is to eliminate the weapons of war or at least to maximize the restraints on war.

The historical record shows that disarmament has worked in many cases to promote an easing of tension and ultimately to bring peace. The Rush-Bagot agreement was one of the foremost cases of a successful approach to disarmament. That agreement, concluded in 1817 between Great Britain and the United States, provided for the naval demilitarization of the Great Lakes. For its time, too, the Washington Naval Disarmament Conference of 1921–22 was a success because it did serve to restrain the buildup of naval armaments among the signatory powers—although for a short period and for certain types of ships.

In one sense, too, we can look at the development of the laws of war as a recognition that the nations of the world are at least aware of the necessity to impose restraints on warfare. In ancient times the victors would take the spoils of war, and the vanquished would lose their freedom, property, and perhaps their lives. In modern times the application of the industrial revolution to military affairs has also coincided with the development of international law governing the conduct of war. Soldiers are not given unrestricted freedom to treat civilians as they might choose but must respect the rights of civilian noncombatants of a hostile state. Prisoners of war, moreover, must be accorded rights and cannot legally be subjected to torture. To be sure, these restraints on power are often violated, but millions of lives have been saved because these rules have been followed.

Awareness. In the past it was feasible to agree with the Prussian military theorist Karl von Clausewitz, who argued in the nineteenth century that war is an instrument of policy. A nation could, consequently, contemplate the use of war for limited objectives. In the period between 1815 and 1914, for example, many small wars were conducted without permanent scars on the world's political landscape.

The experience of World War I, however, demonstrated the dangers of miscalculation in war in modern times. None of the military staffs of the major European powers correctly gauged the character of the war they were about to enter. Had they known, they would have not gone to war. All the military staffs believed that the war would be short. By the time the war was over, however, the prewar governments of Russia, Austria-Hungary, and Germany had toppled. A communist government in Russia, moreover, created a revolutionary force that has transformed world politics.

The world today is aware of the danger of nuclear warfare. It is significant that although both the United States and the Soviet Union possessed nuclear weapons since 1949, neither side resorted to using them during the cold war. At times, such as in the Hungarian uprising of 1956, the Suez crisis of 1956, the Cuban missile crisis of 1962, and the October War of 1973, one side or the other threatened the use of these weapons; but since the defeat of Japan in World War II, neither side used them. So anxious were the United States and the Soviet Union to prevent an accidental war that they instituted a "hot line," a direct communications link between the leaders of the two countries to make certain that nuclear war would not come about as a result of a misunderstanding.

Small powers, too, are aware of the dangers of nuclear warfare. In fact, they have been in the forefront of the movement to reduce the prospects of nuclear warfare. Small powers put pressure on big powers to conclude the Partial Nuclear Test Ban Treaty in 1963, for example. The leaders of the world are not fools and are not anxious to commit either suicide for their own countries or murder against the world.

Technology. It is often assumed that technological innovations do not permit disarmament since a country must keep up with the latest military armaments of its adversary. Measure and countermeasure fuel the arms race, according to this view. Some writers contend that as soon as the 1972 Strategic Arms Limitation Treaty (SALT), which limited certain nuclear weapons systems of the Soviet Union and the United States, was approved, new inventions negated its provisions.

What is often overlooked, however, is that technological innovations are not always detrimental to arms control and disarmament. In fact, they may enhance prospects for the control of the instruments of violence. Satellites and seismic detection devices illustrate this point.

A major difficulty in bringing about arms control agreements in the post–World War II period has been the issue of inspection. The United States insisted from the beginning of the nuclear age that on-site inspection be a prerequisite for any agreements. The Soviets resisted any such American efforts, and agreements were held up for years on this point. Advances in seismic detection and in "spy satellites" made agreement possible. The seismic devices placed in the United States or in countries friendly to the United States could detect a nuclear explosion in the Soviet Union down to small yields in the low kiloton range. The Soviets could use similar devices to check on the United States. Satellites could monitor agreements, too, to the satisfaction of both superpowers. Here were two technological innovations that improved prospects for arms control. Are there not others that can also be helpful? Surely the evidence is clear that technology can benefit the prospect for disarmament.

Cold War. With the disintegration of the Soviet empire and the end of the cold war, the world is at the threshold of an era of peace. As the leader of the communist world, the Soviet Union dominated Eastern Europe and posed a political

and military threat to the United States and its allies.

The political threat was universal. Soviet foreign policy was based on undermining Western alliances and gaining support of Third World countries. By use of subversion, propaganda, and military and economic assistance throughout the world, the Soviet Union created enough insecurity for political leaders and public opinion in the West that an arms race developed. It constructed a powerful military machine and made great strides in new weaponry.

For its part the United States and its allies sought to respond to Soviet challenges. Anticommunist alliances were formed. The West tried to win friends among neutral countries as well as undermine existing communist political systems. The West, too, built powerful military establishments and developed new and sophisticated weaponry.

Each superpower was suspicious of the other, and it was difficult for both the Soviet Union and the United States to build lasting patterns of trust. Consequently, fear and insecurity sparked the arms race.

But now the cold war is over. The Warsaw Pact no longer exists. The fifteen republics that formerly made up the Soviet Union are now independent states. All of them recognize the need to focus on domestic matters of economic development that had been neglected under communism. And so, the greatest threat to peace for the West no longer exists.

Since the United States and its allies have lost their great adversary, they no longer have a need to keep their mighty arsenals. Clearly, arms races can now be seen as a waste of money. It is now possible to turn swords into plowshares.

Disarmament, then, is not a dream of the idealists. It is a practical option that the world should choose.

26/NO   IS DISARMAMENT POSSIBLE?

People who advocate disarmament are probably going to produce the very world situation that they dread. That is, they will, first, undermine the military strength of their own countries to the extent that they influence significant segments of public opinion to focus on "peace" and, con-

sequently, put their own states into weak positions—so weak, in fact, as to make them vulnerable to attack. Second, they will encourage a nonviolent pacifist philosophy, a factor that weakens national security. Effective disarmament is utopian because: (1) wars are a constant element in the history of the world; (2) internal order requires weapons, and it is sometimes difficult to distinguish internal from external weapons; (3) the technical problems of disarmament are insurmountable in the nuclear age; and (4) the collapse of one superpower–the Soviet Union—and the end of the Cold War have resulted in new challenges to peace.

War and History. It is wildly optimistic to believe that a world that has known war since the beginning of history will reform its ways. There is no evidence that war is abating in the nuclear era. The marquee of war in the nuclear age features Korea, Vietnam, Cambodia, Pakistan, India, Israel, Syria, Hungary, Iraq, Iran, Afghanistan, Yugoslavia, and many others.

It is true that the record of disarmament has some successes, and the Rush-Bagot agreement and the Washington Naval Disarmament Conference are two stars in what otherwise is a very dark sky. More often than not, disarmament agreements end in failure. At the Versailles Peace Conference in 1919, for example, disarmament was imposed on Germany. The German army was limited to 100,000 officers and soldiers, and the country was not permitted to manufacture weapons of war. Germany was able to circumvent these restrictions in a variety of ways. German weapons makers entered into agreements with other countries, such as Sweden and the Soviet Union, to produce armaments in those countries. Germany hid its own military production facilities from the inspectors of other countries. It secretly trained soldiers in organizations set up outside the formal military establishment, such as flying clubs and scout organizations.

The record of arms control agreements shows that countries have been ingenious in circumventing the provisions of disarmament treaties. In fact, the record reveals that the most successful disarmament occurs when countries act unilaterally rather than seek accords. At the conclusion of World War II, for example, the world witnessed the most massive voluntary disarmament program in modern history when the United States drastically reduced the size of the armed forces. The United States Army, which had 8,020,000 people on the day Japan surrendered in August 1945, was reduced to 1,889,690 by July 1946.[11] No international agreement

[11]Samuel P. Huntington, *The Common Defense: Strategic Programs in National Politics* (New York: Columbia University Press, 1961), p. 35.

forced this move. The United States acted in this manner because it sought to end its mobilization and to get on with the business of building its peacetime economy. Soon, however, it became apparent that the United States could not return to its prewar isolationist position, and it rearmed to meet a perceived Soviet danger.

The record of history, then, shows that no modern country can afford to disarm. Even countries that are neutral, such as Switzerland and Sweden, have strong military establishments. The familiar picture of the Swiss and the Swedes as peaceful people often overlooks the fact that both peoples devote a considerable amount of their gross national product to defense. Swiss citizens, in fact, have enormous military obligations. No doubt it was because the Swiss were able to mobilize an impressive citizen-army within a twenty-four-hour period that Switzerland was able to maintain its neutrality during World War II.

The nuclear age makes it even easier for states to convert to weapons of war. More states than ever are relying on nuclear energy. It is estimated that, by the year 2000, 20–25 percent of the world's energy will be nuclear, thus making it easy for countries to convert to nuclear weapons. The nuclear-weapons states of the world have shown that they are willing to educate the scientists of the nonnuclear-weapons states in nuclear technology. They have been willing, moreover, to sell the machinery and the expertise by which nuclear weapons could be built. It was widely reported in 1991 and 1992 that some Middle East countries were recruiting nuclear scientists who had worked for the Soviet Union but now needed jobs following the collapse of their country as a political entity. It is foolish to believe that the world will show restraint when temptation is so strong for states to develop their own nuclear weapons systems.

Internal Order. Major conflicts exist within states as well as between them. There is considerable evidence that intrastate violence is greater than interstate violence. In recent years Northern Ireland, Indonesia, Lebanon, Vietnam, Iran, Nigeria, Zimbabwe, and Yugoslavia have suffered civil wars costing thousands, even millions of lives. States need weapons to maintain internal order. It is sometimes difficult to distinguish weapons of internal order from weapons of external disorder. Even the Treaty of Versailles permitted a German military establishment to exist to maintain internal order; and once this kind of necessity is admitted, then the existence of any army is also allowed. Who, then, can prevent staff officers from thinking of noninternal affairs?

If states are not permitted police forces to maintain internal order, then power will go to those elements who possess weapons illegally. A state must have overwhelming military power within its own borders if it is to enforce its laws against those who violate them. Even if weapons are outlawed, then nonweapons will be used as weapons. Gasoline, which can fuel a sports car, can also be used in a Molotov cocktail. A butcher's knife can also kill people. Dynamite, which can be used to dig tunnels, can also be used to destroy them. And chemical weapons of mass destruction can be produced from the same technology employed in manufacturing pesticides. It is unrealistic to think that disarmament is possible without anarchy. To be sure, some anarchists who are opposed to any state would applaud disarmament. There is no evidence to indicate, however, that all human beings in a large, complex industrial society would behave in a peaceful manner in the absence of armed police or military forces.

The Technical Problem. Nuclear weapons are different from conventional weapons. Even if mutual trust characterizes the relations between countries with a history of distrust and war, it is unlikely that the mutual trust would be so pervasive as to lead to complete trust.

Technical problems make disarmament impossible. No one regards inspection systems as so foolproof that they can detect *all* weapons. In spite of all the inspection and search points set up by the British Army in Northern Ireland, for example, bombs are frequently detonated by terrorists. These are conventional bombs that take a constant toll of human life.

Nuclear inspection devices are also imperfect. Inspection must deal with the manufacture and storage of enriched uranium and plutonium—the two key ingredients for nuclear weapons. Since there is and will continue to be large amounts of these components in existence, it will be difficult to locate all of them. It takes just about one pound of enriched uranium for every kiloton of nuclear explosives. With the best inspection devices, it is not possible to account for each and every ounce of this material. Those who want nuclear materials would find it possible to steal it or even hide its existence from inspection devices if it were stolen in small amounts. Even U.N. inspectors in Iraq cannot be sure that Saddam

Hussein did not hide some nuclear weapons in Iraq or in a friendly country.

Then there is the problem of getting rid of existing stockpiles of nuclear weapons if nuclear disarmament is to occur. No inspection system would be foolproof, and the failure to account for each and every nuclear weapon could be catastrophic.

Even when the will is strong to reduce thousands of nuclear weapons—as is the case with Russia since 1991—problems of verification exist. It is possible that, given the turmoil in Russia and the other republics that were once part of the Soviet Union, some of the nuclear weapons could be sold to nonnuclear-weapons countries.

In the real world of the 1990s, it is foolish to think about nuclear disarmament. It is unlikely, moreover, that even if some countries would agree to nuclear disarmament, all countries of the world would approve of inspection devices and give up that part of their sovereignty that would allow international inspection.

In addition to verification problems, there are two other, more traditional problems of disarmament: ratios and convertibility of weapons. Assuming for the moment that the countries of the world agree that disarmament is a good thing, how will the ratios of armaments among the states be apportioned? The Washington Naval Disarmament Conference attempted to deal with this problem with just five principal naval powers. Trying to deal with setting ratios for more than 185 countries would be a virtual impossibility.

Even if ratios could be established, how will the different weapons systems of states be counted? How many nuclear submarines of one country equal how many intercontinental ballistic missiles of another? The mind boggles at the complicated efforts to reach agreement under these conditions. It takes a great deal of time to reach a consensus in the policy-making institutions of every country in the world. Technological innovations, moreover, proceed more rapidly than the ability of states to cope with them.

Even if nuclear disarmament were possible, all that the elimination of nuclear weapons would do is promote the use of nonnuclear weapons, which can take millions of lives. In the fratricidal fighting in Indonesia in 1965, for example, it is estimated that up to half a million lives were taken. The civil war in Nigeria, moreover, may have claimed a million Ibo lives—all without nuclear weapons. The twenty-four-hour saturation bombing of Dresden in World War II took more lives than the bombing of Hiroshima. Conventional methods of destruction may be as grim as nuclear weapons.

Cold War. The end of the cold war has sparked a certain kind of euphoria among advocates of disarmament. Although the demise of the Soviet Union and the virtual end of communism as a force in the world may properly bring comfort to all who love freedom, an objective appraisal of the realities of world politics suggests that disarmament is not a possibility for the future.

First, often ignored about the cold war is the stability that superpowers created for the rest of the world. It is important to keep in mind that Soviet-American relations were marked by a *cold* war and not a *hot* war. For more than four decades, the Soviet Union and the United States were at peace. Whatever maneuvering they did for tactical advantage, neither used nuclear weapons against the other, nor sent its armed forces directly to fight the other.

Second, both the Soviet Union and the United States tried to keep their clients from precipitating conflicts that could get out of hand and cause world war. Whether the volatile issue was communism in Cuba, the Korean War, or the Vietnam War, neither superpower allowed its clients to go too far because of the great dangers of provoking a global war between the superpowers.

Third, for all of its evils, the cold war was able to prevent many of the traditional ethnic and national conflicts from erupting. We now know for sure that during the cold war ethnic resentments were strong in Eastern Europe—not only in the Soviet Union but in other communist countries as well. With the continuing decline of Soviet power and resolve beginning with the emergence of Mikhail Gorbachev, there has been a great explosion of ethnic conflict and civil war in Eastern Europe. Major examples are found in the wars between Armenia and Azerbaijan and between the many ethnic groups in Yugoslavia.

Fourth, wars and hostility have not come to an end with the conclusion of the cold war. Third World countries, such as Iran and Iraq, have sought to acquire weapons of mass destruction. Saddam Hussein demonstrated that he was willing to use chemical weapons against his own people. He also made great strides in his quest for nuclear weapons.

It is foolish, then, to think that the only dangerous conflicts in the world centered on the cold war. New threats to peace based on political, economic, and ideological differences will no doubt emerge that require countries that are in danger to have sufficient armaments for their protection.

Disarmament, then, is the pipedream of idealists. At best, we can hope to regulate weapons, but not to eliminate them.

KEY TERMS

Arms control	International law
Balance of power	Internationalism
Bilateral aid	Isolationism
Collective security	Limited conventional war
Concert system	Limited nuclear war
Containment	Marshall Plan
Diplomacy	Multilateral aid
Disarmament	National character
Divested	National interest
Economic aid	Sanctions
Embargo	Terrorism
General conventional war	Total nuclear war
Grand alliances	Urban guerrilla warfare
Guerrilla warfare	

QUESTIONS

International Politics: Instruments and Constraints

1. Take a foreign policy matter currently in the news and study the instruments of power used by a state involved. Analyze those instruments and evaluate the difficulties of using alternative measures.
2. Who will be the big powers fifty years from now? Why?
3. Do nuclear weapons make collective security obsolete? What are the reasons for your answer?
4. Under what conditions should foreign aid be used as an instrument of foreign policy?
5. What relevance does balance of power have in the nuclear age?

Isolationism

1. What is the relevance of weapons of mass destruction to the U.S. role in world politics?
2. What effect would a U.S. isolationist position in foreign policy have on the economic condition of the United States?
3. What effect would a U.S. isolationist position have on the foreign and defense policy of U.S. allies?
4. What effect would a U.S. isolationist position have on the foreign and defense policy of U.S. enemies?
5. Is isolationism a liberal or conservative policy for the United States? What are the reasons for your answer?
6. Was the U.S. national interest well served by American military participation in the Persian Gulf war? What are the reasons for your answer?

Economic Sanctions

1. What effect do international economic sanctions have on the lives of the people in the targeted country?
2. Under what conditions would sanctions be the most effective? Under what conditions would they be the least effective?
3. What criteria should be used in determining whether a country should apply sanctions? What are the reasons for your answer?
4. What are the difficulties in getting countries to impose economic sanctions against governments that have an extremely brutal record on human rights?
5. What countries today should the United States target for imposing economic sanctions? What are the reasons for your answer?

Disarmament

1. Do arms control agreements strengthen or weaken the prospects for disarmament? What are the reasons for your answer?
2. What is the relationship between arms races and war?
3. How can arms control agreements dealing with nuclear weapons be verified?
4. What effect do chemical and biological weapons have on the prospects for disarmament?
5. What effect would the proliferation of nuclear weapons have on world peace and security?
6. What effect will the end of the cold war have on disarmament?

RECOMMENDED READINGS

International Politics: Instruments and Constraints

BORK, ROBERT H. "THE LIMITS OF INTERNATIONAL LAW." *National Interest*, no. 18 (Winter 1989–90): 3–10. A critique of international law.

CLAUDE, INIS L., JR. *Power and International Relations*. New York: Random House, 1962. An analysis of the balance of power, collective security, and world government.

DEHIO, LUDWIG. *The Precarious Balance: Four Centuries of European Power Struggle*. New York: Knopf, 1962. A historical description of balance of power.

EBERSTADT, NICHOLAS. "Population Change and National Security." *Foreign Affairs* 70 (Summer 1991): 115–31. An assessment of population growth in world politics.

LEVI, WERNER. *Contemporary International Law: A Concise Introduction.* 2d ed. Boulder, Colo.: Westview Press, 1991. An introduction to the subject.

NICOLSON, HAROLD G. *Diplomacy.* 3d ed. London: Oxford University Press, 1963. An analysis of diplomacy.

RUSSETT, BRUCE, and JAMES S. SUTTERLIN. "The U.N. in a New World Order." *Foreign Affairs* 70 (Spring 1990): 69–83. An argument that the United Nations should play a major role in international security in the post–cold war era.

SCOTT, ANDREW M. *The Dynamics of Interdependence.* Chapel Hill, N.C.: University of North Carolina Press, 1982. A study of the interdependence of states.

SMITH, MICHAEL JOSEPH. *Realist Thought from Weber to Kissinger.* Baton Rouge, La.: Louisiana State University Press, 1986. A study of modern realists.

Isolationism

BRZEZINSKI, ZBIGNIEW. "Selective Global Commitment." *Foreign Affairs* 70 (Fall 1991): 1–20. An assessment of the U.S. role in world politics in the post–cold war years.

CARPENTER, TED GALEN. "Uncle Sam as the World's Policeman: Time for a Change?" *USA Today* (Magazine) 119 (January 1991): 21–22. A plea for a less interventionist U.S. foreign policy.

FRIEDMAN, THOMAS L. "Rethinking Foreign Affairs: Are They Still a U.S. Affair?" *New York Times,* February 7, 1992, pp. A1, A10. An overview of the subject.

HARRIES, OWEN, ed. *America's Purpose: New Visions of U.S. Foreign Policy.* San Francisco, Calif.: ICS Press, 1990. Essays viewing U.S. foreign policy in the post–cold war era.

HORMATS, ROBERT D. "The Roots of American Power." *Foreign Affairs* 70 (Summer 1991): 132–49. An argument that unless the United States improves its economy, its power in world politics will decline.

KRAUTHAMMER, CHARLES. "The Unipolar Moment." *Foreign Affairs* 70, no. 1 (1990): 23–33. An argument that the United States has a major role to play in national security in the post–cold war era.

LAYNE, CHRISTOPHER. "Why the Gulf War Was Not in the National Interest." *Atlantic Monthly* 268 (July 1991): 55, 65–68, 70–71, 74, 76–78. A case that U.S. involvement in the Persian Gulf war was unnecessary and counterproductive to U.S. interests.

MAYNES, CHARLES WILLIAM. "Dateline Washington: A Necessary War?" *Foreign Policy,* no. 82 (Spring 1991): 159–77. A case against the Persian Gulf war.

NYE, JOSEPH S. JR. "Why the Gulf War Served the National Interest." *Atlantic Monthly* 268 (July 1991): 54, 56–57, 60–62, 64. A case that U.S. involvement in the Persian Gulf war was necessary and served U.S. interests.

SCHLESINGER, JAMES. "New Instabilities, New Priorities." *Foreign Policy,* no. 85 (Winter 1991–92): 1–24. An assessment of U.S. foreign policy in a less dangerous but more unstable post–cold war world.

TONELSON, ALAN. "What Is the National Interest?" *Atlantic Monthly* 268 (July 1991): 35–39, 42, 44–46, 48–52. A case that the United States should pursue a policy of the national interest rather than internationalism.

Economic Sanctions

BARTLETT, BRUCE. "What's Wrong with Trade Sanctions?" *USA Today* (Magazine) 114 (May 1986): 22–25. A case against sanctions.

COWELL, ALAN. "Sanctions on Iraq Exact a High Price from Poor." *New York Times,* June 9, 1991, p. 14. A description of the effect of sanctions on the Iraqi people.

DOXEY, MARGARET P. *International Sanctions in Contemporary Perspective.* Houndmills, England: Macmillan, 1987. An analysis of recent state practice to elucidate problems of sanctions application and impact.

"Economic Sanctions: A Symposium." *Foreign Service Journal* 67 (November 1990): 21–28. Eight perspectives on the effectiveness of sanctions.

FOSSEDAL, GREGORY A. "Sanctions for Beginners." *New Republic* 193 (October 21, 1985):

18–21. An argument that sanctions can be effective.

HUFBAUER, GARY CLYDE, JEFFREY J. SCHOTT, and KIMBERLY ANN ELLIOTT. *Economic Sanctions Reconsidered.* 2d ed. 2 vols. Washington, D.C.: Institute for International Economics, 1990. A comprehensive analysis of the use of economic sanctions for foreign policy purposes.

LEYTON-ROWN, DAVID, ed. *The Utility of International Economic Sanctions.* New York: St. Martin's Press, 1987. Essays on the subject with case studies.

MOFFETT, GEORGE C., III. "US Sanctions Get Credit for Anti-Apartheid Role." *Christian Science Monitor,* July 2, 1991, p. 7. An assessment of the importance of economic sanctions in ending *apartheid.*

NOSSAL, KIM RICHARD. "International Sanctions as International Punishment." *International Organization* 43 (Spring 1989): 301–22. An assessment of the utility of international sanctions.

U.S. CONG., SENATE. *U.S. Policy in the Persian Gulf.* Hearings before the Committee on Foreign Relations, 101st Cong., 2d Sess., 1990, Pts. 1, 2. A discussion of the methods needed to get Iraq out of Kuwait.

WREN, CHRISTOPHER S. "South Africa Faces Lingering Wounds to Its Economy." *New York Times,* July 14, 1991, sec. IV, p. E3. A description of the effect of sanctions on the South African economy.

Disarmament

BERKOWITZ, BRUCE D. *Calculated Risks: A Century of Arms Control—Why It Has Failed and How It Can Be Made to Work.* New York: Simon and Schuster, 1987. An analysis of arms control.

CRAIG, PAUL P., and JOHN A. JUNGERMAN. *Nuclear Arms Race: Technology and Society.* 2d ed. New York: McGraw-Hill, 1990. A study of the political and technical issues underlying the nuclear arms race.

DUNN, MATTHEW. "Arms Control's Enduring Worth." *Foreign Policy,* no. 79 (Summer 1990): 151–68. An argument that arms control has a role in the post–cold war age.

FINDLAY, TREVOR, ed. *Chemical Weapons and Missile Proliferation: With Implications for the Asia/Pacific Region.* Boulder, Colo.: Lynne Rienner Publishers, 1991. Essays on the prospects for proliferation for chemical weapons and missiles.

GALLIE, W. B. *Understanding War.* New York: Routledge, 1991. A philosophical approach to the study of war.

GRAY, COLIN S. "Nuclear Delusions: Six Arms Control Fallacies." *Policy Review,* no. 37 (Summer 1986): 48–53. An analysis of assumptions about the effectiveness of arms control agreements.

LEVINE, HERBERT M. "What If There Had Been No Cold War?" In *What If the American Political System Were Different?,* ed. Herbert M. Levine. Armonk, N.Y.: M. E. Sharpe, 1992. Chap. 10. An essay speculating about how the United States would have been different had there been no cold war.

NOLAN, JANNE E. *Trappings of Power: Ballistic Missiles in the Third World.* Washington, D.C.: Brookings Institution, 1991. A revelation that the adaptation of technological resources to missile development is occurring in more than a dozen developing countries.

NYE, JOSEPH S., JR. "Arms Control after the Cold War." *Foreign Affairs* 68 (Winter 1989–90): 42–64. An assessment of the subject.

SCHELL, JONATHAN. *The Fate of the Earth.* New York: Knopf, 1982. An examination of the nuclear predicament.

Index